"A PEOPLE BORN TO SLAVERY"

STUDIES OF THE HARRIMAN INSTITUTE
Columbia University

The Harriman Institute, Columbia University, sponsors the Studies of the Harriman Institute in the belief that their publication contributes to scholarly research and public understanding. In this way, the Institute, while not necessarily endorsing their conclusions, is pleased to make available the results of some of the research conducted under its auspices.

"A PEOPLE BORN TO SLAVERY"

RUSSIA IN EARLY MODERN EUROPEAN ETHNOGRAPHY, 1476–1748

Marshall T. Poe

CORNELL UNIVERSITY PRESS

ITHACA AND LONDON

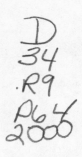

First published 2000 by Cornell University Press

Printed in the United States of America

Library of Congress Cataloging-in-Publication Data

Poe, Marshall.
    A people born to slavery : Russia in early modern European ethnography, 1476–1748 / Marshall T. Poe
        p.   cm.
    Includes bibliographical references and index.
    ISBN 0-8014-3798-9 (alk. paper)
        1. Russia—Foreign public opinion, European.   2. Public opinion—Europe.
3. Russia—Relations—Europe.   4. Europe—Relations—Russia.   I. Title.
    D34.R9 P64   2000
    947—dc21   00-010045

Cornell University Press strives to use environmentally responsible suppliers and materials to the fullest extent possible in the publishing of its books. Such materials include vegetable-based, low-VOC inks and acid-free papers that are recycled, chlorine-free, or partly composed of nonwood fibers. Books that bear the logo of the FSC (Forest Stewardship Council) use paper taken from forests that have been inspected and certified as meeting the highest standards for environmental and social responsibility. For further information, visit our website at www.cornellpress.cornell.edu.

Cloth printing   10 9 8 7 6 5 4 3 2 1

BORIS: But I would say instead, "Whoever barks is a dog." Our neighbors show their envy when they malign us, and we should therefore ignore them. Those who despise should be despised. Whoever thinks I am a barbarian, I consider him a barbarian.

KHREVOI: Brother, you are mistaken. It is easier to say than to do, for whoever ignores the view of the outside world knows neither shame nor honor. He is like some ancient fool who considers himself a philosopher, but who is merely a cynic.

IURII KRIZHANICH, 1663–66

Contents

Acknowledgments

NO ENDEAVOR OF this magnitude is completed without support from many quarters. I received much aid from my mentors. Many years ago, I had the good fortune to be assigned Daniel Kaiser as my freshman tutor at Grinnell College. He introduced me to both the historian's craft and the study of Muscovy. I am accordingly in his debt. Work on this book began at the University of California, Berkeley. So it is only appropriate that I express my heartfelt appreciation to my graduate adviser, Nicholas Riasanovsky. I also thank Reginald Zelnik (University of California, Berkeley) and Robert Crummey (University of California, Davis) for advice in my graduate school years and thereafter. I am particularly grateful to Nancy Shields Kollmann (Stanford) for posing a question that prompted me to rethink and ultimately to completely revise what I had written. Could it be the case, she asked, that the seemingly improbable things the Europeans said about the Muscovites were true? I hope I have answered that question in this book. Finally, I would like to thank Edward Keenan (Harvard), who offered advice and aid at every moment in the evolution of this project.

Many institutions supported my work on this book, and I am indebted to them all: the University of California at Berkeley, Harvard University, the Social Science Research Council, the International Research and Exchange Board, the National Council for Soviet and Eastern European Research, the Kennan Institute for Russian Studies, the Harriman Institute for Russian Studies (Columbia University), and the Institute for Advanced Study.

Many other colleagues and friends generously provided aid and comfort over the years. They all have my thanks. The contribution of Mihi Carol Namkoong was immeasurable. This book is dedicated to her.

M. P.

A Note on Abbreviations

BECAUSE OF THE large number of sixteenth- and seventeenth-century books repeatedly cited in the notes to this work, the following system of abbreviation has been adopted: "[author's last name] ([approximate dates of drafting]), [page numbers]." For example, Sigismund von Herberstein, *Rerum moscoviticarum commentarii. In hijs commentarijs sparsim contenta habebis, candide Lector, Russiae et, que nunc ejus metropolis est, Moscoviae brevissimam descriptionem. De religione quoque varia inserta sunt et quae nostra cum religione non conveniunt. Chorographiam denique totius imperiji Moscici et vicinorum quorundam mentionem. Quis denique modus excipiendi et tractandi oratores disseritur. Itineraria quoque duo in Moscoviam sunt adjuncta* (Vienna, 1549), has been abbreviated in the notes as "Herberstein (1517–49)." For complete bibliographic information about the first edition of the texts cited in this fashion, as well as the editions to which page numbers in the notes refer, see Bibliography 1 at the end of this book.

"A PEOPLE BORN TO SLAVERY"

INTRODUCTION
The History of "Russian Tyranny"

All confess themselves to be the *chlopos,* that is, slaves of the prince.
SIGISMUND VON HERBERSTEIN, 1549

It is not now for the first time that foreigners have been struck with astonishment at contemplating the attachment of this people to their slavery. The following passage, which is an extract from the correspondence of the Baron Herberstein . . . I have found in Karamzin.
MARQUIS DE CUSTINE, 1839

Historians who have written that the tyranny of the tsars conditioned the nation to accept the tyranny of the Communists have missed the fact that Russian habits of obedience have been the cause, not the result, of political autocracy.
NICHOLAS P. VAKAR, 1961

What I am proposing to do here is to construct a psychoanalytic model of the mentality behind both slavish behavior and its cultural signification in Russia.
DANIEL RANCOUR-LAFERRIERE, 1995

IN AUGUST 1953 George F. Kennan—America's foremost Russia expert, author of the policy of "containment," and former ambassador to the Soviet Union—attended a conference on "the problem of Soviet imperialism" sponsored by the School of Advanced International Studies in Washington.[1] Some years earlier, Kennan had broken with the Truman administration over the issue of the nature of Soviet behavior. Since his famous "long telegram" of February 22, 1946, Kennan had consistently argued that the

[1] On the conference, see C. Grove Haines, Foreword to Haines, *Threat of Soviet Imperialism,* v.

sources of Soviet domestic and international policy were a function not only of Communist ideology but also of traditional Russian paranoia.[2] Marxist thought was indeed, Kennan believed, an important and novel force behind Russian actions at home and abroad. But the Bolsheviks were not only Communists; they were also the inheritors of a style of thinking that had been conditioned by centuries of political instability and foreign aggression, or at the very least by the perception of instability and aggression. Though Washington had once accepted Kennan's views, the momentous events of 1949 (the explosion of a Soviet atom bomb, the victory of the Chinese Communists, the formation of the German Democratic Republic) led the American political and policy elite to believe that the Politburo was in fact following a Marxist-inspired "plan" aimed at internal repression and world domination. On the basis of this erroneous assumption, Kennan argued, Truman and Acheson had incorrectly concluded that only a militarized form of containment could halt Soviet "totalitarianism" and "imperialism." Eisenhower and Dulles strayed even further afield, suggesting that the aim of American policy should be the "liberation" of Soviet-occupied areas and Russia itself.[3] Kennan felt that a militant approach would only confirm traditional Russian suspicions about Western aggression, now under the guise of the Communist theory of "capitalist encirclement." Not surprisingly, Kennan's opinions cost him his job, first as head of the Policy Planning Staff in mid-1949 and then in the State Department itself in early 1953.[4]

Having "retired" from the foreign service, Kennan had time to flesh out his thoughts on the long-term Russian historical attitudes that informed much of Soviet policy, and he took the opportunity provided by the conference at the School of Advanced International Studies to air his conclusions. In his nuanced and subtle essay "The Soviet Union and the Noncommunist World in Historical Perspective," Kennan reiterated his conviction that Soviet behavior was motivated not only by Marxist ideology but also by age-old Russian habits. As early as "the days of the Grand Duchy of Muscovy," he wrote, "many things were noted by foreign observers that seem now, in retrospect, to have had a certain prophetic tinge and to have presaged the conflict of our time."[5] "The importance and significance of these observations," he continued, "cannot be denied," for they offered proof that "traits were indeed becoming visible in old Muscovy that were destined later to play an important part in the psychological composition of Soviet power." What were these "traits"?

---

[2] George F. Kennan, "Moscow Embassy Telegram no. 511, February 22, 1946." Kennan later published his views anonymously: X [George F. Kennan], "Sources of Soviet Conduct."

[3] Walter L. Hixton, *George F. Kennan*, 131–54.

[4] Ibid., 89–90, 136.

[5] The citations in this paragraph are from George F. Kennan, "Soviet Union and the Noncommunist World," 5–6.

There was a tendency to a messianic concept of Russia's role in history; an intolerance of foreign outlooks and values; a pronounced xenophobia of Russian officialdom; an insistence on isolating the Russian people from foreign contacts; a secretiveness and deviousness of diplomatic practice; a seeming inability to understand anything in the nature of a permanently peaceful and equal relationship between states; a tendency to view every treaty of peace as being in the nature of a provisional armistice; a tendency to think of conflict as the normal, peace as the provisional and abnormal.

Kennan carefully qualified this striking statement of historical continuity by assuring his readers that many of these Muscovite attitudes "were more common in their own context of time and place than they are today." Nonetheless, he was struck by the prescience of the early European observers, for it could not be denied that the "political habits and outlook" of modern Russians bore a striking resemblance to those described in the accounts of sixteenth- and seventeenth-century European travelers to Muscovy. In a later work, Kennan repeated his contention that in the form of Soviet power, Old Russia had somehow survived into the modern age. Bolshevism, he wrote, reinvigorated "the spirit and practices of the Grand Duchy of Muscovy: the defiant, xenophobic sense of religious orthodoxy, the breakdown of communication with the West, the messianic dreams of Moscow as the Third Rome, the terrible punishments, and the sultry, intrigue-laden air of the stuffy chambers of the Kremlin."[6]

Kennan was neither the first nor the last to find a key to the mysteries of Russian politics in the writings of early modern European travelers. Since the Petrine era, the opinions first formulated by Sigismund von Herberstein, Antonio Possevino, Adam Olearius, and the other early visitors exercised a remarkable hold over both European and Russian consciousness. In the eighteenth century, Western luminaries often contrasted "civilized" Europe with "barbaric" Russia, just as the travelers of the sixteenth and seventeenth centuries had done.[7] In the nineteenth century, Karl Marx, Max Weber, and other Western thinkers refigured the traditional opposition in terms of a theory of historical development in which the West was "progressive" while Russia was "backward," or perhaps even a stagnant "Asiatic despotism."[8] In the twentieth century, Western hostility toward Bolshevism once again led to a reform of the European-Russian distinction: the West now appeared as "democratic" while the Soviet Union was "totalitarian."[9] The opposition between the West and Russia had an even greater impact on Russia's self-understanding.[10] The imperial elite of the eighteenth century idealized the

---

[6] George F. Kennan, *Marquis de Custine and His Russia in 1839*, 130.
[7] Larry Wolff, *Inventing Eastern Europe*.
[8] Bruno Naarden, "Marx and Russia"; Richard Pipes, "Max Weber and Russia."
[9] Abbot Gleason, *Totalitarianism*.
[10] Liah Greenfeld, "Formation of Russian National Identity" and *Nationalism*, 189–274.

West and, paradoxically, incorporated traditional European criticism of Muscovite "barbarity" into its own national identity. In the nineteenth century, this tendency toward self-deprecation before an imaginary West enlivened its opposite: extreme Russian nationalism ("Slavophilism") built on a sense of complete detachment from and even superiority to "corrupt" Europe.[11] The Bolsheviks inherited this peculiar form of national schizophrenia: on the one hand, they were extreme Westernizers who fought to eradicate everything Russian about Russia and replace it with a Western-inspired industrial utopia; on the other hand, the Russian Communists were (as Kennan pointed out) xenophobic patriots who desired to live apart from the "bourgeois" West. One may reasonably doubt that the early travelers were as prescient as Kennan believed, but they were certainly more influential than the careful statesmen understood.

This book attempts to elucidate the origins of the modern image of Russia through an analysis of European accounts of Muscovy written from the late fifteenth to the early eighteenth century. The subject is hardly new. Since the noted imperial Russian historian Vasilii Kliuchevskii wrote his *Foreigners' Tales about the Muscovite State* in the late nineteenth century, many scholars have attempted to trace the general contours of the early modern European image of Russia.[12] The present treatment, however, differs in several significant respects from previous investigations of European thought about Russia. First, this study is focused on one important aspect of European thought about Russia. Europeans wrote many things about the Muscovites, all of which were combined in a general stereotype of Russia and Russians. This book makes no attempt to reconstruct every dimension of that image, but instead concentrates narrowly on the early history of a single, seminal idea—that the tsar was a tyrant who ruled over slave-subjects. This parsimonious approach to the history of European conceptions of Russia is warranted by the fact that "Russian tyranny" was and indeed remains central to the stereotype of Russia. Over the past four centuries, the idea has served as the chief (though by no means only) *differentia* distinguishing Russia from Europe. For this reason, in what follows European comments about Russian government take center stage, while discussions of Muscovite religion, social customs, trade, and so on are broached only in passing. Second, this exploration concentrates on the patterns of thought characteristic of an elite group of European travelers and theorists rather than on general public opinion about Russia. It is true that the mentalities of this select group reflected wider European thought, and that the visitors' writings in turn influenced general beliefs concerning the realm of the tsar. This book, however, makes no claims to offer a complete survey of what "typical Europeans" thought

[11] Nicholas V. Riasanovsky, *Russia and the West in the Teaching of the Slavophiles.*
[12] Marshall T. Poe, *Foreign Descriptions of Muscovy.*

about Muscovy, for it is first and foremost a study of expert opinion. Finally, this investigation attempts to address the question of the correspondence of European perception to Russian reality. This is an important though neglected problem in early modern Russian historiography. Historians of Muscovy have traditionally been of two minds about the value of the European accounts. On the one hand, the travelers' descriptions are seen as essential sources, for they provide information on a host of topics poorly attested in indigenous Muscovite texts. On the other hand, the testimony of Europeans is often viewed with grave skepticism, for it is commonly assumed that they were ignorant of Russian ways, biased against Russian manners, fooled by Russian stagecraft, or misled by their own self-serving desire to create a Russian antipode to the "civilized" nations of Europe.[13] I attempt to shed light on the veracity of the foreign accounts by offering a detailed investigation of the experiences of foreigners in Russia and the ways in which they used European categories to conceptualize Russian society.

The sources treated here are conveniently divided into four types: (1) descriptions written between 1486 and 1549 by Europeans who had never been to Russia; (2) eyewitness accounts drafted between 1549 and 1700 by visiting European diplomats and merchants who remained in Muscovy for relatively short periods of time; (3) eyewitness accounts penned between 1559 and 1699 by European residents who worked in Muscovy for many years; (4) theoretical treatises written between 1576 and 1748 by European scholars who sought to conceptualize Muscovite government in political scientific terms. The approximately ninety accounts discussed represent only a small portion of all European Moscovitica.[14] They have been chosen according to various criteria, depending on their value to particular eras and subjects. In the first half of the sixteenth century, Europeans knew very little about Russia and wrote less. Since only about sixteen accounts written before 1549 survive, all them have been treated. In the second half of the sixteenth century the number of European descriptions increased so rapidly that it is fruitless to attempt to explore them all. For this period, 1549 to 1700, only the thirty or so richest and most influential eyewitness accounts have been selected for analysis. Finally, the number of early modern political scientific accounts touching on Muscovy is quite small, only five, and thus all are discussed here.

The texts in the following survey were written according to the conventions of various early modern genres. Most of them are "ethnographies"; that is, works that offer a general description of Russia according to a standard template of topics—geography, the royal court, the administration, the army, social classes, popular customs and mores, the economy, religion, and

---

[13] Edward L. Keenan, "Muscovite Political Folkways"; Nancy S. Kollmann, *Kinship and Politics*, 146–51; Gabriele Scheidegger, *Perverses Abendland—barbarisches Russland*.

[14] See Poe, *Foreign Descriptions of Muscovy*, where over 600 pieces of European Moscovitica are catalogued.

so on. It is, of course, to some degree anachronistic to call works in this vein "ethnographies," for the word itself never appears in any of the early modern accounts and was, in fact, the invention of a later era. Nevertheless, the similarity of items of this type makes clear that sixteenth- and seventeenth-century authors understood the general description of states to be a distinct *kind* of enterprise, even if they did not have a common name for it. Several of the titles treated here, particularly in the early period of European exploration of Muscovy, are "cosmographies"; that is, works presenting under one cover several brief ethnographic vignettes of important states, principalities, and regions. There is no anachronism in the use of "cosmography" as a name for this genre, for early modern "cosmographers" were sure both of the nature of their discipline and of its title. Naturally, sixteenth- and seventeenth-century authors did not confine themselves to static descriptions of the "present state" (as the titular convention had it) of principalities. When they witnessed momentous events, ethnography and cosmography quickly gave way to another tried and true Renaissance genre, "history." "Histories" were of course narratives detailing significant or (as authors at the time put it) "delightful and instructive" events. Again, there is no hint of anachronism in the use of the term "history," for sixteenth- and seventeenth-century authors often used precisely this word to designate their efforts. A mixed genre sometimes used by the travelers was the "diplomatic report"; that is, a work detailing the progress of an embassy. Like ethnographies, diplomatic reports often contain general observations about the country visited. Like histories, they are basically narratives of events, in this case the events that punctuated the course of an ambassadorial mission. Though diplomatic reports went under various names (*reporte, relazione, Bericht,* etc.), they were all written according to stable generic conventions conditioned by their obviously administrative nature. Finally, the essence of the "political scientific treatise" need hardly be explained. Since the reception of Aristotle's *Politics* in the early Renaissance, theoretically inclined Europeans had been following the Stagerite down the well-trodden road to political wisdom, describing the kinds of commonwealths and their characteristic tendencies. By the mid–sixteenth century, when information about Muscovy first appeared in political scientific tracts, the writing of books in the vein of the *Politics* was hardly an unusual pursuit.

Most of the methods used here to analyze the emergence of the modern image of Russia were invented by other scholars in the field. Leonid Iuzefovich is to be credited with drawing attention to what might be called the "lived experience" of foreign ambassadors in Muscovy and its impact on the nature of their observations.[15] He pointed out that the Muscovite authorities and their guests were locked in a kind of struggle throughout the course of an ambassadorial visit: the Russians strove to impress the foreigners with the

---

[15] Leonid A. Iuzefovich, *Kak v posol'skikh obychaiakh vedetsia.*

might of the tsar and the unanimity of his subjects, while the foreigners attempted to peer through the curtain of court ceremony into the heart of Russian reality. Though Iuzefovich focused on ambassadors, his basic methodological thesis may be extended to all visitors: in order to understand what Europeans said about Muscovy, one must reconstruct their experiences in the country at the hands of Muscovite authorities. Andreas Kappeler, Walter Leitsch, and Samuel Baron are responsible for pioneering the study of borrowing among the European travelers.[16] In a series of fundamental works these three scholars demonstrated that early printed descriptions of Russia, and particularly Herberstein's *Notes on the Muscovites,* exercised significant influence on later accounts. They showed that both the letter and the spirit of Herberstein's seminal book were borrowed by later writers, almost always without acknowledgment. Again, their specific point about Herberstein is valid for all the sixteenth- and seventeenth-century Russia experts: in order to comprehend the character of any given description of Russia, one must take into account the possibility of borrowing from earlier accounts. Finally, Gabriele Scheidegger performed a cardinal service by exploring the ways in which European conceptual baggage shaped the foreigners' understanding of Russian reality.[17] She pointed out that Europeans brought ideas about political power, civility, and religious propriety that powerfully shaped their impressions of the Russians. According to Scheidegger, the Europeans projected their own fears, desires, and fantasies on the Muscovites and (in her striking phrase) viewed "themselves in the other." Though my analysis to some degree diverges from Scheidegger's, her chief methodological point is extremely valuable: in order to understand what the Europeans wrote about Russia, one must take into account the nature of their mental furniture.

This book begins with a discussion of the earliest European descriptions of Russia, all of them drafted by men who had never set foot there and all of them populated by fantastic images. Chapters 2 and 3 turn from fantasy to reality and examine the experience of Europeans in Muscovy and its relation to the evolution of the idea of Russian tyranny. Chapter 2 concentrates on ambassadors and merchants, both of whom visited Russia under special conditions and remained for relatively short periods of time. Chapter 3 explores the experience of European residents in Muscovy, technicians and mercenaries who had traveled to Russia in search of permanent employment. Chapter 4 moves from the analysis of the lived experience of Europeans in Russia to an exploration of the literary forces that influenced their accounts. Specifically, this chapter examines the impact of Herberstein's seminal *Notes on the Muscovites* of 1549 on later descriptions of Russia. The next two chapters turn from literary influence to the impact of political scientific concepts on Euro-

---

[16] Andreas Kappeler, *Ivan Groznyi im Spiegel der ausländischen Druckschriften seiner Zeit;* Walter Leitsch, "Herberstein's Impact on the Reports about Muscovy"; Samuel H. Baron, "Herberstein's Image of Russia and Its Transmission through Later Writers."

[17] Scheidegger, *Perverses Abendland—barbarisches Russland.*

pean thought about Russian civic life. Chapter 5 explores the ways in which European ethnographers conceptualized Russian government within Classical and Renaissance political categories. I conclude the book by asking whether the European ethnographers have anything of value to offer the student of early modern Russia, whether their impression that Russian society was despotic is in any sense valid.

It is perhaps appropriate to close with a few words about terminology. Studies of this kind ordinarily use the term "Russia" to designate the realm of the tsar and "Russian" to indicate those who lived there, and they employ "the West" to signal Europe beyond the Dnieper and "Western" to indicate those who resided there. I follow the former convention but abandon the latter. As any reader of sixteenth- and seventeenth-century Muscovite documents or Renaissance travelers' accounts will know, the most common native and foreign ethnonym for what we call "Russians" was in fact "Muscovites." Two considerations, however, suggest that a certain anachronism is to be permitted here. First, the terminological situation was somewhat confused even in early modern times. One can find both native and foreign documents in which "Russia" and "Russian" are attested, indicating that these terms were semantically similar to the more common "Muscovy" and "Muscovite." Second, both "Muscovy" and "Muscovite" have been supplanted so completely in modern times by "Russia" and "Russian" as to be incomprehensible to all but specialists. Therefore I use "Russia" as a synonym for "Muscovy" and "Russian" for "Muscovite." The terms "West" and "Western" are much more anachronistic. Before the eighteenth century, there was only the faintest idea of the "West" as a term of collective identity in Europe. Certainly papal and Orthodox officials spoke of the "Western" and "Eastern" churches, but this usage is not the equivalent of the modern distinction between the "West" and the "East," nor is it genealogically related to it in any direct way. Proof of the absence of the idea of a distinct "West" and "East" is found on the very pages of the European travelers' accounts. Certainly if those who visited Russia had thought in such terms, they would have called themselves "Westerners," noted that they were passing to the "East," or offered some characterization of the differences between "Western" and "Eastern" culture. But this vocabulary is almost entirely absent from the early modern European accounts of Russia. The writers of the early descriptions of Muscovy preferred to identify themselves with particular kingdoms or kings, and when they used compass orientations (very rarely), they chose "the North" and "the South," Muscovy being an accepted part of the North.[18] It seems obvious, then, that "West" and "Western" must be put aside. In this book I call the men who traveled to Russia in the sixteenth

---

[18] Hans Lemberg, "Zur Entstehung des Osteuropabegriffs im 19. Jahrhundert vom 'Norden' zum 'Osten' Europas." Possevino (1586), 26, identified the Muscovites as one of the "peoples of the northern expanse." Hakluyt (1969), 2:v, placed the English accounts of Muscovy under the rubric of "voyages . . . to the North and Northeast quarters."

and seventeenth centuries "Europeans" and their home "Europe." One might argue that this is simply to substitute one anachronism for another, for it is true that the idea of Europe as a cultural sphere was not well developed at the time, that the travelers do not call themselves Europeans, and that, when they mention Europe, it is in a geographical sense and includes Russia. Nonetheless, there are several reasons to think that "Europe" is the lesser of two evils: the term reflects the fact that the Russians, though in Europe, did not join the wider European system of states until the seventeenth century; it reflects the fact that the Russians had long been isolated from the European cultural stream; and finally, it reflects the collective sense of difference that the travelers felt when they passed over the Muscovite frontier.

1

TERRA INCOGNITA
The Earliest European Descriptions of Muscovy

> In thus entering upon the description of Moscow, which is the capital of
> Russia, and which extends its sway far and wide through Scythia, it will be
> indispensable, candid reader, that I should in this work touch upon many parts
> of the north, which have not been sufficiently known either to ancient authors
> or those of our own day.
>
> SIGISMUND VON HERBERSTEIN, 1549

NEITHER THE HUNGARIAN Jacob Piso nor the Dutchman Albert Campensé had ever been to Muscovy. This was hardly odd in the first half of the
sixteenth century, for at that time Europeans were only beginning to travel
to Russia. What was somewhat unusual about Piso and Campensé is that
both wrote brief descriptions of Muscovy, in fact two of the first accounts of
the northern country ever put to paper by Europeans. Their fascination with
Russia was occupationally inspired: both Piso and Campensé were in the service of the papacy, and the bishop of Rome had taken a keen interest in Muscovy as a possible ally against the advancing Turks. Interestingly, though
they were ostensibly describing the same country, Piso and Campensé offered radically different pictures of Russia. Piso's Russia was a place of universal slavery and barbarity, whereas Campensé's Muscovy was a country of
deep loyalty to a just prince and abiding faith in God.

Why did the two men disagree so sharply about the character of the distant northern land? Like all those who wrote the earliest European descriptions of Russia, Piso and Campensé knew very little about the place. The first
generation of European ethnographers and cosmographers of Russia relied
on occasional interviews with passing Muscovite diplomats, the tales told by
the few Europeans who had traveled to Russia, and, in some cases, the meager stock of written information about Muscovy that slowly built up in the
course of the first half of the sixteenth century. Most important, almost none

of the earliest authors had ever seen Russia with their own eyes. For men such as Piso and Campensé, without reliable intelligence on the very place they were attempting to describe, Russia served as a kind of *terra incognita* upon which they projected their own political desires. For reasons that will become clear in due course, Piso was hostile to the Russians and dismissed the idea of ecclesiastical union or military alliance with them, whereas Campensé saw the Muscovites as the best hope for saving Catholicism from the Reformation and the menacing Turks. Their descriptions were in essence a mirror of their own fantasies. In this chapter we will explore how Europeans first came to write ethnographic and cosmographical accounts of Muscovy and how their hopes, fears, and ignorance led them to produce a variety of confused images of that little-known northern land.

The "Discovery" of Muscovy and the Birth of Renaissance Ethnography

Despite the lore of a long scholarly tradition, Russia was not "discovered" by Europeans in the first quarter of the sixteenth century.[1] By the time Sigismund von Herberstein, the Imperial ambassador often credited with first bringing news of Russia to Europe, traveled to Muscovy in 1517, northern Europeans—Poles, Lithuanians, Baltic Germans, and Scandinavians—had been in continuous contact with the East Slavs since at least the eleventh century. Even southern and central European states—the Italian principalities, the Holy Roman Empire, and Hungary—had known something of the East Slavs since the time of Prince Vladimir. The extent of early Russian-European contact should not, however, be exaggerated. Even at Kiev's zenith, in the eleventh and twelfth centuries, political links between the Riurikid and European princely families were weak, amounting to little more than a few marriages, mostly to Germans and Poles. Almost no Europeans traveled to Russia in medieval times, and those who did were on their way to the Mongol Horde or China. European chroniclers discussed Kievan Russia only in passing. The destruction of Kiev by the Mongols in the thirteenth century further isolated Russia from Europe. Stretching out along the Dnieper, the Kievan realm had been in close proximity to a number of important European polities. In contrast, the Riurikid principalities of the thirteenth and fourteenth centuries were situated in the Oka and Upper Volga basins, far to the north and far off the track beaten by European civilization. It is hardly surprising that in the thirteenth and fourteenth centuries political interaction between Russia and the principalities of southern and central Europe all but ceased, that no Italians, French, or Germans visited the far corner of northeastern

[1] Mikhail A. Alpatov, *Russkaia istoricheskaia mysl' i Zapadnaia Europa XII–XVII vv.*, 27–109.

Europe, or that late medieval annalists of Europe all but forgot about Russia. Only the northern trading cites of Pskov and Novgorod maintained ties to the Baltic and points west during the Mongol period.

In the course of the fifteenth century, a major shift in the geopolitical configuration of western Eurasia slowly eroded the barrier dividing the Oka and Upper Volga regions from Europe. As Byzantium declined and the Mongol Horde fragmented, Muscovy emerged as an important force in northeastern European politics. Under the leadership of Grand Prince Ivan III, the Muscovites attacked their neighbors Sweden, Livonia, and Lithuania. Ivan also formed alliances with courts farther to the west, including Hungary and the Empire, and with the aid of papal officials he succeeded in marrying Sophia, the niece of the last Byzantine emperor. As a result of his military and diplomatic activity, Ivan and the once insignificant principality he ruled were gradually drawn deeper and deeper into European affairs. It is no coincidence that Europeans began to travel to Muscovy at this time.[2] The most numerous visitors were probably merchants, who were attracted to northeastern Russia by the Hanseatic trade in Novgorod. They were followed by the Italian and German craftsmen who built Ivan III's Renaissance palace, by Greeks who made their way to Orthodox Muscovy after the capture of Constantinople in 1453, and by the retainers in Sophia's entourage in 1472. Finally, European diplomats began to travel to Russia in force—Swedish, Livonian, Lithuanian, Italian, Hungarian, Moldavian, and Imperial. A Russian source of the sixteenth century described the influx of foreign envoys who came to pay court to Ivan III.

> And so then, before and after, with God's aid, many emperors, kings, grand princes, and other rulers and potentates—from old Rome from the pope, from the [Holy Roman] emperor, from Constantinople, from the Turkish sultan, from Crimea, from the emperor and other hordes, from the Polish kingdom, from Lithuania . . . and from many other lands—[each] sent [envoys] to the autocrat, to the divinely protected grand prince, Ivan [III] Vasil'evich.[3]

So too did the Muscovites begin to visit Europe. In 1439, Metropolitan Isidor of Moscow traveled with a large Russian entourage to Italy to attend the Council of Florence. After the annexation of Novgorod in 1480, Muscovite ambassadors were dispatched to Livonia, Sweden, and Lithuania. In the late fifteenth century, Muscovite embassies appeared in Hungary, Moldavia, the Empire, and Milan.

---

[2] On foreign visitors to Muscovy in the era of Ivan III, see Gustav Alef, "Origins of Muscovite Autocracy," 255; Norbert Angermann, "Kulturbeziehungen zwischen dem Hanseraum und dem Moskauer Rußland um 1500"; Mikhail N. Tikhomirov, "Ital'iantsy v Rossii XIV–XVI stoletii"; Edgar Hösch, "Die Stellung Moskoviens in den Kreuzzugsplänen des Abendlands"; Robert M. Croskey, "Byzantine Greeks in Late Fifteenth- and Early Sixteenth-Century Russia."
[3] *Polnoe sobranie russkikh letopisei,* 21:554. The passage was written in the mid–sixteenth century and describes events ca. 1491.

The timing of the European "rediscovery" of Russia was fortuitous, at least from the modern historian's point of view, for it was precisely in the late fifteenth and early sixteenth centuries that Europeans first seriously put their minds to the description of foreign peoples. The "Age of Discovery" brought with it the birth of ethnography, and it is thanks to the emergence of the ethnographic genre that we possess the earliest descriptions of Russia. To be sure, medieval Europeans practiced a kind of ethnography. Pilgrimages to the Holy Land, pseudo-scientific explorations such as Sir John Mandeville's, and diplomatic missions by Marco Polo to China, William of Rubruk to the Mongols, and John de Plano Carpini to the Tatars (all in the thirteenth century) produced a small literature on the actual and imagined peoples of distant places. Nonetheless, only the most tenuous lineage can be traced between the works of Piso, Campensé, or Herberstein and these travel descriptions. Rather, Renaissance ethnography was a novel fusion of three disparate streams—newly revived Classical ethnography, emerging diplomatic praxis, and a Humanist interest in the variety of human experience.

The importance of the Classical precedents as an inspiration for early European ethnography may be seen in Herberstein's own apologia for his work. "In ancient days," he informed his readers, "when the Romans sent ambassadors to any distant and unknown country, they are said to have charged them as a duty to commit carefully to writing a description of the manners, institutes, and entire mode of living of the people with whom their embassy brought them in contact." Indeed, he continued, "so much importance was afterwards attached to such descriptions, that upon the termination of an embassy, the ambassador's commentaries were deposited in the temple of Saturn for the instruction of posterity." [4] Though it is not entirely clear whether the Romans ever had such a practice, Herberstein's desire to authorize his own ethnographic work by linking it to the esteemed ancients is transparent. Herberstein would not be the only Renaissance ethnographer to imagine himself continuing the work of Herodotus, Pliny, Tacitus, Ptolemy, and the others, for the names of the Classical geographers appear very frequently in late fifteenth- and sixteenth-century ethnography. [5] The *auctores* provided wide-eyed Europeans with both a method of description and a stable frame of reference within which newly discovered peoples could be placed. Herberstein and his fellows had the greatest confidence that a revival of the ancient art of ethnographic reporting would yield significant benefits. If the Roman practice were followed, he concluded, "we should perhaps have had more light, and certainly less trash, infused into history." [6]

Though Herberstein claimed to be aping Classical statesmen, it is much more likely that he was inspired by modern ambassadors who were, at the very time he was traveling to Muscovy, reinventing diplomatic ethnography.

---

[4] Herberstein (1517–49), 1:clix.
[5] Margaret T. Hodgen, *Early Anthropology in the Sixteenth and Seventeenth Centuries*, passim.
[6] Herberstein (1517–49), 1:clix.

Advice books for envoys had long stressed the importance of careful observation of foreign manners.[7] It was not until the last quarter of the fifteenth century, however, that ethnographic description became a regular part of the ambassador's duties, as can be seen in the appearance of the famous Venetian *relazioni*.[8] The *relazioni* were legally mandated intelligence reports, read before the Venetian senate and recorded in special registers. The accounts were based on the ambassador's personal recollections, information provided by other envoys, local officials and spies, books of various sorts, and preceding *relazioni*. These raw data were crafted into a well-organized analysis of the results of an embassy and the disposition of the state it visited. A typical *relazione* described a principality's geography, ruling factions, military forces, administration, revenues and expenses, and occasionally popular life, customs, and the economy. The *relazioni* grew famous in the sixteenth century. They were copied, collected, circulated, and eventually published. Herberstein's work, in fact, began its life as a kind of Habsburg *relazione*. The emperor had sent Herberstein to Russia not only to make peace between the Lithuanians and Muscovites but also to describe the manners and customs of the Russians for the benefit of his countrymen.[9]

A third force behind Renaissance ethnography was of course Humanism. It was inevitable that the Humanists, having placed man at the center of their interests, would be drawn both to investigate the curious customs reported in the burgeoning ethnographic accounts and to promote the production of new ethnographies. Montaigne, to offer an obvious example, was fascinated by reports of the Brazilians, for they provided not only a picture of another way of life but also a novel perspective on the peculiarities of his native France.[10] Yet Humanist interest was hardly confined to the oddities recorded in treatments of newly discovered regions, for men such as Montaigne realized full well that Europe itself was not sufficiently understood. They urged young men to travel to see for themselves the great variety of peoples that inhabited their native continent and to write accounts of their discoveries. In the first quarter of the sixteenth century, travel instructions, including suggestions on how to observe a foreign land, began to appear in print.[11] The first such textbook of travel went to press in 1518, and by 1550 six more had been published.[12] More books in this vein quickly followed: from 1551 to 1600 forty-two additional textbooks of travel appeared, one of which gave

[7] Garrett Mattingly, *Renaissance Diplomacy*, 212–14; B. Behrens, "Treatises on the Ambassador Written in the Fifteenth and Early Sixteenth Centuries," 617–18.

[8] Donald E. Queller, *Office of Ambassador in the Middle Ages*, 176–81, and "Development of the Ambassadorial Relazioni," 42–43.

[9] Herberstein (1517–49), 1:clxi, notes that Ferdinand encouraged his work on *Notes on the Muscovites*. On his request for a report about Russia in 1526, see Frank Kämpfer, "Herbersteins nicht eingestandene Abhängigkeit von Johann Fabri aus Leutkirch," 3.

[10] Montaigne, "Of Cannibals."

[11] Justin Stagl, "Der wohl unterwiesene Passagier" and "Das Reisen als Kunst und als Wissenschaft."

[12] Hellius E. Hessus, *A profectione ad Des. Erasmum hodoeporicon*. The following figures are drawn from Justin Stagl, comp., *Apodemiken*.

the genre its name, *ars apodemica,* or "art of travel." [13] Further, the Humanists suggested that knowledge of European lands could be of great value, particularly for princes eager to improve their own realms. In the late fifteenth and early sixteenth centuries a spate of books appeared offering detailed analyses of European principalities. Understandably, Italians were the most productive practitioners of what might be called "political ethnography," but they were not alone, as can be seen in the works of Sir John Fortesque and Claude de Seyssel on the governments of England and France, respectively.[14] European political thinkers also began to describe extra-European polities on which sufficient information was available. Beginning in the second half of the fifteenth century, European scholars, statesmen, and travelers invested considerable energy in describing the customs of the peculiarly despotic Turks.[15] A great number of treatises on the Ottomans followed.

In sum, under the leadership of Ivan III the Muscovites not only moved into the European political sphere but also entered European consciousness via the evolving discourse of Renaissance ethnography. These two developments were not unrelated. Had the Russians been more distant from Europe or had they been perceived as a minor power, European ethnographers would probably have ignored them. But, as the rapid and aggressive movement of Ivan III into the eastern fringe of Renaissance civilization demonstrated, the Russians were both uncomfortably near and seemingly very powerful, at least from the point of view of Livonia, Lithuania, Poland, and the Empire. The leaders of these states—and indeed the rulers of principalities farther west—must have been troubled by the almost complete lack of reliable information about the Russians and their intentions. Clearly, more had to be known about the Muscovites if Europeans hoped to deal effectively with them. It was precisely the early ethnographers' task to provide statesmen with the information necessary to make a productive interchange with the Russians possible. As we will presently see, they generally failed to achieve their goal, though for reasons that are at once understandable and characteristic of the age in which they wrote.

The Earliest Renaissance Ethnographies of Russia, 1476–1526

The first Renaissance description of Muscovy was written by an Italian, Ambrogio Contarini. It is often said that Contarini was the first European to travel to Muscovy and return to draft a description of the distant northern land. This account is to some extent true, but it must be understood that the

---

[13] H. Pyrckmair's *Commentariolus de arte apodemica.* On Pyrckmair, see Stagl, *Apodemiken,* 84–85, and Stagl's "Methodizing of Travel in the Sixteenth Century" and "Die Apodemik oder 'Reisekunst' als Methodik der Sozialforschung," 132–33.

[14] Quentin Skinner, *Foundations of Modern Political Thought,* 1:139–44, 2:273–74.

[15] Robert Schwoebel, *Shadow of the Crescent,* 208–9; Carl Göllner, *Turcica.*

Italian did not intend to visit Moscow nor did he really offer a full-blown description of Muscovy. Contarini was a Venetian diplomat and merchant who was dispatched in 1474 to Persia with instructions to form an alliance for the purpose of attacking the Ottomans. On his return trip in 1475 he was forced north and found himself, quite unexpectedly, in Moscow. Contarini remained four months in the capital, but not of his own free will: he was arrested and asked to help the grand prince recover money owed to him by a fellow Venetian. Contarini did as he was told and was eventually released.[16] When he arrived home, the Italian traveler did not write an excited tract about a newly discovered land, for Muscovy was known, if not well, to many Italians. What he did, not surprisingly, was draft a description of his primary mission, a trip to Persia. Muscovy is at best a sidelight in his work. Contarini's book is an itinerary, and thus the Muscovite section appears as a brief episode in the Italian's journey. "On the twenty second of September, 1476," he wrote, "it pleased God that we should enter Russia." Most of the few pages that concern Muscovy continued this sort of narrative presentation: "On the twenty sixth, we entered Moscow . . ."; "On the twenty eighth, I went to visit Marco . . ."; "On the seventh of October, I dispatched Priest Stephano . . . ," and so on.[17] The bulk of Contarini's account of Muscovy is taken up by the story of his internment and heroic escape.

In the middle of his narrative, however, Contarini paused to offer a short ethnographic description of Muscovy.[18] As a merchant-ambassador, Contarini was clearly intrigued by Muscovy's apparent wealth. He informed his readers that the country was rich in produce of every type, all of which could be purchased at a low price. Contarini paid special attention to the Russian fur trade, noting that it was being exploited by Germans and Poles, but unfortunately not by his countrymen. Nonetheless, he was critical of the Muscovites and their institutions. Contarini wrote that the grand prince controlled a large territory and could field a sizable army, although he believed the Russians to be worthless soldiers. The people were handsome but "brutal," and inclined to while away the day in drink and feasting. The Russians were Christians, but their chief priest was a creature of the grand prince and he believed that Catholics were "doomed to perdition." Despite this mild censure, Contarini obviously saw nothing out of the ordinary in Muscovy. He did not call the grand prince a tyrant, the Russian people barbarians, or the Orthodox Church apostate. In fact, he was really not very interested in Muscovite culture at all. The Italian happened upon Russia accidentally, made some incidental observations about it, most of which are focused on commerce, and provided his readers with a pleasant story about his escape. Contarini's lack of enthusiasm reflects a general Italian disinterest in detailed

[16] For sources on Contarini and his mission, see Bibliography 4 below.
[17] Contarini (1476), 158–60.
[18] Ibid., 161–63.

descriptions of Muscovy. Even the curious Venetians left no *relazione* concerning Old Russia specifically. Apparently for Contarini and other Italian merchants, Muscovy was little more than a potential trading partner.

Nonetheless, Italian interest in Russia was growing in the last quarter of the fifteenth century as Muscovite military forces moved westward and Russian diplomats began to call on European princes. The case of Milan offers an example. Since the 1450s, Muscovy and Milan had carried on negotiations over various matters, including the advance of the Turks, the recruitment of craftsmen, and the marriage of Ivan III to Sophia. Yet the Milanese knew very little about the Russians. So, when the Muscovite diplomat Iurii Trakhaniot, an Italianate Greek who had entered Russian service in the 1470s, visited the Szforza court in 1486, Milanese officials were instructed to interview him about the present state of Russia.[19] The product of Trakhaniot's discussions with the Italian officers was a short *relazione* about Muscovy. In typical ethnographic fashion, the Milanese tract describes Muscovy's extent, population, faith, major cities and fortifications, government, language, customs, economy, borders, royal family, slaves, and military.[20] Trakhaniot's comments were, as one might imagine, very positive. According to the Russian diplomat, Muscovy was a large, well-populated, and prosperous kingdom. The country's sovereign was powerful and just, its people were industrious, and its faith was Christian. Trakhaniot, a man with extensive experience in both Muscovy and Italy, knew well the significant cultural differences that separated the realms of Ivan III and the Szforzas. Yet, as the Milanese account itself makes clear, he simply ignored them. The reason is not far to seek. The Muscovites were at the time actively recruiting Italian architects and engineers to work in Moscow. Trakhaniot attempted to depict Russia as an attractive place for Milanese craftsmen to live and labor, and he did so by describing the grand prince's dominions in terms his hosts would understand and appreciate. Ironically, then, the first true Renaissance ethnography of Russia blurs rather than exaggerates the differences between Muscovy and Europe.

In the last decade of the fifteenth century a new, less sanguine image of Muscovy was presented by a Livonian, Christian Bomhover.[21] As the end of the century neared, the Livonians grew increasingly worried by Muscovite aggression in the Baltic region. Naturally, the embattled Order of the Brothers of the Sword—the Teutonic Knights—sought help against the "schismatic Russians" from their patrons in the Empire and Rome. Bomhover played an important role in the Livonians' effort to solicit foreign aid. In 1501 and in 1506 he helped persuade the pope to allow the preaching of crusades against

---

[19] On Milanese-Muscovite relations and the origins of the tract, see Gino Barbieri, *Milano e Mosca nella politica del Rinascimento*.

[20] Trakhaniot (1486).

[21] For sources on Bomhover, see Bibliography 4 below.

the Russians.[22] During these anti-Muscovite campaigns, Bomhover served as commissar of indulgences and organized preaching circuits along the Baltic littoral and in the Empire. It was in connection with this propagandistic effort that Bomhover came to write the *Fine History,* the earliest printed text devoted solely to Muscovite affairs. It is not entirely clear when the account was drafted, but there is some evidence that it was begun in the summer of 1506, at the time of Bomhover's second journey to Rome. The work was apparently pressed in 1508 in Cologne, though the printed version does not survive—only a manuscript comes down to us.

The *Fine History* was written at the behest of the Order and distributed with the permission of the papal curia in the hopes of raising support for the Livonian cause. Its purpose is immediately apparent from the sketch on the cover of the manuscript and presumably the woodcut (see fig. 1) that accompanied the printed version. It depicts the pope seated at the center of the frame with the triple crown, his right hand half raised with two outstretched fingers as a sign of blessing and absolution. To his right is a kneeling knight with the black cross of a crusade on his cloak. Next to the knight stand a cardinal and three bishops, and behind them two other clerics. To the pope's left are three Muscovites with pointed caps and clothed in caftans; in other words, they are dressed like Turks.[23] The text describes the misdeeds of the Muscovites and the valiant efforts of the Order, the "first bastion and shield of all Christianity," to halt the Russians from 1491 to 1508.[24] The Muscovites are not Christians, but heathens; they are barbaric and cruel; their master, Ivan III, is a tyrant; and, worst of all, they have secretly covenanted with the Tatars and the Turks to lay Christendom low. Bomhover devoted little attention to the ethnographic description of Russia. Muscovy, he wrote, is made up of several principalities, in which Moscow is dominant and there are Tatar principalities to the south and east with which the Muscovites sometimes ally.[25]

The Livonians were not alone in attempting to blacken the image of the Muscovites. Since the mid-fifteenth century, Polish clerics had argued that the Russian church, and by extension the Muscovites (or "Scythians," as the Poles sometimes called them), were the enemies of Christendom. In the midst of a protracted conflict with their ascendant eastern neighbor, Polish politicians also found occasion to publicly demonize the Russians. In 1514 King

[22] On the request for and organization of anti-Muscovite crusades, see Leonid Abrusow, "Die Beziehungen des Deutschen Ordens zum Ablasshandel seit dem 15. Jahrhundert."

[23] Abrusow notes that the sketch is taken from the cover of Johannes Sacranus, *Errores atrocissimorum Ruthenorum* (Cologne, 1507), a tract concerning the apostasy of the Orthodox Russians. It was probably written by Bomhover as well. See Abrusow, "Die Beziehungen des Deutschen Ordens zum Ablasshandel," 458.

[24] Bomhover (1508), 135. On Bomhover's depiction of Russia, see Friedrich Benninghoven, "Rußland im Spiegel der livländischen Schonnen Hystorie von 1508."

[25] Bomhover (1508), 118–21, 135.

1. Title page of Johannes Sacranus, *Errores atrocissimorum ruthenorum* (Cologne, 1507). By permission of the Houghton Library, Harvard University.

Sigismund launched a campaign to convince the pope and emperor that the Muscovites were, like the Turks, infidel barbarians being held at the very gates of Christendom by the valiant efforts of the Poles and Lithuanians.[26] To this

26 Ekkehard Klug, "Das 'Asiatische' Russland," 275–77.

end, the Poles sent envoys to Rome to announce the victory at the battle of Orsha, issued a number of panegyrics, and sent two letters to the curia about the war with Muscovy, both of which were published in a collection devoted, significantly, to the crusade against the Turks.[27] The Polish message was similar to Bomhover's: the Muscovites are not Christians; they are cruel and barbaric; they are Asians and not Europeans; they are in league with Turks and the Tatars to destroy Christendom.

The most interesting piece of anti-Muscovite Polish propaganda is Jacob Piso's letter in the Turkish collection. Piso was a Hungarian in papal service who was dispatched by the curia to make peace between Sigismund and Vasilii III and bring the forces of both to bear on the Turks.[28] If we can judge by his writings, Piso was obviously the wrong man for the job, for he was both pro-Jagellonian and anti-Muscovite. Piso somehow made his way into Sigismund's camp and witnessed the conflict at Orsha in 1514. Shortly thereafter he inaugurated a new era in anti-Russian propaganda, issuing the first truly anti-Muscovite broadsheet (*Flugschrift*).[29] His letter in the anti-Turkish compendium was similarly groundbreaking, for it contained the first characterization of the Muscovite government as tyrannical to appear in print. After describing the progress of the battle of Orsha, Piso provided a very brief ethnography of Muscovy. He told his readers that many Muscovites were suffering for their Catholicism at the hands of the grand prince and that "if they were not terrified by the sure tyranny of Moscow, many would flee in all directions." The Muscovites, he wrote, "are oppressed by the most cruel laws— all are born to this condition, all grow to it, and all are reduced to it."[30]

Polish misgivings about the Muscovites apparently found some sympathy in the Empire, as can be seen in the account of Francesco Da Collo. After Emperor Maximilian had made peace with the Poles in 1515, he embarked on an effort to end Polish-Russian hostilities and to forge a united front against the Turks. For this purpose, Maximilian sent Da Collo to Moscow in 1518.[31] Though the Italian failed to make peace between the warring parties, he did provide the emperor with an informative report about the course of the negotiations and the character of Muscovy. Like Piso, Da Collo stressed the absolute power of the Russian ruler over his subjects: the grand prince is the sole proprietor in the realm; the Russians have no written law, only the prince's will; no subject may travel outside the realm without the express permission of the ruler. Moreover, the grand prince controls a cavalry host

[27] The letters, one by Sigismund and the other by Jacob Piso, are found in Ianus Damianus, *Iani Damiani Senensis ad Leonem X. Pont. Max. de expeditione in Turcas Elegia* (Basel, 1515).
[28] For sources on Piso, see Bibliography 4 below.
[29] Jacob Piso, *Die Schlacht von dem kunig Poln. und mit dem Moscowiter. gescheen am tag Marie gepurt.*
[30] Piso (1515), n.p.
[31] On the origins of Da Collo's tract, see Hans B. Uebersberger, *Österreich und Russland seit dem Ende des 15. Jahrhunderts,* 1:105ff. For sources on Da Collo, see Bibliography 4 below.

of 400,000 men armed like Turks.[32] A year after Da Collo's mission failed, Maximilian ordered Herberstein to travel to Muscovy and continue the peace negotiations. Herberstein may have produced a description of Muscovy shortly after his return to Vienna, but this is by no means clear. To be sure, Herberstein's famous *Notes on the Muscovites* of 1549, which was probably based on an earlier diplomatic report, offers an image of Russian tyranny quite similar to that found in Da Collo. Since it seems most probable, however, that Herberstein finished the seminal ethnography in the late 1540s, it falls out of our chronological purview.

Though Rome would occasionally support anti-Russian actions, no amount of Livonian, Polish, or Imperial propaganda could permanently convince the papacy that the Russians were beyond redemption. Persuading the Russians to renounce their "heresy" was, after all, essential to Rome's long-term strategic goal—the unification of the Church and the defeat of the Turks. The Council of Florence in 1439 was the first moment in the papal plan to bring the Muscovites into the fold. Though the Russian delegation to the council agreed to a union of the eastern and western churches, the authorities in Moscow rejected the deal. But Rome never forgot the Russians' initial promise. After the fall of Constantinople in 1453, papal efforts to persuade the Muscovites to join in the defense of Christendom grew more strenuous. Hoping to convince Ivan III that he was the heir of Constantine, the curia arranged a match between the niece of the last Byzantine emperor and Ivan III in 1472. Ivan did not, however, move to recapture his putative patrimony. In 1483 the papacy invited the Muscovites to join the commonwealth of Christian nations with the offer of a papal crown. The grand prince rejected this gesture, explaining that he did not need Catholic recognition to rule his realm. For a time the curia seemed to sour on the Russians, as is perhaps suggested by its support of crusades against the Muscovites in 1496, 1503, and 1506. A peculiar set of events, however, soon raised the prospect of both union and a common front again.

In February 1517 the grand master of the German order, Albrecht von Brandenburg, dispatched Dietrich von Schönberg to Moscow to propose a united front against the Poles. The deal was quickly done, and Schönberg returned home. The treaty, however, was not all he brought to Livonia. While in Moscow Schönberg met with Nicholas von Lübeck, a German doctor in Muscovite service, and others who secretly desired ecclesiastical union with the papacy. The Uniates in Moscow told Schönberg that Vasilii was not in principle opposed to bringing the churches together. Though this report was completely untrue, it fired Schönberg's imagination. Upon his return to Europe in March 1517, he communicated the news about Vasilii's desires to an official of the Order in Rome, who then told Pope Leo X. The papacy's hopes soared and embassies were dispatched to Moscow in 1519, 1520, and 1521 to discuss union and a crusade against the Turks.

---

[32] Dzhuzeppe D'Amato, *Sochineniia ital'iantsev o Rossii kontsa XV–XVI vv.*, 62.

The curia's enthusiasm for its Muscovite project is apparent in the writings of Albert Campensé. Campensé, a Dutch Humanist and official at the curia, had been asked by Pope Hadrian VI (Leo's successor) to draft a report about Russia.[33] His account, however, tells us less about Muscovy than about the Romans' hopes for a Russian savior. Campensé wrote that by ridding the Russians of their apostasy the papacy would gain an ally against the Turks and the "frenzied lunatics," the Lutherans. The entire character of Russian society, he argued, would make conversion a simple task. Campensé noted that the Muscovite grand prince had complete control over his subjects, whom "he rules as slaves, having full power to dispose of their lives and property." No one could hold a living without his writ, leave Russia without his allowance, or contradict him in any way. Russian commoners themselves, he believed, were fanatically loyal to their ruler and, unlike their European counterparts, they were always ready to defend the realm.[34] The grand prince's powers were so extensive and his people so obedient that Campensé was sure that Vasilii could simply order his subjects to become Catholics.

> If we were forced to deal with this issue with the entire people, then we would certainly meet a host of obstacles and difficulties, because it is not easy to convince someone to give up or alter the faith of his ancestors. . . . But here we encounter rather the opposite case. All power is concentrated in the person of the grand prince, who has repeatedly expressed his desire for union of the two faiths.[35]

Moreover, the nature of Russian society and Orthodoxy also suggested that conversion would not be difficult. According to Campensé, the Russians were extremely moral people. "Deception of one another," he wrote, "is considered a terrible, base crime; adultery, violence, and public fighting are very rare; unnatural vices are unknown; oath breaking and blasphemy are unheard of." The Russians were also pious: "In general they deeply honor God and his saints and whenever they meet an image of the crucifixion, they immediately fall to the ground in heartfelt piety." Perhaps more important, the Russian faith was, to Campensé's mind, very much like Catholicism: "The substantive difference between their faith and ours consists of a very few tenets, which by the way in and of themselves are not terribly important for spiritual salvation, and which, according to the words of the Apostle, are more easily suffered than those being extirpated by cruelty or those being preached to people in sin not yet confirmed in the faith." [36] Given all these considerations, Campensé argued, the Muscovites were in a sense waiting to become Catholics.

The papacy was apparently persuaded by Campensé's arguments, for diplomatic overtures continued. In May 1524 Clement instructed Paul Centuri-

[33] For sources on Campensé, see Bibliography 4 below.
[34] Campensé (1524), 9–13, 31–32, 23.
[35] Ibid., 35.
[36] Ibid., 33–34.

one to travel to Moscow and discuss ecclesiastical union with Vasilii. Nothing concrete came of these talks, save Vasilii's promise to send a legate to Rome for further meetings. Pursuant to this pledge, Dmitrii Gerasimov accompanied Centurione to Rome, where they arrived in September 1525. Not surprisingly, Gerasimov's visit did not further the cause of union. It did, however, provide the papacy with an opportunity to learn more about Muscovy. Clement instructed the noted historian Paolo Giovio to interview the multilingual Muscovite diplomat.[37] On the basis of his discussions with Gerasimov, Giovio produced a short description of Muscovy, the second to emerge from Uniate circles. Like Campensé, Giovio argued that clerical union between Rome and Moscow was an integral part of the struggle against the Reformation. And like Campensé, he claimed that the time was right for a papal initiative, for Vasilii was known (so he says) to have pro-Catholic sympathies. Giovio, however, was unwilling to skew his description of Russia so as to suggest that the conversion of the Muscovites would be an easy task. His purpose was to provide an evenhanded ethnographic description of Russia, blemishes and all. He does so in a series of concise surveys of Russian geography, agriculture and trade, religion, physical characteristics, food and drink, the treatment of women, the royal family, the army, and the court. Nowhere in the description does one find any hint that the Muscovites were ready to cross over to the Catholic side. Giovio implicitly denies that the grand prince is a despot. On the contrary, "all Muscovy is governed by the simplest laws, based on the justice of the lord and the impartiality of his lieutenants." About the grand prince he writes: "Vasilii is forty-eight years old, and he exceeds all his predecessors in beauty of body, extent of soul, martial praise, and love and beneficence toward his subjects." He emphasizes Vasilii's familiarity with his men by noting that he frequently dines with them. In fact, the most unusual characteristic of the grand prince's government is not tyranny but fairness: "Generally, in every part of the administration they observe the useful and excellent institution that all according to their services receive eternal reward or eternal shame." Giovio's view of Russian society and Orthodoxy are much more sober than Campensé's. The Russians are devout, but no more so than Catholics: "In all similar dogmas of the faith they hold with the greatest firmness, just as we acknowledge those of our faith." He reviews at great length the not inconsiderable dogmatic differences that divide the churches, and says rightly that "in general the Muscovites observe the same rites as the Greeks, and of course they reject the primacy of the Roman church with impudence and obstinacy."[38]

Others, however, agreed with Campensé about the virtues of the Muscovites. In June 1524 Vasilii III sent Prince Ivan Fedorovich Iaroslavskii and the state secretary Semen Borisovich Trofimov to the court of Charles V in Spain. Their business was completed in August or September 1525, and they left

[37] For sources on Giovio, see Bibliography 4 below.
[38] Giovio (1525), 11, 47, 52–55, 46, 42.

Madrid for Moscow. On their way home, sometime in the late fall of that year, the ambassadorial train stopped at Ferdinand's court in Tübingen, where they were received with full honors. Ferdinand asked the cleric Johann Fabri to interview his guests and produce a report on Muscovy.[39] Fabri was a theologian and jurist by training who made a name for himself in Imperial circles by issuing virulent blasts against the Protestants. He served for many years as a high official in Constance, and in 1521 was called by Ferdinand to serve as councilor in Tübingen, where he devoted most of his time and effort to fighting the Lutheran heresy. Fabri would finally be rewarded for his efforts by being appointed bishop of Vienna. Like Campensé and Giovio, Fabri was interested in Muscovy only insofar as it might serve to strengthen the Catholic cause against the Lutherans and Turks.

Fabri's description of the grand prince's realm was every bit as idealized as Campensé's. He agreed with the Dutchman that the grand prince's authority was unrestricted. "There is no other lordship in the world," Fabri wrote, "that is more subject to its master." Unlike the disobedient Germans, the Muscovites willingly submit themselves to the untrammeled rule of their prince. Even great lords are "ready and eager to execute all the emperor's orders, like the orders of God, even if this might entail the loss of [their] own [lives]." The Russians believe that "unconditional submission to the lord is the highest and most sacred duty of the subject, the fulfillment of which constitutes the primary and valued distinction." They consider that only by means of complete subjection "can one obtain the right to eternal life." According to Fabri, Russian Orthodoxy is the very embodiment of primitive Christianity and the Russians are pious, God-fearing, and devout in the extreme.[40] Fabri concluded his fantastic description with a comparison between his own compatriots and the Russians. Fabri found the Germans wanting:

> About this, your highness, it is difficult not to wonder: how this people, carrying on incessant and terrible wars and thus never knowing peace, could continually and firmly preserve their ancient faith. And our Germans long ago stopped behaving the way they should. Where Russians live, there Germans find death. Where the former [preach] the teachings of God, the latter sow anger and enmity among men. Russians fast when they should, while we go to feasts and banquets. Russians live life strictly and wisely, preserving the sanctity of the marriage bed—and among us? Among the Russians, the performance of the Church's mysteries expiates their sins; among our countrymen, regretfully, this only increases them. And so in all fairness, it must bring sorrow to your highness and the German lords that we, instead of true piety, have given ourselves over to every sort of filth and illegality, in relation to God, in relation to our parents, in relation to our ancestors, and in relation to our fatherland.[41]

---

[39] For sources on Fabri, see Bibliography 4 below.
[40] Fabri (1526), 297–99, 47–48.
[41] Ibid., 66–68.

Fabri hints that not only would the Russians make good allies against the Turks and Protestants, they would also be excellent models for Ferdinand's subjects themselves.

All of the accounts of Muscovy written between 1486 and 1526 are marked by a certain similarity. In the descriptions reviewed above, Muscovy is commonly depicted as a rich northern country, ruled by a powerful prince, and peopled by Christians of the Greek rite. Within these general parameters, however, the accounts are marked by considerable variation. For Contarini and the Milanese officials who interviewed Trakhaniot, Muscovy was an object of commercial interest. In the Italian accounts, Ivan III's realm is imagined as an ordinary kingdom distinguished only by its vast and untapped wealth. A very different image emerges in the Livonian and Polish descriptions. For Bomhover and Piso, the Muscovite grand prince was a tyrant attempting to impose his wayward faith on the true Christians of northern Europe. Those papal and Imperial authors hoping for union with Muscovy provided yet a third picture of Russia. For Campensé and Fabri, Muscovy was an ideal state in which a just despot ruled over a pious, Christian nation. It is clear in each of these instances that the authors projected their interests and desires on an unfamiliar place. Bias of this sort is typical in any age, but the authors of the first generation of European Moscovitica were particularly susceptible to imaginative flights for the simple reason that they lacked reliable information about Russia. Only Trakhaniot had extensive experience in Muscovy. Contarini and Da Collo had visited for a short time, in fact too short to gain any real familiarity with Muscovite culture. The other first-generation authors were compelled to rely on accidental interviews and sketchy written accounts.[42] Sources of the former type clearly predominated in the early treatises: the Milanese officials, Giovio, and Fabri questioned visiting Muscovite diplomats; Piso probably discussed Russian affairs with Polish ambassadors; and Campensé collected information "from several of our merchants, and from my brother and father who lived for quite a time in Muscovy."[43] Outside a few misleading Classical and medieval texts, written sources on Russia were largely unavailable to the first-generation authors: Trakhaniot's interviewers, Contarini, Piso, and Giovio cite no written sources, though in light of the antiquated geographical data in their descriptions it seems clear that they were influenced by Classical authors; Da Collo and Fabri cite Classical and medieval geographers by name and faithfully followed their errone-

---

[42] On Contarini's sources, see Elena Ch. Skrzhinskaia, ed., *Barbaro i Kontarini o Rossii*, 86–89; on Bomhover's sources, see Abrusow, "Die Beziehungen des Deutschen Ordens zum Ablasshandel," 416–18, 458–75; on Maciej z Miechowa's sources, see Anninskii's introduction to Maciej (1517), 12–20; on Da Collo's sources, see D'Amato, *Sochineniia ital'iantsev*, 64; on Campensé's sources, see Andreas Kappeler, *Ivan Groznyi im Spiegel der ausländischen Druckschriften seiner Zeit*, 25, and D'Amato, *Sochineniia ital'iantsev*, 69–70; on Giovio's sources, see Kappeler, *Ivan Groznyi im Spiegel der ausländischen Druckschriften*, 24–25, and D'Amato, *Sochineniia ital'iantsev*, 82–83; on Fabri's sources, see Kappeler, *Ivan Groznyi im Spiegel der ausländischen Druckschriften*, 25.

[43] Campensé (1543), 12.

Table 1. Republication of early ethnographies of Russia

Original text	Republication
Contarini (1487)	Italian: 1524, 1543, 1545, 1559
	Latin: 2 in 17th century (excerpts)
Bomhover (1508)	None
Piso I (1514)	Latin: 1586
Piso II (1514)	None
Giovio (1525)	Latin: 1537, 1545, 1551, 1551, 1555, 1557, 1557, 1571, 1600
	Italian: 1545, 1545, 1549, 1583
	German: 1563, 1567, 1576
Fabri (1526)	1582, 1600
Campensé (1543)	Italian: 1559, 1583

ous geographical and ethnographic teachings; and Bomhover may have used contemporary printed texts about Muscovy, but these works related more about Orthodoxy than about Russia's land and people.

Though the impact of the early accounts after 1526 is difficult to gauge, one rough measure of their later influence is the number of times each text was printed and translated. Table 1 provides a brief overview of the early modern publishing history of each text. Judging by the relative frequency of republication, one can see that the only ethnography to have a lasting impact on European consciousness of Russia was Giovio's. The remaining accounts were largely forgotten. Contarini's book, though it was plagiarized at least once in the sixteenth century (by Josaphat Barbaro), seems to have exercised little or no influence.[44] Fabri was recalled by Herberstein, but by no one else.[45] No references to Bomhover, Piso, or Campensé are to be found in later European writings on Muscovy.

Muscovy in the Early Cosmographies, 1517–1544

Though they were divided over the nature of Russian society, the men who wrote the earliest Renaissance descriptions of Muscovy succeeded in providing Europeans with their first glimpse of the northern Russian dominion. After 1526, one major ethnography of Russia—Giovio's—was widely available to the educated public, and several others were in limited circulation. Nonetheless, the ethnographies were not the only or even the primary sources of enlightenment about Russia before the publication of Herberstein's *Notes on the Muscovites* in 1549. Like ethnography, cosmography was a burgeoning genre in the first half of the sixteenth century.[46] It was designed to provide curious readers with a brief introduction to the various parts of the

[44] Barbaro (1488–89). On his plagiarism, see Skrzhinskaia, *Barbaro i Kontarini*, 96–104.
[45] Herberstein (1517–49), 1:clx.
[46] Hodgen, *Early Anthropology*, 111–61.

world, with particular attention to little-known or newly discovered areas such as Muscovy. Sebastian Münster, perhaps the greatest cosmographer of the era, advised his readers that it was not necessary to "wander all over the world to observe and experience the conditions of countries, cities, rivers, mountains, valleys, and the customs, habits, laws, and governments of men as well as the property and nature of animals, trees, and creatures." Münster insisted that one could "find these things in books, and indeed learn and experience more of this or that land than someone who has spent a year and a day in it." [47] To facilitate such a mental journey around the globe, the cosmographers (in the words of Johann Boemus, another early practitioner) "collected, abridged, digested, compacted together the manners and façions, the Lawes, Customes and Rites" of many countries. [48] The product of the cosmographer's work was, as the French scholar Jean Bodin wrote, a compendium "which contains the origins, conditions, changes and fall of not only illustrious peoples, but also of all peoples, yet with a brevity such that one can see almost at a glance what was the established form of each state." [49] Though the cosmographers were sometimes men of vast experience, they tended to rely on printed ethnographies for information about particular countries. As Münster admitted, "what I have not seen myself, and indeed this is much, I will take from the writings left behind by learned and experienced men." [50] As we will presently see, a series of short ethnographies of Muscovy appeared in European cosmographies between 1517 and 1544. The images of Russia they present vary widely, largely because their authors appropriated passages from first-generation ethnographies that depicted Russia in various ways.

Maciej z Miechowa's Account of the Two Sarmatias, Asian and European (Cracow, 1517) may rightly be considered the first cosmographical work to include information about Muscovy. Maciej was a geographer, medical doctor, and historian who made his career at the esteemed University of Cracow. [51] He seems to have traveled in the same elite circle out of which emerged the Polish anti-Muscovite propaganda of 1516 and 1517. Yet his intention in writing a description of the "two Sarmatias" was not, at least in the first instance, publicistic. He was primarily interested in eradicating the errors of the Ptolemaic cartography of his day. In his Account, Maciej z Miechowa assures his audience that the great rivers of Muscovy do not find their headwaters in the "Ryphei" or "Hyperborei" mountains because no such mountains exist. European Sarmatia is a vast plain out of which flow the Don and Volga. Despite his focus on geography, Maciej devotes some

[47] Münster (1544), Vorrede.
[48] Johann Boemus, The fardle of façions conteining the aunciente maners, customes, and Lawes, quoted in Hodgen, Early Anthropology, 131–32.
[49] Jean Bodin, Method for the Easy Comprehension of History, 21.
[50] Münster (1544), Vorrede.
[51] For sources on Maciej z Miechowa, see Bibliography 4 below.

energy to dispelling ethnographic myths: there is no race of happy "Hyper-bornians"; the Muscovites speak one language ("Russian or Slavic"); the Russians hold one faith ("Greek"); some northerners are idolaters. His trea-tise, however, is not entirely bound up in revision, for he confirms what his countryman Piso said about the tyrannical rule of the grand prince. "In the Muscovite state, as in the lands of the Turks," he tells his readers, "people are thrown from place to place and from province to province for coloniza-tion, and to replace [those who have departed] they send and settle others." Maciej implies that the grand prince, like the Ottoman sultan, treats his sub-jects like slaves. Muscovites are not even free to leave the realm: "There are guards everywhere so that not only slaves and prisoners, but freemen and visitors will not depart without an edict from the prince." And he believes that the political slavery of the Muscovites has penetrated their social life. "Slaves," he writes, "are sold by lords like cattle, and with them their wives and children; more than that, poor people born free but not having food sell their sons and daughters, and sometimes themselves, in order to obtain from the lord any kind of food, albeit gross." [52] Though he offers no detailed com-mentary on Russian governance, Maciej hints that there is something strange and perhaps threatening about Muscovite civic life.

Maciej z Miechowa was hardly the only European scholar interested in the cosmographical description of the Slavic inhabitants of northern Europe. Soon after the Polish geographer published his *Account,* Albert Krantz's cos-mographical treatment of the Slavs, *Wandalia* (Cologne, 1519), appeared in print. Krantz was educated in the Hanseatic town of Rostock and later be-came rector of the university there. [53] Thereafter he served the Hansa in vari-ous cities, holding one post or another in the league for the rest of his active life. From 1500 to 1504 he devoted himself to the study of northern, central, and eastern European history. One of the products of his labor was *Wanda-lia*. He completed the work before 1504, but it was not published until 1519. Krantz, who had served in Livonia, pays special attention to the Baltic lit-toral. It is in this connection that we find several brief relations about Mus-covy, all focused on Russian aggression in the region. Krantz recalls that Ivan III plundered Novgorod in 1487, exiling and killing many of its citizens. Since then, he continues, Russian-Hanseatic relations had been going badly: the Russian grand prince had imprisoned Hanseatic merchants, stolen their goods, and invaded Livonia. [54] The picture is brief but clear—Ivan III is a tyrant, and a danger to both the League and the Livonian Order.

As news about the Russians spread west, German cosmographers deeper in the Empire became interested in the realm of the grand prince. The work of Johann Boemus provides an example. Boemus was born in Aub and stud-

[52] Maciej (1517), 45, 115–17, 112.
[53] For sources on Krantz, see Bibliography 4 below.
[54] Krantz (1504), bk. 1, chap. 2; bk. 13, chap. 15; bk. 14, chap. 22.

ied in Leipzig, Frankfurt an der Oder, and Tübingen.[55] He entered the German order and became a Latin scholar in the Humanist circles in Ulm, Augsburg, and Nuremberg. Little else is known about him, other than that he had a rather progressive penchant for cosmography. His *Mores, Laws, and Rites of All Peoples* (Augsburg, 1520) was groundbreaking: he gathered out of many books information about a host of peoples and reduced said data to pithy vignettes.[56] Boemus's book has rightly been called the first ethnographic encyclopedia. He remained true to his role as an editor and not author, for his brief section on Muscovy is almost entirely derivative of Maciej z Miechowa. As a member of the German order he certainly would have been sympathetic to Maciej's view of what he undoubtedly saw as the "schismatic Muscovite."

The 1530s witnessed a new wave of cosmographical writing on Muscovy that arrived, strangely, by way of German chauvinism.[57] Early in the sixteenth century German scholars began to show interest in the historical geography of the Empire. Ancient texts containing less than flattering pictures of the Germans were printed and the image of the "barbaric" Germans spread throughout learned Europe. German geographers attempted to demonstrate the nobility of their ancestors. The first effort in this direction was Enea Silvio's *Germania* of 1457. It was followed by many attempts to recapture the Germanic past and ennoble the Germanic present, not the least of which was Konrad Celtis's project to produce a *Germania illustrata* on the plan of Biondo's famous *Italia illustrata*. Though Celtis's project was never completed, it inspired others to write cosmographies of central Europe. One of them was the famous Hebraist and cosmographer Sebastian Münster.[58] Münster began to pursue geographical projects in the mid-1520s. His first major work in this vein, *Description of Germany* (Basel, 1530), was a long commentary on the old map of Nicolas Cusanus rather than a full-blown cosmographical description. He did, however, mention Muscovy in the book. As we might expect, Münster discusses the Imperial struggle with the grand prince, but his actual rendering of Russia is brief and neutral in tone.[59] This is interesting, because the section on Muscovy in *Description of Germany* is essentially an abridgment of Maciej z Miechowa and Giovio. Münster chose to reflect neither the former's subtle criticism of Muscovy nor Giovio's sanguine view of Muscovite civic life. The reasons may have had to do with the neutrality of Münster's science, but it seems just as likely that he selected only what he found interesting in the two texts with little regard for evenhandedness.

Much more interesting is the description of Muscovy found in the Humanist Willibald Pirckheimer's *Germany Described from Various Sources* (Nu-

[55] For sources on Boemus, see Bibliography 4 below.
[56] Boemus (1520).
[57] Gerald Strauss, *Sixteenth-Century Germany*.
[58] For sources on Münster, see Bibliography 4 below.
[59] Münster (1530), 39–40.

remberg, 1530).[60] Like Münster, Pirckheimer drew inspiration from Celtis's *Germania illustrata*. He described the Muscovites in connection with the German *Ostraum*. In a section of his book devoted to the Germans beyond the Vistula in European Sarmatia, Pirckheimer relates that long ago many Teutonic tribes—Goths, Alans, Vandals, and so on—invaded the area. After them came a multitude of Slavs (*"Schlevini"*), who occupied the lands of the Germans and sometimes forced them out completely. Among the various Slavs he identifies the "Russians or Muscovites," and explains that their empire spreads to the Don and beyond. Indeed, there is nothing unusual here, and Pirckheimer momentarily forgets the Muscovites and moves on to an account of Prussia and Livonia. This section, however, suddenly breaks off and Pirckheimer abruptly launches into a brief description of Muscovy. The realm of the grand duke is enormous, he writes, extending from the Baltic to the Volga and into Asiatic Scythia. Ivan III greatly expanded his empire, adding Perm, Correlia, and Uyguria to his already sizable holdings. The people inhabiting the latter region are the ancestors of the Hungarians, and to this day are very primitive, living without bread or money, and offering tribute to the grand prince in pelts. Other conquests of Ivan III include Novgorod and Smolensk. Moscow is the capital of the realm, and it is entirely built of wood, except for the fortress and palace of the grand princes. Pirckheimer offers a particularly harsh view of Muscovite society: "This nation is rude and completely barbarous, and moreover they are subject to extreme servitude, such that, as among the Turks, all property is accounted as belonging to the rulers. And the prince of Moscovia holds everything to be his property: he relinquishes only profit and use [of his property] to his subjects, and not for longer than he desires." [61]

Some of Pirckheimer's obvious disgust with the Russians no doubt derived from his fear, shared by many in the Empire after the events in Livonia, of Muscovite aggression. It is possible, however, that Pirckheimer was also influenced by Herberstein, for both saw all Muscovites as slaves to the grand prince. In writing *Germany*, Pirckheimer solicited information from a wide circle of correspondents. One of them was the well-known Humanist, poet, and reformer Ulrich von Hutten. Pirckheimer asked Hutten whether it was true that the river the Russians called the Volga was the ancient Rha, as he had read in "a book about the two Sarmatias," which is of course Maciej z Miechowa's *Account*. In a letter to Pirckheimer dated October 25, 1518, Hutten responded that he too had read Maciej and wondered about the Volga and the Rha. Hutten explained: "As I researched this question with the care it deserved, it luckily happened that I became acquainted with the knight Sigismund von Herberstein, an adviser of the emperor. In the past winter he served as the emperor's ambassador to the prince of Moscow, and he traveled over

---

[60] For sources on Pirckheimer, see Bibliography 4 below.
[61] Pirckheimer (1530), 105.

much of Scythia and made his way into barbarian Asia." [62] It seems that Hutten met Herberstein at the Diet of Augsburg, which both attended in the summer of 1518.[63] Herberstein informed Hutten that Maciej z Miechowa was correct in writing that the Rhyphei and Hyperborei mountains existed only in the imaginations of the ancient geographers, but the Polish geographer had made a serious mistake concerning the Volga: it is called the Rha in Ptolemy, but it flows "into the Black and not the Caspian sea."[64] Pirckheimer indeed incorporated Herberstein's geographical corrective into his account of Muscovy.[65] Whether Herberstein also provided Pirckheimer via Hutten with the master-slave description of Russian society is an open question.

As in the case of Maciej z Miechowa, Pirckheimer's rendering of Muscovy inspired followers. The German theologian Sebastian Franck published a cosmography in 1534 that contained passages borrowed from both Maciej and Pirckheimer. Franck's cosmography would seem to be modeled on Boemus's *Mores, Laws, and Rites of All Peoples,* for it is heavy with ethnography and light on mathematical geography. And like Boemus, Franck made no effort to hide the fact that he was merely compiling the work of others into a more convenient form. Thus Franck included Boemus's section on Muscovy, itself drawn from Maciej, and Pirckheimer's vignette on Russia from his *Germany.* The former is a more or less verbatim translation, but in the latter we see some interesting variations. The most important of these alterations is found in Franck's reworking of Pirckheimer's passage on Muscovite society.

> In sum, the people of the Muscovite state are rude, and furthermore they are subject to great servitude and tyranny, such that, as is the case among the Turks, anything anyone has is considered to be the king's own, and the king holds everything as his property. As a master allows his slaves the profit and use [of his property], so he allows his subjects, and not longer than he desires, and on the condition that they give him what, when, and however much he wants, including themselves, their wives, and children.[66]

This was a significant elaboration of Pirckheimer's statement. Pirckheimer described a regime of property rights not dissimilar to what he might have understood as feudalism: all lands are legally granted by the monarch and held of him as conditional tenures. Only temporary use is transferred. Such may have been the case under Charlemagne, and partial remnants of this system remained in the law of France, England, and the Empire. Living exam-

---

[62] The letter is reprinted in Willehad P. Eckert and Christoph von Imhoff, *Willibald Pirckheimer,* 336–49 (hereafter cited as Hutten); the quotation is on 348.

[63] Hajo Holborn, *Ulrich von Hutten and the German Reformation,* 103–5. For Herberstein, see Berthold Picard, *Das Gesandtschaftswesen Ostmitteleuropeas in der frühen Neuzeit,* 168. Also see Theodor G. von Karajan, "Selbstbiographie Sigmunds Freiherrn von Herberstein," 135ff.

[64] Hutten, 348.

[65] Pirckheimer (1530), 104–5.

[66] Franck (1534), 30.

ples of despotic feudalism, he seemed to say, might be found only in Turkey and Muscovy. Significantly, Franck added the notion of slavery to this analysis. The Muscovite grand duke is a *dominus* in his realm. He rules both the lives and property of his subjects, who are here figured as slaves. Why Franck chose this interpretive route is difficult to guess. He may have felt some animosity toward the Muscovites, but there is nothing in his biography to indicate that he did, save the fact that he was a subject of the Empire.[67] It is also possible that his alteration of Pirckheimer's text was motivated by empirical considerations. Franck had translated and published a late fifteenth-century description of Turkey in 1530.[68] The account of Turkish government may have provided him with material for the elaboration of Pirckheimer.[69] In addition, we can see the influence of Maciej z Miechowa via Boemus. Recall that Maciej and Boemus drew attention to the practice of slavery, and especially self-sale, in Muscovy. Franck, of course, reproduced these passages, and so they were readily at hand when he translated and emended Pirckheimer.[70] This would seem to be the source of his interpolation into Pirckheimer regarding the surrendering of self and family to the grand prince.

Following Franck, Münster again enters the picture. Since his *Description of Germany* of 1530, Münster had widened his horizons somewhat, and in 1536 he made bold to issue what claimed to be an all-European description— *Map of Europe* (Frankfurt, 1536).[71] Despite its title, the book was not a mere commentary on a map, but was instead an ethnographic description of all European countries. The vast majority of the material in *Map of Europe* is drawn from his *Description of Germany,* and most experts agree that the former should really be seen as a popular, expanded version of the latter. The section on Muscovy is different from that in *Description of Germany* but ultimately is based on the same sources. Münster seems to have relied on Boemus or Franck, but it is impossible to tell which was his primary source, for Franck repeated Boemus verbatim. And as I pointed out above, Boemus's information on Muscovy was drawn from Maciej. Thus the source for the Muscovy sections in *Description of Germany* and *Map of Europe* is ultimately Maciej z Miechowa.

Three years after Münster published his *Map of Europe,* another geographical text bearing a brief description of Muscovy entered the stream of European Moscovitica. This was the Swedish bishop Olaus Magnus's *Sea Map and Description of Northern Regions* (Venice, 1539).[72] *Sea Map* is primarily a description of Scandinavia, but it includes the Muscovite territories along the Baltic littoral north of Ivangorod and slightly to the east of the Baltic lordships. Specifically, the three most easterly quadrants of his map

[67] For sources on Franck, see Bibliography 4 below.
[68] Georgius de Hungaria, *Chronica, Abconterfayung und Entwerffung der Turckey.*
[69] Franck's description of Turkish government is in his *Chronica,* chap. 7.
[70] Franck (1534), 57.
[71] Münster (1536).
[72] Magnus (1539). For sources on Magnus, see Bibliography 4 below.

(C, F, and I) show parts of Muscovy. In the commentary appended to the map, Muscovy is mentioned eight times (C.d, C.f, C.o, C.p, F.f, F.n, I.a, I.e). Topics covered include geographical curiosities, Muscovite pirates, fishing and hunting rights, trade, shipbuilding, and rivers. *Sea Map* contains no analysis of Muscovite society, but it reflects the attitudes of the Swedes toward what they perceived as Muscovite aggression. In three sections of the commentary, corresponding to three icons on the map, the conflict between Muscovy and Sweden, Livonia, and Lithuania is discussed. In section F.f., the map shows Swedish fortifications being built "against the Muscovites." In commentary F.n., which discusses a picture of Muscovite and Swedish forces attacking one another, Magnus offers a brief characterization of what he believed to be the root cause of the conflict: "Here are the Swedish knights fighting the Muscovites on the ice; around the same water and on other rivers they defeated them in the summer. The origin of the war is the anger of both sides that part of the land is under the Greek [religion] and the other part under the Latin." Finally, in commentary A.i., indicating Livonia on the map, Magnus excludes the Orthodox Russians from the greater Christian commonwealth. "In this final section under the small letter 'A' [is] Livonia (Leifland), which has been placed under the German Order of Our Lady for the purpose of defending and protecting daily the Christian religion against the Russians and Muscovites."

In Magnus's map one sees a rather late echo of the campaign against the Muscovites first initiated by the Livonians and Poles. Magnus accepted the two key elements in the Baltic position on the Muscovites: that they were schismatics and that they were bent on seizing the Baltic rim from its rightful Christian lords. In Magnus's major work, *History of Northern Peoples* (Rome, 1555), the Muscovites and their defenders receive even harsher treatment, but this book falls out of the range of our present concerns.[73]

The final pre-Herbersteinian cosmography to include a description of Muscovy is Münster's enormously influential *Cosmography* of 1544. In its organization and purpose, this work is an almost grotesque elaboration of Boemus's modest *Mores, Laws, and Rites of All Peoples*. It also represents the fruition of Münster's dream of an encyclopedic cosmography. Unlike his previous publications, *Cosmography* was an ostensibly universal description, presenting the reader with the entire panoply of human culture. The entries in *Map of Europe* provided Münster with a base for the European section of *Cosmography*. His basic technique seems to have been to take the pertinent section from *Map of Europe* and add new material, producing an expanded, improved vignette. This is precisely what we find in the case of his description of Muscovy.[74] The new account is quite long in comparison with those found in *Description of Germany* and *Map of Europe*, running a full six pages

---

[73] Magnus (1555).
[74] Münster (1544), 1029–34.

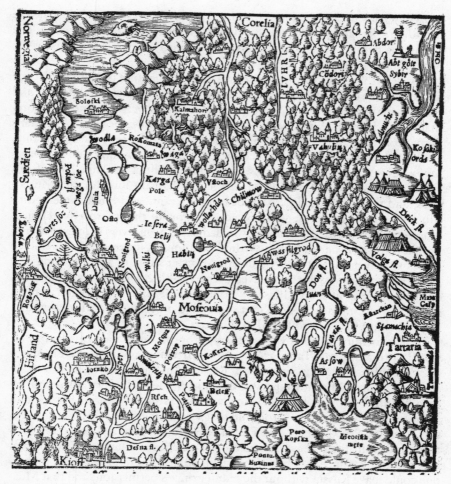

2. Muscovy. Sebastian Münster, *Cosmographia* (Basel, 1544).

with accompanying woodcuts and a map (see fig. 2). It is for the most part based on Maciej z Miechowa and Giovio, both of whom are cited. To these sources Münster adds two more: Ivan Liatskii ("Johannes Latzki"), a Muscovite official who had fled the grand prince's court after the death of Vasilii III; and Anton Weid ("Anthonius Weid"), a Lithuanian artist in Polish service. Actually the two sources are in a sense one: Liatskii provided Weid with information he needed to draft a map of Muscovy, which in turn Münster reproduced in *Cosmography*. Though Münster expanded both his entry on Muscovy and the circle of sources for it, we find nothing new about Russian society in the vignette. All we learn is that there are many principalities in

Muscovy, each under the rule of the grand prince.[75] Interestingly, the passage regarding self-slavery in *Map of Europe* was removed for *Cosmography*. The account is neutral in tone and content, and this is apparently precisely the way Münster meant it.

It is clear that there was no consensus about the nature of Muscovite civic life among the early cosmographers. Two of the early texts (Pirckheimer and Franck) plainly describe Muscovy as a place of universal despotism, foreshadowing Herberstein. Five of them (Maciej, Krantz, Boemus, Münster's *Map of Europe,* and Magnus) contain elements of this view, such as tyranny and self-slavery. Finally, Münster's *Description of Germany* and *Cosmography* paint a neutral or even positive picture. Politics explains part of this variation. The Polish Catholic Maciej surely had no love for the Muscovites, and the same could perhaps be said of Krantz and Pirckheimer. Anti-Muscovite bias, however, will not account for all the interpretive choices represented in the texts. Franck was dedicated to universal tolerance and probably did not share any anti-Orthodox animus. Nonetheless, he depicted Muscovy in very dark tones. Similarly, Münster's text of 1530 includes the Muscovite propensity for self-slavery, whereas his books of 1534 and 1544 do not. There is little in Münster's political biography that would explain such a shift. It stands to reason that something other than political prejudice stands behind the discord found in the texts.

That something is borrowing—the appropriation of passages from previously printed items. Table 2 describes borrowing among early European cosmographies including vignettes of Russia. Among the first-generation accounts, Maciej z Miechowa proved the most influential: every cosmography save Krantz borrowed from his *Account,* or, as in the case of Franck and Münster, received passages from the text via another work. Part of the reason Boemus, Pirckheimer, and Franck described Muscovy as a tyranny is to be found in their heavy reliance on Maciej as a source. He told them that the grand prince was free to move his subjects about the realm, that no one could leave Russia without the grand prince's permission, and that Muscovites often sold themselves and their family members into slavery. Boemus repeated this claim, Pirckheimer used it as a basis for his conclusion that Muscovite government was similar to Turkish despotism, and Franck simply plagiarized Pirckheimer's reworking. Magnus and Münster, though they knew Maciej, avoided his statements about forced migration, the prohibition on exit, and self-slavery. Magnus did so for purely practical reasons: it would have been inappropriate to offer a digression on Muscovite civic life in the course of a map commentary. Münster's motives are more difficult to guess. He may have noted that Maciej's claims were not corroborated by Giovio, his second source on Muscovy, and therefore rejected them on em-

---

[75] Ibid., 1030–31.

Table 2. Borrowing among cosmographies including Moscovitica

Text	Source
Miechowa (1517)	Unknown
Krantz (1504)	Unknown
Boemus (1520)	Maciej
Pirckheimer (1530)	Maciej (and Herberstein?)
Münster (1530)	Maciej and Giovio
Franck (1534)	Pirckheimer and Boemus
Münster (1536)	Boemus or Franck
Magnus (1539)	Maciej and Giovio
Münster (1544)	Maciej and Giovio

Table 3. Republication of cosmographies including Moscovitica

Original text	Republication
Maciej (1517)	Latin: 1518, 1521, 1532, 1537, 1542, 1555, 1582, 1588, 1600
	German: 1518, 1534; Polish: 1535, 1541, 1545
	Italian: 1561, 1562, 1584, 1606, 1634
	Dutch: 1563
Krantz (1519)	Latin: 3 (to 1600)
Boemus (1520)	Latin: 4 (1536–1621)
	French: 10 (1538–58)
	Italian: 10 (1542–85)
	Spanish: 1 (1556)
	English: 2 (1555, 1611)
	German: 1 (1604)
Pirckheimer (1530)	Latin: 1532, 1610
	German: 1606
Münster (1530)	Latin: 1574, 1673
Franck (1534)	German: 1542, 1567
	Dutch: 1560, 1562, 1583, 1595
Münster (1536)	German: 1536, 1537
Magnus (1539)	None
Münster (1544)	Latin: 5 (1550–1572)
	German: 20 (1545–1628)
	French: 6 (1552–1575)
	Italian: 3 (1558–1575); Czech: 1 (1554)

pirical grounds. Or perhaps he simply objected to the harsh characterization of Russia found in Maciej z Miechowa.

The early cosmographies were a crucial means of spreading information about Muscovy in the sixteenth and early seventeenth centuries. This is suggested by Table 3, which tracks republications of early cosmographies with Muscovite vignettes. If we may judge by the frequency of reprinting, the cosmographies were much more influential than the ethnographies of Russia. The former, comprising nine titles, were printed in over a hundred editions, the vast majority before 1600. The latter, comprising seven titles, were issued in only thirty-four editions. Further, a few cosmographies enjoyed disproportionate popularity: Maciej, Boemus, and Münster (1544) were printed over eighty times, whereas all other cosmographies were issued only twenty-two times.

Conclusion

For the men who sought to describe Russia in the first half of the sixteenth century, Muscovy was a mysterious place that existed more as an artifact of the imagination than a flesh-and-blood reality. Without the benefit of direct observation, they were compelled to rely on passing conversations with visiting Russians, the tales told by the few Europeans who had seen Muscovy with their own eyes, and the meager literature on the realm of the grand prince. Given the paucity of their sources, it is no wonder that they could not agree on any general characterization of Russian life. More than simple ignorance, however, skewed their descriptions in all directions. Among the early ethnographers, one can see obvious preconceptions of a political nature at work. Hoping for Muscovite relief from the Turks and Lutherans, many Catholics produced wildly positive images of Russia. They imagined Russia to be a fantastic place ruled by a mighty prince who would lead his wayward people back into the papal fold and against the enemies of the Church. Swedes, Lithuanians, Poles, and Livonians, fearful of military action by the Muscovites, offered a more sober though no less inventive view of the Muscovites. In their writings Russia emerges as a tyranny in which a malevolent prince rules over barbaric subjects. A bias of a more prosaic type divided the picture of Muscovy in the texts of early sixteenth-century cosmographers. They were scholars committed at least nominally to the collection and distribution of accurate information about little-known places. Unfortunately, the sources available to them were few and contradictory. Without any real yardstick with which to measure the accuracy of this or that account, the early cosmographers were compelled to repeat whatever they found in ethnographic Moscovitica. If they possessed a positive description of Muscovy, then they themselves produced a positive description; if their library contained only a negative account, then they rehearsed it in all particulars. Some emendation might be called for, but generally speaking they believed it best to repeat whatever they had at hand. And this they did, producing a series of texts that both reflected and complicated the already confused picture presented by the early ethnographers.

✺ 2

LEGATUS AD MOSCOVIAM
European Ambassadors and the Origin of "Russian Tyranny"

> I have written these things and handed them down to the memory of posterity,
> not only as an ear, but as an eye-witness and that not with any disguise in my
> description, but openly and freely.
>
> SIGISMUND VON HERBERSTEIN, 1549

THE IMPERIAL AMBASSADOR Sigismund von Herberstein was familiar with the work of his colleague Johann Fabri in the field of Russian ethnography. As we have seen, in 1525 Fabri had interviewed a passing Russian diplomat about Muscovy and his slight report had found its way into Herberstein's hands in 1526.[1] Then on his way to Moscow, Herberstein must have read Fabri's treatise on Muscovy with great interest, for it had a tangible impact on the envoy's own description of Russia, *Notes on the Muscovites*. Yet as even a cursory comparison of the two works suggests, Herberstein also found much to disagree with in Fabri's account. Fabri had painted Muscovy in glowing terms as a kind of monarchical utopia: the prince was wise, his authority unopposed, and each of his men faithful and obedient.[2] Herberstein agreed with Fabri that the grand prince's power was unrestricted, but to the mind of the Habsburg ambassador this condition was due to the Russian prince's cruel tyranny rather than to the voluntary submission of his men. And though he concurred with Fabri that Russian magnates were eager to follow the prince's orders, Herberstein believed that theirs was the obedience of fear rather than love.

Why did the two Imperial servants disagree so fundamentally about the nature of Russian government? The answer is found in their contrasting ex-

---

[1] Frank Kämpfer, "Herbersteins nicht eingestandene Abhängigkeit von Johann Fabri aus Leutkirch," 1–3.

[2] Fabri (1526), 297–98.

periences. Fabri had heard about the realm of the grand prince from visiting Russian servitors, whereas Herberstein had seen the place for himself. Fabri's Russian informants doubtless painted the realm of their sovereign in the best possible light, so it is little wonder that the Italian cleric gained the impression that Russia was a place in which an unbridled, wise king ruled loyal subjects. It was an appealing image, particularly to a Catholic hierarch fascinated by the prospect of ecclesiastical union and the possibility of involving the Russians in an anti-Turkish crusade. In contrast, Herberstein's knowledge of Russia was immeasurably richer and more objective than Fabri's. Having traveled to Russia twice as a member of Imperial diplomatic missions, he had not only seen the grand prince's court but also interrogated numerous Russian officials about Russian affairs. Again and again he stressed that the information in *Notes on the Muscovites* was credible because it was based on his own observations. "And in order that my opinion in this matter may not be looked upon with suspicion or considered presumptuous," Herberstein wrote, "I assert with all honesty, that not once only, but repeatedly, . . . I have seen and investigated Moscow, as it were under my very eyes." [3] What Herberstein saw and heard convinced him that Russia was hardly the political paradise of which Fabri dreamed. Rather, Muscovite government showed every sign of being, at best, an overmighty monarchy and, at worst, a heartless tyranny.

Herberstein's case was hardly unique. Nearly all sixteenth- and seventeenth-century ambassadors to Russia emphasized that their accounts were based on what they had seen and heard in Muscovy and, like the Habsburg ambassador, they concluded that the Russian government was tyrannical. This chapter reconstructs the experience of European envoys and itinerant merchants in Moscow and explores the ways in which their observations there molded the European understanding of Russia. Muscovite officials were quite suspicious of foreign envoys and thus took steps to ensure that they did not learn too much about Russian affairs or receive the "wrong" impression of the tsar's realm. Accordingly, visiting ambassadors were kept in special quarters, surrounded by officially appointed attendants, and discouraged from wandering about or engaging Muscovites in discussions. Moreover, the court presented visiting diplomats with a variety of propagandistic rituals designed to emphasize the authority of the tsar, the wealth of the realm, and the subservience of the population. Despite the government's efforts to isolate and indoctrinate the envoys, they succeeded in gathering a mass of "unauthorized" information about Russian government, society, and culture. In collecting these ethnographic data, envoys employed a kind of plan for investigation, a set of political and social categories that they used to guide their observations and subsequent expositions of Muscovite ways. Pursuing

---

[3] Herberstein (1517–49), 1:1. See Christine Harrauer, "Beobachtungen zu Darstellungsweise und Wahrheitsanspruch in der 'Moscovia' Herbersteins," 186ff.

these topics, they explored several key facets of Russian government: the tsar's power, the condition of the nobility, the system of state service, and the state of the commons. After assiduous examination, the envoys and merchants concluded that the Russian tsar was a kind of tyrant and his subjects were bound in servile subjection.

Envoys and Itinerant Merchants in Muscovy

Muscovites were weary of European diplomats and visiting merchants. The court considered them potential spies; Russian merchants sometimes felt threatened by European competition; and the Orthodox Church and its flock believed those of foreign faiths to be heretics.[4] Nonetheless, the Russian authorities realized that diplomacy and mercantile relations with European powers were necessary accouterments of great power status, and in the second half of the fifteenth century, European envoys and traders began to appear in Moscow. The Italian city-states, the Hungarians, the Moldavians, and the Habsburgs sent missions to Muscovy at various times beginning in the 1460s. Swedes, Livonians, and Lithuanians began to visit Moscow regularly in the later 1470s. As for merchants, the Hanseatic entrepôt at Novgorod, as well as the trade opportunities provided by Pskov, drew Baltic merchants into Muscovy in the last quarter of the fifteenth century. It was in this period that the Muscovites first developed a coherent program for hosting visiting envoys and itinerant merchants from Europe.[5] Their policy was based on two principles—restricted entry and segregation. Foreign merchants were generally free to trade in border towns (Kazan, Arkhangelsk, Ivangorod, etc.), but, with the exception of nations and organizations that had special allowances (e.g., the English Muscovy Company), they were not permitted to travel into the interior of the country. As for other groups, the Muscovite borders were closed to all but invited diplomatic parties and technical specialists (craftsmen, doctors, and mercenaries) whom the court wished to take into service. Permission to pass into the interior of the country could be granted only by the highest authorities in Moscow. Once envoys and itinerant merchants crossed the frontier, the authorities insisted that they conduct their business and depart as rapidly as possible. In the seventeenth century, the Muscovites permitted some ambassadors to remain as residents, but seemingly only as exceptions.[6] As can be seen in Table 4, most of the major itinerant (that is, not resident) ethnographers remained in Russia for about a year, though there were exceptions such as Peyerle, Maskiewicz, Olearius, and Paul of Aleppo, all of whom lived in Muscovy about two years.

[4] A. S. Muliukin, *Priezd inostrantsev v Moskovskoe gosudarstvo*, 33, 36–37, 49–50, 58.
[5] Ibid., 1–30.
[6] Sergei V. Bakhrushin and Sergei D. Skazkin, "Diplomatiia v novoe vremia," 1:248–49. See Olearius (1656), 179–80, on residents in Moscow.

Table 4. Major sixteenth- and seventeenth-century itinerant European authors

Author	Dates in Muscovy	Time In Muscovy	Written/ printed	Genre
Herberstein (1486–1566; Imperial diplomat)	March 1517– November 1517 April 1526– November 1526	1 yr., 5 mos.	1517–49/1549	Ethnography
Chancellor (d. 1556; English navigator)	August 1553– March 1554	8 mos.	1553/1589	Ethnography
Jenkinson (1530–1611; English merchant)	July 1557– July 1558	1 yr.	1557–58/1589	Ethnography
Barberino (1532–1582; Italian merchant)	July 1564– July 1565	1 yr.	1565/1658	Ethnography
Printz (1546–1608; Imperial diplomat)	November 1575– February 1576	4 mos.	1578/1668	Ethnography
Ulfeldt (d. 1593; Danish diplomat)	June 1578– November 1578	6 mos.	1579/1608	Dip. report/ ethnography
Possevino (1533/ 34–1611; papal diplomat)	August 1581– March 1582	8 mos.	1586/1586	Dip. report/ ethnography
Fletcher (1546– 1611; English diplomat)	October 1588– August 1589	11 mos.	1588/1589	Ethnography
Peyerle (German merchant)	May 1606– August 1608	2 yrs., 3 mos.	1606–08	History
Maskiewicz (fl. 1580–1632; Polish officer)	September 1609– June 1612	2 yrs., 10 mos.	1594–1621	Diary/ ethnography
Olearius (1603– 71; Holsteinian diplomat)	June 1634– January 1635 March 1636– October 1636 June 1638– April 1639 July 1643– October 1643	2 yrs., 5 mos.	1639–47/1647	Ethnography
Paul (fl. 1636– 66; archdeacon of Aleppo)	July 1654– June 1656	1 yr., 11 mos.	1655–56	Ethnography
Meyerberg (1612–88; Imperial diplomat)	April 1661– October 1662	1 yr., 7 mos.	1661–63/1663	Dip. report/ ethnography
Wickhart (Imperial diplomat)	August 1675– November 1675	4 mos.	1675/1675	Dip. report/ ethnography
Tanner (Polish diplomat)	April 1678– September 1678	6 mos.	1678/1680?	Dip. report/ ethnography
"Neuville" (French agent)	July 1689– December 1689	6 mos.	1690?/1698	Dip. report/ ethnography
Korb (1670–174; Austrian diplomat)	April 1698– August 1699	1 yr., 5 mos.	1698–99/1700	Dip. report/ ethnography

Note: Dip. = Diplomatic. All dates are approximate. Several authors (Petreius, for example) traveled to Russia on numerous occasions for short periods of time, and others (Paul of Aleppo) visited for extended periods after they wrote their ethnographies. Neither short visits before accounts were drafted nor long visits afterward are listed here. For sources on each author, see Bibliography 4 below.

While the visitors were in Muscovy the government attempted to sequester them so as to limit their opportunities to mix with the Orthodox population and to gather intelligence. When ambassadors arrived at a designated
entry point on the Russian border (often Smolensk, Putivl', or Arkhangelsk),
they stated their business to the local official (*voevoda*), who then sent word
of their arrival and intentions to Moscow.[7] "For it is the custom in Russia,"
explained Olearius, "that when foreign ambassadors reach the frontiers they
must declare their business and then wait until the ruler of the country is
notified by courier of their arrival and sends the governor of the province
instructions for receiving and entertaining them."[8] Envoys sometimes
complained of being held for inordinate periods at the border.[9] Daniel Printz
wrote that an envoy who did not have the proper papers, or even if he did,
might be "held like a prisoner" at the frontier.[10] Once permission to enter
the country was granted, envoys were met by escorts (*pristavy*), who supplied them with provisions and guided them to Moscow.[11] During trips to
the capital, the ambassadors were generally sequestered, sometimes outside
villages and towns along the way. When Herberstein's attendants requested
that his party billet outside Smolensk, he objected that he was "not accustomed to live in the woods like the wild beasts."[12] The legates were not allowed to purchase goods from the local population. Jacob Ulfeldt complained
that his party was "not permitted to buy anything from traders because of
the proximity of the natives."[13] Casual contact with local people was forbidden. Barberino, for example, was dismayed that the attendants would not
permit his party "to speak with anyone along the road" to Moscow.[14]

[7] On receptions at the Muscovite border, see Herberstein (1517–49), 2:112–14; Adams/
Chancellor (1553), 250; Barberino (1565), 2:13–14; Ulfeldt (1575), 6–9; Printz (1578), 73;
Possevino (1589), 14–15; Peyerle (1608), 176, 198; Bussow (1611), 56–57; Petreius (1615),
182, 281–82; Olearius (1656), 45–49; Aleppo (1655), 1:259; Meyerberg (1661), 30–33;
Reutenfels (1671), 106; Wickhart (1675), 46; Tanner (1678), 28–30; Korb (1700), 1:59ff.

[8] Olearius (1656), 40.

[9] On complaints of being unduly held at the border, see Herberstein (1517–49), 2:115–16;
Adams/Chancellor (1553), 250; Barberino (1565), 2:13–14; Printz (1578), 73; Petrieus
(1615), 281; Meyerberg (1661), 10, 32–33; Tanner (1678), 33.

[10] Printz (1578), 73.

[11] On escort parties and provisioning, see Adams/Chancellor (1553), 250; Ulfeldt (1575),
11, 13, 25; Printz (1578), 49; Horsey (1584–1621), 302; Staden (1586), 65, 72–73; Possevino
(1586), 21; Margeret (1607), 42, 44; Bussow (1611), 56–57; Massa (1614), 46–47, 49, 65,
71; Petreius (1615), 182, 282; Olearius (1656), 47; Aleppo (1655), 1:269–70, 280, 287, 360,
364, 2:22, 303; Meyerberg (1661), 34, 61, 175; Reutenfels (1671), 73, 105–6; Wickhart (1675),
54–55, 74, 126; Tanner (1678), 33, 39; Neuville (1698), 11–12; Korb (1700), 1:87ff., 138.

[12] Herberstein (1517–49), 2:116. On sequestration of ambassadorial parties from the border to Moscow, see also Barberino (1565), 2:13–14; Ulfeldt (1575), 6–9, 11, 12, 14, 15, 41;
Printz (1578), 51; Possevino (1586), 16–17; Massa (1614), 191; Aleppo (1655), 1:359; Meyerberg (1661), 43; Reutenfels (1671), 105–6; Tanner (1678), 31; Gordon (1661–99), 43; Korb
(1700), 1:71

[13] Ulfeldt (1575), 11. On the prohibition against buying items from local merchants, see also
Herberstein (1517–49), 2:118, 212; Adams/Chancellor (1553), 250; Barberino (1565) 2:13–
14; Juusten (1569–72), 57; Ulfeldt (1575), 41.

[14] Barberino (1565) 2:13–14.

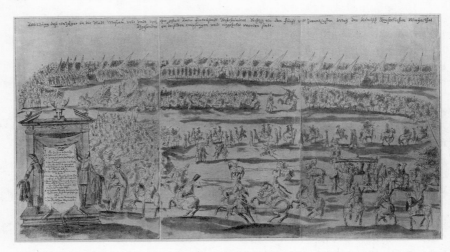

3. An ambassadorial entrance. Augustin Freiherr von Meyerberg, *Al'bom Meierberga: Vidy i bytovyia kartiny Rossii XVII veka* (St. Petersburg, 1903).

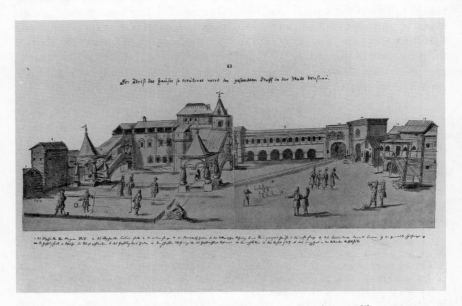

4. The Ambassadorial Court. Augustin Freiherr von Meyerberg, *Al'bom Meierberga: Vidy i bytovyia kartiny Rossii XVII veka* (St. Petersburg, 1903).

Once the envoys had been ceremonially received in the capital (see fig. 3), they were held in closely guarded government apartments called (at least in the seventeenth century) the "ambassadorial court" (see fig. 4). The visitors were also provided with attendants who catered to their needs and spied on them.[15] Members of embassies and trade delegations often bitterly complained that they were confined like common criminals. "It is the custom of this people, unfamiliar with more enlightened laws," wrote Printz in 1578, "to hold the ambassadors of foreign governments almost like prisoners so they will not be able to learn what they are doing."[16] Over half a century later, Paul of Aleppo wrote that his party was "in great distress, perplexity, and doubt; particularly as we were shut up in close confinement, without a single person to inform us what the emperor was doing, or where he was, or what was passing in the world."[17] Envoys and sequestered merchants were allowed out of their quarters for official functions such as audiences, negotiations, and banquets. Antonio Possevino wrote that even his drivers were not allowed to leave the compound "to water their horses."[18] When ambassadors were permitted to venture forth, they were always attended by guards. Jacques Margeret explained that the Russian authorities did not "allow anyone to leave who [did] not have a guard with him to see where he goes, what he will do, and what he will say."[19] Naturally, the Russians could not prevent the ambassadors from occasionally exiting, and several envoys of the second half of the seventeenth century noted that freedom of movement and reception was occasionally granted, but only after the conclusion of their first audience with the tsar.[20] Olearius, for example, was shocked when his attendants "advised that His Tsarist Majesty granted [the Holsteinian embassy] permission to go out [and] . . . to visit and receive the Swedish ambassadors and their party. This was a great surprise," he explained, "for customarily neither ambassadors nor their attendants were allowed to go out alone while they resided in Moscow." The Muscovites told Olearius that his legation was the first "to have the right to go out freely."[21]

The government ordered residents of Moscow to avoid contact with foreign envoys. Possevino wrote that as a general rule Russian subjects "are not allowed to associate with foreigners unless the prince has been informed and given his personal permission."[22] Local people were not allowed to visit the

---

[15] On sequestration in Moscow, see Herberstein (1517–49), 2:120–21; Barberino (1565), 2:13–14, 21; Ulfeldt (1575), 36, 37; Staden (1578), 71; Printz (1578), 51; Horsey (1584–1611), 273; Possevino (1586), 17, 47, 49; Margeret (1607), 42; Peyerle (1608), 212, 214; Massa (1614), 49, 131, 191; Petreius (1615), 284–85, 294; Aleppo (1655), 1:366, 2:21, 218, 295; Olearius (1656), 66, 180; Meyerberg (1661), 80–81, 184–85; Reutenfels (1671), 106–7; Wickhart (1675), 71–73; Tanner (1678), 49–50; Neuville (1698), 8, 10; Korb (1700), 1:93, 158, 238.

[16] Printz (1578), 51. The prison metaphor was not unique to Printz. See Juusten (1569–72), 61; Peyerle (1606), 212, 214–15; Petreius (1615), 284–85, 294.

[17] Aleppo (1655), 1:359.

[18] Possevino (1586), 49. On the prohibition on exit, see also Barberino (1565), 2:13–14; Ulfeldt (1575), 36; Massa (1614), 191; Petreius (1615), 284–85, 294; Aleppo (1655), 1:365; Olearius (1656), 180; Aleppo (1655), 1:365; Neuville (1698), 10; Korb (1700), 1:93, 158, 238.

[19] Margeret (1607), 42. See also Petreius (1615), 284–85; Aleppo (1655), 2:21, 218.

[20] Olearius (1656), 180; Meyerberg (1661), 80–82; Neuville (1698), 8; Korb (1700), 1:238.

[21] Olearius (1656), 66, 180.

[22] Possevino (1586), 49. Also see the incidents cited in Herberstein (1517–49), 2:118, and Ulfeldt (1575), 41.

ambassadors' quarters.[23] Russian guards, Margeret wrote, "do not permit anyone to enter the ambassador's residence except those who are assigned to do so."[24] Russian officials explained to Augustin von Meyerberg that guards had been provided so the embassy "could sleep safely at night," but he knew it was to keep the local populace at bay.[25] The restriction on visitors seems to have been relaxed in the second half of the seventeenth century: Paul of Aleppo and Johann Korb explained that envoys could receive visitors after their audience.[26] Further, Russians were not to approach the envoys in the street. If Peter Petreius is to be believed, Russian attendants were instructed to prevent local residents from talking with the envoys and were under orders to report any conversations that occurred.[27] And if Russians happened to talk to foreigners, they were not to reveal anything of the tsar's business. "They will tell nothing to a foreigner whatever, either good or bad, of their own affairs," Paul of Aleppo wrote. Why? Paul explained that Russians were bound by a religious oath not to speak of the tsar's business to visitors.[28]

It was probably not difficult for the government to enforce the restriction on contact with foreigners, for Orthodox commoners believed visitors to be "unclean."[29] Several envoys claimed that frightened peasants ran away from foreigners and considered contact with them impure.[30] Many more reported that they were not allowed to enter Russian churches because the Muscovites believed their places of worship would be defiled by foreign contact.[31] Ulfeldt was denied access to an Orthodox church "because [the Russians] believed that we were not worthy enough to enter."[32] Olearius noted that "as the church is a holy, pure place, nothing impure may enter," including foreigners. When members of his entourage "unwittingly went into a church to have a look," they "were escorted out again by the arm, and the floor was swept after us with a broom."[33] A bit later in the seventeenth century Meyerberg confirmed that the Russians swept churches that had been entered by foreigners.[34] Several ethnographers reported that foreigners could not be buried

---

[23] On the prohibition on visitors, see Barberino (1565), 2:13–14; Ulfeldt (1575), 37; Possevino (1586), 17; Margeret (1607), 42; Massa (1614), 49; Aleppo (1655), 1:365, 2:21; Olearius (1656), 180; Meyerberg (1661), 80–82; Neuville (1698), 8; Korb (1700), 1:238.

[24] Margeret (1607), 42.

[25] Meyerberg (1661), 80–82.

[26] Aleppo (1655), 1:365; Korb (1700), 1:238.

[27] Petreius (1615), 284–85.

[28] Aleppo (1655), 1:359.

[29] Lev P. Rushchinskii, *Religioznyi byt russikh po svedeniiam inostrannykh pisatelei XVI i XVII vv.*; Scheidegger, *Perverses Abendland—barbarisches Russland.*

[30] Ulfeldt (1575), 24, 41; Olearius (1656), 51, 53, 54, 254.

[31] Barberino (1565), 2:1; Ulfeldt (1575), 10; Possevino (1586), 28, 78; Margeret (1607), 22; Bussow (1611), 59; Massa (1614), 132, 137; Aleppo (1655), 1:382; Olearius (1656), 50–51, 73, 263; Meyerberg (1661), 40; Collins (1667), 40, 99; Reutenfels (1671), 171–75; Wickhart (1675), 224–25; Tanner (1678), 35, 83–84; Neuville (1698), 63; Korb (1700), 2:175.

[32] Ulfeldt (1575), 10.

[33] Olearius (1656), 263.

[34] Meyerberg (1661), 40.

with or married to Russians unless they converted to the Russian church.[35] The visitors also said that European Christians who did convert had to be rebaptized.[36] The envoys believed that even the tsar felt soiled by foreign contact. According to several foreigners, the grand prince washed his hands after contact with those of alien faiths.[37] "They say that the prince believes that in giving his hand to an ambassador of the Roman creed," Herberstein wrote, "he gives it to an unclean and impure person; and that, therefore, after their departure, he immediately washes his hands."[38]

Because of their physical and social isolation, the visitors' primary source of information was the Muscovite government and its agents. In its dealings with the foreigners, and particularly ambassadors, the Russian court had a clear and singular purpose—to display the dignity and might of its prince. An envoy's visit was punctuated by dramatic events—entries, receptions, audiences, banquets—all designed by the court to overawe visitors.[39] The accounts of diplomats and some merchants are replete with detailed descriptions of every manner of official occasions.[40] In addition to diplomatic

---

[35] On the prohibition against being buried among Russians, see Jenkinson (1557), 443; Schlichting (1571a), 258–59; Staden (1578), 107; Petreius (1615), 158; Korb (1700), 1:143. On the prohibition against being married to Russians, see Printz (1578), 63; Petreius (1615), 157; Olearius (1656), 246–47; Meyerberg (1661), 82, 87–89; Collins (1667), 35–36; Reutenfels (1671), 102; Gordon (1661–99), 47, 54; Korb (1700), 2:18.

[36] Printz (1578), 37–38; Possevino (1586), 85; Fletcher (1591), 280, 285; Margeret (1607), 21; Aleppo (1655), 2:296; Olearius (1656), 233, 242, 246–47; Meyerberg (1661), 3, 77–78, 87–89; Collins (1667), 5–6, 35–36; Neuville (1698), 62; Korb (1700), 2:174.

[37] Herberstein (1517–49), 2:125; Possevino (1586), 28, 47; Petreius (1615), 286; Aleppo (1655), 382; Olearius (1656), 63; Meyerberg (1661), 49, 64; Reutenfels (1671), 106–7; Korb (1700), 2:248.

[38] Herberstein (1517–49), 2:125. Though many foreigners reported this custom, only Possevino (1586) claimed to have seen it: "As they are withdrawing he always washes his hands in a silver bowl placed openly on a bench in general view, as though he were performing a rite of expiation" (47). Leonid. A. Iuzefovich, *Kak v posol'skikh obychaiakh vedetsia,* argues that the handwashing custom was myth invented by Europeans.

[39] On Russian diplomatic spectacles, see Leonid A. Iuzefovich, "Russkii posol'skii obychai XVI veka" and *Kak v posol'skikh obychaiakh vedetsia.*

[40] On receptions at the border, see Herberstein (1517–49), 2:112–14; Ulfeldt (1575), 6–9; Printz (1578), 73; Possevino (1589), 14–15; Peyerle (1608), 176, 198; Bussow (1611), 56–57; Petreius (1615), 182, 281–82; Aleppo (1655), 1:259; Olearius (1656), 45–49; Meyerberg (1661), 30–33; Reutenfels (1671), 106; Wickhart (1675), 46; Tanner (1678), 28–30; Korb (1700), 1:59ff.

On entry into Moscow, see Herberstein (1517–49), 2:120–21; Adams/Chancellor (1553), 255; Ulfeldt (1575), 26; Printz (1578), 52; Peyerle (1608), 176, 180–82; Bussow (1611), 34–35, 56–57; Massa (1614), 59, 127ff.; Petreius (1615), 156, 158–59, 167, 180–81, 283–85; Aleppo (1655), 1:363–64, 2:208–9, 218–21; Olearius (1656), 59, 61–64, 68–70, 72–75, 96, 101; Meyerberg (1661), 56ff.; Reutenfels (1671), 73, 106–7; Wickhart (1675), 65–70; Tanner (1678), 42–48; Gordon (1661–99), 56; Korb (1700), 1:80ff.

On audiences, see Herberstein (1517–49), 2:123–25; Chancellor (1553), 226–27; Jenkinson (1557), 420; Barberino (1565), 1:15; Randolfe (1568), 102–7; Ulfeldt (1575), 28–29; Printz (1578), 53–54; Horsey (1584–1611), 273, 302–3, 324–25; Possevino (1586), 16, 47–48; Peyerle (1608), 176–77, 182–85, 201–9, 223–27; Petreius (1615), 159–61, 270–73; Aleppo (1655), 1:379–88, 2:219, 221, 275–77; Olearius (1656), 68–75; Meyerberg (1661), 63ff.; Reutenfels (1671), 107–8; Wickhart (1675), 83–95, 116–17, 120–23, 212–13; Tanner

ceremonies, the foreigners were occasionally treated to mass religious rituals in which the tsar played an important role, such as the "blessing of the waters" and the Palm Sunday procession.[41] The court sometimes succeeded in using ceremony to give an impression of overwhelming power. Richard Chancellor was beguiled by the spectacle presented at his first audience: "This so honorable an assemblie, so great a Majestie of the Emperour, and of the place might very well have amazed our men, and dashed them out of countenance."[42] Bernard Tanner, having witnessed a massive military parade, exclaimed, "Who would not be amazed at this wondrous spectacle!"[43]

The government's attempt to impress visitors, however, was not confined to vast spectacles. From the moment they crossed the border to the moment they departed the country, most visitors were in the constant company of commissioners, the *pristavy*. In the course of all their duties, these officials were to maintain the honor of the tsar. What Jacob Reutenfels said of Russian ambassadors—that they were "ordered, under threat of severe punishment, to carefully guard the tsar's dignity and majesty"—was equally true of the commissioners, who were, incidentally, in the employ of the Ambassadorial Chancellery (see fig. 5).[44] The commissioners' duty to safeguard the honor of their sovereign had an important impact on the perception of the foreigners. It guaranteed that visitors would be continually surrounded by officials who were behaving in a scripted fashion, not only in organized ceremonies but also in everyday interactions. The foreigners often complained, for example, that their attendants refused to yield on the slightest point of protocol even during mundane affairs. "This had always been a point of great difficulty at the reception of ambassadors," Korb remarked, "the Muscovites having the ambition to pretend to this exceedingly empty prerogative."[45] Be-

(1678), 50–54, 92–95; Gordon (1661–99), 56; Korb (1700), 1:161ff.

On royal banquets, see Contarini (1478), 164–65; Herberstein (1517–49), 1:90, 2:128, 130; Chancellor (1553), 227; Adams/Chancellor (1553), 256–58; Barberino (1565), 1:5, 2:18; Jenkinson (1557), 421, 428; Printz (1558), 54–56; Ulfeldt (1575), 30–31; Possevino (1586), 15; Margeret (1607), 55; Peyerle (1608), 188–90; Maskiewicz (1611), 45; Bussow (1611), 24; Massa (1614), 50, 60; Petreius (1615), 288; Aleppo (1655), 1:389–90, 407–8, 2:153–54, 249, 291; Olearius (1656), 200–201; Reutenfels (1671), 108; Neuville (1698), 23; Korb (1700) 1:189–91, 2:154; Perry (1716), 227–29.

[41] On the "blessing of the waters," see Jenkinson (1557), 422, 432; Ulfeldt (1575), 18; Printz (1578), 48; Possevino (1586), 55; Fletcher (1591), 292; Margeret (1607), 22; Aleppo (1655), 1:310, 353–55, 2:169–70, 238–39; Olearius (1656), 53; Reutenfels (1671), 171–75; Tanner (1678), 90–91; Korb (1700), 1:145, 224–28. On the Palm Sunday procession, see Jenkinson (1557), 434ff.; Printz (1578), 40; Bussow (1611), 160–61; Maskiewicz (1611), 59; Aleppo (1655), 2:88–93; Meyerberg (1661), 187ff.; Collins (1667), 16ff.; Reutenfels (1671), 171–75; Wickhart (1675), 177.

[42] Adams/Chancellor (1553), 255.

[43] Tanner (1675), 44.

[44] Reutenfels (1671), 105. For a similar statement, see Olearius (1656), 144.

[45] Korb (1700), 1:82. See also Herberstein (1517–49), 2:112–13; Ulfeldt (1579), 26–28; Juusten (1569–72), 62; Printz (1578), 60–61; Bowes (1583), 254; Mniszek (1605), 150ff.; Oleśnicki (1606), 199; Peyerle (1606), 182, Olearius (1656), 45–47, 137; Meyerberg (1661), 33, 38; Reutenfels (1671), 105–6; Wickhart (1675), 46; Tanner (1678), 42–48; Korb (1700), 1:159, 2:172ff.

5. The Ambassadorial Chancellery. Adam Olearius, *Vermehrte newe Beschreibung der muscowitischen und persischen Reyse* (Schleswig, 1656).

cause of their seemingly unreasonable punctiliousness, the commissioners came in for harsh treatment in the travelers' accounts. Olearius expressed a common opinion when he wrote that the Russians were "very arrogant":

> Far from concealing this, they openly demonstrate it by their facial expressions, words, and deeds, especially in the relations with foreigners. Just as they have less regard for foreigners than their own countrymen, similarly they consider no ruler in the world comparable to theirs in wealth, power, greatness, distinction, and virtue. They refuse any letter addressed to His Tsarist Majesty if the slightest detail of his title is omitted, or [if anything included] is strange to them.[46]

Whether their censure was justified or not, it is clear that, encircled as they were by the commissioners, most envoys would have limited opportunity to observe what might be called vernacular Russian behavior. Rather, they witnessed a kind of political theater played out during everyday contact.

---

[46] Olearius (1656), 137. See also Herberstein (1517–49), 2:113ff.; Ulfeldt (1575), 11; Printz (1578), 49; Possevino (1586), 16–17; Olearius (1656), 138; Meyerberg (1661), 33; Reutenfels (1671), 105–6, 141–42, 147–48; Wickhart (1675), 248; Korb (1700), 1:82, 104–5, 2:194–95.

The Course of Ethnographic Investigation

The itinerant ethnographers were sophisticated men—gentlemen, courtiers, and experienced diplomats. They understood only too well that the Muscovites were trying to prevent them from learning about their realm. Sequestration was only the most obvious sign of the government's effort to keep the envoys in the dark. But the authorities' policy, the envoys suspected, went far beyond simply denying them freedom of movement. As many envoys agreed, the Muscovites looked askance at any sort of questioning. Possevino remarked that the Russians "possess highly suspicious temperaments."[47] Paul of Aleppo and other envoys concurred that the Muscovites would divulge nothing about their affairs.[48] Why? Possevino believed that Russians were afraid. "Since [Ivan IV] tries to find out everything his subjects do," the Italian ambassador wrote, "very few of them dare to say anything, and they speak only to curry favor or avoid punishment."[49] Paul of Aleppo, characteristically, saw loyalty behind Muscovite silence. "Every Muscovite," he claimed, "is sworn upon the Cross and the Gospel, and bound, on pain of excommunication by the Patriarch, not to reveal their national affairs to foreigners."[50] Both men were probably right: in Ivan IV's day, as Albert Schlichting said, "it [was] not safe to converse at court," and even in the seventeenth century under milder tsars, Muscovites were obliged to report seditious or even suspicious speech to the authorities.[51] Many of the foreigners wrote that Muscovites bore a duty to spy for their sovereign.[52] Possevino was no doubt correct when he called his attendants "spies," for it is certain that they reported the substance of conversations with visiting envoys to their superiors.[53] A humorous example of Muscovite suspicion was provided by Meyerberg: an Italian doctor was called to account by the authorities when an attendant heard him mention the "Crimean tatars," when in fact he had said "cream of tatar."[54] Korb reported that even the enlightened Peter I was "suspicious of frequent meetings between the magnates and foreigners."[55]

Questioning was suspect, but even looking around could put the Muscovites on guard. Paul of Aleppo wrote that "whenever they see any person . . .

[47] Possevino (1586), 26.
[48] Aleppo (1655), 1:359.
[49] Possevino (1586), 49.
[50] Aleppo (1655), 1:359.
[51] Schlichting (1571a), 219. On the obligation to report speech concerning the "sovereign's word and deed," see Ann M. Kleimola, "Duty to Denounce in Muscovite Russia." Possevino (1586), 47, called the attendants "spies."
[52] On denunciations in the travelers' accounts, see Ulfeldt (1575), 41; Printz (1578), 29–30, 66; Aleppo (1655), 1:359, 2:73, 119; Meyerberg (1661), 4–5, 87–88; Korb (1700), 1:125, 136–37, 198–99, 217, 2:137.
[53] Possevino (1586), 47.
[54] Meyerberg (1661), 87–89. The story is repeated in Gordon (1661–99), 53.
[55] Korb (1700), 1:244. Similarly, see Neuville (1698), 10, where Neuville is suspected for meeting with magnates.

looking attentively at a cannon or examining a fort, they seize him on the spot, and carry him away to Siberia, saying: 'You are surely a spy, Sir, introduced among us from the country of the Turks.'" And he recounted the story of a Russian whom the authorities "had seen going round, looking about the walls." The fellow in question was brought before a minister and stripped, and they "carried him round the whole city, with his hands tied behind his back; whilst the executioner followed behind, armed with an instrument made of a bull's nerve, with which he struck him continually—crying aloud, that he was a spy, and that this was his reward—until he beat him out of his senses."[56] Neuville in fact caught a Russian official spying on him after he had, "contrary to the custom of that country and the honour of my rank, paid several private visits to this prince [Vasilii Golitsyn]."[57]

Even when one did succeed in hearing or seeing something of ethnographic value, the itinerant visitors realized that nothing was really quite as it seemed. The foreigners understood that statements made by Muscovite officials and Russians in general about Russian practices had to be taken with a grain of salt. Again and again the visitors remarked that the Russians were not to be trusted to speak the truth about their affairs. "Since the Russians resort to craftiness and treachery in many things, and do not keep faith with one another," Margeret wrote, "it may be imagined how they feel about foreigners, and how difficult it is to trust them."[58] Similarly, the foreign envoys did not believe that the well-orchestrated ceremonies to which they were often treated were a true reflection of the power of the state, but rather a kind of political show. Herberstein, for instance, guessed that his Russian hosts were carefully stage-managing the Habsburg embassy's entrance into Moscow.

> For it is the custom amongst these people, that on all occasions when distinguished ambassadors from foreign kings and princes are to be conducted to the court, the lower class of nobles, stipendiaries, and soldiers assemble together by command of the prince, from the neighboring and surrounding districts. All the taverns and shops of the city are on such occasions shut up, all buyers and sellers are expelled from the market place, and the citizens gather together to the scene of display from all quarters. The result of this is that the power of the prince appears very great in the eyes of foreigners, from such an immense concourse of men as his subjects.[59]

Many of the envoys made similar cynical comments about Russian attempts to impress them during the course of their visits.[60] And it was not only in mass

---

[56] Aleppo (1655), 1:268, 2:119.

[57] Neuville (1698), 10; also see 57.

[58] Margeret (1607), 86. See also Jenkinson (1557), 423; Ulfeldt (1575), 11; Possevino (1586), 35; Fletcher (1591), 305–6; Petreius (1615), 315; Olearius (1656), 137; Meyerberg (1661), 38; Tanner (1678), 87; Neuville (1698), 11; Korb (1700), 1:135–36.

[59] Herberstein (1517–49), 2:123.

[60] Aleppo (1655), 2:208–9. For similar statements about the contrived arrangement of entrance ceremonies, political displays, and deception generally, see Staden (1578), 71; Possevino

ceremonies that the Muscovites attempted to deceive. The envoys were also skeptical about the meaning of the peculiar slavishness of Russian subjects in the presence of the tsar. Possevino, like many ambassadors, was astonished at the groveling of Russian courtiers, but suspected that all their grotesque fawning was disingenuous and designed expressly to overawe him.[61] "The Muscovites," he wrote, "are greatly impressed by outward show." He, for one, was not, and he warned other ethnographers not to give more "credit to appearances than they should." [62] In the next century, Olearius noted that "it is [the Russians'] custom and manner to be servile and to make a show of their slavish disposition." [63]

The skepticism with which the envoy-ethnographers approached their investigative task suggests that they were not naive observers duped by the tricks of Russian stage management. Sequestration, suspicion of questioning and observing, ostentatious displays of power, and a tendency to prevarication were, to the visitors, all part of the court's plan to hide its business from prying foreign eyes. With this in mind, the ethnographers viewed their task as one of peering through the veil of government suspicion, propaganda, and deception so as to arrive at the "truth" about Russia. Though none of the ethnographers ever spelled out in synoptic form the various techniques they used to penetrate this screen, numerous hints scattered throughout their accounts allow a general reconstruction of investigative methods. These techniques can conveniently be divided into three classes, depending on the source of the information: gathering of testimony, observing behavior, and reading Russian materials.

It is clear that much of what the foreigners learned in Muscovy came from discussions with Russians. The foreigners often attempted to confirm claims by noting that they were told this or that personally by a Russian. Herberstein, for example, knew that his readers would not believe that Russian servants understood beating to be a sign of affection, so he emphasized that he had personally heard them complain about a lack of abuse.[64] To gain further credibility, the envoys identified their informants by name: Herberstein cited a number of informants; Possevino records having had lengthy discussions with Ivan IV; Maskiewicz tapped the boyar Vasilii Golovin for information; Paul of Aleppo received much of his data from Patriarch Nikon; one

---

(1586), 4, 15, 77; Peyerle (1608), 187, 221; Bussow (1611), 12–13, 34–35, 57; Massa (1614), 42, 46–47, 58, 159; Petreius (1615), 167; Aleppo (1655), 1:340, 2:22, 208–9; Olearius (1656), 44–47; Meyerberg (1661), 36, 52; Collins (1667), 114–15; Reutenfels (1671), 86, 89–90, 101–2, 105; Neuville (1698), 5; Korb (1700), 1:104–5, 2:154.

[61] See especially Possevino (1586), 11, where the Jesuit suggests that the Russian courtiers "do not really believe" what they say about the authority of the prince.

[62] Ibid., 65, 4.

[63] Olearius (1656), 147.

[64] Herberstein (1517–49), 1:106–7. For other examples, see ibid., 2:84; Chancellor (1553), 228–29, 235; Jenkinson (1557), 423–24, 441; Barberino (1565), 2:8; Ulfeldt (1575), 11–13; Horsey (1584–1611), 304–6; Peyerle (1608), 214; Possevino (1586), 30; Margeret (1607), 78; Maskiewicz (1611), 55–56; Aleppo (1655), 2:33–34; Olearius (1656), 50, 114.

Petr Mikliaev explained to Olearius the meaning of the sign of the cross; Neuville had frequent discussions with the magnate Vasilii Golitsyn and Nikolai Spafarius, a Moldavian in the employ of the Russian Ambassadorial Chancellery.[65] The envoys sometimes sought the corroboration of several witnesses: Herberstein interrogated "a great number of people"; Ulfeldt relied on the testimony of "many trustworthy people"; Printz claimed the authority of "several people"; Paul of Aleppo interviewed "persons of strictest veracity"; Carl Wickhart relied on various "trustworthy" sources.[66]

The envoys also did a good deal of looking around. The visitors often claimed at the onset of their accounts their testimony was based primarily on what they personally witnessed.[67] But beyond such programmatic statements, the envoys also frequently strengthened particular claims of fact by noting that they had "seen" this or that.[68] Herberstein, for instance, wanted to convince his audience that felonious priests were under the jurisdiction of the secular authorities. So he wrote that he "saw some drunken priests publicly whipped at Moscow, whose only complaint was, that they were beaten by slaves, and not by a gentleman."[69] For particularly outrageous contentions, the envoys reserved the authenticating device "I have seen this with my own eyes." Paul of Aleppo, for example, was certain that his readers would not believe there existed a Muscovite ritual in which a man hosting guests presented his wife in ceremonial clothing and commanded her to kiss the visitors and offer them vodka. So he introduced his description of the rite with the following device: "And now I have to mention a strange thing, which I witnessed on this occasion; a thing which we had been told of, but which we would not believe. I saw it, however, with my own eyes; and it was this."[70] Seeing something several times confirmed that it was a custom rather than something accidental. Olearius, for instance, was amazed that Russians of both sexes bathed together at public baths. To assure his readers that this scandalous practice was not unusual in Russia, he noted that his party "*several times* saw men and women come out of public baths to cool off, and as naked as God created them."[71] The envoys were also careful to warn their

---

[65] Herberstein (1517–49), 2:34; Possevino (1586), 67–79; Maskiewicz (1611), 55–56; Aleppo (1655), 2:60–66; Olearius (1656), 252; Neuville (1698), 10, 65–71.

[66] Herberstein (1517–49), 1:clxi; Ulfeldt (1575), 13–14; Printz (1578), 29; Aleppo (1653), 1:404; Wickhart (1675), 205.

[67] Herberstein (1517–49), 1:1; Barberino (1565), 1:5–6, 2:34; Possevino (1586), 1; Collins (1667), 2–3; Reutenfels (1671), 9; Wickhart (1675), Vorrede, 188; Korb (1700), 2:180–81, 274–75.

[68] For "I/we saw," see Chancellor (1553), 235; Jenkinson (1557), 421; Barberino (1565), 2:10, 26; Ulfeldt (1575), 11, 13–14, 16, 55; Printz (1578), 69; Maskiewicz (1611), 55–56; Aleppo (1655), 1:274, 304, 316–17, 347–48, 359, 372, 382, 410, 2:73, 111, 119, 389–99; Olearius (1656), 142, 145, 146, 231; Meyerberg (1661), 59, 70; Reutenfels (1671), 117–19, 167–69; Tanner (1678), 71, 101, 106; Korb (1700), 1:209, 2:108–10.

[69] Herberstein (1517–49), 1:56.

[70] Aleppo (1655), 2:285.

[71] Olearius (1656), 142; emphasis added. See also Ulfeldt (1575), 13–14; Aleppo (1655), 2:111; Meyerberg (1661), 70.

audience when they reported something that they had not witnessed. Anthony Jenkinson was shown the coffin of Saint Sergei and told that "he healeth many diseases, and giveth the blind their sight, with many other miracles." Yet the Englishman was incredulous, writing that he "was hard of belief because [he] saw him worke no miracle whilest [he] was there."[72] In order to give their readers a more detailed understanding of what they had seen, the envoys routinely accompanied their accounts with illustrations of various kinds. Meyerberg, for example, offered an entire sketchbook of Russia life, including such ethnographic curiosities as depictions of types of Russians (see fig. 6).

Though most of them understood little Russian, several of the envoy-ethnographers turned to written sources for guidance. The outstanding example is Herberstein, who could read Russian and had access to a wide variety of documents.[73] The Habsburg ambassador investigated chronicles, religious texts, legal codes, and geographical notes.[74] Herberstein approached the Russian texts with a skeptical eye. After reviewing a series of improbable phenomena cited in a Russian geographical source (e.g., the cult of the "Golden Hag," cenocephali, fish-men), Herberstein interjected a note of doubt:

> Hitherto, whatever I have related has been literally transcribed by me from a Russian itinerary, which has been placed at my service; and although in my narrative some things may appear to be fabulous and scarcely credible, . . . yet I myself, in spite of diligent investigation respecting them, have not been able to get certain information from any one who has seen them with his own eyes, although by universal report they are held to be true.[75]

Other envoys occasionally mentioned reading Russian papers. Printz cited Russian "chronicles" and claimed to have had access to "the archives of the leading men"; Possevino mentioned a variety of religious texts; Paul of Aleppo referred to a Russian "history" of Ivan IV; Olearius claimed to have used the Council Law Code of 1649 to render a picture of Russian legal practice; Meyerberg, Wickhart, and Korb mined Muscovite chronicles and law codes for information.[76]

---

[72] Jenkinson (1557), 441. For a similar statement, see Wickhart (1675), 177.

[73] Herberstein knew Slovenian natively, and when in Russia he apparently quickly assimilated at least a working knowledge of Russian. For more information, see Chapter 4 below.

[74] Herberstein (1517–49), 1:7ff., 55–58, 66–73,102–4, 2:37ff. On the nature of these sources and the large literature devoted to Herberstein's use of chronicles, see Anna L. Khoroshkevich, "Die Quellen Herbersteins" and "Sigizmund Gerbershtein i ego Zapiski o Moskovii"; and the notes to Sigizmund von Gerbershtein, *Zapiski o Moskovii*, 288–89 (n. 59), 309 (n. 244), 312 (n. 268), 312 (n. 270), 319 (n. 330), 332 (n. 523).

[75] Herberstein (1517–49), 2:42.

[76] Printz (1578), 2, 8–9; Possevino (1584), 49; Aleppo (1655), 2:2; Olearius (1656), 227–28; Meyerberg (1661), 47, 100, 120; Reutenfels (1671), 103; Wickhart (1675), 248ff.; Korb (1700), 2:187.

6. Types of Russians. Augustin Freiherr von Meyerberg, *Al'bom Meierberga: Vidy i bytovyia kartiny Rossii XVII veka* (St. Petersburg, 1903).

On occasion one can witness the envoy-ethnographers actually gathering information and attempting to puzzle out what they had seen, heard, or read. The envoys, for example, frequently reported questioning Russians about particular subjects: Barbarino asked Muscovites about the significance of breaking a cup on the floor at the conclusion of a marriage ceremony; Ulfeldt interrogated numerous Russians about Orthodoxy; Paul of Aleppo posed "scrutinizing questions" to his hosts on a range of topics; Meyerberg queried his *pristav* on religious matters, only to be called an "idiot"; Wickhart made a point of asking about the details of Russian religious services; Tanner asked about the sign of the cross and inquired as to why the Russians jumped into the Moskva River after the blessing of the water.[77] Not only did the diplomats take the trouble to question Russians, they also went out of their way to view aspects of Russian life necessary for any thorough ethnographic description: Barberino stole into a Russian church "twice, once in the day and once at night," to investigate the interior; during a short absence from Moscow, Possevino left two subordinates "to make numerous observations"; Olearius bribed officials for information and "went incognito" to see a Russian public bath; Tanner went to a bath "for the sake of curiosity"; Wickhart traveled to see the place in Moscow where the rebel Stenka Razin was executed.[78] Many of the envoys made a point of visiting the homes of Muscovite magnates and observing domestic life in Russia.[79]

The Ethnographic Template and the Description of Muscovite Government

Though the ethnographers' interests were broad, they were not and could not be universal: even within the parameters set by Muscovite suspicion, the envoys and itinerant merchants saw and heard far more than they were capable of recording. There was simply too much to relate. Jenkinson, having described a single banquet, warned his reader that there were "many other things [he] sawe that day, not here noted."[80] Theorists of travel and travel description sensibly recommended that those who journeyed to distant lands concentrate their attention on things that were of importance. The great scientific methodologist Francis Bacon, who took a keen interest in the explo-

---

[77] Barberino (1565), 2:7; Ulfeldt (1575), 19; Aleppo (1653), 1:404; Meyerberg (1661), 101; Wickhart (1675), 225–26; Tanner (1678), 91, 104–6.

[78] Barberino (1565), 2:1; Possevino (1586), 1; Olearius (1656), 161, 226; Tanner (1678), 106; Wickhart (1675), 115.

[79] For examples of envoys visiting magnates, see Maskiewicz (1611), 52–53, 57; Olearius (1647), 42, 158, 169; Aleppo (1655), 2:285–86; Meyerberg (1661), 37; Wickhart (1675), 257–58; Tanner (1678), 101; Korb (1700), 2:37, 207.

[80] Jenkinson (1557), 421. Also see Neuville (1698), 55.

ration of foreign lands, suggested that "the Things to be seene and observed [by foreign travelers] are"

> The Courts of Princes, specially when they give Audience to Ambassadours: The Courts of Justice, while they sit and heare Causes; And so of Consistories Ecclesiasticke: The Churches, and Monasteries, with the Monuments which are therein extant: The Wals and Fortificqation of Cities and Townes; And so the Havens and Harbours: Antiquities, and Ruines: Libraries; Colledges, Disputations, and Lectures, where any are: Shipping and Navies: Houses, and Gardens of State, and Pleasure, neare great Cities: Armories: Arsenals: Magazens: Enchanges: Burses; Whare-houses: Exercise of Horseman-ship; Fencing; Trayning of Souldiers; and the like: Comedies; Such wherunto the better Sort of persons doe resort; Treasuries of Jewels, and Robes; cabinets, and Rarities: And to conclude, whatsoever is memorable in the Places; where they goe. After all which, the Tutors or Servants, ought to make diligent Enquirie. As for Triumphs; Masques; Feasts; Weddings; Funeralls; Capitall Executions; and such Shewes; Men need not to be put in minde of them; Yet are they not to be neglected.[81]

The theorists of ethnography further suggested that travelers "always have a Table-book at hand to set down every thing worth remembering, and then at night more methodically transcribe the Notes they have taken in the day."[82] Once the traveler returned from his voyage, he was instructed to "methodize" his notes and produce an ethnography that would be, in James Howell's phrase, "applyable to the publique utility of ones own country."[83]

There is every indication that the envoys intuitively followed the suggestions of ethnographic theorists in analyzing Muscovite life. The ambassadors began their investigation with a mental picture of an ideal monarchy and its basic institutions. All of them knew or assumed that Muscovy, like other kingdoms, would have a prince who ruled through a royal council and estate-representative institutions, and whose authority was limited by law; that there would be a nobility serving the prince in a military and administrative capacity; and that this nobility would own estates, perhaps "held of the king" but in fact private property. When researching Muscovite government, the foreigners employed the categories provided by this standard template to direct their explorations. They wanted to know how powerful the Muscovite prince was vis-à-vis institutions that might limit his authority, what sort of position the nobility occupied vis-à-vis the prince, and how this nobil-

---

[81] Francis Bacon, "Of Travaile," 55–56. For similar lists of observational "heads," see Robert Johnson, "Of Travell," chap. 9; Awnsham Churchill and John Churchill, eds., *A Collection of Voyages and Travels*, 1:lxxv.

[82] Churchill and Churchill, *Collection of Voyages*, 1:lxxv. A "tablebook" is of course a device for note-keeping. It is synonymous with "commonplace book."

[83] James Howell, *Instructions for forreine travell*, 73.

ity maintained its "estate." All of them took notes under these rubrics. Herberstein, Barbarino, Olearius, and Meyerberg all quite explicitly state that they made (in the words of Herberstein) "numerous notes" in daily registers.[84] Once their "data" were collected in notebooks, the ethnographers then "methodized" their findings into appropriate categories.[85]

Giles Fletcher's *Of the Russe Commonwealth* provides the best example of the use of a descriptive template for empirical exploration and exposition. Upon his return from Russia, Fletcher "reduced [his observations] into some order," the results of which can be seen in the "Table, let downe before the beginning of the Booke," which exactly diagrams the contents of the treatises (see Table 5).[86] Fletcher's description of Russian government—"the ordering of their State"—is embedded in a larger account of Russian "pollicy," by which he understood the manner or art of governance in general. He begins with a description of the royal family (the "stocke of the Russe Emperour," "the manner of inauguration"), analyzes the extent of sovereign power ("the forme or manner of their pubilique government") and then details what might be called "auxiliary" government institutions—representative bodies, the nobility, provincial administration, the royal council, revenues, and the political condition of the commons. Though Fletcher's analysis of Russian society is much more clearly articulated than that found in any other Muscovite ethnography, the categories he used were hardly unique to either ethnography of Russia or European ethnography in general. Similar systems of description were at work in most of the accounts of Russia left to posterity by the envoys.[87] Just as the topics described in the ethnographies were similar, so too was the analysis of Russian government in particular. Like Fletcher, Herberstein, and Olearius, many of the ethnographers began by detailing the power of the tsar, rendered a characterization of the political elite and important governmental institutions, and then offered details about the state administration. It is to these descriptions of Russian government that we now turn.

Russian Government in the Eyes of the Envoys

At the center of the Muscovite political system was of course the tsar, and it is not surprising to find that all the envoys commented on the extent of his

[84] Herberstein (1517–49), 1:clx; Barberino (1565), 1:5–6; Adam Olearius, *Vermehrte Newe Beschreibung der Muscowitischen und Persischen Reyse*, xvi; Meyerberg (1661), 177.

[85] On the systemization of travel descriptions, see especially Justin Stagl, "Methodizing of Travel," 312–16 (see fig. 3, 307, for an example).

[86] On "reduction to order," see Fletcher (1591), 169.

[87] It is difficult to agree with Richard Pipes's thesis that Fletcher's use of the schema "distinguishes [*Of the Russe Commonwealth*] from all other foreign accounts." See Pipes's introduction to *Of the Russe Commonwealth*, ed. Pipes and John Fine, 23. It is precisely the presence of the schema that indicates its generic similarity to other accounts.

Table 5. Fletcher's outline of *Of the Russe Commonwealth*

The sum of this discourse conteining the	1. Cosmographie of the Country		1. The breadth and length of the Countrie, with the names of the Shires. 2. The Soyle and Clymate. 3. The native commodities of the Countrie. 4. The Cheife cities of Russia.
	2. Pollicy	1. The ordering of their State.	5. The house or stocke of the Russe Emperour. 6. The maner of inauguration of the Russe Emperours. 7. Their forme or manner of their publique government. 8. Their Parliamentes and manner of holding them. 9. The Russe Nobilitie, and meanes whereby it is kept in an under proportion agreeable to that State. 10. The manner of governing their Provinces, or Shires. 11. The Emperors privie Counsell. 12. The Emperors Customes and other Revenues, and what they amount unto, with the Sophismes practised for the encrease of them. 13. The Russe communaltie and their condition.
		2. Their iudicial proceeding.	14. Their publique Iustice and manner of proceeding therein.
		3. Their warlike provisions.	15. The Emperours forces for his warres, with the officiers and their Salaries. 16. Their manner of mustering, armour, provision for vitaile, encamping, &c. 17. Their order in marching, charging, and their martiall discipline. 18. Their colonies and pollicie in mainteyning their purchases by conquest. 19. Their borderers, with whom they have most to doo in warre and peace. 20. Of the Permians, Samoites, and Lappes.
		4. Their Ecclesiastical State	21. Their Church offices, and degrees. 22. Their Leiturgie or forme of Chuch service, with their manner of administering the Sacraments. 23. The doctrine of the Russe Church. 24. Their manner of solemnizing marriages. 25. The other Ceremonies of the Russe Church.
	3. Oeconomie or private behaviour		26. The Emperours domestique or private behaviour. 27. The Emperours houshold, and offices of his house. 28. The private behaviour, and manners of the Russe people.

Source: Fletcher (1591), 171.

power. In general, however, they are quite vague on this score, noting only that the tsar's authority was universal or nearly so. Sixteenth-century envoys uniformly described it in this fashion: Herberstein believed that the grand prince dominated the "lives and property of all his subjects"; Jenkinson wrote that Ivan IV "keepeth his people in great subjection"; Barbarino commented that the Russian "people fear their lord and are more obedient to their rulers than any other people in the world"; Printz said that the Muscovites "live in the most extreme slavery"; Possevino remarked that the tsar "enjoys unrestricted power over his people"; and Fletcher characterized the tsar's rule as "plaine tyrannical." [88] Seventeenth-century envoys offered similar characterizations of the tsar's authority over his realm and its people: Olearius proclaimed that "the tsar, or grand prince, alone rules the whole country"; Meyerberg wrote that Aleksei Mikhailovich "rules everything himself"; Wickhart believed that "the Muscovites are all the slaves of the grand prince"; Korb agreed that "the whole Russian race is rather in a state of slavery than of freedom." [89] The only discordant voice was that of Paul of Aleppo, whose Orthodox religious sympathies and strident Russophilia made it impossible for him to characterize the tsar as anything other than a servant of the church. [90]

The foreigners generally failed to offer a detailed list of the tsar's powers. Fletcher was the only sixteenth-century ethnographer to attempt to provide a catalog.

> Concerning the principall points and matters of State, wherein Soveraintie consisteth (as the making and annulling of publike Lawes, the making of Magistrates, power to make warre or league with any forraine State, to execute or to pardon life, with the right of appeale in all matters, both civil and criminal) they doo so wholy and absolutely pertaine to the Emperour, and his Counsell under him, as that hee may be saide to be both the Soveraine commaunder and executioner of all these. [91]

A half a century later, Olearius gave a less coherent account of the Russian sovereign's authority: the grand prince "is not subject to the law and may, as he desires and deems fit, publish and establish laws and orders"; he "appoints and removes officials, and even expels and executes them as he pleases"; he "alone has the right to declare war on foreign nations and may conduct it as he sees fit"; he "distributes titles and honors, making princes of those who

---

[88] Herberstein (1517–49), 1:32; Jenkinson (1557), 423; Barberino (1565), 2:8; Printz (1578), 29–30; Possevino (1586), 27; Fletcher (1591), 194.
[89] Olearius (1656), 173; Meyerberg (1661), 116; Wickhart (1675), 246; Korb (1700), 2:193–94.
[90] See, for example, Aleppo (1655), 2:59, 230, where he views the tsar as a slave to the patriarch.
[91] Fletcher (1591), 195.

have rendered services to him or to the country, or whom, in general he considers worthy of his favor"; and he "coins his own money." [92] The envoys were unable to offer anything more than a general characterization of the tsar's might for good reason, for the powers of the grand prince were *formally* unlimited. Neither constitution nor custom provided the visitors with any idea of what the tsar might or might not do. They may have turned to Muscovite officials for guidance in this matter, but it seems unlikely that a question concerning the extent of royal power would have been fully understood by the tsar's men. Russian authorities were probably unfamiliar with the divisions of and limitations on authority that Herberstein, Fletcher, and Olearius—who clearly had European governance in mind—imposed on Muscovite monarchy.

The envoys were, however, specific on one point—the tsar was the ultimate holder of all landed property in Muscovy. We have already seen that Herberstein remarked that Vasilii III possessed "unlimited control" over the land of his subjects. Later sixteenth-century commentators implied the same thing: In the 1550s, Chancellor wrote that the lands of all those who died without heirs reverted to the fisc; Printz described the same practice twenty years later; Possevino maintained that no land could be inherited without the prince's approval.[93] Seventeenth-century commentators followed their sixteenth-century predecessors in proclaiming the tsar a universal owner: Olearius wrote that Muscovites did not truly own their property; Paul of Aleppo called the tsar "universal heir"; Korb wrote that even Peter I disposed "as freely of the property of private individuals, as if nature had produced everything for his sake alone." [94]

Why did the envoys insist that the tsar held both unrestricted political and proprietary authority? The answer is simple: the Russians themselves said so. It is apparent that the Muscovites felt obliged to demean themselves and praise the tsar in answer to questions about royal authority in Russia. Possevino rightly observed that "the Muscovites [were] astonishingly prone to exalting their grand princes." "The deference universally accorded the prince," he said, "is something the mind can scarcely comprehend." [95] If the envoys are to be believed, the Muscovites possessed an entire catalog of stock phrases that they deployed to describe the tsar's unrestricted power. Herberstein, who was the first to memorialize what might be called Russian political folk sayings about the tsar's authority, wrote that the Muscovites "openly confess that the will of the prince is the will of God; on this account they call him God's key-bearer and chamberlain, and in short they believe that he is the executor of the divine will." "If anyone inquires respecting some doubt-

---

[92] Olearius (1656), 176–79. For a similar characterization, see Reutenfels (1671), 101.
[93] Printz (1578), 65; Chancellor (1553), 232; Possevino (1589), 9.
[94] Olearius (1656), 174; Aleppo (1653), 1:400–401; Korb (1700), 2:193–94.
[95] Possevino (1568), 27, 11.

ful and uncertain matter," the Habsburg ambassador continued, "the common answer is, 'God and the great prince know.'"[96] Olearius noted that

> beginning very early, they teach their children to speak of His Tsarist Majesty as of God, and to consider him equally lofty. Thus they say, 'God and the grand prince [alone] know that.' The same idea is expressed in others of their bywords: they speak of appearing before the grand prince as 'seeing his bright eyes.' To demonstrate their humility and sense of duty, they say that everything they have belongs not so much to them as to God and the grand prince.[97]

Other envoy-ethnographers of both the sixteenth and seventeenth centuries reported that the Russians claimed that all they owned was God's and the grand prince's; that the tsar was God, but not God, a man, but more than a man; that he did not burn up or sink at sea; that he knew everything and could do everything; that as God rules in heaven, so the grand prince ruled on earth; that one must not alter the word of God or the grand prince, but obey both without fail.[98] "In brief," observed Meyerberg, "they speak of him as a God, and many believe this."[99]

Despite the willingness of Muscovites to attribute complete power to their sovereign, the foreigners recognized that the tsar ruled with the aid of a royal council.[100] This is understandable, for every time the envoys attended an audience, they saw the "*Boarstva dumna,*" as Fletcher called it.[101] At audiences, the envoys often noted the presence of boyars who were members of the council. "Along the walls around to the left [and right], and opposite the tsar," Olearius wrote, "sat over fifty distinguished and splendidly dressed boyars, princes, and state counselors; on their heads were tall black hats of fox fur, which, as is their custom, they did not remove" (see fig. 7).[102] Several of the visitors were able to accurately enumerate ranks within the royal council and to offer lists of its members (see fig. 8).[103] It seems reasonable to assume

[96] Herberstein (1517–49), 1:32.

[97] Olearius (1656), 174.

[98] Chancellor (1553), 232; Printz (1578), 29–30; Olearius (1656), 147, 174, 176, 214; Meyerberg (1661), 116–17; Wickhart (1675), 246; Tanner (1678), 74; Korb (1700), 2:155.

[99] Meyerberg (1661), 116. For similar characterizations, see Aleppo (1655), 1:400, 2: 72; Olearius (1656), 137, 174, 176, 236–37; Wickhart (1675), 246; Korb (1700), 1:159, 2:155, 157.

[100] On the "Boyar Council," see Marshall T. Poe, "Boyar Duma," and the literature there cited.

[101] Fletcher (1591), 211.

[102] Olearius (1565), 63. For similar descriptions, see Herberstein (1517–49), 2:123–25; Chancellor (1553), 226–27; Jenkinson (1557), 420; Barberino (1565), 2:15; Randolfe (1568), 102–7; Ulfeldt (1575), 28–29; Printz (1578), 53–54; Horsey (1584–1611), 273, 302–3, 324–25; Possevino (1586), 16, 47–48; Peyerle (1608), 176–77, 182–85, 201–9, 223–27; Petreius (1615), 159–61, 270–73; Aleppo (1655), 1:379–88, 2:219, 221, 275–77; Olearius (1656), 68–75; Meyerberg (1661), 63ff.; Reutenfels (1671), 107–8; Wickhart (1675), 83–95, 116–17, 120–123, 212–13; Tanner (1678), 50–54, 92–95; Gordon (1661–99), 56; Korb (1700), 1:161ff.

[103] On ranks within the Boyar Council, see Fletcher (1591), 211; Olearius (1656), 219–20. On lists of counselors, see Possevino (1586), 11; Fletcher (1591), 202, 211; Aleppo (1656), 2:

Audience des Ambassadeurs chez le Czar de Moscovie.

7. The tsar receives the Holstein ambassadors. *Voyages du Sr. Adam Olearius* (Amsterdam, 1727). Courtesy of the Division of Rare Books and Manuscript Collections, Cornell University Library.

that Russian officials informed the visitors about the structure and composition of the council, and they may have even used official lists. The foreigners were less clear about the role councilors played in government. Most of them recognized that members had judicial responsibilities: Ulfeldt was told that the royal councilors reviewed petitions addressed to the prince; Possevino noted the presence of "twelve senators who hear cases"; Fletcher said that "All matters there both civill and criminall, are heard and determined in the several courtes, held by some of the said Counsell"; Olearius claimed that boyars served as "judges." [104] Moreover, the envoy-ethnographers generally agreed that the councilors had administrative duties. Fletcher, Olearius, Wickhart, and Korb identified by name members of the royal council who were in charge of major administrative organs (*prikazy*).[105] Again, this

74–75; Olearius (1656), 218–21; Meyerberg (1661), 166; Wickhart (1675), 87, 198, 206–8; Korb (1700), 2:242ff.

[104] Ulfeldt (1571), 20; Possevino (1586), 11; Fletcher (1591), 208; Olearius (1656), 227. Also see Wickhart (1675), 248; Korb (1700), 186–92.

[105] Possevino (1586), 12, is vague on this score. However, Fletcher (1591), 205, Olearius (1656), 221–27, and Korb (1700), 242–56 list chancelleries (*prikazy)* and the men who headed

information could have been gained from the testimony of Russian authorities or from official lists, though the envoys do not cite their sources.[106]

Despite their acknowledgment that Russian magnates held limited judicial and administrative authority, the visitors almost universally claimed that the Boyar Council itself had little or no political power. Herberstein wrote that "not one of [the grand prince's] counselors has sufficient authority to dare to oppose him, or even differ from him, on any subject."[107] Fletcher insisted that "the Emperours of Russia give the name of councellours to divers of their cheife Nobilitie, rather for honors sake, then for any use they make of them about their matters of state," adding that "they are seldom or never called to any publique consultations."[108] Olearius characterized the tsar's use of the council in the following terms:

> He consults with the boyars and counselors . . . , but in the manner of Xerxes, the Persian emperor, who assembled the Asian princes not so much to secure their advice on the proposed war with the Greeks as to personally declare his will to the princes and prove that he was a monarch. He said then that he had, in truth, assembled them in order that he not do everything at his own discretion, but at the same time they were to understand that their business was more a matter of listening than of advising.[109]

Meyerberg believed that the grand princes asked the council's opinion "for show in order to divert from themselves on to it the hatred for the unfair things done by them."[110] "Those that are admitted to the dignity of the privy council," wrote Korb, "assume the lofty name of magnates, and come next in rank after their sovereign, have merely more splendid bonds of slavery."[111]

The foreigners needed no positive evidence to demonstrate that the Boyar Council was powerless, for this conclusion followed from their belief that the tsar held complete authority. In any case, it is difficult to imagine a sane Muscovite official explaining to a foreigner that the council ruled together with the prince, for, as we have seen, the entire point of Russian diplomatic theater was to highlight the tsar's omnipotence. Nevertheless, the foreigners' observation of the Boyar Council seemed to confirm that it was indeed without authority. The visitors noted that during their audiences with the tsar, the boyars played little or no substantive role in the proceedings, sitting mute and largely motionless. Herberstein was amazed at the silence of the courtiers: "During this time, not a single one of those who stood around [the

---

them. Also see Aleppo (1655), 2:122; Meyerburg (1661), 166–67; Wickhart (1675), 206–13; and Korb (1700), 1:110, all of whom provide brief overviews of the chancelleries.

[106] In the seventeenth century Russian authorities kept regular records of chancellery personnel. On them, see Natalia F. Demidova, *Sluzhilaia biurokratiia v Rossii XVII v. i ee rol' v formirovanii absoliutizma,* and Borivoj Plavsič, "Seventeenth-Century Chanceries and Their Staffs."

[107] Herberstein (1517–49), 1:32.

[108] Fletcher (1591), 211.

[109] Olearius (1656), 177.

[110] Meyerberg (1661), 166.

[111] Korb (1700), 2:193–94.

1. Bojar Boris Jvanowitz Morosou.
2. Bojar Boris Nikita Jvanowitz Romanou.
3. Bojar Jvan Wasilowitz Morosou.
4. Bojar Kneß Jvan Andreowitz Gallizin.
5. Bojar Kneß Nikita Jvanowitz Odoouski.
6. Bojar Kneß Jacob Kudenietewitz Tzerkaski.
7. Bojar Kneß Alexei Nikitowitz Trubetzkoi
8. Bojar Gleeb Jvanowitz Morosou.
9. Bojar Wasili Petrowitz Tzeremetou.
10. Bojar Kneß Boris Alexandrowitz Reppenim.
11. Bojar Michael Michailowitz Soltikou.
12. Bojar Wasili Jvanowitz Streesnou.
13. Bojar Kneß Wasili Simonowitz Projorouski.
14. Bojar Kneß Fedor Simonowitz Kurakin.
15. Bojar Kneß Grigori Simonowitz Kurakin.
16. Bojar Kneß Jürgi Petrowitz Buhnessou Rosiouski.
17. Bojar Jvan Jvanowitz Soltikou.
18. Bojar Grigori Wasilowitz Puskin.
19. Bojar Kneß Fedor Fedorowitz Volchonski.
20. Bojar Laurenti Demitriowitz Soltikou.
21. Bojar Kneß Jürgi Alexeowitz Dolgorukoy.
22. Bojar Jlia Danilowitz Miloslauski.
23. Bojar Wasili Wasilowitz Butterlin.
24. Bojar Kneß Michail Petrowitz Pronski.
25. Bojar Kneß Jvan Petrowitz Pronsky.
26. Bojar Kneß Jvan Nikitowitz Gavenski.
27. Bojar Kneß Fedor Jürgiowitz Chworostiny.
28. Bojar Wasili Borissowitz Tzeremettou.
29. Bojar Nikita Alexeowitz Susin.

Nach diesen folgen die Ocolnitzen/aus welchen die Bojaren erwehlet werden.

1. Ocolnitza Kneß Andre Fedrowitz Litwinow Masalskoy.
2. Oc. Kneß Jvan Fedrowitz Chilkou.
3. Oc. Mikifor Sergeowitz Zabackin.
4. Oc. Kneß Demetri Petrowitz Lewou.

5. Oc.

8. A list of members of the Boyar Council. Adam Olearius, *Vermehrte newe Beschreibung der muscowitischen und persischen Reyse* (Scheswig, 1656).

hall] showed the least mark of respect to us; but on the contrary, if we happened in passing to salute or speak to any one with whom we were familiarly acquainted, he would make no reply, just as if he had never known any of us, or had never received a salute from us before." [112] Possevino remarked that during his audiences the Russian notables "never say a word and hang upon the ruler's every expression and gesture." [113] Seventeenth-century envoys reported similar behavior at their audiences.[114] Even during negotiations, the boyars appeared to be powerless. "Whenever I proposed a new item," Possevino wrote of his negotiations, "not daring to respond on their own initiative all the councilors would immediately repair to the prince, ask him what their reply should be, and bring back and present an accurate digest of his views." When Possevino accompanied Muscovite ambassadors to Italy he noted that they "were unprepared for the degree of freedom they enjoyed in Venice, accustomed as they are to referring everything to their prince." [115] Again, only Paul of Aleppo was willing to assign considerable authority to the Boyar Council.[116]

Some of the foreigners were also aware that Muscovy had, in addition to a royal council, some sort of estate-representative institution.[117] Fletcher offered the most systematic and idealized description of the body.

> Their highest Court of publike consultation for matter of State, is called the *Zabore,* that is, the *Publike Assembly.* The states and degrees of persons that are present at their Parliaments, are these in order. 1. The Emperour himselfe. 2. Some of his Nobilitie about the number of twentie being all of his Councel. 3. Certain of the cleargy men, &c. about the same number.[118]

Generally speaking, however, the foreigners' knowledge of the so-called *zemskie sobory* (a term invented by nineteenth-century Russian historians to denote large, quasi-representative councils) was quite imperfect. Most of the ethnographers were unaware of their existence. Printz, for example, did not mention them, but did note the absence of urban assemblies: "In the towns there are no councils, no senators—the names of which the Russians do not even know." [119] Most of those who discussed national councils could have learned about them only through word of mouth, for no envoy-ethnographer

---

[112] Herberstein (1517–49), 2:124.

[113] Possevino (1586), 48.

[114] Peyerle (1608), 176–77, 182–85, 201–9, 223–27; Petreius (1615), 159–61, 270–73; Aleppo (1655), 1:379–88, 2:219, 221, 275–77; Olearius (1656), 68–75; Meyerberg (1661), 63ff.; Wickhart (1675), 83–95, 116–17, 120–23, 212–13; Tanner (1678), 50–54, 92–95; Korb (1700), 1:161ff.

[115] Possevino (1586), 16, 23.

[116] Aleppo (1655), 2:74–75.

[117] On this body, see Richard Hellie, "Zemskii Sobor," and the extensive literature there cited.

[118] Fletcher (1591), 196.

[119] Printz (1578), 65.

ever attended one. Since they were extraordinary assemblies, it seems probable that even Muscovite officials did not view them as a regular part of Russian government and therefore would have had no reason to describe them to the ethnographers in the course of conversations about the structure of the state. What little was known about the assemblies, together with the general presumption that the tsar ruled without counsel, suggested to the foreigners that they were without authority. Fletcher observed with disgust that the assemblies contained no "Burghers or other to represent the communaltie."[120] According to the English ambassador, even those who were represented in the general council had no authority, "for as touching any Lawe or publique order of the Realme, it is ever determined of before any publique assemblie or Parliament bee summoned."[121] In the first half of the seventeenth century national councils played an important role in Muscovite governance. Large assemblies of some kind elected Mikhail Romanov, approved major war taxes, discussed relations with Poland and the Crimean Tatars, and helped formulate the Council Law Code of 1649. The last assembly was held in 1653 to deliberate the annexation of Ukraine. Interestingly, seventeenth-century envoys were almost completely unaware that the institution had ever existed. Even Olearius, who was in Muscovy in the 1630s, when the assembly was active, did not discuss the institution in his detailed description of Muscovite government. He did note that the tsar summoned "the wisest heads of all stations" to formulate the Council Law Code of 1649, but he clearly believed that this assembly was extraordinary.[122]

Another institution that drew the foreigners' attention was the law.[123] Most often their interest in Russian statutes was purely ethnographic, as in the case of Herberstein, who offered his readers an excerpt from the Law Code (*Sudebnik*) of 1497.[124] Later visitors, and particularly the English merchants of the Muscovy Company, gained practical experience with Muscovite courts in the course of suing Russian traders.[125] Several seventeenth-century envoys mentioned or offered discussions of the Council Law Code of 1649.[126] In general, the envoys were more concerned with measuring the fairness of Russian law and the extent to which it was followed than in providing a catalog of legal provisions, something that would have been far beyond the competence of most of them. Some commentators praised Russian

[120] Fletcher (1591), 196. Also see ibid., 224.
[121] Ibid., 195.
[122] Olearius (1656), 227.
[123] On Muscovite law, see Richard Hellie, "Sudebniki" and "Ulozhenie of 1649," and the extensive literature cited in both overviews. For a treatment of Russian law in the accounts of foreigners, see Walter E. Butler, "Foreign Impressions of Russian Law to 1800."
[124] Herberstein (1517–49), 1:102–3.
[125] The English documents reproduced in Hakluyt are full of legal wrangling. See, for example, Hakluyt (1903–5), 3:324–30.
[126] Olearius (1656), 227; Meyerberg (1661), 91–92; Wickhart (1675), 248ff.; Korb (1700), 2:187.

law for its simplicity, pointing out that Muscovy had no attorneys.[127] Most foreigners, however, held Russian law in low regard. They pointed out that the law was not respected and that Muscovite judges (and administrators generally) were corrupt. "Although the prince is very severe," Herberstein commented, "nevertheless all justice is venal, and that without much concealment."[128] Sixteenth-century envoys noted that not only was the law poorly observed and unfairly enforced, it was also unstable, for the prince could alter any statute at his pleasure.[129] Seventeenth-century commentators agreed. The tsar himself was unrestrained by any legal code, for his will was the law.[130] Like the envoys' belief that neither the Boyar Council nor the national assemblies held any significant power, the proposition that the will of the prince was law was founded less on observation than on inference: if the tsar was omnipotent, he would have to be the author of laws, not subject to them. Precisely this reasoning led Fletcher to conclude that Muscovy had no substantive written law at all, something he knew to be false.[131]

The lack of institutional and legal restraint on the authority of the tsar disturbed the foreigners, but more unsettling was the way the Russian ruler treated his nobility. Men such as Herberstein, Fletcher, Olearius, and Korb were members of the elite in their countries of origin. They took it for granted that nobles would be treated by their monarchs in a fashion consistent with their dignified status. It is likely that the ethnographers expected Russian notables—the men who accompanied them throughout their visits—to be afforded the same degree of deference by the tsar. Yet the Europeans constantly observed the tsar treating his subjects, particularly magnates and officials, with the greatest disrespect. Some of the visitors noted that humiliation of the nobility was a regular part of Russian ceremonies. Peyerle, for example, recorded "the manner in which the tsar . . . wanted to display to the ambassadors his greatness":

> Having called the most notable senator, Ivan Vasil'evich Shuiskii, he ordered him to place before him a bench and to place his feet on it; he ordered his brother, Dmitrii Shuiskii to do the same; then he dismissed them both with some sort of order. In their place he ordered other notable boyars to support him by the arms. He sent these away and called other princes to him. In such a

[127] On the lack of lawyers, see Chancellor (1553), 233; Adams/Chancellor (1553), 263; Barberino (1565), 2:9; Fletcher (1591), 229; Olearius (1656), 227; Korb (1700), 2:187. Adams/Chancellor (1553), 264, praised the grand prince for hearing legal cases himself.

[128] Herberstein (1517–49), 1:105. See also Herberstein (1517–49), 1:89; Adams/Chancellor (1553), 264; Fletcher (1591), 230; Olearius (1656), 202, 226; Meyerberg (1661), 79–80; Wickhart (1675), 254; Korb (1700), 1:110, 297, 2:13, 188–89.

[129] Barberino (1565), 2:8–9, Printz (1578), 65; Fletcher (1591), 169–70, 195.

[130] Olearius (1656), 176; Meyerberg (1661), 116–17; Korb (1700), 2:187.

[131] Fletcher (1591), 169–70. Fletcher does recognize the existence of procedural law. See ibid., 232.

manner he summoned and dismissed his magnates several times. They were all supposed to execute orders that our lords do not give to even the last noble.[132]

It was not only in diplomatic rituals that the foreigners had opportunities to witness the tsar's lack of proper regard for his nobility. Many foreigners were shocked to see that Russian notables (and clergy) were subject, just like commoners, to corporal punishment for infractions as slight as failure to pay a debt in a timely fashion.[133] Printz observed that even "for mild offenses they are stripped to the waste, led out to the street, and beaten with the knout." He added that "even the boyars and clergy are often subjected to this punishment."[134] "One can judge of the boyars' slavery," concluded Olearius, "by the barbaric punishments meted out to them for offenses" (see fig. 9).[135] Far more horrific examples of the tsar's abuse were observed by the foreigners during Ivan IV's reign of terror in the *oprichnina* era. Several of the envoys witnessed Ivan's outrages at firsthand and left detailed accounts of his many atrocities, the majority of which were directed against nobles.[136] The envoys were clearly shocked by Ivan's behavior and understood it to be beyond the pale. Royal abuse of the wellborn, however, was not unique to Ivan's bloody reign. Even the pious Aleksei Mikhailovich was observed mistreating his nobles. Meyerberg, for instance, described an incident in which Aleksei demanded that his boyars be bled for medical purposes. One magnate refused and was attacked by the grand prince.

> "You worthless slave!" said Aleksei in anger. "You will not do what your sovereign will? The blood flowing in you is more valuable than mine? And why do you place yourself above your equals, and even your betters. . . ?" Not saying a word he threw himself on him, striking him many times with his fists until blood flowed, giving him many kicks with his foot.[137]

Later envoys witnessed similar incidents of physical and verbal abuse at the hands of the tsar.[138] Most surprising to the envoys was the fact that Russian magnates sometimes thanked the tsar for striking them. "Even when beaten

[132] Peyerle (1606), 187. Also see Peyerle (1608), 221.

[133] For corporal punishment of nobles, see Barberino (1565), 2:10; Fletcher (1591), 219, 232; Aleppo (1655), 1:260–61; Olearius (1656), 135, 147, 173, 230; Meyerberg (1661), 55, 58, 116–17, 168–69; Tanner (1678), 77; Korb (1700), 1:110, 160, 174, 182, 191, 217, 2:29, 163. For corporal punishment of clergymen, see Herberstein (1517–49), 1:56 and 58; Ulfeldt (1575), 24; Olearius (1656), 230; Reutenfels (1671), 167–69; Neuville (1698), 60; Korb (1700), 1:172, 2:179.

[134] Printz (1578), 66.

[135] Olearius (1656), 147.

[136] Ulfeldt (1575) and Printz (1578).

[137] Meyerberg (1661), 55.

[138] Aleppo (1655), 1:260–61; Olearius (1656), 135, 147, 173; Meyerberg (1661), 55, 58, 116–17, 168–69; Tanner (1678), 77; Korb (1700), 1:110, 160, 174, 182, 191, 217, 2:29, 163.

9. Muscovite punishments. *Voyages du Sr. Adam Olearius* (Amsterdam, 1727).
Courtesy of the Division of Rare Books and Manuscript Collections, Cornell University Library.

to the point of death," Possevino wrote, "they will sometimes say that the prince has done them a favor by chastising them." [139]

Not only did the tsar demean his nobility, but they, remarkably, also demeaned themselves. Almost without exception, the foreigners were shocked to find that Russian notables and officials called themselves the tsar's "slaves." [140] Herberstein was the first to record this custom, in 1517, when he obliquely stated that "all confess themselves to be the *chlopos,* that is, serfs of the prince." [141] Fletcher noted correctly that, according to Muscovite legal protocol, petitioners called themselves *kholop* (slave) in the titular formula of "anie publike instrument of private petition which they make to the Emperour." Such undignified deference, Fletcher observed, was not only due to the tsar. Commoners, the English envoy wrote, "subscribe themselves *Ko-*

[139] Possevino (1586), 11. See also ibid., 50; Olearius (1656), 147; Meyerberg (1661), 116–17; Wickhart (1675), 203; Korb (1700), 1:198–99.

[140] Muscovite sources report this practice. See, for example, Kotoshikhin, *O Rossii v tsarstvovanie Alekseia Mikhailovicha,* fols. 186–88. See Marshall T. Poe, "What Did Muscovites Mean When They Called Themselves 'Slaves of the Tsar'?" and Nancy S. Kollmann, "Concepts of Society and Social Identity in Early Modern Russia."

[141] Herberstein (1517–49), 1:95.

lophey, that is, their villains, or bondslaves," in petitions and other papers "to any of the Nobles of chiefe officers of the Emperours." [142] Olearius recorded this habit in the second quarter of the seventeenth century:

> All subjects, whether of high or low condition, call themselves and must count themselves the tsar's *kholopi,* that is slaves and serfs. Just as the magnates and nobles have their own slaves, serfs and peasants, the princes and the magnates are obliged to acknowledge their slavery and their insignificance in relation to the tsar. They sign their letters and petitions with the diminutive form of their names, such as Ivashka instead of Ivan, or "Petrushka, *tvoi kholop* [your slave]." Also, when the grand prince speaks to anyone, he employs diminutive names.[143]

Meyerberg offered a long ethnographic description of Russian petitionary formulas, accompanied by an illustration (see fig. 10).[144] Those who failed to abase themselves properly were punished, as Korb related: "He that should happen to subscribe his name in the positive degree to petitions or letters to the tsar would be publicly tried for treason. This was a crime imputed to the military engineer Laval," wrote Korb of a foreign officer, "by which the ministers contended that he had deserved the tsar's hatred; for that he ought to write and style himself the grand duke's *cholop,* or most abject and vilest slave, and acknowledge that all the goods and chattels he possessed were not his, but the monarch's." [145]

The envoys also witnessed Russian nobles prostrating themselves before the tsar (see fig. 11). Herberstein offered the first account of this practice. He observed that if anyone "desires to offer his thanks to the grand duke for any great favor, or to beg anything of him he then bows himself so low as to touch the ground with his forehead." [146] In 1556 Raffaelle Barberino noted the same custom, adding that the Muscovites prostrated themselves so readily and so vigorously that "many of them have calluses on their heads." [147] Some year later, Printz correctly remarked that the Muscovites "use the phrase 'to strike the forehead'" to denote ritual prostration.[148] Possevino noted that Muscovite envoys in Rome "were quick enough to do obeisance whenever they heard any remark they thought touched upon the interests of their grand prince, for the Muscovites throw themselves at the feet of their bishops and strike their foreheads on the ground, and in behaving thus they show them a respect which the early Christians reserved solely for the Apos-

[142] Fletcher (1591), 199, 224.
[143] Olearius (1656), 147. Also see Olearius (1647), 173; Aleppo (1655), 2:203; Korb (1700), 2:194–95.
[144] Meyerberg (1661), 116–17.
[145] Korb (1700), 2:193–94.
[146] Herberstein (1517–49) 2:125.
[147] Barberino (1565), 2:12.
[148] Printz (1578), 67.

10. A Russian petitionary ritual. Augustin Freiherr von Meyerberg, *Al'bom Meierberga: Vidy i bytovyia kartiny Rossii XVII veka* (St. Petersburg, 1903).

tles." [149] Fletcher added that Russian commoners prostrated themselves not only to the tsar and chief clerics, but to "his Nobilitie, chief officers, and souldiers." "When a poore Mousick," wrote the English ambassador, "meeteth with any of them upon the high way, he must turne himselfe about, as not

[149] Possevino (1568), 26.

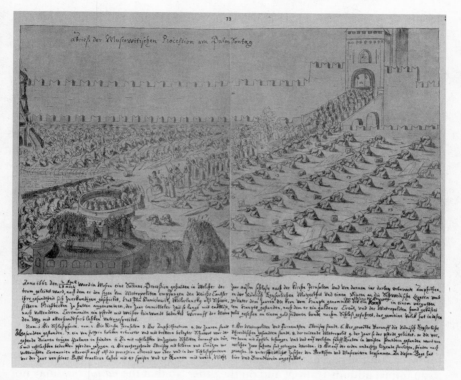

11. Prostration during a Palm Sunday procession. Augustin Freiherr von Meyerberg, *Al'bom Meierberga: Vidy i bytovyia kartiny Rossii XVII veka* (St. Petersburg, 1903).

daring to looke him on the face, and fall down with knocking of his head the very ground, as he doth unto his Idoll." [150] Paul of Aleppo characteristically approved of prostration.

> A remarkable custom in this country is, that when any person presents himself with a petition before the emperor, or a governor, patriarch, bishop, or priest, and after humbling himself in supplication, finds that his prayer is not conceded to his many metanoias, he then beats his head on the ground, and thus perseveres; refusing to raise it, until his petition is granted.[151]

All other seventeenth-century envoys to Russia interpreted the rite more critically. For European visitors, prostration was proof that Russians were, in Olearius's words, "serfs and slaves." [152] "The Muscovites are all the slaves of

[150] Fletcher (1591), 224.
[151] Aleppo (1655), 1:352.
[152] Olearius (1656), 147.

the grand prince," Wickhart concluded, "in that they fall before him and rest their foreheads on the ground."[153]

In the eyes of the visitors, the tsar's mistreatment of his nobility was not confined to verbal or physical abuse. Indeed, the entire system by which the grand prince provided for his servitors was seen as exploitive. Many foreigners reported with amazement (and occasionally admiration) that there was no class of privileged freemen in Russia—all Muscovite nobles and gentry were obliged to serve their prince in some capacity.[154] Herberstein, speaking of the gentry, remarked that in times of war "each and all are compelled, both as stipendiaries and as aspirants to the prince's favour, to go to battle."[155] Those who followed Herberstein agreed that noble military service was mandatory and that those who did not fight for the tsar were severely punished.[156] Moreover, as Olearius remarked, noblemen were obliged to supply the tsar "according to the number to their estates . . . a certain number of foot soldiers and cavalrymen."[157] Chancellor, Paul of Aleppo, Meyerberg, and Korb concurred that Muscovite magnates were required to provide troops for their sovereign.[158] The envoys also noted that Russian magnates were compelled to serve as administrators and provincial governors, all of whom were, in the opinion of the envoys, corrupt.[159] The foreigners often observed that there were no powerful local officials in Russia: the court itself appointed local vicegerents (*namestniki*) and only for limited tenures.[160] Olearius explained the logic behind short appointments: "This practice is followed, on the one hand, so that a locality may not be subjected too long to an unjust administration, and on the other, so that the *namestnik* may not become too friendly with the inhabitants and be tempted to neglect his

[153] Wickhart (1675), 246.
[154] On the service requirements of various elements of the Muscovite population, and particularly the nobility and provincial gentry, see Richard Hellie, *Enserfment and Military Change in Muscovy*, 36ff., and "Dvorianin," 77–79.
[155] Herberstein (1517–49), 1:95–96.
[156] Chancellor (1553), 231; Barberino (1565), 2:24–25; Printz (1578), 65; Fletcher (1591), 233, 238; Olearius (1656), 198.
[157] Olearius (1656), 198.
[158] Adams/Chancellor (1553), 260; Aleppo (1655), 2:295; Meyerberg (1661), 181; Korb (1700), 1:232–33, 2:144.
[159] On service in the central administration, see Fletcher (1591), 205; Aleppo (1655), 2:122; Olearius (1656), 221–27; Meyerberg (1661), 166–67; Wickhart (1675), 206–13; Korb (1700), 1:110, 2:242–56. On provincial administration, see Herberstein (1517–49), 1:30–31; Staden (1578), 8, 63–64; Fletcher (1591), 194–96, 207, 219, 244–46; Aleppo (1655), 1:262, 2:12; Olearius (1656), 176–77; Meyerberg (1661), 91–92; Korb (1700), 2:163–64. On corruption in central administration, see Chancellor (1553), 233–34; Barberino (1565), 2:10, 21; Fletcher (1591), 207–8; Olearius (1656), 202, 205, 226, 227; Meyerberg (1661), 79–80; Wickhart (1675), 254; Korb (1700), 1:110, 297, 2:13, 188–89. On corruption in provincial administration, see Ulfeldt (1575), 25; Printz (1578), 65; Fletcher (1591), 207–8, 218; Aleppo (1655), 1:276–77, 2:236–37; Meyerberg (1661), 91–92.
[160] Herberstein (1517–49), 1:30–31; Fletcher (1591), 194–96, 207, 219, 244–46; Aleppo (1655), 1:262, 2:12; Olearius (1656), 176–77; Meyerberg (1661), 91–92; Korb (1700), 2:163–64.

duty." [161] The ethnographers also observed that Russian magnates were compelled to suffer less prestigious and even servile offices. For example, the visitors often noted with amazement that Russian magnates were obliged to appear at court ceremonies, and to come appropriately dressed. [162] Olearius wrote that before the reign of Aleksei Mikhailovich "the *gosti* [wealthy merchants] and magnates, who were supposed to turn out at public audiences in sumptuous dress, were beaten on the bare back with the knout, like slaves, if they failed to appear without good reason. Now, however, they get off with a two- or three-day confinement in prison, depending upon [the influence of] their patrons and intercessors at court." [163] The envoys were surprised to learn that the grand prince was in the business of lending ceremonial robes to impecunious nobles. "If insufficient means do not allow some one to dress in this fashion," wrote Meyerberg, "then it is loaned to them, relative to their status, by the tsar's treasury, for a small fee." If the clothes were damaged or lost, Meyerberg continued, then the lendee "must pay a large sum for his infraction" and "he must suffer to be beaten with cudgels." [164]

What was more remarkable to the envoys, particularly those who visited in the reign of Ivan IV, was that the gentry seemed to serve without proper monetary compensation. "Whoever receives his [Vasilii III's] orders to attend at court, or to go to war, or upon any embassy," Herberstein wrote, "is compelled to undertake whatever it may be at his own expense, with the exception of the younger sons of nobles of slender fortune, whom he sends for every year, and maintains with a fixed but inadequate stipend." [165] If a servitor was too poor to do the grand prince's bidding, Herberstein said, he was punished. [166] Later authors agreed that Muscovite servitors were forced to serve without sufficient compensation. [167] It must be said that the visitors' observations about the lack of monetary compensation in the second half of the sixteenth century are to some extent contradicted by Muscovite documents of the period that imply that entitlements (*oklady*) were, at least occasionally, paid to warriors. By the end of the century, the envoys had become aware that the crown granted its servitors some sort of monetary compensation. Fletcher's account reflected this practice.

> Of these 15000. horsemen, there are three sorts or degrees, which differ as well in estimation, as in wages, one degree from another. The first sort of

[161] Olearius (1656), 177.

[162] Adams/Chancellor (1553), 258–59; Barberino (1565), 2:24–25; Printz (1578), 53; Possevino (1586), 14, 48; Olearius (1656), 60, 62, 128, 173; Meyerberg (1661), 58, 62, 175; Wickhart (1675), 247; Neuville (1698), 5, 17, 37.

[163] Olearius (1656), 173.

[164] Meyerberg (1661), 58.

[165] Herberstein (1517–49), 1:30–31.

[166] See Herberstein (1517–49), 1:31, for a story about a state secretary (*d'iak*) who claimed he did not have the means to serve as ambassador.

[167] Adams/Chancellor (1553), 260; Printz (1578), 31; Possevino (1586), 12.

them is called *Dworaney Bulshey,* or the company of head Pensioners, that have, some an hundred, some fourscore rubbels a yeere, and none under 70. The second sort are called *Seredney Dworaney,* or middle ranke of Pensioners. These have sixty, or fiftie rubbels by the yere, none under fourtie. The third and lowest sort are the *Deta Boiarskey,* that is, the lowe Pensioners. Their salarie is thirty rubbels a yere for him that hath most, some have but five and twentie, some twentie, none under twelve.[168]

Seventeenth-century commentators described a similar system of monetary remuneration or implied that one existed.[169]

The envoy-ethnographers learned, undoubtedly in conversations with their attendants or other officials, that Muscovite gentry were compensated with estates.[170] "If any man behave himselfe valiantly in the fielde to the contention of the Emperour," wrote Chancellor in 1553, "he bestoweth upon him in recompense of his service, some farme, or so much ground as he and his may live upon."[171] Fletcher correctly identified these grants as *"Pomestnoy* (as they call it) that are helde at the Emperours pleasure."[172] Though they were rather vague about the nature and organization of these prebendal estates (*pomest'ia*), later sixteenth- and seventeenth-century envoys demonstrated a general awareness of their existence as a means of payment for services rendered to the crown. The visitors, however, were clear on one point—tenures held of the tsar were quite precarious.[173] Printz explained that those who held conditional estates did not dare claim to own them: "If you ask anyone about his estate, he will say 'All that is the grand prince's and mine.'"[174] This was because, as Possevino explained some time later, "the prince formally declares himself to be the residuary legatee of all the land in his country and everything upon it. He assigns goods and estates to whomever he wishes and confiscates them from whomever he desires whenever he pleases."[175] In the seventeenth century, Olearius and a variety of other ambassadors confirmed Printz's statement, noting that Russians "say that everything they have belongs not so much to them as to God and the grand

[168] Fletcher (1591), 233–34.

[169] Aleppo (1655), 2:60–64; Olearius (1656), 159, 200, 202; Meyerberg (1661), 175–76; Tanner (1678), 70; Korb (1700), 1:191, 2:136. All of these sources mention salaries for military personnel.

[170] On prebendal estates, see Hugh F. Graham, "Pomest'e," and the literature there cited.

[171] Adams/Chancellor (1553), 259. On granted estates and their administration, see also Printz (1578), 31, 65; Possevino (1586), 12; Aleppo (1655), 2:61; Olearius (1656), 222; Meyerberg (1661), 175.

[172] Fletcher (1591), 201; also see 205.

[173] On Muscovite property law, see George G. Weickhardt, "Due Process and Equal Justice in Muscovite Law" and "Pre-Petrine Law of Property" and the literature there cited. The foreigners' thesis that Muscovite property was very insecure is not necessarily supported by the Russian statutes Weickhardt discusses. Whether these statutes were followed in practice is unknown.

[174] Printz (1578), 29.

[175] Possevino (1586), 49.

prince." [176] The Holsteinian envoy explained that Muscovites "came to use such expressions partly in consequence of the violent acts perpetrated by the tyrant Ivan [IV] Vasil'evich and partly because they and their property indeed are in that condition." [177] Paul of Aleppo remarked that "all the estates of the churches and convents are in the hands of the emperor; so that the heads of the clergy have no power over such estates or their revenues." Secular landholders, according to Paul, could sell their property, but "when the family of an archon is extinct, and he has left no heir to his property, it reverts wholly to the emperor; for he is the universal heir." [178] Though Korb claimed that Peter the Great had made great strides in reforming Russia, even he viewed his subjects' property as a source of revenue, for "this absolute master uses his subjects at his will, and their wealth in what share he pleases." [179]

Envoys of the second half of the sixteenth century often noted that Ivan IV, as universal proprietor, could confiscate estates and indeed other property seemingly at will. If, for example, a Muscovite ambassador had received personal gifts during an embassy, the goods were said to be the property of the grand prince and were placed in the treasury.[180] If a servitor did not perform his requisite duties, his estates were attached, sometimes at the behest of his fellows. Chancellor explained this practice: "If there be any rich man among them who in his owne person is unfit to the warres, and yet hath such wealth, that thereby many Noble men and warriours might be maintained, if any of the Courtiers present his name to the Emperour, the unhappy man is by and by sent for, and in that instant, deprived of all his riches." [181] Barbarino claimed he was told by Russians that Ivan frequently extorted estates from his men in the following way:

> The sovereign suddenly demands a sum of money from his vassals, and if it occurs to anyone to excuse himself on the grounds that he does not have the sum, or something like that, the sovereign, irritated by the refusal, immediately orders the man's house and everything in it seized . . . and after that nothing more is heard of him. Not even his family will discuss him. In this arbitrary fashion he rules the state.[182]

Possevino believed that Russian servitors did not flee Ivan IV's tyranny because "their children would be killed on the spot and all their property would

---

[176] Olearius (1656), 174, and also see 147; Meyerberg (1661), 116–17; Korb (1700), 2:155.

[177] Olearius (1656), 174.

[178] Aleppo (1655), 1:316–17, 400–401.

[179] Korb (1700), 2:153; also see 193–94.

[180] Herberstein (1517–49), 1:31, and Possevino (1586), 9. For seventeenth-century examples, see Reutenfels (1671), 105, and Korb (1700), 1:89.

[181] Adams/Chancellor (1553), 260.

[182] Barberino (1565), 2:9.

be immediately confiscated."[183] Fletcher added that the seizure of land "upon such as are in displeasure" provided the tsar with a sizable income. The English envoy believed that Ivan IV used confiscation to destroy the Muscovite nobility: "Having thus pulled them and seased all their inheritaunce, landes, priviledges, &c. save some verie small part which he left to their names, he gave them other landes of the tenour of *Pomestnoy* (as they call it) that are helde at the Emperours pleasure, lying farre of in an other country, and so removed them into other of his Provinces, where they might have neyther favour, nor authoritie, not being native nor well knowen there."[184] Though later envoys insisted that seventeenth-century tsars were, like their predecessors, universal proprietors, they were for the most part silent about capricious confiscation of estates and other property.[185] "And it is remarkable," Meyerberg wrote, "given [Aleksei Mikhailovich's] supreme authority over his people, brought by its rulers into complete slavery, he never encroached upon anyone's estate, life, or honor."[186]

Foreign envoys of the second half of the sixteenth century also noted that there was no sure right of entail on prebendal estates. Upon the death of the holder, granted estates were attached by the crown and could be ceded to heirs only with the crown's allowance. "Also, if any gentleman or man of living do die without issue male," Chancellor wrote, "immediately after his death the Duke entreth his land."[187] According to Chancellor, Ivan IV attached the property of abbots who had passed on.[188] Printz was more exact, correctly distinguishing between hereditary and prebendal estates: "If one has a hereditary estate one may pass it to his nearest relative, but if the land has been granted by the grand prince out of beneficence . . . on the death of the land holder the land reverts to him [the grand prince]."[189] "Lands and villages assigned to individuals," Possevino agreed, "cannot be bequeathed by them to their descendants without the prince's approval. The result of this policy," the Italian cleric concluded, "is that no one can really say what actually belongs to him, and every man, whether he wishes it or not, exists in a state of dependency upon the prince."[190] Some years later under Tsar Fedor Ivanovich, Fletcher confirmed that the crown had to approve the passage of estates from father to son, but he noted approval was regularly granted. "When they are of yeers able to beare armes, they come to the office of Roserade, or great Constable, and there present themselves: who entreth their names, and allotteth them certeine lands to maintein their charges, for

[183] Possevino (1586), 11.
[184] Fletcher (1591), 218, 201.
[185] For one seventeenth-century example, see Korb (1700), 2:163.
[186] Meyerberg (1661), 115.
[187] Chancellor (1553), 232. Also see Adams/Chancellor (1553), 260; Printz (1578), 65; Possevino (1586), 9, 49.
[188] Chancellor (1553), 238. Also see Adams/Chancellor (1553), 268.
[189] Printz (1578), 65.
[190] Possevino (1586), 9.

the most part the same that their fathers enjoyed." [191] Though envoys of the seventeenth century continued to argue that the tsar was universal proprietor and that the estates he granted were conditional, they did not discuss the necessity of gaining the tsar's approval for inheritance. Paul of Aleppo, for example, simply stated that in the absence of heirs, estates reverted "wholly to the emperor; for he is the universal heir." [192]

Finally, all the European envoys agreed that the Russian commons were held in the most abject servitude by landholders and the crown.[193] Several visitors commented that the nobility had an almost unrestricted right to exploit and punish peasants, whom they treated little better than slaves: Herberstein wrote that peasants were "in a very wretched condition, for their goods are exposed to plunder from the nobility and soldiery"; Printz said it was "incredible how they [the nobility] oppress the unfortunate people and deprive them of their property"; Fletcher believed that the grand prince had given "the Nobilitie a kind of iniust and unmeasured libertie, to commaund and exact upon the commons and baser sort of people in all partes of the realme where so ever they come." [194] Seventeenth-century commentators confirmed that landowners oppressed their peasants. Paul of Aleppo, for instance, wrote that "the peasants indeed have the appearance of slaves. For they sow the ground for their masters, ploughing it with his horses, and carrying the produce in his wagons to whatever place he directs them, and whithersoever he is pleased to call them, even to the transport of fire-wood, timber, stones, and other materials, for the building and service of his mansions, and of everything else that he wants." [195] Olearius went further, noting that commoners not only appeared to be slaves but were in fact all "serfs and slaves." [196] The grand prince and his officials also preyed on the commons. According to the envoys, the tsar compelled peasants to perform onerous services and pay heavy taxes.[197] The foreigners described local governors (voevody) as particularly corrupt and rapacious, a fact even acknowledged by the government.[198] Fletcher reported that these officials arrived "fresh and hungrie upon [the people] lightly every yeare, they rack and spoile them without all regard of iustice, or conscience." [199] Some of the foreigners had the opportunity to observe the oppression of the peasantry at firsthand. For

[191] Fletcher (1591), 232.

[192] Aleppo (1653), 1:400–401.

[193] On the lower orders in the accounts of foreigners, see Elisabeth Harder–von Gersdorff, "Die niedere Stände im Moskauer Reich."

[194] Herberstein (1517–49), 1:106; Printz (1578), 65; Fletcher (1591), 194.

[195] Aleppo (1653), 1:400.

[196] Olearius (1656), 147. Also see Meyerberg (1661), 65.

[197] Barberino (1565), 1:10; Ulfeldt (1575), 24, 25; Printz (1578), 30, 71; Fletcher (1591), 224–25; Olearius (1656), 206; Korb (1700), 2:153.

[198] Herberstein (1517–49), 1:30–31; Ulfeldt (1575), 25; Printz (1578), 65; Fletcher (1591), 207–8, 218; Olearius (1656), 177; Aleppo (1655), 1:276–77, 2:122–23; Meyerberg (1661), 91–92; Korb (1700), 2:163–64.

[199] Fletcher (1591), 207–8.

example, all the ambassadors would have witnessed Muscovite officials ex-
tracting transport (*podvody*) and provisions from the local population.[200]
Sometimes these extractions required force. "I was present when my pur-
veyor requested something at the hands of a certain prior," wrote Herberstein, "and finding that he persisted in refusing to comply with his request,
he threatened to have him beaten."[201] Ulfeldt noted his attendants "beat [the
local people] with whips, sticks, and cudgels until they were forced to give
us the necessary items."[202] And sometimes the foreigners themselves, as Iurii
Krizhanich reported, "beat the poor peasant drivers mercilessly, saying:
'These people are barbarians, and barbarians must be beaten if one hopes to
derive any good from them.'"[203] Herberstein, Olearius, and others believed
that just as magnates thanked the tsar for beatings, Russian servants thanked
their masters.[204] Indeed, several of the envoys said that the Russians' disposition was such that they needed a heavy hand and that in this sense they
were fit for slavery.[205] And several of them noted that Russians sometimes
sold themselves and their family members into slavery, evidence that they
preferred a servile condition.[206]

Conclusion

Gathering ethnographic information was no easy task for the sixteenth-
and seventeenth-century envoys in Russia. The visitors, however, did not
shrink from their task in the face of these difficulties. They did their best to
amass the information necessary for what they imagined to be a complete
ethnography. Though the envoys and itinerant merchants by and large did
not achieve a deep understanding of Russian ways, they rendered something
more than a superficial description of Muscovite society and government. In
investigating the nature of a variety of institutions—the tsar's power, the state
of the nobility, the system of state service, and the condition of the lower orders—they came to a clear understanding that monarchical power was much
stronger in Russia than in their homelands. Fletcher made the contrast explicit in his dedication to Queen Elizabeth:

[200] Adams/Chancellor (1553), 250; Barberino (1565), 1:10; Ulfeldt (1575), 24, 25; Aleppo
(1655), 1:269, 361, 2:282; Wickhart (1675), 186–87; Tanner (1678), 34; Korb (1700), 2:18.
[201] Herberstein (1517–49), 1:58.
[202] Ulfeldt (1575), 25.
[203] Krizhanich (1663), 491.
[204] Herberstein (1517–49), 1:106–7; Possevino (1586), 11, 50; Olearius (1656), 147;
Meyerberg (1661), 116–17; Korb (1700), 1:198–99, 2:209.
[205] Horsey (1584), 310; Olearius (1656), 147; Meyerberg (1661), 116–17; Reutenfels (1671),
116–17; Korb (1700), 1:179–80, 2:194–95.
[206] Maciej (1517), 112; Herberstein (1517–49), 1:95; Adams/Chancellor (1553), 264;
Jenkinson (1557), 423–24; Fletcher (1591), 230; Olearius (1656), 151; Korb (1700), 2:
200–201.

In the manner of their government, your majesty may see both: A true strange face of a Tyrannical state, (most unlike to your own) without true knowledge of GOD, without written Lawe, without common iustice: save that which proceedeth from their Speaking Lawe, to wit, the Magistrate who hath most neede of a Lawe, to restraine his owne iniustice. The practise hereof as it is heavy, and grievous to the poore oppressed people, that live within those Countreyes: so it may give iust cause to my selfe, and other your Maisties faithfull subiects, to acknowledge our happines on this behalfe, and to give God thankes for your Maiesties most Princelike, and gracious government: as also to your Highnesse more ioy, and contentment in your royall estate, in that you are Prince of subjects, not of slaves, that are kept within duetie by love, not by feare.[207]

As Fletcher's "us-and-them" depiction suggests, he and the other envoys were in some measure guilty of projecting an inverted image of their own governments (or idealizations of their governments) on Muscovy: their rulers were "kings," whereas the Muscovite sovereign was a "tyrant"; their governments were moderated by law and custom, whereas the will of the grand prince was unrestrained; their nobles were proud men of ancient lineage, whereas Muscovite magnates were rootless servants; their estates, though they might be "held of the king," were secure, whereas the properties of Russians could be seized at a moment's notice; their commons were respected, whereas Muscovite folk were little more than slaves. Yet it would be a mistake to conclude that the envoys' picture of Russia was simply a fantasy, for it was not. They were experienced men, subtle observers, and, in many cases, persistent investigators. The visitors knew the difference between truth and fiction and took it as their task to pursue the former and vanquish the latter in their ethnographic explorations. They offered what they believed to be a true picture of what they had observed in Muscovy.

[207] Fletcher (1591), 169–70.

🎋 3

NECESSARIUM MALUM
European Residents and the
Origin of "Russian Tyranny"

> I must point out that I know the history in depth, seeing that I have lived
> in Moscow, the capital of that country, for the past eight years; and being
> very curious, I was in a position to find out everything in consequence of
> my relations with a number of nobles and secretaries of the court, whose
> friendship I continually sought.
>
> ISAAC MASSA, 1614

RAFFAELLE BARBERINO AND Heinrich von Staden arrived in Muscovy in the summer of 1564, just in time to witness Ivan IV divide his realm
into two halves—the *oprichnina* and *zemshchina*—in February 1565 and
begin a ruthless assault on his own court. It is hardly surprising, then, that
both travelers agreed the Russian prince was a tyrant nearly unparalleled in
the annals of history. Yet, while Barberino and Staden reached the same conclusion concerning Ivan's abuse of monarchical power, they did so in very
different ways. Barbarino's account of Muscovy is distinctly that of an isolated outsider. He was unable to speak Russian, sequestered by royal guards,
without significant Russian contacts, and permitted to remain in Muscovy
for less than a year. Though he did his best to "describe everything from the
beginning," he succeeded in supplying only the most general information
about Russian life and the affairs of Ivan IV.[1] It is telling, for example, that
he does not seem to have been aware of the founding or even of the existence
of the *oprichnina*. Staden, in contrast, was clearly an insider. After approximately five years' service in Livonia, the native of Westphalia entered Russia
and asked to be employed by the tsar. If his account is to be believed, he was
immediately taken into service and given money, provisions, and estates.[2]

[1] Barberino (1565), 1:5–6.
[2] Staden (1578), 101–2.

Staden remained in Russia over a decade, and in the course of his stay he learned Russian, became intimately familiar with the details of Russian life and royal administration, and developed numerous Russian and foreign contacts. The German adventurer knew much about the *oprichnina*, for he himself was a member for a time.[3] Naturally, he was able to supply details about the operation of the government that were completely unavailable to envoys and itinerant merchants such as Barberino. Many envoys had noted that the tsar had almost unbelievable control over his subjects' "lives and property" (in the seminal words of Herberstein). But, as we will presently see, Staden and other long-time residents of Muscovy were able to move behind generalities about royal power in Russia and, at least in some instances, provide detailed intelligence about the mechanisms of Russian governance.

The Resident Experience in Muscovy

By all evidence, most Russians of the sixteenth and seventeenth centuries were, to say the very least, weary of resident Europeans. As in the case of diplomats and itinerant merchants, the state feared that European residents were, in essence, spies; Russian merchants resented the competition offered by foreign merchants; and the church and Orthodox population believed the Europeans to be spiritually bankrupt.[4] Nonetheless, Muscovite policy makers knew that foreigners would have to be allowed to enter the realm in reasonably large numbers and to remain in Muscovy for lengthy periods if Russia was to become competitive in the European system of states. The authorities viewed the visitors, as Patrick Gordon put it, as "*necessaria malia* [sic]."[5] Krizhanich, with characteristic xenophobia, called resident Europeans "the diseased parts of the state and the body politic."[6] Beginning in the reign of Ivan III, the Russian court recruited European specialists, particularly craftsmen, doctors, and mercenaries, to serve its needs. In the reign of Ivan IV, the government began to grant merchants (English, Swedish, and Dutch) the right to keep houses in various cities, including Moscow.[7] Simultaneously, the Russians evolved a policy aimed at limiting foreign contact with the native population. In a general sense, the government's plan concerning resident Europeans rested on the same two principles as that pursued vis-à-vis diplomats and itinerant merchants—restricted access and segre-

---

[3] The exact dates of Staden's tenure in the *oprichnina* are unclear. He made it seem that he was made a member of the institution immediately after his arrival in Russia in 1565 (ibid., 103), but an examination of his account indicates that he was not a member until late 1569. See Thomas Esper's Introduction, ibid., xxi.

[4] On all these points, see the literature cited in notes 7–9 in Chapter 2 above.

[5] Gordon (1661–99), 47.

[6] Krizhanich (1663–66), 643.

[7] A. S. Muliukin, *Priezd inostrantsev v Moskovskoe gosudarstvo*, 58–248.

gation. Just as many diplomats had done, resident merchants and specialists often pointed out that the Muscovite border was for all intents and purposes closed. "Russia is not a free country," explained Margeret, "which may be entered to learn the language and to become informed of certain matters and then leave."[8] In theory, potential residents could enter Russia only with the permission of the grand prince himself, and such permission was granted only to those traders who were members of privileged national groups or companies, or to those specialists who had particularly valuable services to offer the tsar.[9] The major resident ethnographers were all privileged merchants or specialists or members of their families, as may be seen in Table 6.

While living in Muscovy, the foreigners were subject to a great variety of special regulations concerning their legal status, the conduct of business, relations with the native population, and the practice of their "heretical" faiths.[10] The most important of these restrictions was the requirement that they live in a "foreign settlement" (*nemetskaia sloboda*), the name given to several suburbs that intermittently existed in various areas of Moscow from the mid-sixteenth to the beginning of the eighteenth century.[11] Though the settlement definitely existed by the 1570s, its early history is obscure. The suburb was formally disbanded around 1610 and reestablished in 1652, although it probably existed in an unofficial capacity throughout the seventeenth century.[12] Many of the residents (as well as nonresidents) described some sort of "foreign" settlement in the capital.[13] Staden, to give but one example, briefly noted the existence of a suburb outside the Kremlin on the left bank of the Iausa River—Bolvanovka—"where the German horsemen" were given houses "after Moscow was burned" in 1571.[14]

Though the government's policy of isolating foreigners in settlements may have succeeded in some general sense, it does not seem to have been effective in hampering the investigations of the resident ethnographers. In fact, almost none of the residents who left descriptions of Muscovy lived in the

---

[8] Margeret (1607), 84. See also ibid., 26; Petreius (1615), 142–43; Krizhanich (1663–66), 540, 616, 650; Reutenfels (1671), 131, 145–46; Neuville (1698), 1, 54; Gordon (1661–99), 47.

[9] On Russian policy concerning the entry of merchants, see Muliukin, *Priezd inostrantsev v Moskovskoe gosudarstvo*, 60, 170–248. On Russian policy concerning the entry of specialists, see especially ibid., 39–40, 110–69.

[10] On the status of foreign residents, see Dmitriii V. Tsvetaev, *Protestantstvo i protestanty v Rossii do epokhy preobrazovanii*; A. S. Muliukin, *Ocherki po istorii iuridicheskogo polozheniia inostrannykh kuptsov v Moskovskom gosudarstve*; Joseph T. Fuhrmann, *Origins of Capitalism in Russia*, 218–42.

[11] Muliukin, *Priezd inostrantsev v Moskovskoe gosudarstvo*, 58.

[12] For an overview of the history of the foreign settlement, see Lindsey A. J. Hughes, "Foreign Settlement."

[13] For mentions and descriptions of the foreign settlement, see Schlichting (1571a), 224 (in Kolomna); Boch (1578), 99–100; Horsey (1584–1611), 299–300; Margeret (1607), 23; Staden (1578), 66, 84; Bussow (1611), 14; Massa (1614), 62; Aleppo (1655), 2:22; Olearius (1656), 30, 279–81; Reutenfels (1671), 93–94, 144; Wickhart (1675), 100–101, 119–20, 125–26, 184, 259–62; Tanner (1678), 68–71; Gordon (1661–99), 45 and passim; Korb (1700), 106, 223ff.

[14] Staden (1578), 66, 84.

Table 6. Major sixteenth- and seventeenth-century resident European authors

Author	Dates in Muscovy	Time in Muscovy	Written/ printed	Genre
Taube and Kruse (Livonian nobles)?	1559–August 1571 (Taube)	12 yrs., 8 mos.	1571/1582	History
	August 1560– August 1571 (Kruse)	11 yrs.		
Staden (b. 1542?; German mercenary)	May 1564–1576?	12 yrs., 8 mos.	1578–79	Ethnography
Schlichting (German translator)	November 1564– October 1570	6 yrs., 1 mo.	1571	History
Horsey (1573–1627; English merchant/ diplomat)	? 1573–October 1591	18 yrs., 10 mos.	1589–1621	History
Massa (1587–1643; Dutch merchant)	? 1600–? 1609	10 yrs.	1610–14	History
Margeret (1565?– 1619; French mercenary)	June 1600– September 1606	6 yrs., 4 mos.	1607/1607	Ethnography
Bussow (d. 1617; German mercenary)	April 1601–? 1611	10 yrs., 9 mos.	1611–17	History
Petreius (1570–1622; Swedish agent/ diplomat)	December 1601– November 1605	6 yrs.	1615/1615	Ethnography
	July 1607– April 1608			
	December 1609– ? 1610			
Collins (1619–70; English doctor)	December 1659– ? 1669	10 yrs., 1 mo.	1661–67/ 1671	Ethnography
Krizhanich (1618?–83; Croatian scholar)	September 1647– January 1648	18 yrs., 7 mos.	1663–66	Political theory
	January 1659– November 1677			
Reutenfels (nephew of court doctor)	? 1670–? 1672	3 yrs.	1672–80?/ 1680	Ethnography
Gordon (1639–99; Scottish mercenary)	August 1661– d. November 1699	38 yrs.	1661–99	Diary

Note: All dates are approximate. Several authors (Petreius, for example) traveled to Russia on numerous occasions for short periods of time, and others (Aleppo) visited for extended periods after they wrote their ethnographies. Neither short visits before accounts were drafted nor long visits afterward are listed. For sources on each author, see Bibliography 4 below.

suburb. Foreign servitors in the second half of the sixteenth century and the beginning of the seventeenth century were granted plots in Moscow, though not necessarily in a foreign ghetto, and they were given estates outside the capital where they sometimes lived for extended periods.[15] Johann Taube

[15] See ibid., 65–66, for an excellent description of the procedure for recruitment and remuneration of foreign servitors in the second half of the sixteenth century. On the recruitment and provisioning of foreign specialists in the seventeenth century, see Margeret (1607), 42; Bussow (1611), 16–17; Petrieus (1615), 303–4; Aleppo (1655), 2:256, Krizhanich (1663–66), 518–19; Reutenfels (1671), 125.

and Elbert Kruse, for instance, never mentioned a suburb. After they entered Russian service in the 1570s, both were assigned houses in Moscow, given the right to run taverns, and granted provincial estates.[16] Staden had several residences in various areas of Moscow, including taverns, and estates in the countryside.[17] Albert Schlichting made no mention of a foreigners' suburb.[18] He probably owned a residence in Moscow and perhaps lands in the Moscow region. It is unclear where Margeret kept his house, but it is known that he received a land grant of nearly a thousand acres upon his enlistment as a foreign mercenary in 1601.[19] The location of Konrad Bussow's residence in Moscow also is unknown, but it is sure that he held several estates in various parts of central Russia.[20] The only mercenary to leave an account of Muscovy who definitely resided in the ghetto was Patrick Gordon, who kept a house in the "Slabod, or village where the strangers live."[21] Though merchants were more likely than mercenaries to live in the foreign suburb in this era (Massa may have lived there),[22] not all did. Jerome Horsey, as a sometime officer of the Russia Company in Moscow, probably lived in the "English House," not far from the Kremlin, at least from 1573 to 1584.[23] Specialists such as Petrus Petreius, Samuel Collins, and Johann Rosenberg (Jacob Reutenfels's probable host), all of whom were doctors at court, may have resided in a suburb, but this is by no means clear from their accounts.[24] Iurii Krizha-

[16] Taube and Kruse (1571), 55–56, vaguely mention receiving the grand prince's favor, honor, and riches. Staden (1578), 114–15, confirms that Taube owned an estate in Rzhev and the village of Spitsyno. Henning (1590), 48v, records that both Taube and Kruse were granted the right to trade in *meth und brantwein*. Both Staden (1578), 66, 104, and Boch (1578), 100, confirm that in the era of Ivan IV residents ofthe foreigners' settlement were routinely allowed to truck in alcohol. For the beginning of the seventeenth century, see Margeret (1607), 23. For the reign of Aleksei Mikhailovich, see Krizhanich (1663–66), 645.

[17] Staden may have kept a tavern in the foreign settlement, but he also mentions having several houses in other parts of Moscow, in both the *zemshchina* and *oprichnina*. See Staden (1578), 103–11. On his various estates, see 102 ("Tesmino with all its villages"), 108 ("the villages of Krasnoe and Novoe were *votchiny*, and six villages were *pomest'ia*"), and 115 ("the village of Spitsyno").

[18] He did, however, note a foreign suburb in Kolomna. See Schlichting (1571a), 224.

[19] See Dunning's introduction to Margeret (1607), xviii, and Dunning, "Margeret, Jacques (1565?–1619)," 97.

[20] See Bussow (1611), 95.

[21] Gordon (1661–99), 45.

[22] See Orchard's introduction to Massa (1614), x.

[23] The "English House" is mentioned in Horsey's account, though he does not say he lived there. See Horsey (1584–1611), 300, 307. On Horsey's employment in the "English House," see Donald L. Layton, "Horsey, Sir Jerome," 81.

[24] Iurii A. Limonov and Viktor I. Buganov speculate that Petreius, who seems to have been a Swedish diplomatic agent, served as a doctor. See their introduction to Petreius (1608), 13. Petreius himself wrote vaguely that he "served the grand prince" for four years ([1615], 143). Limonov and Buganov claim that Petreius lived in the suburb. See the introduction to Petreius (1608), 10. Collins does not mention the foreign suburb, but he does note the rivalry of the English and Dutch in Moscow: "The Dutch, like Locusts, swarm in *Mosco,* and eat bread out of the English-mens mouths, they are more in number, and richer, and spare no gifts to attain their ends" ([1667], 128). Reutenfels wrote nothing about where he resided, but it seems likely that he would have lived with his uncle, Johann Rosenberg. On their connection, see the editor's introduction to Reutenfels (1671), iv–v.

nich lived for decades in exile in Tobol'sk.[25] In short, the government could not isolate the resident ethnographers from the populace. They lived among the Orthodox (with whom they could converse, for all knew Russian well),[26] developed countless close personal contacts with Muscovites, traveled widely throughout the realm, and, as their accounts demonstrate, became intimately familiar with the details of Russian culture.

The court was even less successful in shielding the residents from the workings of the state. Though the tsar and his ministers were aware of the perils of permitting foreigners to observe their affairs, they also realized that if their mercenaries and specialists were to be effective, they would have to be allowed into key court, governmental, and military institutions. Indeed, the biographies of the major resident ethnographers demonstrate the government's resolve in this matter, for many of them held very important posts in Russian service over many years. Johann Taube and Elbert Kruse were advisers and diplomatic agents of Ivan IV from 1564 to 1571; Heinrich von Staden was a member of Ivan's *oprichnina* and served the tsar from 1564 to 1572; Albert Schlichting was employed as an interpreter for a foreign doctor at Ivan's court from 1568 to 1570; Jacques Margeret held important military commands under Boris Godunov, False Dmitrii I, and Vasilii Shuiskii from 1600 to 1606; Bussow commanded troops under Godunov and False Dmitrii I from 1601 to 1606; Petreius served the court, perhaps as a doctor, from 1602 to 1606; Collins was a physician to Tsar Aleksei Mikhailovich from 1659 to 1669; Gordon commanded Russian and foreign forces in major campaigns under Aleksei, Fedor, Sophia, and Peter from 1661 to 1699.[27] Interestingly, Krizhanich complained that foreigners seemed to "manage the most important affairs [of state]."[28] Thus the resident ethnographers worked on a daily basis in Russian institutions, personally knew Russian servitors high and low, moved freely all over the country on service assignments, and, as is evident in their writings, gained a deep knowledge of the operation of the Muscovite governmental apparatus.

The magnates realized that after years of service in the upper reaches of the government, some foreigners knew too much about Russian affairs of state. This concern, combined with the feeling that the residents (and particularly highly ranked mercenaries) were an important asset, led the Russians to attempt to prevent some foreign hirelings from returning to their homelands.[29] The resident ethnographers, and particularly those of Ivan IV's era,

[25] For a brief account of Krizhanich's life in Russia, see Josip Bozicević, "Krizhanich, Yurii (1618?–83)."

[26] The residents often bragged about their facility with Russian. See Staden (1578), 102; Schlichting (1571a), 214; Horsey (1584–1611), 263; Margeret (1607), 4, 85; Collins (1667), 98–99.

[27] On the service biographies of all these figures, see Bibliography 4 below.

[28] Krizhanich (1663–66), 501.

[29] Muscovite authorities recruited foreign specialists for both temporary contracts (*po godam*) and lifetime service (*na imia gosudarevo* or *na vechnuiu sluzhbu*). Muliukin points out that in fact both arrangements allowed for the departure of the servitor under various conditions, but

did their best to warn all those Europeans who sought employment in Russia that departure would be difficult. If a foreigner, Staden wrote, "is caught trying to flee the country, then only God can help him." The German mercenary added that "it seldom happens that a foreigner manages to flee the country, since the road into the country is broad and clear, but the way out is extremely narrow."[30] Antonio Possevino, though not himself a resident, noted that "many foreigners had been officially granted freedom of movement, but if they asked to return to their own country they were condemned and executed on the spot."[31] Ivan's immediate successors were apparently no more lenient. In 1606 Margeret warned his countrymen that it was difficult to escape the Russian realm:

> All routes out of Russia are so closed that it is impossible to leave without the permission of the emperor. They have not allowed any of those who carry arms to leave the country in our times; for I was the first. Even if there is a war against the Poles, they do not cast out Poles although they have a goodly number of them. Instead, they send them to the frontiers of Tartary. They do likewise with the other non-Russian peoples among them, out of fear that these foreigners will run away or surrender to the enemy.[32]

Bussow recounted the story of a group of Livonian refugees who, having sought protection from the Poles in Muscovy near Pskov, were "asked" to enter Muscovite service. They resisted at first, because, as Bussow explained, "they were free people, [and] they did not want to fall into perpetual servitude." But a Russian abbot, undoubtedly doing the bidding of the crown, "urged them in conscience not under any circumstances to reject such great kindness, or persist in their refusal any longer; for in confidence he could not conceal from them that, in the event that they rejected the tsar's kindness, and refused to go to Moscow of their own accord, not one of them would be allowed to return to Livonia but they would be arrested as spies and taken bound hand and foot to Moscow." The foreigners were enlisted as mercenaries and made to swear that they would remain in the country and report any seditious speech they happened to hear.[33] Isaac Massa reported that when Godunov "freed" the Livonians "whom the tyrant Ivan once led into slavery," he did so "with the stipulation that they must not leave the empire." He also noted that "those who take service in Muscovy are hired only on condition that they stay there all their lives."[34] Later in the seventeenth

---

that the government often held its hirelings even when they wished to depart. See Muliukin, *Priezd inostrantsev v Moskovskoe gosudarstvo,* 146ff. and especially 154–60.

[30] Staden (1578), 70.

[31] Possevino (1586), 17.

[32] Margeret (1607), 26.

[33] Bussow (1611), 20–21, 23.

[34] Massa (1614), 62, 153. This was formally untrue, but the fact that many foreigners hired on a temporary basis were pressed into more or less permanent service may have led Massa to conclude that all service was de facto for life. See Muliukin, *Priezd inostrantsev v Moskovskoe gosudarstvo,* 146ff.

century, as the number of foreign condotieri mounted in connection with government attempts to modernize the Russia military, the restrictions on exit were relaxed. Yet the resident ethnographers reported that it remained difficult to leave Muscovy even in this more liberal era. Reutenfels said that foreigners who "accept the Russian faith may never leave Moscow."[35] Some Germans in Russian service attempted to enlist the envoy Bernard Tanner with offers of "a great salary, advancement, piles of gold. I was first transfixed by the money," he wrote, "but I knew from other Germans that whoever enters the service of the tsar will become a slave with his whole household for the rest of his life, and so I soon respectfully answered, that golden freedom is more valuable to me than golden promises."[36] Augustin von Meyerberg pitied "those people of the Catholic faith who, in expectation of slight mercantile advantages or for military service, move to Moscow . . . without any hope that they would ever be released from there."[37] Krizhanich criticized the Russian government for holding its foreign hirelings against their will.[38] Even at the end of the century Johann Korb would write that "foreigners whom chance or choice has led into Muscovy [the Russians] condemn to the same yoke, and will have them be slaves of their monarch. Should they catch and bring back any of them departing furtively," he claimed, "they punish them as runagates."[39]

As with the German ghetto, the policy of blocking foreign servitors from leaving the country might have been successful in some instances, but it did not prevent most of the resident ethnographers from decamping and informing Europe about life in Russia. Schlichting fled to Poland in 1570; Taube and Kruse, who disingenuously claimed they had been held captive for their entire stay, "escaped" to Poland in 1571; Staden was (according to his story) forgotten in the muster of 1572 and seemed to have left of his own accord in 1576; Petreius departed, apparently without interference, in 1605 and returned several times in a diplomatic capacity; Margeret was released from service by Shuiskii in 1606, wrote *The Russian Empire and the Grand Duchy of Muscovy,* returned to serve False Dmitrii II in 1609, and left the empire finally in 1611; Bussow, who had been allowed to retire on his estates in 1606, quit Russia in 1611; Collins left Muscovy in 1669, only to expire one year later; Reutenfels made his way out of the country in 1672; Krizhanich petitioned Aleksei Mikhailovich to be released from exile and to be allowed to depart, which he did in 1677. Only Gordon was held all his life in Russia. Immediately upon his arrival in 1661, the Scotsman "began in good earnest to consider how [he] might ridd [himself] of this countrey, so farr short of [his] expectation, and disagreeing with [his] humour." Everyone he met, however, "alleadg[ed] it impossible" to quit Russia. Why? Several merce-

[35] Reutenfels (1671), 171–75; also see 123–24, 146–47.
[36] Tanner (1678), 70.
[37] Meyerberg (1661), 103–4.
[38] Krizhanich (1663–66), 640.
[39] Korb (1700), 2:195.

naries explained that if a foreign servitor asked to leave, the Russians would suspect he "was come to spy out their countrey only, and then returne." They thought that Gordon might be dismissed, as requested, but "to Sibiria or some remote place" rather than to Europe. Despite these warnings, Gordon persisted in his requests to leave. In 1686 he petitioned to leave Russia so as to serve as English envoy. The authorities could not let him go, for, as they explained, "he is to be in the great army in this expedition against the Turks and Tatars."[40] After Gordon died in 1699, his massive diary remained in Russia and with it all he had learned about Russian ways.

The Course of Investigation

Like their ambassadorial counterparts, the residents were apprised of the fact that Russian authorities did not appreciate having foreigners snoop around, even if they were employees of the crown. In the era of Ivan IV, Schlichting explained, any sort of exploration could be dangerous to the investigator: "Foreigners visiting Moscow were traders who never saw the prince; those who did meet him hesitated to investigate his actions because they feared the tyrant. If he conceived the slightest suspicion he would subject foreigners to appalling tortures."[41] Ivan was not the ultimate cause of the mistrust noted by Schlichting. Rather, as Margeret explained in the first years of the seventeenth century, suspicion of foreigners was a Russian characteristic—the Muscovites, he wrote, were the "most distrustful and suspicious nation in the world."[42] Massa was afraid to ask for aid in producing a map of Muscovy, for had he requested assistance, Russian officials "would have quickly seized [him] and delivered [him] over for torture, thinking that in making such a request [he] must be contemplating treason. This people is so suspicious in this regard," he concluded, "that nobody would have been so bold to undertake the task."[43] Petreius also felt Russian eyes, noting that the Muscovites did "not allow anyone to learn of their affairs and dealings."[44] Among his other efforts at intelligence gathering, Reutenfels attempted to collect information about royal weddings, but was unable to do so because "the Muscovites will not permit anyone to learn" about them.[45] Collins knew why: "For the people are very jealous, and suspect those who

---

[40] Gordon (1661–99), 47, 48, 162. Gordon was dispatched to England in 1665 and 1685, and on either of those occasions he could have quit Russian service. But he had married in Russia in 1664 and again before 1686, and he had children by both wives; his departure would probably have had serious consequences for his family.

[41] Schlichting (1571a), 213.

[42] Margeret (1607), 26.

[43] Massa (1614), 130.

[44] Petreius (1615), 143.

[45] Reutenfels (1671), 82.

ask them any questions concerning their Policy, or Religion."[46] So deep was the tsar's distrust that, according to the English doctor, he had filled Moscow with informants and indeed even spied himself.

> In the night season the *Czar* will go [about] and visit his Chancellors Desks, and see what Decrees are pass'd, and what Petitions are unanswer'd. He has his spyes in every corner, and nothing is done or said at any Feast, publick Meeting, Burial or Wedding but he knows it. He has spyes also attending his Armies to watch their motions, and give a true account of their actions: These spyes are Gentlemen of small fortunes who depend on the Emperours favour and are sent into Armies, and along with Embassadors, and are present on all publick occasions.[47]

Gordon, as we have seen, knew he would be accused of being a spy if he sought to leave Russia.

Given that the residents knew their Russian hosts were suspicious of foreigners, it stands to reason that they would be skeptical about Russian pronouncements. According to Schlichting, Ivan's paranoia made it difficult for any Russian to tell the truth. "Muscovites," he concluded, "are inherently spiteful."

> They habitually bring secret charges, slander each other to the tyrant, display mutual hatreds, and thus destroy one another. Such behavior is highly pleasing to the tyrant, since he delights in listening to informers and slanders. He does not care whether their information is true or false, if only it provides him with the opportunity to destroy people, who are often totally unaware that charges have been made against them. It is not safe to converse at court. Let a man speak loudly or quietly, grumble, laugh or frown, or become gay or sad, the tyrant will ask him why he is laughing and rejoicing, or scowling, or feeling happy or dejected, and then falsely charge, 'you have concerted with my enemies and are plotting against me.'[48]

Later residents agreed that it was difficult to credit many of the things Russians said. Margeret, for example, told his readers that "Russia is a nation of liars, without law, without conscience."[49] Petreius agreed that the Muscovites were "untrustworthy."[50] Krizhanich admitted that in Russia, as in other Slavic countries, "there is great mendacity."[51] Not only did the residents suspect the Russians of not being completely forthcoming in conversation, they also understood very well that state ceremonies were designed

---

[46] Collins (1667), 2–3. Also see Neuville (1698), 57.
[47] Collins (1667), 116.
[48] Schlichting (1571a), 219.
[49] Margeret (1607), 86.
[50] Petreius (1615), 315.
[51] Krizhanich (1663–66), 491.

to deceive foreigners. All of them knew, for example, that foreign envoys were guarded and sequestered so that they would learn as little as possible about the country.[52] The residents were also aware—perhaps even more so than European envoys—that the Muscovites presented visitors with an elaborate political theater designed to put the best face on the Russian realm. All the residents knew that Muscovite courtiers were under strict orders to appear well dressed at diplomatic ceremonies, and that if the servitors did not own the proper attire, the treasury would rent robes to them.[53] But many of the residents were more specific about the form and rhetoric of state rituals. Staden, for example, recorded that Ivan IV ordered foreign ambassadors to be led "along only those roads where peasants are living, to the place where the grand prince will give him an audience, so that [they would] not learn the right route and see how desolate the country is."[54] Bussow detailed a similar government-organized effort to hide conditions of hunger from visiting Imperial ambassadors in 1604:

> Boris [Godunov] gave orders that in those places through which the embassy passed, no beggar should be seen. He also ordered emergency supplies to be brought to the markets in those towns, lest foreigners notice any scarcity. Since it was necessary to meet the ambassador and receive him ceremoniously half a mile from Moscow, each of the princes, boyars, Germans, Poles, and all other foreigners who had lands and peasants was ordered, on pain of forfeiture of annual salary, to array himself richly and splendidly as possible, in velvet, silk and brocade, wearing his best garments in honour of the tsar, and to come out and meet the Imperial ambassador and to take part in his entry into Moscow.[55]

On another occasion, Godunov used a different method to send a rather pointed message to visiting ambassadors:

> There was also drawn up a considerable body of artillery, about a hundred pieces of large calibre (there are quite a few of them in this country, and they are so splendidly large and so fine that it is scarcely to be believed here among the German nation), firing in order to impress the Persian and Tatar embassies, which had arrived there and which were to have audience in the field. In this manner so much powder was expended, and such splendour and magnifi-

---

[52] Staden (1578), 71; Horsey (1584–1611), 273; Margeret (1607), 42; Peyerle (1608), 212, 214; Massa (1614), 49, 131, 191; Petreius (1615), 284–85, 294; Reutenfels (1671), 106–7; Neuville (1698), 8, 10.

[53] Staden (1578), 66, 102; Horsey (1584–1611), 273, 289; Margeret (1607), 42; Peyerle (1608), 232; Bussow (1611), 16, 22, 24–25, 34; Massa (1614), 58, 124–25; Petreius (1615), 286, 315; Collins (1667), 61; Wickhart (1675), 247; Neuville (1698), 5, 17, 37; Gordon (1661–99), 46.

[54] Staden (1578), 71.

[55] Bussow (1611), 34–35.

cence was shown, that both ambassadors were overawed with the great power of the Muscovites, their weaponry, power, and riches, and they doubtless said there was no lord equal to this one in the whole wide world.[56]

Massa also observed that Godunov designed special martial ceremonies to impress foreign envoys with "his power and his grandeur."[57] Krizhanich claimed that the only reason "German" soldiers were maintained in Moscow was to "show them in parades and at ambassadorial receptions."[58] Several seventeenth-century residents noted that the court attempted to maintain its dignity by rarely appearing in public. "The Russian tsars appear to the public very rarely," Reutenfels remarked, "and truly, if all that is unknown is considered magnificent, then they, given all their seclusion, are respected by their subjects almost like Gods, unseen and unapproachable."[59]

It seems evident, then, that the residents were no more naive observers than were most visiting envoys. Like the envoy-ethnographers, the residents consciously aimed to penetrate the curtain of court suspicion, deception, and propaganda and thereby to render an accurate picture of Muscovite life. They accomplished this task by gathering testimony from Russian and foreign sources, closely observing the behavior of Russians, and reading Russian materials.[60] Over the course of their long service in Russia, the residents developed many personal contacts with Russian officials and commoners and, it must be assumed, had frequent conversations on countless topics with their hosts. In order to authorize their accounts, the residents again and again stressed their reliance on trustworthy oral testimony.[61] Massa was typical of the entire group, emphasizing that he drew his information from "nobles and secretaries of the court, whose friendship I continually sought."[62] Russians were not their only informants. Bussow noted that he gathered testimony "not only from Muscovites, but also from Germans who had lived in Russia for many years, and who had noted down these events as they occurred."[63] Similarly, the residents repeatedly emphasized that they personally had seen much of what they reported.[64] "These things which I have de-

---

[56] Bussow (1611), 12–13. Bussow reported that this display took place in 1597.

[57] Massa (1614), 42.

[58] Krizhanich (1663–66), 646; also see 500.

[59] Reutenfels (1671), 86. Also see Collins (1667), 114–15; Reutenfels (1671), 89–90.

[60] Like the envoys, residents also read previous accounts of Russia written by Europeans. The influence of printed European Moscovitica on the impressions of ambassadors and residents is treated in Chapter 4 below.

[61] Schlichting (1571b), 272; Horsey (1584–1611), 263; Petreius (1615), 143; Reutenfels (1671), 9.

[62] Massa (1614), 4.

[63] Bussow (1611), 172.

[64] Taube and Kruse (1571), 29; Horsey (1584–1611), 314; Margeret (1607), 84; Bussow (1611), 172; Massa (1614), 4, 180–81; Petreius (1615), 142–43; Collins (1667), 2–3; Reutenfels (1671), 9.

scribed to Your Royal Highness," Schlichting wrote typically, "are what I saw
with my own eyes in Moscow." [65] Finally, the residents often claimed to have
read Russian materials in their search for the truth about the northern country. Taube and Kruse quoted a "special oath"; Staden was intimately familiar with all manner of administrative documentation; Horsey cited "chronicles"; Margeret provided detailed information about the salaries of various
ranks of government personnel that could have come only from Russian administrative documents; Bussow, like Taube and Kruse, cited verbatim an
oath given by Vasilii Shuiskii to a man hired to poison the rebel Ivan Bolotnikov; Massa quoted a list of the moneys that False Dmitrii I sent to Poland;
Petreius published the Russo-Swedish treaty of 1611; Krizhanich had a large
library of Russian materials with him in Tobol'sk; Collins provided an excellent description of Russian petitions; both Petreius and Reutenfels cited
Russian "chronicles" as sources. [66]

The residents also conducted focused investigations of particular questions during their time in Russia. In order to flesh out his account of the famine of 1604, Bussow questioned "chancellery officials and merchants" about
the number of deaths in Moscow. [67] Massa, as we have already seen, made
"great efforts to procure a faithful representation of [Moscow]," and though
he met with resistance in this endeavor, finally managed to obtain a map of
the city. [68] Krizhanich reported the sum and substance of conversations with
many people on economic matters. [69] The most extensive and interesting in-
quiries made by the residents, however, concerned the true identity of the man
who claimed to be Tsarevich Dmitrii. Margeret, who knew the man personally, explored the question in great detail and concluded that he was not
Grishka Otrep'ev, as many people claimed, but the true son of Ivan IV who
had reportedly been murdered in Uglich on May 15, 1591. "As for the opinions of those who do not hold Dmitrii Ivanovich to be or to have been the son
of Ivan Vasil'evich, surnamed the Tyrant, but rather an impostor," Margeret
wrote, "I shall respond to them with my own views on the matter." The
French mercenary then provided a point-by-point refutation of all the arguments mustered to demonstrate that Dmitrii was an impostor: Dmitrii was
not murdered by Boris but spirited away to Poland by his clever relatives;
Grishka Otrep'ev—the defrocked monk who many said had impersonated
Tsarevich Dmitrii—did come from Poland to Russia, but he was not "False

---

[65] Schlichting (1571a), 266. Also see ibid., 214, and Schlichting (1571b), 272.

[66] Taube and Kruse (1571), 35; Staden (1578), 122; Horsey (1584–1611), 263, 285; Margeret (1606), 46–47; Bussow (1611), 98; Massa (1614), 149–50; Petreius (1615), 258–70;
Collins (1667), 44–45; Petrieus (1615), 296; Reutenfels (1671), 26, 124.

[67] Bussow (1611), 33. The information Bussow received, if he reported it correctly, was inaccurate, for the "chancellery officials and merchants" reported 500,000 persons had died, a
number in excess of the total population of the capital at the time.

[68] Massa (1614), 130.

[69] Krizhanich (1663–66), 416–19, 479, 505, 511, 586.

Dmitrii," for the real Dmitrii was with him when he crossed the border; and Dmitrii was neither Polish nor a Polish pawn, for he spoke Russian as would a Russian boy raised in Poland and received little Polish aid.[70] Bussow took considerable pains to set forth the "genuine and factual truth" about the man's identity and concluded that he was indeed an impostor. He questioned several key figures: Petr Fedorovich Basmanov, "Dmitrii's" one-time lieutenant, told him "in strict secrecy" that though the man who claimed to be Dmitrii was a great leader, he was not the real tsar; "a certain apothecary," who had seen the real Tsarevich Dmitrii as a child, informed Bussow "in confidence" that the man who claimed to be Ivan IV's son was a liar; a "certain noblewoman" who had been witness to Tsarevich Dmitrii's birth offered Bussow similar testimony; a Muscovite who had guarded Tsarevich Dmitrii when he was a boy likewise stated "in confidence" that the man who claimed to be Dmitrii was "not the son of Ivan the Terrible"; Jan Sapieha, a Polish general, boasted to Bussow that the Poles had placed False Dmitrii on the throne.[71] For Massa, there was no question that Grishka Otrep'ev was the man who had falsely assumed the identity of the deceased Tsarevich Dmitrii. Massa was rather intrigued by the rumor that False Dmitrii had survived the massacre of the Poles in Moscow in May 1606. He investigated the question carefully and drafted a list of "arguments of those who asserted that Dmitrii was still alive, and refutations of these arguments."[72] Massa concluded that False Dmitrii was indeed dead: he himself had seen the body of the man and "recognized him readily"; the contention that the dead man had long hair and False Dmitrii had short hair rested on a false premise, for the impostor always wore a hat; the dead man had several distinguishing marks, for example, a mole on his face that identified him as False Dmitrii, and so on.

Generic Templates and the Description of Muscovite Government

Just as the ambassadors had done, the residents occasionally complained that they had gathered more information than they could possibly relate in their treatises. Schlichting explained, for instance, that he "would need whole volumes to tell of the events that took place in other cities, towns, and fortresses."[73] And like the ambassadors, the residents turned to stock organizational devices for help in their effort to bring order to their massive and unruly observations. Two such devices can be seen operating in the residents' accounts: the historical narrative and the ethnographic template. Sev-

[70] Margeret (1607), 80–91.
[71] Bussow (1611), 82–83.
[72] Massa (1614), 30–32, 156–59. On Tsarevich Dmitrii's death, see Massa (1614), 30–32. On Otrep'ev's rise, see ibid., 68–69.
[73] Schlichting (1571a), 266.

eral of the residents chose to arrange their observations within a narrative framework because they understood, to put it plainly, that they had the material for a good story, and one that was important to their audience. Taube and Kruse, for example, suspected that a tale of Ivan IV's assault on his own realm would be pleasing to Polish officials arrayed against the Muscovites in Livonia. In fact, they explicitly suggested that, given the Muscovites' weak state, the time was right for a Polish offensive.[74] Staden digressed from his strategic description of Russia to tell the lurid story of Ivan's outrages against his people, a tale he knew would interest Emperor Rudolph II, to whom the mercenary dedicated his work. Like Taube and Kruse, Staden argued that Russia could easily be conquered and provided a plan for the undertaking.[75] Similarly, Schlichting wrote entirely in a narrative mode about Ivan's bloody tyranny, perhaps at the request of his Polish handlers, who intended to use his account to convince papal officials that Russia was beyond the pale.[76] The residents who had lived in Russia around 1600 also had a penchant for narratives. The "murder" of Tsarevich Dmitrii, the rise and "tragic" fall of Godunov, and the troublesome question of the identity of the man who claimed to be Dmitrii were the very stuff of "history" as it was then understood—a "mirror for princes," a fount of stories that simultaneously delighted the reader and provided instructive examples.[77] "For he who carefully reads history," Ulfeldt wrote, "has ever before his eyes examples by which he can guide his business, and from the examples of others he may learn to live in order so as to honor God, so as through eternal life not to fall in divine disfavor and justified punishment."[78] Massa and Bussow were very conscious of the twin requirements of historical writing. In order to bring greater drama to their stories, both men took significant liberties with the facts. In Bussow's telling, for instance, "Dmitrii" (who, as we have seen, Bussow believed was actually Grishka Otrep'ev) was hired by Prince Adam Wiśniowiecki, a Polish magnate and Dmitrii's future patron. While serving the prince in his bath, the young servant failed to fulfill some minor duty and was slapped by his master. Bussow continued: "Then the youth made an expression, as if he took all this very much to heart, and wept bitterly in the bathroom, saying to the prince: 'If only you, Prince Adam, knew who I am, you would not have abused me and called me a whoreson, neither would you have borne so heavily upon me for such a triviality. But since now I find

---

[74] Taube and Kruse (1571), 30–31, 59. Their text was dedicated to Jan Chodkiewicz, then Polish commander in Lithuania. See ibid., 29, where the Livonians suggest that Ivan's rule might be broken and all the territories he had captured in Livonia might be taken by a Polish assault.

[75] Staden (1578), 17–36, 75–96.

[76] On the background of Schlichting's essay, see Hugh Graham, "Schlichting, Albert."

[77] On the "delight and instruct" trope, see Timothy Hampton, *Rhetoric of Exemplarity in Renaissance Literature*, 8–9. The trope is rehearsed, for example, by Reutenfels's seventeenth-century editor. See Reutenfels (1671), 2–3.

[78] Ulfeldt (1575), 1–2.

myself here as your servant, I must bear this with patience.'"[79] As the touch-ing scene concluded, Dmitrii "revealed" himself as tsarevich and won the prince's heart. The event may have occurred as described, but it is hard to imagine how this information—and particularly the direct speech—made its way to Bussow. Moreover, the scenario's fit with Bussow's literary purpose strongly suggests fictionalization. The scene becomes easier to comprehend when it is placed in a literary context. Bussow used two standard rhetorical techniques to give his story additional drama: anagnorisis—the uncovering of a crucial but hidden fact; and peripeteia—the fashioning of a turning point in a story. Massa and Bussow also understood that their histories should provide lessons. Massa told his patron that the story of False Dmitrii could serve as an admonition for those who were insufficiently mindful of Satan's cunning:

> I earnestly pray that you will cherish this account, which contains only facts
> I have witnessed during my stay in this country, for the purpose that has
> prompted it, and that you will not regard it as a useless and insignificant gift.
> Consider it also as a warning. It will in fact show you how Antichrist, with
> the aid of Satan, has long sought by insidious snares to oppress God's holy
> church, and being unable to assail it from one side, is trying to surprise it
> on another.[80]

For Bussow, Dmitrii's story was one of hubris: "Into this tragic mirror all rulers and sovereigns would do well to look, and if any such tendencies [as exhibited by the arrogant Dmitrii] begin to appear in themselves, they should correct them in good time, so as not to give the Good God cause to visit such wrath upon them, for it is said: 'What has happened to one can happen to many; similar causes have similar effects.'"[81]

Less commonly, the residents cast their treatises in the form of ethnog-raphies.[82] Margeret, for example, clearly invoked the purpose ascribed to ethnographic description by the theorists of the genre in this dedication to the king, much as Herberstein had done in his dedication to *Notes on the Muscovites.*

> If the subjects of your majesty who travel in faraway countries were to give
> a true account of what they saw and noted there of great interest, their own
> gain would be turned to the public advantage of your state: not only to have
> that which is good and industrious in other countries shown, examined, and
> imitated (it being very true that God had ordered all things in such a way that
> in order to improve relationships among men, some of them find elsewhere

[79] Bussow (1611), 28–29.
[80] Massa (1614), 180–81.
[81] Bussow (1611), 79.
[82] On the ethnographic template, see Chapter 2 above.

that which they do not have at home); but also this would give heart to a
number of idle and stay-at-home young men to seek out and learn the virtue
in the laborious but useful honorable exercise of travel and foreign military
service.[83]

This appeal to the "personal and public" utility of travel description was, as
we have seen, a common trope of the ethnographic genre. So too was the use
of "heads" to guide investigation and govern the array of information in subsequent accounts. This device is also evidenced in several of the descriptions
of Russia written by residents. Petreius, for example, offered his readers a
clear summary of the subjects he explored in Russia and the topics treated
in his lengthy ethnography:

> As far as I have traveled—and not without great danger to my life—I have
> carefully observed and recorded their religion and ceremonies, government
> and policy, and in addition all of their customs, usages, activities, business
> and trade, [their] manner and art of warfare, the fertility of the land in grain,
> cattle, wild [animals], birds and fish, the beautiful flowing rivers, streams and
> springs, the merry forests and glades with all the various trees there growing,
> the fragrant meadows and fields, the populous cities and towns, the fortified
> castles and houses, [and] the recent wars and transactions between the Swedes,
> Poles, and Russians.[84]

Once the residents had collected information on these (and other) topics,
they "methodized" the data according to a definite descriptive template.
Collins, for instance, produced copious notes on his life in Russia, but (so
his editor, Robert Boyle, complained) he did not succeed in "methodizing"
them before an "unkinde disease put a period to that and his life."[85] Boyle
brought order to the manuscript himself.[86] The "method" found in all the
ethnographies may be witnessed in the common series of topical heads into
which almost all the treatises are divided. Though the order of the rubrics is
somewhat different in each case, the set of topics covered is quite similar—
chorography (regional ethnographic description), history, government and
administration, social customs, economy, and religion. The residents understood that, according to the theory of travel description, a well-formed ethnography should cover each of these topics. Collins, for example, omitted
chorography in violation of common generic convention. He knew that his
readers would expect a discourse on the geography of Muscovy in a treatise

[83] Margeret (1607), 3.

[84] Petreius (1615), 143.

[85] Collins (1667), A4. Indeed, Collins claimed "not to be an exact Historian, or Methodist,
and so must beg my Readers pardon" (30).

[86] On the origins and redaction of Collins's notes (actually, letters to Robert Boyle), see Leo
Loewenson, "The Work of Robert Boyle and 'The Present State of Russia' by Samuel Collins,"
470–85.

titled *The Present State of Russia,* and so he included an explanation of its absence: "As for the Situation of *Russia,* it is so well known, that it would be a needless labour for me to let it down; my design at present is to Survey the Religion and Manners of the inhabitants." [87]

Russian Government in the Eyes of the Residents

The residents often worked at court, and they clearly understood the tsar to be the center of political power in Russia. They generally agreed that the authority of the Muscovite prince was unlimited. Staden wrote that "he alone rules," that "everything he orders is done and everything he prohibits is not done," such that "no one, neither cleric nor layman, stands against him." [88] Margeret described the "absolute power" of the tsar in the following terms: "Strictly speaking, . . . there is no law or council save the will of the emperor, be it good or bad. He has the power to put all to fire and sword, be they innocent or guilty. I consider him to be one of the most absolute princes in existence." [89] Petreius wrote that "none may presume to go against him, in word, council, or deed." [90] Collins simply called the rule of the tsar "Perfectly Monarchical." [91] Krizhanich was of the opinion that God had blessed Russia with a great gift—"absolute autocracy." [92] Similarly, Reutenfels described the power of the tsar as "unlimited by any laws and sovereign to the extent that it may fairly be called equal if not superior to the imperial power of the ancient Assyrians and Greeks and to the contemporary Turks, Persians, and Tatars." Reutenfels is unique among the residents in supplying a list—albeit vague—of the tsar's several spheres of authority: "And indeed the tsar possesses not only the most complete right to promulgate and abrogate laws, to conclude and break unions and peace treaties, to appoint and dismiss administrators, to lower and raise taxes, but he gladly controls completely of the life and death of his subjects and their property, such that he can, if he wants, seize from them their entire fortune and life without explaining his actions." [93] The residents were unable to supply a detailed account of the tsar's specific powers because, as they well knew from their own observations of the prince's behavior and that of his courtiers, there were no constitutional limits on his authority. Certainly they recognized that certain tsars had more or less power vis-à-vis various forces (and particularly the elite) in society: Taube and Kruse, Schlichting, and Staden personally wit-

---

[87] Collins (1667), 1.
[88] Staden (1578), 55–56.
[89] Margeret (1607), 28.
[90] Petreius (1615), 300.
[91] Collins (1667), 44.
[92] Krizhanich (1663–66), 481, 540, 549, 616.
[93] Reutenfels (1671), 101.

nessed the horrible extent of Ivan's might, while Massa and Bussow clearly perceived Godunov's weakness and, a bit later, False Dmitrii's inability to stop the coup that brought him down. Nonetheless, the residents agreed that the tsar's authority over his subjects was unrestricted in principle and ordinarily in fact.

Like the ambassadors, though, the residents did specify one unusual power possessed by the tsar—he seemed to be the de facto proprietor of all land in Muscovy.[94] In the narratives describing Ivan IV's reign of terror composed by Taube and Kruse, Schlichting, and Staden, this authority is implied by the fact that the "terrible" tsar granted estates at will (indeed, all these men received conditional properties) and appropriated the goods of his servitors with similar ease. The residents of the second half of the sixteenth century recognized that, at least in principle, allodial estates (*votchiny*) existed in Russia, but they concurred that in actual fact such properties were not protected from Ivan's incursions.[95] Staden, as we saw above, clearly distinguished between *votchiny* and conditional properties; however, he remarked that *votchiny* could be and in fact were subject to arbitrary confiscation by the tsar.[96] Later authors were also aware that there was some sort of difference between allodial and conditional properties, but they were either unable to describe the distinction or considered it unimportant. Margeret, for example, never discussed allodial holdings, but he did take the time to detail the operation of the Service Land Chancellery (*pomestnyi prikaz*):

> Besides that, there are two more offices. One handles the land grants and is called the *pomestnyi prikaz*. For each grant the recipient must give two, three, or four rubles, according to the extent of the land of which he takes possession. Then if one of these landholders falls into disgrace, the revenue from said land returns to the *pomestnyi prikaz* until the emperor grants the land to someone else.[97]

Significantly, Margeret described the "nobility" as the class receiving an "annual salary and possessing lands from the emperor."[98] Petreius confirmed that servitors' properties were held of the crown and therefore were subject to confiscation if a man proved unable to fulfill his duties.[99] Collins was more absolute in his judgment: "He is master of every man's Estate, the Son does alwaies petition for his fathers Land. They hold all in *Capite*."[100] Reutenfels,

---

[94] On Muscovite property law, see the literature cited in Chapter 2, note 173, above.

[95] Schlichting (1571a), 232–33, 240–41, 244–45; Taube and Kruse (1571), 35–38; Staden (1578), 18, 31; Horsey (1584–1611), 273.

[96] Staden (1578), 31.

[97] Margeret (1607), 35–36.

[98] Ibid., 30.

[99] Petreius (1615), 297.

[100] Collins (1667), 59.

as we have already seen, noted that it was fully within the power of the tsar to confiscate the estates of his servitors.[101]

Unlike the envoys, who knew comparatively little about Russian politics and perhaps less about the Russian property regime, the residents were well acquainted with both. Several of them lived in the shadow of the court and received estates in exchange for their services. Yet, like the ambassadors, they found additional evidence that the tsar's power was untrammeled and that he was a universal proprietor in the testimony of Muscovites themselves. The residents commonly heard the Russians demean themselves and extol the power of the tsar, often using the same phrases reported by the envoys. Staden reported two Russian proverbs (significantly, in Russian): "The lord does not burn up and does not sink at sea" and "God watches over the sovereign."[102] Petreius recorded several sayings about the tsar's authority: "As God reigns in Heaven, so the grand prince rules on Earth"; "What is God's will is also the will of the grand prince"; "God knows and the grand prince."[103] On one occasion, Collins was "curious to see the fine buildings for the Flax and Hemp," so he "ask't to what end they were built." The workmen there responded only that "God and the Emperour know best."[104] Reutenfels reported that Muscovite subjects "openly acknowledge that they and all their property belong to God and the tsar." In another place he claimed the Russians "continually and openly acknowledge that God and the tsar know and can do everything, that they are ready to give everything and even their lives to God and the tsar."[105] Gordon—who was perhaps the most experienced resident in Russia and surely the most highly placed— knew well the proper way to address the Muscovite sovereign. His petition to Sophia requesting that he be allowed to serve as English envoy was writ- ten, he said, "in as submissive terms and expressions as could be done to God Almighty."[106]

As servitors of the court, many of the residents realized that the tsar, de- spite his overwhelming authority, did not rule alone: ostensibly he was ad- vised by a body of magnates. Schlichting and Bussow called this institution the Boyar Council.[107] Some of the residents seem to have been well informed about the council—understandably, since many of them, particularly those

---

[101] Reutenfels (1671), 101. Reutenfels does mention (122) "hereditary" and "granted" lands, but only to make the point that the tsar required the holders of both to provide taxes and services.

[102] Staden (1578), 40.

[103] Petreius (1615), 300: "Then they began to say that the voice of the people was the voice of God; whoever was chosen [tsar] by all the people was undoubtedly chosen by God." See Bus- sow (1611), 11.

[104] Collins (1667), 117.

[105] Reutenfels (1671), 101, 142–43.

[106] Gordon (1661–99), 160–61.

[107] Schlichting (1571a), 255; Bussow (1611), 38. Krizhanich (1663–66), 579, mentions a "council."

who stood high in the court administration and military, were personally acquainted with members of the body. Staden, Collins, and Reutenfels provided lists of members; Margeret and Reutenfels offered an overview of ranks within the body; several of the residents were able to identify specific members of the council with specific administrative posts; and Margeret, in a unique instance, described the council's daily schedule:

> The nobility . . . maintain this regimen: During the summer they ordinarily get up at sunrise and go to the castle (if they are in Moscow), where the council meets [from five A.M. until ten A.M.]. Then the emperor, attended by the council, goes to hear the church service. This lasts from eleven until noon. After the emperor leaves the church, the nobles go home to eat dinner, and after dinner they lie down and sleep for two or three hours. At about [six P.M.] a bell rings, and all the lords return to the castle, where they remain until two or three hours after sunset. Then they retire, eat supper, and go to bed.[108]

The residents cited many instances that indicated that the council could be an important advisory and administrative body. Schlichting, for instance, noted that during Ivan's terror, "certain noblemen" sought "to restrain the tyrant from brutally destroying his subjects, who were clearly innocent of wrongdoing." [109] Their reproaches, according to Schlichting, stayed the tsar's hand, but only for a time. Staden reported that members of the council "held the entire government in their hands." These men, he said, "sat in every court of law and every other chancellery." [110] Margeret believed that the tsar met with his council "in matters of great consequence." [111] Massa wrote that in the fall of 1605, False Dmitrii ordered an attack on Narva, but "leading lords argued vigorously against this expedition, so he gave the idea up for some reason or other." Massa also believed that after the coup that deposed False Dmitrii I, members of the boyar elite "elected a tsar from their own number," Vasilii Shuiskii.[112] Collins wrote that though Aleksei Mikhailovich was an "absolute Monarch," he possessed a "Council both general and particular to advise with." [113] Reutenfels remarked that the members of the council were powerful because they had "free access to the tsar." [114] Gordon reported that at the election of the patriarch in August 1690, the "old boyars" succeeded in choosing their own candidate over that of Tsar Peter.[115]

Although the residents were willing to attribute more power to the coun-

---

[108] Margeret (1607), 30, and see 27–28. See also Staden (1578), 6–10; Collins (1667), 46; Reutenfels (1671), 99–100, 121–23.
[109] Schlichting (1571a), 217.
[110] Staden (1578), 9.
[111] Margeret (1607), 27.
[112] Massa (1614), 120, 146.
[113] Collins (1667), 46.
[114] Reutenfels (1671), 99–100.
[115] Gordon (1661–99), 169.

cil and its members than visiting envoys were, several of them expressed the opinion that the body was without significant authority. In the narratives concerning Ivan's reign we find frequent allusions to the tsar's oppression of his high nobles and even of his explicitly ignoring their advice. Under the heading "Criticism of His Tyranny," Schlichting described how "the chancellor, Ivan Mikhailovich Viskovatyi, kept telling the prince to think of God, not to shed so much innocent blood, and, above all, not to exterminate his nobility." In Schlichting's telling, Ivan rebuked Viskovatyi, called the councilor his "slave," and later ordered him tortured and killed.[116] Staden was the only resident of the *oprichnina* era to issue a general pronouncement on the issue of councilor power, claiming vaguely that "no one, neither cleric nor layman, stands against [Ivan IV]."[117] Authors who wrote during the Time of Troubles were similarly dismissive of the council's general power. Bussow wrote that False Dmitrii "sat daily with his boyars in the council chamber, demanding resolution of many matters of state, attentively following each speech, and after each had at length expounded his own opinion, said with a smile: 'You have taken counsel for so many hours and so racked your brains, and have nevertheless not reached any conclusion. Here is how it should be.'"[118] Margeret believed that neither law nor council could bridle the will of the tsar. False Dmitrii, said the French mercenary, was a "schoolteacher to all his council."[119] In the second half of the seventeenth century, Reutenfels issued a similar opinion. "Every week," he wrote, "several boyars, the patriarch, the metropolitan with the bishops meet at the palace for private conferences, in which the patriarch crosses the forehead and cheeks of the tsar when he comes and goes." All offered their opinions, he said, and then deferred to the prince. "If [the grand princes] sometime discuss matters with their boyars," he concluded, "then this is not to seek their approval, but so that they may profit by their experience and submission."[120]

The residents also demonstrated a greater awareness of the so-called *zemskii sobor,* Muscovy's irregular national assembly, than did visiting envoys and merchants. Residents from Schlichting in 1571 to Reutenfels in 1671 alluded to the congress, though it must be said that none of them offered a systematic description and none was convinced that the assemblies had any sustained political authority. Schlichting, for example, recorded that in 1566 "more than 300 nobles, members of the tyrant's court, met to hold discussions with the prince," Ivan IV. The German resident may have witnessed the event, and if he did not, he probably heard about it from courtiers who did. According to Schlichting, the assembly rebuked Ivan for his abuses: "'Our

[116] Schlichting (1571b), 272; (1571a), 259, 272.
[117] Staden (1578), 55–56.
[118] Bussow (1611), 51.
[119] Margeret (1607), 27–28, 70.
[120] Reutenfels (1671), 103, 101.

lord, most illustrious tsar, why do you order the deaths of our innocent brothers? We all serve you devotedly and shed our blood for your sake, yet you set your retainers upon us as recompense for our service. They kidnap our brothers and relatives, insult, harass, beat, ruin and kill us.'" Schlichting claims that Ivan responded in typically tyrannical fashion: "Flying into a rage, the tyrant imprisoned and held all of them for five days, after which he had them brought before him; tore out their tongues, lopped off their hands and feet, and beat them." [121] Horsey, obviously thinking in an English mode, recalled that after Ivan IV had abdicated in favor of a puppet tsar in 1575, "his clergy, nobility, and commons" begged the tsar to return to the throne "upon many conditions and authentical instruments confirmed by act of parliament in a very solemn new inauguration." [122] Ivan agreed to return but nothing more was heard of the "conditions." Margeret claimed that after the death of the last Riurikid, Tsar Fedor Ivanovich, in 1598, the regent Godunov planned to "convoke in due course the estates of the country—namely, eight or ten persons from each town, to the end that all the land would have a voice" in the election of a new tsar. The French mercenary, however, did not mention the convening of a popular assembly before Godunov's accession, and he emphasized throughout that Boris used cunning to gain the throne rather than any constitutional procedure.[123] Bussow did provide an account of the convening of an assembly of "all the estates of the land" to elect a new tsar in 1598. According to the German resident, Godunov skillfully manipulated popular sentiment within the body and was "elected" against the wishes of the "great lords, princes, and boyars." [124] Margeret recorded that False Dmitrii was also capable of using the *zemskii sobor* for his own purposes. For example, the Frenchman implied that Dmitrii convoked an assembly of "persons chosen from all estates" in June 1605 in order to gain the conviction of Prince Vasilii Shuiskii for spreading rumors that he was an impostor.[125] A year later Dmitrii had been overthrown by the forces of this same Shuiskii. Realizing that he needed at least the nominal support of a national assembly to become tsar, Shuiskii convened a rump *zemskii sobor* composed, as Bussow wrote, of "as many as could be considered his accomplices in the murders and treasons, all those merchants, piemen, cobblers, and a few princes and boyars who happened to be present." Shuiskii was elected tsar but, Bussow concluded, "without the knowledge or the consent of the assembly of the land." [126] Massa agreed that Shuiskii had been chosen not by a national council but by "magnates." [127] After Shuiskii him-

---

[121] Schlichting (1571a), 248–49.

[122] Horsey (1584–1611), 275.

[123] Margeret (1607), 18. Margeret did write that "the people begged Boris . . . to receive the crown" (19). Exactly who "the people" were is unclear.

[124] Bussow (1611), 10–11.

[125] Margeret (1607), 68.

[126] Bussow (1611), 84.

[127] Massa (1614), 146.

self had been overthrown by a coup in July 1610, Bussow described how "the estates" selected Władysław, son of Sigismund of Poland, to become emperor; but a coalition of Russian forces threw the Poles out of Moscow in October 1612 and chose Mikhail Romanov to be tsar. In his brief mention of Mikhail's election, Bussow, significantly, did not recall the convening of any assembly of the land.[128] Shortly after the Time of Troubles ended, Petreius wrote that if there is no heir to the throne in Muscovy, "the estates elect one of the prominent lords who would seem to be fit for rule." He knew from his reading (and plagiarizing) of Bussow, however, that such elections were the exceptions rather than the rule, so he included the possibility that a man could assume the Russian throne "by the sword," as several had done in the preceding decades.[129] In the reign of Aleskei Mikhailovich, the assemblies fell into disuse, and thus it is no wonder that Reutenfels was dismissive of them: "As concerns popular assemblies, they are very rarely held among the Muscovites, because the tsar summons and dismisses them." He added that there were no popular councils in urban centers such as those found in Europe.[130] Krizhanich called for a reinvigoration of national assemblies, but under his plan they would be convened only upon the accession of a new tsar.[131]

Because they lived and worked in the empire for many years, the residents were of course familiar with Russian law. Several of them, and particularly those who wrote in the ethnographic mode, were able to provide brief overviews of Russian legislation, general procedures used in courts of law, and punishments.[132] Horsey admired the legislative activity of Ivan IV: "This emperor reduced the ambiguities and uncertainties of their laws and pleadings into a most perspicuous and plain form of a written law, for every man universal to understand and plead his own cause without any advocate. . . ."[133] Yet his was a voice in the wilderness, for nearly all of the residents agreed that the law was not properly followed in Muscovy. "They had law books that should have been used to determine fair judgments," Staden admitted, but "they were not used."[134] Margeret knew well that there were laws in Muscovy, but he said that they did not restrain the grand prince, for "strictly speaking there is no law or council save the will of the emperor, be it good or bad."[135] Petreius reported that Muscovite judges did not rule according to "made and written laws" but ruled according to the grand prince's will

[128] Bussow (1611), 145–46, 167.

[129] Petreius (1615), 277.

[130] Reutenfels (1671), 103, 130.

[131] Krizhanich (1663–66), 617; also see 669.

[132] Staden (1578), 9ff.; Margeret (1607), 28–30; Petreius (1615), 318ff.; Collins (1667), 44, 71–74; Reutenfels (1671), 114–19.

[133] Horsey (1584–1611), 311.

[134] Staden (1578), 8.

[135] Margeret (1607), 28. Also see Barberino (1565), 2:8–9; Printz (1578), 65; Fletcher (1591), 169–70, 195.

and what they believe to be "right and good." [136] Collins called Muscovite
justice "Arbitrary, for they have very few written Laws." [137] Reutenfels reported that the "tsar possesses . . . the most complete right to promulgate
and abrogate laws." [138] Not only was the prince above the law and the law
not followed, but the residents generally felt that Muscovite judges were corrupt. Staden provided a long bill of complaints against corrupt Russian officials and judges, such as Grigorii Shapkin in the "Criminal Affairs Chancellery": "When someone was arrested for murder anywhere in the country—in
districts, cities, villages, or on the highways—and could pay off, he was
egged on [by members of the chancellery] and forced to accuse a merchant
or a rich peasant of having helped him murder. The great got money in this
way." Officials (*prikazchiki*) of the "lower law court" (*zemskii dvor*), Staden
wrote, "could right a wrong in the street before a person was brought to this
court, and on the other hand, could also wrong a right." Other court officers
(*nedel'shchiki*) who were dispatched to arrest people accused in lawsuits
were similarly corrupt: "If the accused gave money [to the *nedel'shchik*], he
was acquitted even if he was guilty." [139] Margeret noted that Godunov imposed extreme penalties on judges who took bribes, but "notwithstanding
this punishment, these officials [did] not stop taking [gifts]." [140] Collins wrote
that Russian judges "go much upon Precedent," but added that "money is
their best Precedent, which overthrows all the former." The English doctor
admitted, however, that there was nothing particularly unusual about the
bribe-taking of Russian judges, for in this respect "they are like other Nations, ready to act any thing for Bribes or Money, and to deceive as many as
they can." [141] Krizhanich claimed that Russian judges and officials were un-
derpaid and therefore compelled to "live by trading in the law." [142] Reutenfels said that among Russian officials "deception and bribery have become
so rife that it has become normal to corrupt and be corrupted." [143] Gordon
described a Russian official who delayed paying him his salary "in expectation of a bribe, which is not only usual here, but, as they think, due." [144]

According to the common opinion of the residents, then, the tsar's power
was largely, if not completely, unrestrained by any constitutional body or legal regime. To be sure, they viewed the extent of the tsar's power as unusual;
but it would be a mistake to conclude that they understood his overwhelming authority to be necessarily evil. Absolutist government was praised by
important political philosophers of the day (Bodin, Bossuet, Hobbes) and

[136] Petreius (1615), 318.
[137] Collins (1667), 44.
[138] Reutenfels (1671), 101.
[139] Staden (1578), 10, 11.
[140] Margeret (1607), 28. On a similar campaign by False Dmitrii I, see Bussow (1611), 52.
[141] Collins (1667), 44, 125; also see 10, 71, 73.
[142] Krizhanich (1663–66), 584.
[143] Reutenfels (1671), 110.
[144] Gordon (1661–99), 46.

pursued by the monarchs of major states (Louis XI, Philip II, James I). If used judiciously, the residents agreed, absolute power might well be a force for good. Staden, for example, noted that "although Almighty God has punished Russia so severely and heavily that it is beyond description, still the present grand prince has managed so that in all of Russia, in his government, there is one faith, one weight, and one measure, that he alone rules, that everything he orders is done and everything he prohibits is not done." [145] Though Ivan IV was for a time wicked, Horsey argued, he achieved much: he conquered Kazan, Astrakhan, and Siberia; he improved Russian law and judicial administration; he "established and published one universal confession of faith"; he gave alms to the poor; he "did build in his time 155 castles in all parts of his kingdoms"; he founded "300 towns in waste places and wildernesses"; he created a postal system; and he fortified Moscow.[146] In the accounts of the Time of Troubles, Godunov came in for similar praise.[147] Collins admired the fact that absolute power had succeeded in homogenizing Russia: "The mode of men and women, rich and poor, are all one, all over the Empire, from the highest to the lowest, and their Language one, yea and Religion too, which certainly must hugely tend to their peace and preservation." He contrasted the uniformity of Russian customs to "our own unhappy divisions and differences in opinions." [148] Later in the seventeenth century, Reutenfels offered guarded praise for the regime of Aleksei Mikhailovich.[149]

What troubled the residents most was not Russian absolutism but the abusive manner in which the tsar often treated his nobility. The residents were generally not of the same high social standing as visiting European envoys, but they shared the belief that the nobles should be afforded privileged treatment by their sovereign even if he were an absolute monarch. In Russia, they all agreed, this intrinsic right was often not respected. The residents of Ivan IV's court repeatedly witnessed the "terrible" tsar humiliating, beating, torturing, and publicly murdering his nobles. Take, for example, the murder of Viskovatyi as Schlichting described it:

> Making a sign with his hand the tyrant cried: 'Seize him.' They stripped him naked, passed a rope under his arms, tied him to a traverse beam, and let him hang there. Maliuta went to the tyrant and asked who was to punish him. The tyrant replied: 'Let the most loyal punish the traitor.' Maliuta ran up to the man as he hung from the beam, cut off his nose, and rode away on his horse; another darted up and cut off one of Ivan's ears, and then everyone in turn approached and cut off various parts of his body. Finally Ivan Reutov, one of the tyrant's clerks, cut off the man's genitals and the poor wretch expired on the spot. . . . The body of Ivan Mikhailovich was cut down and laid on the ground;

---

[145] Staden (1578), 55–56.
[146] Horsey (1584–1611), 312–13.
[147] Massa (1614), 94–95; Bussow (1611), 13, 26; Margeret (1607), 18–19.
[148] Collins (1667), 66.
[149] Reutenfels (1671), 73.

the retainers cut off the head, which had neither nose nor ears, and hacked the rest of it to pieces.[150]

Taube, Kruse, and Staden witnessed or heard rumors of the same execution, and though their description of Viskovatyi's death are less detailed than Schlichting's, they generally corroborate his account.[151] All of the residents were certain of Ivan's chief (though not exclusive) target: "worthy princely and boyar clans," according to Taube and Kruse; "men of ancient and distinguished lineage," Schlichting said; "the chief men of the *oprichnina* and *zemshchina*," Staden wrote; his "chief nobility and richest officers and other the best sort of his merchants and subjects," Horsey had it.[152] The "terrible" tsar's attack on his people, and particularly the nobility, became lore among all those who wrote about Russia in the later sixteenth and seventeenth centuries.[153] Ivan's immediate successor, Fedor Ivanovich, was feeble-minded, and according to all reports, he did not repeat the tyranny of his father. Boris Godunov, however, was quite another story. The writers of the Time of Troubles of course implicated Godunov in the murder of Tsarevich Dmitrii.[154] But more than that, they were certain that he had rather ruthlessly exiled and eliminated his rivals at court.[155] "Boris and his family," Horsey wrote, "a-growing mighty and very powerful, suppressing and oppressing by degrees, and making away most of the chief and ancient nobility, whom he had wonderfully dispensed, long tormented with all impunity to make himself redoubtable and fearful."[156] Margeret reported that in his

---

[150] Schlichting (1571a), 259–60. The residents' descriptions of Ivan's atrocities are too numerous to cite here. They may be found scattered through the pages of Taube and Kruse (1571), Schlichting (1571a), and Staden (1578), all of whom were eyewitnesses. For an analysis of the foreigners' testimony concerning Ivan's murders, see Ruslan Skrynnikov, *Oprichnyi terror.*

[151] Taube and Kruse (1571), 51; Staden (1578), 28.

[152] Taube and Kruse (1571), 33–34; Schlichting (1571a), 214; Staden (1578), 36; Horsey (1584–1611), 270. The residents' thesis that Ivan specifically attacked the nobility has been called into question by modern historians. See Stepan B. Veselovskii, *Issledovaniia po istorii oprichniny;* Aleksandr A. Zimin, *Oprichnina Ivana Groznogo;* Skrynnikov, *Oprichnyi terror.*

[153] Horsey (1584–1611), 266–69, 273, 278–79, 283–84, 292, 293, 299–300; Fletcher (1591), 219; Margeret (1607), 16, 23; Massa (1614), 15–16; Peyerle (1608), 153; Maskiewicz (1611), 27, 55–56; Aleppo (1655), 2:2; Olearius (1656), 92; Collins (1667), 48–49, 101–2; Reutenfels (1671), 60ff., 94, 116–17, 154–56; Tanner (1678), 60; Neuville (1698), 65; Gordon (1661–99), 44–45; Korb (1700), 2:42–43, 114, 153–54, 156. In an interesting instance, Gordon mentioned briefly Ivan's atrocities and referred "to those who have written at large thereof" (44). For more information on folkloric Ivaniana, see Maureen Perrie, *Image of Ivan the Terrible in Russian Folklore,* chap. 3. On the spread of Ivaniana in the European (and especially German-language) press, see four works by Andreas Kappeler: "Die deutschen Flugschriften über die Moskowiter"; "Die deutschen Russlandschriften der Zeit Ivans der Schrecklichen"; "Die letzen Oprichninajahre"; and *Ivan Groznyi im Spiegel der ausländischen Druckschriften seiner Zeit.*

[154] Horsey (1584–1611), 358; Peyerle (1608), 153–54, 202; Maskiewicz (1611), 57; Margeret (1607), 17; Bussow (1611), 8; Massa (1614), 30ff.; Petreius (1615), 148.

[155] Horsey (1584–1611), 322–23, 330–31; Margeret (1607), 17, 53, 60; Bussow (1611), 8–9, 26–27; Massa (1614), 31, 36, 40, 44, 45, 55–56, 73–74.

[156] Horsey (1584–1611), 361.

paranoia, Boris ordered many significant people "tortured, sent into exile, and poisoned." [157] According to Massa, Boris sought "diverse means of destroying the noblest Muscovite families." He was kind to the common folk, "but when it came to people from the leading families, he condemned them on false evidence, then rid himself of them secretly by suffocation, drowning, or assassination, or by giving them the monkish tonsure, always with the aim of destroying the nation's high nobility and replacing them with this own relatives and creatures." [158] False Dmitrii behaved in a similar fashion. Massa reported, for example, that Dmitrii "resolved to kill all the Muscovite lords and great families," though he did not get a chance to do so.[159] Later residents recorded no similar campaign of terror against the nobility by a Russian monarch. They did, however, note (as sixteenth-century commentators had done) that magnates, high officials, and even clergymen were subject to corporal punishment.[160] "The . . . knout and club are generally used, and are even known to boyars," Reutenfels remarked.[161] Interestingly, Krizhanich suggested that "all wellborn [people] should forever be freed from knouting, whipping, and disgraceful punishments." [162] Peculiarly, several of the residents noted that Russians, including nobles, thanked the tsar for the physical punishment they received.[163]

The residents' tendency to believe that the nobility was in a state of subjection to the tsar was reinforced by their observation of two Russian customs. As I noted above, Schlichting recorded that Ivan IV called his courtiers "slaves." [164] Later residents observed that Russians, and even Russian magnates, called themselves "the tsar's slaves." Margeret, for example, considered the Russian tsar "to be one of the most absolute princes in existence, for everyone in the land, whether noble or commoner, even the brothers of the emperor, call themselves *kholopy gosudaria,* which means 'slaves of the emperor.'" [165] Reutenfels remarked that "as a consequence of the fact that the tsar enjoys supreme and condescending power over his subjects, the rights of the nobility and the commoners are almost identical"; indeed, "all call themselves his slaves." [166] Krizhanich pointed out that foreign criticism of this ritual rested on a kind of double standard: the "Germans" claimed it

---

[157] Margeret (1607), 61.

[158] Massa (1614), 36, 44.

[159] Massa (1614), 142, and see 116. See also Margeret (1607), 68; Bussow (1611), 54–55, 112.

[160] On corporal punishment of the elite, see Schlichting (1571a), 240–41, 252; Staden (1575), 39; Margeret (1607), 28–30, 65, 79; Bussow (1611), 34–35, 38; Massa (1614), 15–16, 119. On corporal punishment of clergy, see Taube and Kruse (1571), 43–44; Massa (1614), 148.

[161] Reutenfels (1671), 117–19; also see 154–56, 167–69.

[162] Krizhanich (1663–66), 604.

[163] Schlichting (1571a), 247–48, 252; Massa (1614), 15–16; Petreius (1615), 313; Reutenfels (1671), 117–19.

[164] Schlichting (1571b), 272.

[165] Margeret (1607), 28.

[166] Reutenfels (1671), 121; also see 143.

was shameful for Russians to call themselves "the sovereign's slaves," though they thought nothing of terming themselves *"knecht"*—"that is, slave." Nonetheless, Krizhanich recommended that the usage of "the tsar's slave" be abandoned. The grand prince's subjects high and low, the Croatian scholar advised, should be called "'servitors,' 'courtier,' 'wellborn people,' and not 'slaves.'" He also found the common Muscovite term "service people" (*sluzhilye liudi*) to be a "vile, undignified expression that diminishes the manliness of warriors." Krizhanich, together with Reutenfels, noted that servitors used diminutives of their names when they petitioned for the tsar's grace. Characteristically, the Croatian disapproved of this usage and suggested it be eradicated.[167]

Furthermore, the residents were surprised to see Russians of every estate prostrate themselves before the tsar. Schlichting, for example, remarked vaguely that an officer of Ivan IV "greeted his lord with the profound traditional bow."[168] The exact nature of this rite was made clear by Margeret:

> The Russian way of showing reverence is to remove one's hat and to bow low. This is not done in the fashion of the Turks or the Persians and other Mohammedans, who put their hand on their head or on their chest, rather it is done by lowering the right hand to the ground, or not so low, according to the respect which they wish to show. However, if an inferior wishes to entreat something from his superior, he will prostrate himself before his master, with his face against the ground as they do in their prayers before some [icons]. They know no other signs of respect.[169]

When Godunov refused the crown, Bussow observed, people of every station "lay with their faces to the ground, and from time to time arose, crying and begging: 'Have pity on us, have pity. Have mercy, Lord, have mercy and be our tsar!'"[170] Massa remarked that after the accession of Godunov's successor, False Dmitrii, "all the people prostrated themselves on the ground, begging his pardon, excusing themselves for all the crimes they appeared to have committed, and wishing good fortune to Dmitrii Ivanovich, Tsar and Grand Prince of all the Russias."[171] Collins believed that the haughty Poles "bow not so much as the Russians."[172] "When the tsar goes past," Reutenfels remarked, "then all bow to him, falling down and touching their heads to the very ground." He correctly identified this act of ritualized abasement as *bit' chelom* and believed it to be of "Asian" origin. The purpose of the rite, Reutenfels explained, was "to show the tsar great honor . . . , a fervent desire to please him, and limitless servility."[173] Krizhanich was a proponent of

[167] Krizhanich (1663–66), 442, 121, 143, 545–46, 603. See also Reutenfels (1671), 121, 143.
[168] Schlichting (1571a), 250.
[169] Margeret (1607), 33.
[170] Bussow (1611), 12; also see 29, 50, 78–79; Petreius (1615), 193–94, 279–80, 287.
[171] Massa (1614), 105; also see 15, 38–39, 122, 146.
[172] Collins (1667), 99.
[173] Reutenfels (1671), 86, 147, 142–43.

neither "limitless servility" nor rituals denoting it. Bowing to the ground, he said, was appropriate only before "God and the holy icons." [174]

In the eyes of the residents, the submission of the elite to the tsar was not entirely symbolic. When Russian nobles called themselves slaves, they were not greatly exaggerating the treatment they received from the grand prince, for he required all of them to serve him in various capacities. The residents agreed that there were no "freemen" in Muscovy, a fact that they, as servitors of the tsar, were able to appreciate far better than visiting envoys who reported the same thing. "No one in the entire country," Staden observed, "not even one who had received nothing from the grand prince, was free from service." Ivan IV, according to the German mercenary, was intent on forcing all his landholding nobles into military service. He described in some detail how the grand prince expropriated those men whose ancestors had not fought with proper vigor. Military service was the hereditary obligation of the landholding class: "All the sons of the princes and of boyars who were twelve years old were also given estates and were entered on the military muster roll; and if they failed to appear at muster in person, they were punished just like their fathers." [175] Over twenty-five years later, Petreius described a similar regime of universal military service.

> When war is at hand, all must appear in the field who are enlisted and indicated on the grand prince's register, young and old, and no one is spared, be he ever so old, sick or weak, he must appear, regardless of the fact that he can hardly go. This does not matter: he will not be allowed to substitute another in his place. The son is also not permitted to ride or serve for his father, but when he is strong and grown, he must ride and serve for himself, and the father for himself. [176]

And half a century after Petreius, Reutenfels provided a somewhat more nuanced account of the upper order's service requirement. The noble estate, he wrote, is divided into three classes: "princes," who "serve the tsar just as everyone else"; "boyars," who either serve the tsar as counselors or simply hold the title; and "*deti boiarskie,*" who serve in the central offices, the provinces, or the army. Reutenfels remarked that service was both impossible to avoid and hereditary. [177] Krizhanich recorded with approval that in Muscovy "no one is allowed to live idly, no one can free himself from general public service, be it at court, in government offices, or in the military campaigns." [178] The residents noted that the tsar required service from other estates as well: wealthy nobles, the church, merchants, and peasant communities were

---

[174] Krizhanich (1663–66), 603; also see 587.
[175] Staden (1578), 55, 18, 55.
[176] Petreius (1615), 297.
[177] Reutenfels (1671), 122, 124–25.
[178] Krizhanich (1663–66), 540. Yet in his proposal for reform, Krizhanich granted the governing classes freedom from burdensome "court services and permanent attendance at court" (606).

obliged to supply soldiers for the tsar's army.[179] Military service was not the only obligation of the nobility. According to several of the residents, the high nobility was required to be in Moscow, at court, and under the watchful eye of the tsar at all times. "The magnates lead a fairly unhappy life in this country. Obliged to be at court continually and remain standing for days on end before the emperor, they scarcely have one day of rest in three or four. The more they are raised in honour, the wearier they are out of anxiety and fear, and yet nevertheless they are constantly seeking to mount higher."[180] When servitors were on assignment outside the capital—as provincial governors, for example—they were given short tenures, presumably so they would not build up power in the countryside.[181] Reutenfels described the subjugation of governors in the following terms:

> When they are dispatched on a governorship the tsar gives them a staff, as a symbol of power, or perhaps as a reminder of future punishment, because they are easily deprived not only of their office and freedom, as revenge, but of their lives if they raise any suspicion or receive any complaints against them for malfeasance. Earlier they were required to leave their wives and children in Moscow so that the tsar would trust them more. Today they are dispatched to the province, as accompaniment, with legates and secretaries, so that mutual fear and official competition will powerfully dissuade them from unfair activities.[182]

Finally, the residents remarked that high nobles were required to participate in court ceremonies of all types, and they were to be well dressed under threat of punishment. If a magnate did not have the means to purchase the proper attire, the treasury would rent it to him.[183]

Having spent years in service to the crown, the residents knew that the tsar compensated his men with monetary salaries, a fact that many envoys registered only vaguely, particularly in the first half of the sixteenth century.[184] They also understood that service men were granted estates. As we saw earlier, Taube and Kruse, Schlichting, Staden, and other residents were given landed properties upon entering Russian service. Nonetheless, the foreigners

---

[179] On the obligations of wealthy landholders, see Staden (1578), 7; Margeret (1607), 46; Reutenfels (1671), 125. On the obligations of the church, see Staden (1578), 38–39, 40; Bussow (1611), 83; Massa (1614), 74, 172; Reutenfels (1671), 125, 167–69. On the obligations of merchants, see Margeret (1607), 50. On the duties of peasants, see Staden (1578), 40; Margeret (1607), 50; Massa (1614), 168.

[180] Massa (1614), 95. Also see Staden (1578), 45–46; Margeret (1607), 27; Reutenfels (1671), 102.

[181] Staden (1578), 8, 63–64; Massa (1614), 45, 195; Reutenfels (1671), 102, 110–11.

[182] Reutenfels (1671), 110–11.

[183] Staden (1578), 66, 102; Horsey (1584–1611), 273, 289; Margeret (1607), 42; Peyerle (1608), 232; Bussow (1611), 16, 22, 24–25, 34; Massa (1614), 58, 124–25; Petreius (1615), 286, 315; Collins (1667), 61.

[184] Staden (1578), 13, 65–66, 101–2; Horsey (1584–1611), 286; Margeret (1607), 30, 35, 40–41, 46–47; Bussow (1611), 16–17, 24–25, 34–35; Petreius (1615), 297, 300; Reutenfels (1671), 108–9, 125; Krizhanich (1663–66), 445, 551; Gordon (1661–99), 46.

clearly had the impression that the proffered estates—like all other property in Russia—were quite precarious and subject to confiscation for little reason. The residents of Ivan's court witnessed repeated confiscations, and their accounts are replete with descriptions of Ivan's appropriation of both the allodial and conditional properties of his highborn servitors.[185] Authors of the seventeenth century also mention occasional capricious confiscations (particularly by Godunov and False Dmitrii),[186] but for the most part they stress that estates were attached only for a serious infraction, such as a crime, failure to serve, or disfavor. Margeret, for example, remarked that if the holder of a prebendal estate was for whatever reason "disgraced," his lands were seized by the crown.[187] Bussow noted that Godunov confiscated the estates of those servitors who were remiss in their military obligations.

> Those other princes, boyars, and all those who were under obligation to go on campaign but had remained at home, he [Godunov] ordered to be chased out of their estates by his officers to join the forces in the field. He ordered the estates of several of those who had been disobedient to be confiscated, and some were cast into prison, while others were punished with the whip until their skin was so torn that nowhere on their backs was there left a patch of whole skin large enough that the point of a needle might be placed upon it.[188]

When the rebel Bolotnikov threatened, Massa reported, Shuiskii took similar measures: "He sent letters to every town commanding that all the boyar sons, or gentry, be summoned, together with all the able-bodied men who were still in the fields, not having left for the army, and threatening recalcitrants with forced recruitment and confiscation of goods."[189] Petreius simply stated that those who did not appear for military musters had their estates confiscated.[190] Even Reutenfels reported late in the seventeenth century that the tsar, as universal landholder, could "seize from them [his subjects] their estates and lives without explaining his actions."[191] The practice aroused Krizhanich to indignation: no one, he insisted, should have "their property confiscated without due process of law."[192] Such things were known to occur under Peter. Gordon reported that on January 10, 1690, the property of the boyar Andrei Ivanovich Golitsyn was confiscated after his mother-in-law spoke ill of Peter.[193]

The residents were for the most part servitors of the court, so it is hardly

---

[185] For just a few examples, see Schlichting (1571a), 232–33, 240–41, 244–45; Taube and Kruse (1571), 35–38; Printz (1578), 65; Staden (1578), 18, 31; Horsey (1584–1611), 273.

[186] Margeret (1607), 35–36; Bussow (1611), 26–27, 34–35, 38, 108; Massa (1614), 44, 168; Petreius (1615), 161; Gordon (1661–99), 167.

[187] Margeret (1607), 35–36.

[188] Bussow (1611), 38.

[189] Massa (1614), 168.

[190] Petreius (1615), 297; also see 304.

[191] Reutenfels (1671), 101.

[192] Krizhanich (1663–66), 605.

[193] Gordon (1661–99), 167.

surprising that they were able to write at great length and with convincing authority about life among the service elite. At the same time, as city dwellers, estate holders, and commanders of large detachments of Russian soldiers, the residents also gained a considerable appreciation of the condition of the Muscovite commons. And when they wrote about the state of townspeople and peasants, they expressed a single opinion: the commons were oppressed both by the tsar and by the service elite. The writers of the *oprichnina* era made clear that though Ivan's anger was directed primarily toward the nobility, he did not spare people of lesser estates. According to Schlichting, Ivan "slew 2770 Novgorod nobles and wealthy men," and also "persons of lesser rank and an uncountable number of the lower classes." [194] Such outrages were not unknown after Ivan's death. Bussow, for example, described the "dreadful and merciless vengeance" wreaked on peasants who had supported False Dmitrii I. Bussow had personal experience with the suffering of peasants during the Time of Troubles, for several estates that he owned were plundered and their inhabitants killed or captured.[195] The foreigners believed that abuse of the commons was not confined to occasional outrages but was a systematic part of Muscovite governance. Staden described the rule of provincial governors over simple people in dark terms:

> These military leaders and others like them took turns being governors, *voevody,* or commanders for two years in certain lands and city regions in the country. . . . When the two years were up, they were changed. All the sins, burdens, outrages, oppression, and exploitation that they had inflicted upon the peasants and merchants and had forgotten were completed by their replacements.[196]

According to the residents, the tsar compelled peasants to perform onerous services, dragooned them into the army, and forced them to pay heavy taxes.[197] Landholders, agents of the tsar, were also hard on peasants, beating and exploiting them at will.[198] Several residents theorized that the abuse meted out by the government and its servants against the commons was not necessarily pernicious, for Russians required a heavy hand to prosper. "For this people does not prosper unless it is oppressed by the mighty," Massa

---

[194] Schlichting (1571a), 234. For other examples of the oppression of the poor by Ivan and his servitors, see ibid., 224–25, 229, 233, 234, 238, 249–50; Taube and Kruse (1571), 35–36, 44–45; Staden (1578), 8, 33, 67.

[195] Bussow (1611), 41, 120–122.

[196] Staden (1578), 8; also see 64–65; Margeret (1607), 28; Krizhanich (1663–66), 584; Reutenfels (1671), 110–11.

[197] On the requirement that peasants supply transportation, see Staden (1578), 65, 72–73; Horsey (1584–1611), 302; Margeret (1607), 42; Bussow (1611), 56–57; Massa (1614), 46–47, 49; Petreius (1615), 283. On dragooning, see Staden (1578), 40; Margeret (1607), 50; Massa (1614), 168. On taxes and other duties, see Taube and Kruse (1571), 35–36, 40; Staden (1578), 38–39; Reutenfels (1671), 125–26, 138.

[198] Staden (1578), 33, 67, 122–23; Petreius (1615), 314; Collins (1667), 14.

wrote, "and it is in slavery that it becomes rich and happy." [199] The residents were hardly surprised to learn that Russian commoners readily sold themselves into slavery.[200]

Conclusion

Like the envoys who attempted to provide Europeans with accurate information about Russia, the resident ethnographers and historians found that Russia was a difficult place to observe. The residents, however, were far better able to overcome the hurdles placed in the way of their investigations than were European envoys and itinerant merchants. They moved with relative freedom throughout the realm, lived among the Orthodox population, and worked near the center of authority. Thus they had ample opportunity to observe Russian life, and particularly Russian government, at close quarters over long periods of time. Perhaps most important, they had the means to understand much if not all of what they heard and saw. After living in the empire for years, they gained an intimate familiarity with the basic patterns of Russian government and society. To be sure, they were not natives, but it would hardly be an exaggeration to call them—or at least the most skilled of them—insiders. Because the envoy-ethnographers were ignorant of the native culture and in the country for a relatively short period, they had to make a conscious effort to investigate the Russian state and the society it ruled. The residents conducted investigations as well, for they were, like the envoys, aware of the basic rules guiding contributions to the genres of history and ethnography. But in addition to what they learned in the course of their positive explorations, they possessed something the envoys did not—a deep reservoir of personal experience, a mass of ingrained knowledge that they could and did use to construct a detailed depiction of Russia.

What is perhaps surprising is that the image they constructed was in general quite similar to that found in the writings of the envoys and itinerant merchants. The residents clearly felt that the governmental regime they observed in Russia was quite distinct from that which obtained in their homelands. Schlichting, for example, concluded that "in character and generosity our king is as different from the tyrannical prince of Muscovy as the sun is from the moon. Whenever our king summons a man to his presence," the German wrote, "it is remarkable to observe how his heart swells with pride and his spirits soar." In contrast, "whenever the prince orders a man to report to him, be he noble senator or common soldier, in preparation for the meeting he takes leave of his wife, children and friends, assuming that he will never see them again because he will either be beaten to death or beheaded,

---

[199] Massa (1614), 185. Also see Horsey (1584), 310; Reutenfels (1671), 116–17, 176–78.
[200] Krizhanich (1663–66), 605.

although he knows that he is guilty of no crime." [201] A century later, Reutenfels offered a similar contrast:

> Although the obligations of officials among the Muscovites carry names similar to those of the Poles, in the execution of the better part of them it is clear, from one or another angle, that there is a difference. Among the Poles everything is directed to the freedom of the notables; in Muscovy, it is generally said, everyone is in sad, servile subjection. A few higher officials who once had a semblance of freedom have either had it taken by the tsars or had their power and majesty limited, so that today even the boyars, who are called senators of the state, cannot be considered the equals of even private councilors. [202]

In such comparisons one can certainly detect a tendency to overdraw the distinction between European and Russian rule, to contrast an idealized "us" against a demonized "them." Yet even when we take this tendency into consideration, it is apparent the sometimes confused and inaccurate observations of the residents marked out a real difference between the basic patterns of European and Russian government. The residents were by no means naive men, nor were they simply Russophobic ideologues. They were experienced observers concerned to provide a factual—if not always completely objective—account of what they had seen in Russia.

[201] Schlichting (1571a), 219. Also see Peyerle (1608), 187.
[202] Reutenfels (1671), 110–11.

4

RERUM MOSCOVITICARUM
Herberstein and the Origin
of "Russian Tyranny"

> Upon his death [Ivan III] in 1504, his son and successor, Gavriil, known
> to posterity as Vasilii [III], brought into submission all the remaining princes
> of the Muscovite clan and regained Smolensk, and emboldened by these
> conquests, began to nourish higher ambitions and adopted for himself the
> imperial title, according to the testimony of Herberstein, the ambassador of
> the Roman Emperor Maximilian I.
>
> AUGUSTIN FREIHERR VON MEYERBERG, 1661

NEITHER JOHN MILTON nor Jodocus Crull had ever been to Muscovy,
yet both wrote descriptions of the country. Interestingly, the two stay-at-
home ethnographers offered strikingly different images of Muscovite government. In *A Brief History of Muscovy,* the famous English poet stressed the
efficiency and fairness of Russian government. All Russian subjects, Milton
assured his readers, served the tsar loyally and were rewarded according to
their merits. "Any rich man," Milton wrote admiringly, "who through age,
or other impotence is unable to serve the Publick, being inform'd of, is turn'd
out of his Estate, and forc'd with his family to live on a small Pension, while
some other more deserving, is by the Duke's authority put into possession." [1]
Milton's paean to Muscovite governance was virtually unique among
seventeenth-century European descriptions of Russia. In contrast, Crull's
Ancient and Present State of Muscovy echoed the far more common opinion
that Muscovy was ruled despotically. "The State of Muscovy, or its Political
Government," Crull believed, "is not only Monarchical, but also Despotical
or Absolute; forasmuch as the Czar being sole and absolute Master over all
his Subjects, disposes without Controul of their Lives and Estates." [2]

[1] Milton (1648), 336–37.
[2] Crull (1698), 169.

Why did Milton and Crull disagree so strongly about the nature of Muscovite government? The answer cannot lie in differing experiences because neither man had ever set foot on Russian soil. Neither is an explanation to be found in contrasting political perspectives, for Milton surely would have joined Crull in condemning tsarist tyranny had he believed that the Russian prince was a tyrant. Rather, Milton and Crull could not agree because their sources could not. Milton based his description on early and, by seventeenth-century standards, very unusual accounts, namely, those by Paolo Giovio and Richard Chancellor.[3] Both men had praised the fairness of the Muscovite monarchy, and Milton blindly followed them.[4] Like so many ethnographers of the later sixteenth and seventeenth centuries, Crull relied on Herberstein's *Notes on the Muscovites* of 1549 and works that had borrowed information from it.[5] Herberstein had written that the grand prince holds "unlimited control over the lives and property of all his subjects"; slightly rephrasing the Habsburg ambassador, Crull repeated that the tsar "disposes of the Lives and Fortunes of his subjects at his pleasure."[6]

As we shall see, *Notes on the Muscovites* was in some measure responsible for convincing not only Crull but many Europeans that Muscovy was ruled by a despot and peopled by slaves. Herberstein did not invent the image of Russian despotism, but his depiction of it was the first to be grounded in personal experience. Whereas his predecessors had based their sketchy understanding of Russia on wishful thinking or brief interviews, Herberstein had been to Moscow, seen the Russian court with his own eyes, and met with men who served the grand prince. His observations convinced him that though Muscovy had once been a balanced monarchy, Ivan III and Vasilii III (Herberstein's host) had transformed Russia into a kind of tyranny. The Habsburg ambassador's picture of Muscovite political life around 1525 was broadcast throughout Europe via the printing press. In a period starved for intelligence about Russia, Herberstein's book proved tremendously popular, and it was often reprinted in the second half of the sixteenth century. Soon after its initial publication, his tome became the major European source of

---

[3] Milton's information was, as the subtitle of his book relates, "Gather'd from the Writings of several Eye-witnesses" (331). The "Eye-witnesses" were primarily the sixteenth-century English travelers who had contributed to Hakluyt, among whom one finds Chancellor. Milton called Giovio a "Pattern or Example" to be used by writers of ethnographies (327).

[4] Milton copied, almost verbatim, Adams/Chancellor (1553), 260. Chancellor's statement received partial corroboration in Giovio (1525), 55: "In every part of the administration they [the Muscovites] observe the useful and excellent institution that all according to their services receive eternal reward or eternal shame."

[5] It seems that Crull had Olearius (1656) and Reutenfels (1671) at hand, both of whom were heavily dependent on Herberstein.

[6] Herberstein (1517–49), 1:32; Crull (1698), 169. In fact, Crull recognized that Giovio was wrong in praising Muscovite monarchy. He wrote (apparently unaware that the Italian cleric had authored his treatise in 1525) that "Ivan IV" was not "a good and devout Christian," as Giovio had written. Giovio, of course, had Vasilii III in mind. Crull then repeated (330–31) Herberstein's thesis that Ivan III was the original architect of Muscovite despotism.

information on Muscovy and, more generally, the interpretive lens through which men of the late Renaissance viewed Russia. Almost every serious student of Muscovy read *Notes on the Muscovites* and was influenced by the image of Russian government it presented.

Herberstein's Image of Russia

Any discussion of the growth of European knowledge about Russia in the second half of the sixteenth century must begin with Herberstein's *Notes on the Muscovites* (see fig. 12). The facts of Herberstein's life are well known. He was born in 1486 at Wippach, in Styria, to a prominent German family. Slovenian was spoken in that region of the Habsburg domain, and Herberstein's familiarity with the South Slavic language would be significant later in his career. In 1499 he entered the University at Vienna, where he studied philosophy and law. During his days as a student, he may have come into contact with Konrad Celtis, who taught at Vienna and was, as we noted earlier, one of the pioneers of the new Humanist science of "chorography," or regional ethnographic description.[7] In 1506 Herberstein became an officer in the Imperial army and served with distinction in several campaigns. He was knighted by Emperor Maximilian I in 1508 and entered the Imperial Council in 1515. That year also marked the beginning of his long and storied diplomatic career. From 1515 to 1553, Herberstein carried out something on the order of sixty-nine foreign missions for his Habsburg masters, traveled throughout much of Europe, and became acquainted with the personalities and practices of courts too numerous to mention here.[8] He was lauded for his achievements: the Habsburgs granted him estates and titles, and books and collections of panegyrics were dedicated to him.

Herberstein first journeyed to Muscovy to make peace between Russia and Lithuania. Aware that Sigismund I, ruler of Poland and Lithuania, was consolidating his hold on the Hungarian throne, Maximilian initiated an anti-Polish coalition, of which Vasilii III was to be a member. In early 1514 the grand prince, already at war with the Lithuanians, agreed to an alliance with the Habsburgs. Sigismund soon learned of the Imperial-Russian pact and realized that he was in desperate straits. At the Council of Vienna in 1515, Sigismund made peace with Maximilian and agreed to a dynastic marriage that ensured the Habsburgs would receive the coveted Hungarian crown. With this rapprochement between the Habsburgs and Poland, the Rus-

[7] On Celtis and early Humanist chorography, see Gerald Strauss, *Sixteenth-Century Germany,* 12–26.

[8] There is no full-length, modern biography of Herberstein, though much has been written in various places about his activities. For sources on Herberstein, see Bibliography 4 below. The best treatment of Herberstein's diplomatic activities is Berthold Picard, *Gesandtschaftswesen Ostmitteleuropas in der frühen Neuzeit.*

RERVM MO=
SCOVITICARVM COM=
mentarij Sigismundi Liberi Ba-
ronis in Herberstain, Neyperg,
& Guettenhag:

Quibus Rusiæ ac Metropolis eius Moscouiæ descriptio, Cho-
rographicæ tabulæ, Religionis indicatio, Modus excipiendi &
tractandi oratores, Itineraria in Moscouiam duo,
& alia quædam continentur.

HIS NVNC PRIMVM ACCEDVNT,

SCRIPTVM RECENS DE GRAECO
rum fide, quos in omnibus Moscorum natio
sequitur:

ET

COMMENTARIVS DE BELLIS MOSCORVM AD-
uersus finitimos, Polonos, Lituanos, Suedos, Liuonios, & alios gestis,
ad annum usque LXXI, scriptus ab Ioanne
Leuuenclaio.

Cum Cæs. & Regiæ Maiest. gratia & priuilegio
ad decennium.

BASILEAE, EX OFFICINA OPO-
RINIANA. 1571.

12. Title page of Sigismund von Herberstein, *Rerum moscoviticarum commentarii*
(Basel, 1571).

sian war with Poland-Lithuania lost value for Maximilian; therefore, he dispatched Herberstein in 1517 to arrange a truce between the two parties. Though Herberstein remained nine months in Moscow, he was unable to persuade the parties to reconcile their differences. In 1522 a second Imperial embassy under Francesco Da Collo culminated in the signing of a five-year truce between the Poles and Muscovites. Herberstein was sent to Moscow for a second time in 1526 to secure the renewal of that treaty.

The earliest version of Herberstein's account of Muscovy was probably written between 1517 and 1527. Though no early manuscript of *Notes on the Muscovites* has been found, several facts point to the existence of some sort of proto-text. In the first edition of the book, Herberstein recollected that during his diplomatic missions he had made numerous notes "doubtless worthy of being commemorated in print." Herberstein also remarked that he gave the emperor a "description of the customs and ceremonies of the Russians," but it is unclear whether this account was written or oral.[9] The ambassador mentioned an early report on Muscovy in his autobiography, but again it is not certain whether it was written or oral.[10] There is another possible reference to a written treatise in 1518, but what relation it bears to *Notes on the Muscovites* is unknown.[11] A letter from Ferdinand to Herberstein of 1526 asked the ambassador to produce a formal account of his experiences in Russia.[12] The original report may have remained unattended in the Habsburg archives until Herberstein began the revision of it, perhaps in the 1530s.[13] It was only then, as Herberstein explained, that he found time away from his "various embassies and other labors" to revise his manuscript.[14]

Herberstein succeeded in producing the first detailed, eyewitness ethnography of Muscovy. His account was in every way more trustworthy and complete than those of his predecessors, largely due to the great variety of sources he used.[15] Herberstein carefully reviewed the existing literature on Russia including works by Maciej z Miechowa, Paolo Giovio, Alberto Campensé, Johann Fabri, Anton Weid, Olaus Magnus, and Sebastian Münster. The Habsburg diplomat viewed all their opinions skeptically, for he realized that the early ethnographers and cosmographers had not had the opportunity to visit Russia and see "what no one but an ambassador could have be-

---

[9] Herberstein (1517–49), 1:clx, 2:158.

[10] Theodor Georg von Karajan, ed., *Selbstbiographie Sigmunds Freiherrn von Herberstein*, 135.

[11] The reference occurred in a letter from Ulrich Hutten to Pirckheimer. See Willehad P. Eckert and Christoph von Imhoff, *Willibald Pirckheimer*, 336–49.

[12] Frank Kämpfer, "Herbersteins nicht eingestandene Abhängigkeit von Johann Fabri aus Leutkirch," 1–3.

[13] Walter Leitsch, "Westeuropäishe Reiseberichte über den Moskauer Staat," 159–60, and "Herberstein's Ergänzungen zur Moscovia in späteren Auflagen," 186–87.

[14] Herberstein (1517–49), 1:clxi.

[15] The best general treatment of Herberstein's sources is Anna L. Khoroshkevich, "Die Quellen Herbersteins und die Moscovia," 179–244.

come acquainted with." [16] Unlike many ethnographers of his age, Herberstein was no plagiarist: he read the early descriptions of Muscovy critically and compared what they had to say with his own observations. Herberstein's treatment of Fabri is a case in point. In *Notes on the Muscovites* he responded—both positively and negatively—to many points made in Fabri's book.[17] While in Muscovy, Herberstein employed his knowledge of Slavic to interrogate a sizable circle of Russians on a host of topics.[18] The ambassador proclaimed that he "daily availed [himself] of every opportunity to converse much upon such matters with a great number of people." Even here Herberstein exercised caution, making sure that all the intelligence he gathered from Russians was well corroborated. "I made myself acquainted with the greater part of the talented and trustworthy men of the place," wrote the Habsburg diplomat, "and did not rely upon this or that man's account, but trusted only to the unvarying statements of many." The various Russian written sources that Herberstein investigated provided him with details about Russian culture completely unavailable at the time in Europe, even to those such as Giovio and Fabri who had interviewed visiting Russian diplomats. But as a rule, the ambassador fully trusted only his own senses. Again and again he stressed that the information in *Notes on the Muscovites* was credible because it was based on his own observations. "And in order that my opinion in this matter may not be looked upon with suspicion, or considered presumptuous," he wrote, "I assert with all honesty, that not once only, but repeatedly, . . . I have seen and investigated Moscow, as it were under my very eyes." [19]

Herberstein described a remarkable range of topics: existing literature on Muscovy, Russia's languages, its name and borders, Russia's ancient history, the grand prince's mode of rule, his titles and coronation ceremonies, the history of Muscovite relations with Poland-Lithuania and the Empire, Russian religion, domestic affairs (women, servants, peasants), the grand prince's army, the administration of justice, the condition of the gentry and commons, Russia's economy and geography, the condition of the Tatars on Russia's southern and eastern frontiers, the vast and little-known northern territories, the Russian court's treatment of ambassadors, and, finally, the course of Herberstein's own embassies to Russia. Herberstein's book was a veritable encyclopedia of Moscovitica. Its contents were finely tuned to the interests of the day. Merchants hoping to trade in the east would find the best chorography of Muscovy, Tataria, and Lithuania available anywhere. Persons concerned with religious affairs and particularly the question of ecclesiastical union could read in *Notes on the Muscovites* a detailed, even-handed treat-

[16] Herberstein (1517–49), 1:clx–clxi.
[17] Kämpfer, "Herbersteins nicht eingestandene Abhängigkeit von Johann Fabri," 1–27.
[18] Anna L. Khoroshkevich, "Sigizmund Gerbershtein i ego Zapiski o Moskovii," 32–37.
[19] Herberstein (1517–49), 1:clxi, 1. See Christine Harrauer, "Beobachtungen zur Darstellungsweise und Wahrheitsanspruch in der 'Moscovia' Herbersteins," 186ff.

ment of the Russian Orthodox faith. Envoys could use the long description of Muscovite diplomatic practice to prepare themselves for embassies to Russia.

Notes on the Muscovites, however, was not merely a collection of facts. Herberstein offered a coherent theory of Russian political culture. At the center of Herberstein's perception was the overwhelming power of the grand prince and the servility of his subjects. As we have seen, the observation that the Muscovite monarchy was despotic was not new: Campensé and Fabri, both of whom Herberstein read, had stressed the unfettered authority of the grand prince over his people.[20] There is little doubt that Herberstein's description of Muscovite government was influenced by these early accounts. Campensé noted that the grand prince had "full power to dispose of [his subjects'] lives and property," and Herberstein's formulation was almost identical.[21] Similarly, Fabri insisted that "there is no other realm in the world that is more subject to its master"; Herberstein told his readers exactly the same thing.[22] But Herberstein's understanding of Muscovite civic life, while formally similar to that of his predecessors, was in fact radically different. Campensé and Fabri held up an idealized depiction of Muscovy as a mirror to what they believed were the corrupt polities of Europe. The Russians, they claimed, were fanatically loyal to their grand prince and were willing to sacrifice all to fulfill his orders. Europeans, in contrast, showed great disrespect for their kings and knew nothing of civic pride. Herberstein may have traveled to Muscovy with this fantasy in mind, but what he learned there quickly disabused him of the thought that there was anything virtuous in the rule of the grand prince.

Herberstein arrived in Moscow at the end of a fundamental shift in the political life of the East Slavic territories. In the first half of the fifteenth century, northeastern Russia was overgrown with a tangle of principalities, appanages, and republics. Though most of these jurisdictions were ruled by a single, loosely knit dynasty of East Slavic princes—the Riurikid—and though all the Riurikid princes were nominally subordinate to the senior member of their line, the grand prince of Vladimir, northeastern Russia was anything but united. Several principalities acted as sovereign entities; some of these entities were subdivided into semi-independent appanages under the control of junior members of the ruling line; and Novgorod, a city-state in the north, refused direct control by the Riurikid altogether. During the second half of the century, the political heterogeneity of northeastern Russia ended as Moscow rose to prominence. Ivan III brought the once sovereign principalities of Iaroslavl', Rostov, and Tver to heel; he severely restricted the rights of the appanage princes in the Moscow line; and he violently ended the independence of Novgorod. The princes of Russia and their high-

[20] On Herberstein's conception of Russia, see Samuel H. Baron, "Herberstein's Image of Russia and Its Transmission through Later Writers."

[21] Campensé (1524), 32; Herberstein (1517–49), 1:32.

[22] Fabri (1526), 298–99; Herberstein (1517–49), 1:30.

born retainers came to Moscow to serve Ivan as his dependents. In 1493 Ivan declared himself "sovereign of all Russia," and thus Muscovy—a new East Slavic kingdom and European state—was born.

The Habsburg ambassador probably knew little of these events when he first traveled to Moscow in 1517. No histories of Muscovy were available in Europe, and it is unlikely that many Europeans who had been to Moscow or who were conversant with Muscovite affairs—men the ambassador might have interviewed—took an interest in the past of a country whose present was so dimly understood. Herberstein felt, however, that no description of a nation could be complete without at least a brief history, and thus he invested considerable energy in reading Russian chronicles and interviewing his Muscovite attendants about the *res gestae* of their country. What Herberstein discovered must have shocked him, for his investigations made it clear that Russia had suffered a violent political struggle and that Muscovy had emerged only very recently as the dominant power in the region. Herberstein's reading of the chronicles suggested that "from the time of Vladimir Monomach," who ruled Kiev in the twelfth century, to the reign of Vasilii II, prince of Moscow from 1425 to 1462, "Russia had no monarch." The ambassador emphasized that before the mid–fifteenth century, discord and division had torn the Riurikid house apart. According to Herberstein, the man responsible for unifying Russia was Ivan III, Vasilii II's son, whom the Habsburg ambassador characterized as a cruel tyrant, a drunk, and a misogynist. Herberstein went to great lengths to describe Ivan's efforts to bring all the sovereignties of Russia under his high hand. After marrying the sister of "Michael, Grand Duke of Tver, he drove out his brother-in-law, and took possession" of the principality; he "reduced the inhabitants [of Novgorod] to abject servitude"; he forced the princes of the "province of Severa" to surrender "themselves up to the government of Russia"; he exiled "the citizens [of Pskov] through the colonies, and sending Muscovites into their place, he utterly abolished their liberty"; he "thrust out and banished" the princes of Rostov; he "drove" the lords of Suzdal' from their territories. At the conclusion of Ivan's "plan of ejecting all princes and others from the garrisons and fortified places," all the formerly independent princes of Russia, "being either moved by the grandeur of his achievements or stricken with fear, became subject to him." Having forced all his rivals into submission, Ivan "assumed the title of Grand Duke of Vladimir, Moscow, and Novgorod" and declared himself "monarch of all Russia."[23]

According to Herberstein, Vasilii III, Ivan's son and the ambassador's host, continued the policies of his tyrannical father (see fig. 13). Vasilii reduced the remaining independent principalities, for example, seizing Riazan' and dis-

[23] Herberstein (1517–49), 1:20, 23–24, 29, 33, 44, 30, 21. Herberstein attributes the conquest of Pskov to Ivan III, though it actually occurred under his son.

Russorum Rex & Dominus sum, iure paterni
Sanguinis: imperij titulos à nemine, quauis
Mercatus prece, uel precio: nec legibus ullis
Subditus alterius, sed Christo credulus uni,
Emendicatos alijs aspernor honores.

13. Vasilii III. Sigismund von Herberstein, *Rerum moscoviticarum commentarii*
(Basel, 1571).

persing "a great portion of [its population] through different colonies, so that the strength of the entire principality was loosened and broken."²⁴ Vasilii, Herberstein wrote, "certainly grants no fortresses to his relations, nor even puts them in charge of any, but oppresses nearly all of them with close confinement." He compelled all the magnates to serve him at their own expense. Vasilii appointed local governors for brief tenures, presumably so that no provincial leaders could arise to challenge his authority, and he exacted tribute from each region annually. He appropriated gifts made to ambassadors at foreign courts and, in general, reserved the right to confiscate the goods of any servitor who dared to question his authority. He exercised complete control over the clergy, appointing whomever he pleased to all ecclesiastical offices.²⁵ The commons were similarly ill treated. Vasilii and his men systematically exploited and abused the peasantry. Common folk had little recourse to legal remedies, for they were granted no access to the prince but were forced to turn to his councilors, who either ignored their grievances or exacted bribes from them. Indeed, the simple people had been held down so long, Herberstein theorized, that they had grown to "enjoy slavery more than freedom" and to understand beating as a sign of affection. Finally, Herberstein was struck by the fact that all Russians—both high and low—were incredibly obsequious to Vasilii, calling themselves his slaves, prostrating themselves before him, and claiming that he was like God.²⁶

Why did Herberstein take such a dim view of Ivan III and Vasilii III? To answer this question it must be borne in mind that Herberstein was a jurist and important member of the local nobility in his native Styria. As such, he was fully aware of both the carefully prescribed limits of Imperial power in his native Habsburg lands and the legally protected rights of provincial magnates in the sundry localities of the Empire. Given his knowledge and experience, he could not have interpreted what he read in the Russian chronicles about Ivan III's activities as anything but the unlawful destruction of a loose confederation of semisovereign principalities by a power-hungry tyrant. Moreover, as the representative of an ancient provincial family, he doubtless felt sympathy for his unfortunate Russian peers. While in Russia he was surrounded by men who clung to their identities as the princes of formerly independent sovereignties, some of whom he named. The principality of Iaroslavl', for example, "was forcibly taken by the same monarch [Ivan III]; and although there still remain dukes of the province called *knesi* [princes], yet the prince usurps the title to himself, the country being granted to the *knesi* as to subjects."²⁷ He went on to identify three of these former princes, all de-

²⁴ Ibid., 2:11. The remaining citations in this paragraph are from 1:30–32, unless otherwise noted.
²⁵ Ibid., 54.
²⁶ Ibid., 95, 105–7, 2:125.
²⁷ Ibid., 2:34.

Table 7. Descendants of Vasilii Davidovich of Iaroslavl'

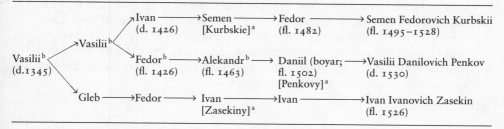

[a] New (cadet) line.
[b] Senior prince of Iaroslavl'.

scendants of Prince Vasilii Davidovich of Iaroslavl' and all of whom Herberstein had met—Prince Semen Fedorovich Kurbskii, Prince Vasilii Danilovich Penkov, and Prince Ivan Ivanovich Zasekin.[28] Their lineages are traced in Table 7. Semen Fedorovich Kurbskii's father, Fedor Semenovich, entered Muscovite service as early as 1482. Semen himself became an important commander in the Muscovite army. It is unclear how Herberstein became acquainted with Semen, but the biographical details he relates indicate that the ambassador probably knew him well. Vasilii Danilovich Penkov's grandfather, Aleksandr Fedorovich, was the last sovereign prince of Iaroslavl'. Aleksandr ceded his rights and properties to Ivan III in 1463 or 1471.[29] Vasilii's father, Daniil Aleksandrovich, had entered Muscovite service by 1485 and was made a boyar by 1500.[30] Vasilii himself enjoyed a distinguished military and diplomatic career in Muscovy. According to Herberstein, Vasilii escorted the Habsburg legation to and from the royal palace during Herberstein's visit in 1526. It is known from Muscovite records that Vasilii sat across from Herberstein at an official banquet on October 18, 1526.[31] Very little is known about the ancestors of Ivan Ivanovich Zasekin beyond the fact that they represented a junior branch of the Iaroslavl' line. In any case, Ivan was active in the Muscovite army and ambassadorial corp. He had been sent on a mission to Emperor Charles V in 1524, and from January to April 1526 he accompanied Herberstein on his journey from Vienna to Moscow. Though none of these men could personally have recalled an independent Iaroslavl', they would have learned about the existence of such a place from the testimony of their fathers, court chronicles, and genealogical registers. There would

[28] All the biographical information on these three persons is drawn from Aleksandr A. Zimin, *Formirovanie,* 83–98, and Herberstein (1517–49), 2:34, unless otherwise noted.
[29] On the incorporation of the principality of Iaroslavl', see Lev V. Cherepnin, *Obrazovanie russkogo tsentral'izovannogo gosudarstva v XIV–XV vekakh,* 825–30.
[30] Nancy S. Kollmann, *Kinship and Politics,* 226–27.
[31] Khoroshkevich, "Sigizmund Gerbershtein i ego *Zapiski o Moskovii,*" 33.

seem to be little doubt that the Iaroslavl' princes and others like them were very conscious of the loss their families had suffered at the hands of Ivan III. And it is hardly difficult to imagine that proud men such as Semen, Vasilii, and Ivan—all of whom spent considerable time with the Habsburg embassy—told Herberstein tales of their once mighty ancestors and their dispossession by Ivan III. In short, all of the data Herberstein gathered in Russia pointed to one conclusion: Vasilii III was a despot.

The Popularity of Notes on the Muscovites

In the 1550s and 1560s, Europeans' interest in Muscovy grew appreciably, primarily in connection with the opening of Muscovite trade by the English, the onset of the Livonian war, and the terror of Ivan IV.

Since the waning years of the fifteenth century, the Muscovites had been frustrated by the Hansa's and the Livonian Order's virtual monopoly on Russian-European trade through the Baltic. Ivan III, Vasilii III, and Ivan IV had all struggled with only marginal success to break the "Germans'" hold on commerce in the region. Thus when the English merchant-adventurer Richard Chancellor appeared unexpectedly (and accidentally, for he was looking for the northeastern passage to China) at the mouth of the Northern Dvina River in 1553, the Russians were very pleased.[32] The English offered Ivan IV an opportunity to circumvent the Hanseatic and Livonian merchants, and he quickly granted them advantageous trading privileges. Ivan's generosity was met with enthusiasm in England: in 1555 approximately two hundred investors formed what would be called the Muscovy Company, Englishmen began to travel to Russia in ever larger numbers, and goods began to flow between the two countries. And not only goods, but information as well—the English, it seems, were fascinated by the Muscovites. English pilots, merchants, and ambassadors produced some of the first and best European ethnographies of Russia, notably those by Richard Chancellor, Anthony Jenkinson, Jerome Horsey, and Giles Fletcher—all of which were published (entire or in part) in what was the largest early modern collection of Moscovitica ever issued, Hakluyt's *Principal navigations*.[33] News of the Muscovites spread far and wide throughout English society.[34] Famously, Shakespeare included a "masque of the Muscovites" in *Love's Labour's Lost*.[35]

Ivan's hopes of solving the Baltic question were not pinned solely on the English. The White Sea trade was rather a diversion, an ancillary move in his

[32] The literature on the English discovery of Muscovy and the activities of the Muscovy Company is large. See Chester S. Dunning, "Russia Company."

[33] Adams/Chancellor (1553), Chancellor (1553), Jenkinson (1557), Horsey (1584–1611), Fletcher (1591), and Hakluyt (1969).

[34] Karl H. Ruffmann, *Das Russlandbild im England Shakespeares*.

[35] William Shakespeare, *Love's Labour's Lost* (c. 1600), V.ii.79–265.

larger strategic aim—the conquest of the Baltic littoral itself. Frustrated by the continued recalcitrance of the Livonians and believing that the Order was crumbling, Ivan attacked Livonia in 1558. The Livonian elite immediately began to make desperate appeals to their patrons in the Empire for aid against the "godless" Muscovites.[36] Soon fearful talk of the Livonian conflict again entered Imperial correspondence.[37] Once more furtive discussions of the Russian threat were held in Imperial diets.[38] In a brief span, Muscovy became the object of intense interest in northern and central Europe and remained so until the war ended in 1585.[39] The fascination that Muscovy held for the inhabitants of the Baltic, the Polish-Lithuanian Commonwealth, and the Empire is reflected in the rather sudden appearance of Russian news in the burgeoning pamphlet press and in the entry of Muscovy into European historiography. During the first half of the sixteenth century—particularly in connection with the Turks and the battles of the Reformation—a proto-news press had developed in central Europe. Part propaganda and part hard fact, *Flugschriften* or "pamphlets" provided common readers with printed information on events of the day.[40] Beginning in the 1560s, pamphlets concerning the course of the Livonian war began to appear in central Europe, often issued by Imperial authorities for partisan purposes. They were generally anti-Muscovite in tone, as the title of the very first pamphlet, printed in Nuremberg in 1561, suggests: "Very gruesome, shocking, unheard-of true new tidings of the cruel tyranny of the Muscovite committed against the Christian prisoners abducted from Livonia, both men and women, virgins, and small children . . ."[41] Directly under this title is a well-wrought woodcut graphically depicting the Muscovite atrocities mentioned in the text (see fig. 14). It displays (according to the text) how the Muscovites slaughtered young children, "nailing their tender little hearts to trees," and how they

---

[36] For Livonian correspondence, see Friedrich G. Bienemann, ed., *Briefe und Urkunden zur Geschichte Livlands in den Jahren 1558–1562;* Carl C. G. Schirren, ed., *Quellen zur Geschichte des Untergangs livländischer Selbständigkeit* and *Neue Quellen zur Geschichte des Untergangs livländischer Selbständigkeit.*

[37] For correspondence among princes in the Empire, see August Kluckhohn, ed., *Briefe Friedrichs des Frommen,* 1:64ff., 70, 211; Georgii V. Forsten, ed., *Akty i pis'ma k istorii Baltiskogo voprosa,* 130ff., 153ff.; and Pierre de Vaissière, *Charles de Marillac,* 378ff.

[38] Karl H. von Busse, ed., "Deutsche Reichtags-Verhandlungen über Livland." Also see Eduard Reimann, "Das Verhalten des Reiches gegen Livland," and Gustav Sommerfeldt, "Die Betrachtung über ein Kreuzzug gegen Russland und die Türkei."

[39] Walter Platzhoff, "Das erste Auftauchen Rußlands und der russischen Gefahr in der europäischen Politik," and Erich Donnert, *Die livländische Ordensritterstaat und Russland.* Both of these treatments are to be used with great care. Platzhoff's ringing Russophobia may be taken as evidence of the persistence of the *russische Gefahr* through more than three centuries. Donnert's doctrinaire Marxist treatment goes to the opposite extreme—fear of Muscovy (*"diese künstlich gezüchtete russische Gefahr,"* as he calls it) was *wholly* the product of Livonian propaganda and was accepted by the reactionary German "ruling classes" alone.

[40] On early *Flugschriften,* see Margot Lindemann, *Deutsche Presse bis 1815,* 64–69; Robert E. Prutz, *Geschichte des deutschen Journalismus,* 98–116; and Matthias A. Shaaber, *Some Forerunners of the Newspaper in England.*

[41] Konstantin Höhlbaum, "Zeitungen über Livland," 121.

14. Title page of a German pamphlet depicting Muscovite atrocities in Livonia, 1561. Andreas Kappeler, *Ivan Groznyi im Spiegel der auslandischen Druckschriften seiner Zeit* (Bern, 1972).

raped "the most beautiful noble and common virgins" and afterward made a game of shooting their "privy parts."[42] In the course of the second half of the sixteenth century, nearly sixty such pieces were issued: fourteen from 1561 to 1570, thirty-four from 1571 to 1580, and nine from 1581 to 1582.[43] The vast majority of the pamphlets were in German and printed in Imperial cities; several were published in Livonia, Poland, and Italy. During the war, German, Polish, and Livonian historiography began to reflect the basic message of the pamphleteers—that Ivan was a godless, cruel invader, bent on destroying Livonia and indeed all Christendom.[44] During the first two decades of the conflict, references to Ivan and the Livonian war are found in only a handful of histories. In the next two decades—the 1580s and 1590s—the number of histories more than doubled. Approximately thirty historical texts—local histories, histories of the war, universal histories, historical compendia—over the entire period (1562–99) contain critical references to Ivan and the Livonian conflict.

Events within Muscovy also drew the attention of Europeans. In the 1570s, printed reports from diplomats, merchants, and resident tradesmen began to appear, telling of unspeakable atrocities perpetrated by Ivan IV at the Muscovite court (see fig. 15). The earliest such account is *Truthful New Tidings* (n.p., 1571), a product of official Polish propaganda: a one-time Polish prisoner of war in Moscow was deposed by a Polish border officer, who then sent the critical report to Sigismund. The Polish pamphlet of 1571 describes Ivan's punitive raids on the Russian cities of Tver, Novgorod, and Pskov.[45] This item was followed by *Actual Truthful Description* or *Brief Trustworthy Tidings* (Frankfurt, 1572), which, though of unclear provenance, seems to be the work of one or more eyewitnesses. Like the *Truthful New Tidings*, it reports Ivan's attack on Tver, Pskov, and Novgorod as well as other activities.[46] The *News from Diverse Places in the World* (Florence, 1572) is also of mysterious origins. The anonymous author wrote of a conspiracy against Ivan involving a group of nobles and the Poles.[47] Further information regarding Ivan's murderous experiment was made available in two printed works of the 1580s. The first was by Alessandro Guagnini, an Italian who entered

---

[42] Höhlbaum, "Zeitungen über Livland," 121.

[43] For a bibliography, see Andreas Kappeler, *Ivan Groznyi im Spiegel der ausländischen Druckschriften seiner Zeit*, 253–58. Five of the pamphlets have no date and have been omitted.

[44] Ibid., 37–38, 44–45, 51–53, 69–73, 77–82, 87–91, 102–4.

[45] *Warhaftige Newe Zeitung* (n.p., 1571). See Kappeler, *Ivan Groznyi im Spiegel der ausländischen Druckschriften*, 40–41, and Kappeler, "Die letzten Oprichninajahre," 6–7.

[46] *Eigenliche Warhaftige Beschreibung* or *Kurtze glaubwürdige Zeitung* (Frankfurt, 1572). See Kappeler, *Ivan Groznyi im Spiegel der ausländischen Druckschriften*, 41–42, and Kappeler, "Die letzen Oprichninajahre," 7–12.

[47] *Avisi di diversi luoghi del Mondo* (Florence, 1572). *Avisi*'s source may be one of Schlichting's reports regarding Muscovite affairs then in currency in Italy. See Kappeler, *Ivan Groznyi im Spiegel der ausländischen Druckschriften*, 43.

15. Ivan IV as portrayed in a German pamphlet, second half of the sixteenth century. Andreas Kappeler, *Ivan Groznyi im Spiegel der auslandischen Druckschriften seiner Zeit* (Bern, 1972).

Polish military service about 1556. In addition to being a soldier, he evidently had scholarly pretensions, and it was this combination, together with his life in the service of the Polish crown, that led him to write and publish his influential *Description of European Sarmatia* (Cracow, 1578).[48] Guagnini's account of the murderous activities of Ivan IV's *oprichnina* was drawn from the unpublished writings of Albert Schlichting, a German in Polish military service during the first phase of the Livonian war.[49] Schlichting was probably captured with Lithuanian forces at Ozerishche in late 1564 and taken to Moscow, where he served as an assistant to the tsar's doctor until he fled to Poland in 1570. While in Moscow he witnessed the height of the *oprichnina* terror, and upon his return to Poland he drafted two reports describing how "the grand prince executed his nobles and citizens."[50] The second eyewitness account of Ivan's excesses printed in the 1580s was by Johann Taube and Elbert Kruse.[51] Taube and Kruse were Livonian officials who fell into Muscovite hands at the onset of the war and became *oprichniki*. In 1571 Taube and Kruse fled to Poland, where they wrote *The Shocking, Cruel, and Unheard-of Tyranny of Ivan Vasil'evich* (n.p., 1582) (see fig. 16).[52] This tract, like Schlichting's and Guagnini's, is an inflammatory indictment of Ivan's merciless tyranny.

Despite growing interest in Muscovy in the 1560s and 1570s, little new information beyond that found in the accounts of the first half of the sixteenth century was available to European readers. Not counting some bawdy poems published by George Turberville in 1587,[53] only one of the English ethnographic reports mentioned above was printed before the appearance of Hakluyt's compendium in 1589—a mysterious version of Chancellor edited and translated by one Clement Adams.[54] The anti-Muscovite pamphlets produced in the course of the Livonian conflict provided shocking accounts of the misbehavior of Russian soldiers and their tsar, but offered no overview of Muscovite life. The same might be said of the printed European descriptions of Ivan IV's putative reign of terror: they overflowed with bloody *personalia* but were bereft of more general ethnographic information. Before the ap-

---

[48] Guagnini (1560). On Guagnini, see the sources cited in Bibliography 4 below.

[49] On Guagnini's reliance on Schlichting, see Kappeler, *Ivan Groznyi im Spiegel der ausländischen Druckschriften*, 54, and Hugh Graham, "Guagnini, Alessandro," 174.

[50] Schlichting (1571b), 272. On Schlichting, see the sources cited in Bibliography 4 below.

[51] On Taube and Kruse, see the sources cited in Bibliography 4 below.

[52] The identity of the authors was long confused by a manuscript attributed to a certain "Georg von Hoff." Adelung, for example, considered Taube / Kruse and Hoff as separate pieces. See Friedrich von Adelung, *Kritisch-literarische Übersicht der Reisenden in Russland*, 1:350. That "Hoff" is a textual variant of Taube and Kruse's treatise was demonstrated by A. I. Braudo, "Poslanie Taube i Kruze k gercogu Ketleru."

[53] Turberville (1568).

[54] Adams's translation was apparantly published in 1554, but no copy of it survives. An English version of the text appears in Eden (1555), 256ff., and was reprinted in Hakluyt (1589). Hakluyt reported that Chancellor's account was "written in the Latine tongue, by that learned yong man Clement Adams" (Adams/Chancellor [1553] 239).

Erſchreckliche/ greuliche

vnd vnerhorte Tyranney Iwan Waſilowitz/
jtzo regierenden Großfürſten in Muſcow/ſo er vorruckter Jar
an ſeinen Blutsuerwanten Freunden / Vnderfürſten/Baioaren vnd ge-
meinem Landtuolck vnmenſchlicher weiſe/ wider Gott vnd Recht erberm-
lich geübet. Den jenigen/welche ſeines theils/vnd ſich böſer mei-
nung an jhnen zubegeben willens/ zur warnung
in druck verfertiget.

Anno M. D. LXXXII.

16. Title page of Johann Taube and Elbert Kruse, *Erschreckliche greuliche und unerhorte Tyranney Iwan Wasilowictz jtzo regierenden Grossfürsten in der Muscow* (1582), depicting the atrocities of Ivan IV. Andreas Kappeler, *Ivan Groznyi im Spiegel der auslandischen Druckschriften seiner Zeit* (Bern, 1972).

pearance of Guagnini's account in 1578—itself largely based on Schlichting and Herberstein—interested readers had no place to turn for an accurate survey of Muscovite society but *Notes on the Muscovites*. Only three monographs about Russia had gone to press before 1550—Giovio, Fabri, and Campensé—and they were issued a total of five times. Additional informa-

tion on Muscovy was available in printed compendia such as Maciej z Miechowa's and Münster's, but these works did not offer extensive descriptions
of Russia. It is not unlikely that most European readers of the 1550s to 1580s
welcomed *Notes on the Muscovites* as the first printed book about Russia.

The high level of interest in Russia and the paucity of ethnographic information made Herberstein's book very popular. From 1549 to 1611, twenty-
two editions or substantive excerpts were printed in eight major cities.[55] The
only monograph explicitly devoted to Russia that was published with com-
parable frequency (eleven times) in the same period was Giovio's, largely because it was often appended to editions of *Notes on the Muscovites*. By the last
quarter of the century, Herberstein's book was recognized as the authoritative description of Russia. In 1568, for example, Turberville recommended
Herberstein in the highest possible degree:

> A dieu friend Parker, if thou list, to know the Russes well
> To Sigismundus booke repaire, who all the trueth can tell:
> For he long earst in message went unto the savage King,
> Sent by the Pole, and true report in each respect did bring,
> To him I recommend my selfe, to ease my penne of paine,
> And now at last do wish thee well, and bid farewell again.

Many eyewitness ethnographers of the second half of the sixteenth century
took Turberville's advice and turned to Herberstein's work for information
about Russia.[56] In most cases, Herberstein's influence was ambient and its
impact on later descriptions is therefore difficult to trace with exactitude. In
the 1550s and 1560s, many authors seem to have read Herberstein before
their departure for Russia or at the time they wrote their accounts after their
return home. They often borrowed freely from *Notes on the Muscovites* without acknowledgment. As Table 8 demonstrates, the only major sixteenth-
century ethnographer who seems not to have been influenced by Herberstein
was Heinrich von Staden, a German mercenary in the employ of Ivan IV.

Herberstein's influence was still stronger among ethnographers of the seventeenth century. His book was the most widely disseminated description of
Russia in the sixteenth century, and though the pace of reprinting of *Notes
on the Muscovites* slowed around 1600, the book remained extremely popular in the seventeenth century. Thus the fame of its author and the availabil-
ity of his book would have made it hard for any would-be ethnographer to
overlook *Notes on the Muscovites*. Moreover, the most widely disseminated
descriptions of Russia published after 1549—Possevino and Olearius—were
heavily dependent on Herberstein: the former was published eight times in
two languages and the latter was printed approximately twenty-five times in

[55] Herberstein, *Zapiski o Moskovii*, 389–91.
[56] Baron, "Herberstein's Image of Russia and Its Transmission" and "Influence in Sixteenth-
Century England of Herberstein's *Rerum moscoviticarum* commentarii"; Walter Leitsch, "Herberstein's Impact on the Reports about Muscovy."

Table 8. Printed sources of chief sixteenth-century eyewitness ethnographies

Author	Source
Chancellor	[Herberstein]
Jenkinson	[Herberstein]
Barberino	[Herberstein]
Randolph	[Herberstein]
Guagnini	[Herberstein], Schlichting
Printz	Herberstein
Possevino	Giovio, Campensé, Herberstein
Fletcher	[Herberstein], Horsey, Hakluyt items
Horsey	Fletcher, Hakluyt items

Note: Bracketed sources not acknowledged but probably used.

five languages.[57] Even readers who were ignorant of *Notes on the Muscovites* itself were likely to receive information from it via Possevino or Olearius. An investigation of the sources used by the major seventeenth-century ethnographers suggests that Herberstein was indeed very influential, as Table 9 indicates. Among the major eyewitness ethnographers of the seventeenth century, only Paul of Aleppo and Bernard Tanner seem not to have been directly influenced by *Notes on the Muscovites*. Paul probably did not know Herberstein's book: he was a Syrian cleric entirely unfamiliar with the corpus of Renaissance Moscovitica. It stands to reason that Tanner, an educated Habsburg official, would have at least been aware of the existence of *Notes on the Muscovites*. Indeed, he claimed that nothing in his work was new, suggesting he had read some account of Russia before writing his description.[58] Moreover, there is some slight evidence that he was told of Herberstein's tome (or some work like it) by resident Germans in Moscow who are known (from Krizhanich) to have possessed European descriptions of Russia, including Herberstein's.[59] Textual comparison, however, indicates that Tanner's work was independent of any printed book on Muscovy. As for the rest of the seventeenth-century ethnographers, all of them cited Herberstein directly or relied on a text that had drawn information from *Notes on the Muscovites*.

[57] On the publication of Possevino, see Graham's introduction to Possevino (1591), xxix. On the publication of Olearius, see Baron's preface to Olearius (1656), viii–ix.

[58] Tanner (1678), 3.

[59] Tanner's editor made this suggestion (ibid., vii–viii). Tanner's dependence on Herberstein is hardly certain, though. One does find parallel passages in Herberstein (1517–49), 2:4, and Tanner (1678), 69, both of which concern the part of Moscow called Naleika, literally "Pour," a place where foreigners are supposed to have imbibed. Yet Tanner's knowledge of Naleika need not have come from Herberstein: it was probably folklore within the foreigner community, and information on it was available in a variety of accounts; for example, Thevet (1575), 16; Fletcher (1591), 186; Olearius (1656), 116; Reutenfels (1671), 60–61, 94. On the possession of Renaissance Moscovitica by Germans living in Moscow, see Krizhanich (1663–66), 488.

Table 9. Printed sources of chief seventeenth-century eyewitness accounts

Account	Source
Massa, Bussow?	*[The Legend of the Life and Death of Dmitrii]* [a]
Margeret	[Bodin, Herberstein] [b]
Petreius	Maciej, Giovio, Herberstein, [Bussow]
Olearius	Giovio, Herberstein, Guagnini, Ulfeldt, Possevino, Petreius
Paul of Aleppo	
Collins	Thevet, [Herberstein]
Meyerberg	Herberstein, Guagnini, Possevino, Oderborn, Olearius
Reutenfels	Giovio, Fabri, Magnus, Herberstein, Possevino, Bussow, Petreius, Olearius
Wickhart	Herberstein, Olearius
Tanner	
Neuville	[Herberstein, Avril] [c]
Korb	Wickhart [Herberstein, Olearius] [d]

Note: Bracketed sources not acknowledged but probably used.

[a] *La Légende de la vie et de la mort de Démétrius, dernier Granc-Duc de Moscovie* (Amsterdam, 1606). On Massa's use of this obscure text, see G. Edward Orchard's introduction to Massa (1614), xxii–xxiii.

[b] In his introduction to Margeret (1607), Chester Dunning writes (xxv) that Bodin's "popular and influential works were certainly known to Margeret, whose portrayal of Muscovite absolutism echoes Bodin's ideas." This may be an overstatement. As an educated man, Margeret probably knew Bodin, but his description of Muscovite government is somewhere different from Bodin's. Bodin ([1576], 201) classified Muscovy (citing Herberstein) as a seigniorial monarchy; that is, a system in which the king is master of slave-subjects. Margeret, in contrast, simply writes ([1607], 28) that the Muscovite tsar is "absolute" and that his subjects call themselves slaves. Nowhere does he cite Bodin or offer a formal (Aristotelian) characterization of Muscovite government. If Margeret read Bodin's description of Russia in *Six Books,* then he knew of Herberstein's book, for Bodin cites it explicitly.

[c] On Neuville's use of Avril and Herberstein, see Lindsey Hughes's introduction to Neuville (1698), xxvii–xxviii.

[d] See the borrowing from Herberstein (1517–49), 1:32 and 95, in Korb (1700), 2:155–56, and the probable borrowing from Olearius (1656), 177, in Korb (1700), 2:163–64.

Notes on the Muscovites proved more popular among cosmographers than among ethnographers—understandably so, when we consider that cosmographers had no firsthand experience in Muscovy and thus were compelled to rely on visitors' accounts for information. Cosmographers had traditionally based their brief descriptions of Muscovy on Maciej z Miechowa or Giovio, the two most popular printed descriptions of Russia. In the second half of the sixteenth century, however, Herberstein's book supplanted all older texts and became the source of choice among the "Universal 'Geographistorians,'" as Bodin called those who "combined the history of the peoples with the geography." [60] The influence of *Notes on the Muscovites* may be seen in the cosmographies of William Cunningham, Alexander Guagnini, Abraham Ortelius, François de Belleforet (where, incidentally, we find one of the last

[60] Jean Bodin, *Method for the Easy Comprehension of History,* 38, 367.

positive descriptions of Muscovite kingship), André Thevet, David Chytreaus, Michael Neander, Giovanni Botero, Pierre d'Avity, Peter Heylyn, Herman Conring, and Samuel Pufendorf.[61]

Herberstein's stamp can also be seen on collections of travels to newly discovered or little-known areas of the world. Materials on Muscovy had been
included in travel compendia since Johannus Hutichius's aptly named *New
World* of 1532, which excerpted both Miechowa and Giovio. Similarly, Antonio Manuzio's *Voyages Made by Venice* (Venice, 1541) included reprints of
Barbaro and Contarini. The first compendium of travel to borrow large sections from *Notes on the Muscovites,* however, was Richard Eden's *Decades
of the Newe World* (1555), which consisted of a translation of a cosmography by Peter Martyr together with a large collection of travel accounts.
Among them one finds, in the section titled "Of Muscovy, Cathay and the
North Regions," selections "out of the books of Sigismundus Librus."
Though the first edition of Giovanni Battista Ramusio's pathbreaking *Concerning Navigations and Voyages,* published in 1559 (vol. 2), makes no mention of Herberstein, the second edition, issued in 1574, contained a complete
Italian translation of *Notes on the Muscovites.* Ramusio's work was the inspiration for Richard Hakluyt's well-known *Principall navigations* of 1589,
which, thanks largely to the efforts of the men of the English Muscovy Company, included a large collection of Moscovitica. The first edition did not
mention Herberstein, but the second, issued in 1598, republished an extract
from *Notes on the Muscovites* borrowed from Eden.[62] In the last quarter of
the century, two compendia devoted solely to Muscovy appeared, both of
which included material from Herberstein.[63] In 1630, *Notes on the Muscovites* and texts dependent on it were excerpted in two more compilations of
European Moscovitica.[64]

The Transmission of Herberstein's Image of Russia

It seems clear that knowledge of Herberstein was nearly universal among
late sixteenth- and seventeenth-century ethnographers, cosmographers, and
editors of travel compendia. But how did they use the text and to what extent were they influenced by its general interpretation of Muscovite government? Most ethnographers, particularly those with wide experience in Muscovy, did not follow Herberstein blindly. By the late 1570s, ethnographers

[61]Cunningham (1559), 18; Guagnini (1559); Ortelius (1570); Belleforest (1565), 1038; Belleforest (1575), 1824; Thevet (1575), 109–10; Chytreaus (1586); Neander (1586); Botero
(1591), 93–94; Avity (1637); Heylyn (1652), 510; Conring (1660s), 433–45; Pufendorf
(1682), 377–82.
[62]Hakluyt (1969), 2:405–12.
[63]Łasicki (1582); *Rerum* (1600).
[64]*Russia sue Moscovia* (1630); Boxhornius (1630).

had begun to use Herberstein as a measure by which they judged their own observations. Daniel Printz, for instance, wrote in 1578 that "great changes have occurred in many ways" since Herberstein described the Russians' treatment of ambassadors under Vasilii III, and he felt it necessary "to describe in brief how [men in his party] were received and maintained." [65] Possevino found that Herberstein's treatment of Muscovite religion was "not particularly useful for refuting or converting the Muscovites." In addition, the Italian cleric remarked with disgust that later German editions of Notes on the Muscovites had been so adulterated by "heretics" (i.e., Protestants) that their descriptions of Russian Orthodoxy were of even less value.[66] Olearius "did not find that Russian wives regard frequent blows and beating as a sign of intense love," as Herberstein contended.[67] Meyerberg remarked that Herberstein was wrong about the date of St. Sergei's death.[68] As the years progressed, some seventeenth-century ethnographers went further, arguing not only that Notes on the Muscovites contained erroneous details but that its general interpretation of Muscovite government might be outdated.[69] Olearius, for example, castigated those who thoughtlessly repeated the obsolete opinions of "old writers such as Herberstein" about the barbarity of the Russian prince.[70]

Yet despite occasional scuffles over minutiae and even occasional protestations of obsolescence, the ethnographers of the second half of the sixteenth and seventeenth centuries generally presented a picture of Muscovite government that was quite consistent with the view that was put forward in Notes on the Muscovites. Herberstein described Russian civic life in terms of four qualities:

1. Absolutism: the grand prince possesses complete control over the various political, administrative, and military organs of the realm.
2. Despotism: the grand prince exercises complete control over the property, particularly the landed property, of his subjects.

---

[65] Printz (1578), 47. Possevino ([1586] 14) disagreed.

[66] Possevino (1586), 37.

[67] Olearius (1656), 170.

[68] Meyerberg (1661), 100. For further examples of criticism of one ethnographer (or ethnographic opinion in general) by another (not necessarily Herberstein), see Barberino (1565), 2:20; Schlichting (1571a), 213; Ulfeldt (1575), 25; Staden (1578), 4; Printz (1578), 47; Possevino (1586), 3; Massa (1614), 8–9, 16; Petreius (1615), 143–44, 194; Aleppo (1655), 2:285–86; Olearius (1656), 175; Meyerberg (1661), 106–7, 117–19; Collins (1667), A3–4, 85; Reutenfels (1671), 2–3, 66, 108, 116–17, 121, 167, 199; Wickhart (1675), 185, 188, 214–15; Korb (1700), 1:284.

[69] On signs of Westernization in the European accounts, see Olearius (1656), 175; Collins (1667), 92–93; Reutenfels (1671), 60–61, 65, 73–74, 85, 88, 156–60; Wickhart (1675), 206–7, 244–45; Neuville (1698), 9, 13, 21, 40, 54, 54, 67; Korb (1700), 1:82–83, 106, 139–40, 156, 159, 170–71, 223, 244–45, 255, 264–65, 273, 2:129–30, 133–34, 137, 157–58, 197–98, 226.

[70] Olearius (1656), 175. Also see Korb (1700), 1:82–83.

Table 10. Interpretation of Russia as despotism in chief eyewitness accounts

Author	Written/printed	Absolutism	Despotism	Subjects as slaves	Quasi divinity
Herberstein	1517–49/1549	+	+	+	+
Chancellor[a]	1553–54/1589	+?	+		
Jenkinson[a]	1557–58/1589	+?			
Barberino[a]	1564–65/1658	+?			
Staden	1578–79	+	+		
Guagnini[b]	1578?/1578	+	+	+	+
Printz[b]	1578/1668	+	+	+	+
Possevino[b]	1586/1586	+	+	+	+
Fletcher[b]	1588–89/1591	+	+	+	
Margeret[a, c]	1607/1607	+	+	+	
Petreius[b]	1615/1615	+	+	+	+
Olearius[b]	1639–47/1647	+	+	+	+
Paul of Aleppo	1655–56		+		+
Meyerberg[b]	1661–63/1663?	+	+	+	+
Collins[a, c]	1667/1667	+	+	+?	+
Reutenfels[b]	1672–80/1680	+	+	+	+
Wickhart[b]	1675/1675			+	+
Tanner	1678/1680?				
Neuville[a]	1690?/1698	+?		+?	
Korb[b]	1698–99/1700	+	+	+	+

+ = characteristic is present in account; +? = characteristic is weakly present in account.
[a] May have known Herberstein's *Notes on the Muscovites*.
[b] Cited Herberstein's *Notes on the Muscovites* or borrowed its text verbatim.
[c] Cited or used a book reliant on Herberstein's *Notes on the Muscovites*.

3. Subjects as slaves: the subjects of the grand prince are his slaves.
4. Quasi divinity: the subjects of the grand prince worship him as they did God.

Table 10 indicates the presence or absence of these characteristics in major eyewitness ethnographies written between 1549 and 1700.

The distribution of the despotic interpretation among the later sixteenth- and seventeenth-century accounts suggests two things. First, when ethnographers used Herberstein (or some Herbersteinian text), the image of despotism tends to be present. Of the twelve authors who cited either Herberstein or a text that drew on it, eleven—the only exception being Carl Wickhart—recapitulated three or more of the basic characteristics of the despotic view.[71]

[71] Wickhart (1675) cited *Notes on the Muscovites* and, perhaps under the book's influence, wrote that "the Muscovites are all the slaves of the grand prince, whom they worship almost as a God" (246). Yet Wickhart did not ascribe universal power to the tsar or claim that Aleksei Mikhailovich had complete control over the property of his servitors. Rather, he described Aleksei's government as composed of high ministers who supervised the daily affairs of the state. At their head was Artemon Sergeevich Matveev, to whom Wickhart attributes significant power. Characteristically, Wickhart calls Matveev Aleksei's "primarius minister" (206). About private property or the lack of it Wickhart related nothing.

The degree to which ethnographers in this set were indebted to Herberstein for the specific terms of the despotic image varied considerably. Guagnini and Reutenfels represent one extreme: both cited *Notes on the Muscovites* extensively and both repeated almost verbatim Herberstein's description of the tsar's authority.[72] At the other extreme are Margeret and Collins: neither probably knew *Notes on the Muscovites* directly and neither characterized Muscovite despotism in terms similar to those found in Herberstein. Between these poles one encounters a wide range of degrees of dependence. Though each case should be investigated independently, it stands to reason that *direct* influence decreased over time. The authors of the early descriptions—certainly Guagnini and probably Printz, Possevino, and Fletcher—relied heavily on Herberstein, for his was the only major ethnography available. Moreover, no widely accepted stereotype of Russian rule was at hand. But as the image presented in *Notes on the Muscovites* became commonplace, lines of influence between Herberstein and later ethnographers grew increasingly indistinct. By the first quarter of the seventeenth century, it was not necessary to read *Notes on the Muscovites* to learn that the tsar was a despot whose slave-subjects worshiped him as a god—this idea was available in any number of Herbersteinian descriptions, and furthermore, it was "common knowledge" among educated Europeans. Thus, unless an ethnographer simply borrowed text from *Notes on the Muscovites* (e.g., Guagnini) or his characterization of Muscovite government was strikingly different from Herberstein's (e.g., Margeret), it is very difficult to determine whether a given depiction of despotism came from Herberstein, a text dependent on Herberstein, or common opinion. All that can be said is that with the spread of Herberstein's image, unmitigated influence became less likely.

The second conclusion that follows from Table 10 is this: ethnographers who did not know Herberstein omitted or gave scant attention to the despotic interpretation. None of the six eyewitness ethnographers who were ignorant of *Notes on the Muscovites* or who were only slightly familiar with the book repeated three or more of the elements of the despotic view. Chancellor, Jenkinson, and Barberino, for example, may have been aware of *Notes on the Muscovites*, but their understanding of Muscovite government was not influenced by it. They all offered a juridical depiction of the grand prince's authority—he personally made all judgments—which is both different in character from and weaker than Herberstein's understanding of tsarist tyranny.[73] Among the three early ethnographers, Chancellor alone followed Herberstein in suggesting that the grand prince was a universal landlord. Unlike Herberstein, however, the English captain heartily approved of this in-

---

[72] Guagnini (1560), 27; Reutenfels (1671), 101.

[73] Chancellor (1553), 233–34; Jenkinson (1557), 423; Barberino (1565), 2:8; Herberstein (1517–49), 1:32.

stitution, arguing that it ensured subservience among the Russian nobility. Would that English monarchs possessed such power:

> Oh that our sturdie rebels were had in the like subjection to knowe their duety towarde their princes. They may not say as some snudges in England say, I whould find the Queene a man to serve in my place, or make his friends tarrie at home if money have the upper hand. No, no, it is not so in this countrey: for hee shall make humble sute to serve the Duke.[74]

It is somewhat ironic that several decades after Chancellor praised what might be called Russian feudalism as a model, his countryman Fletcher—an avid reader of Herberstein—would condemn the same system as barbarous despotism.

Paul of Aleppo, Staden, Tanner, and Neuville provided additional accounts that did not follow the Herbersteinian model, perhaps because they were ignorant of *Notes on the Muscovites* or texts influenced by it. Paul, as we have seen, was a Middle Eastern cleric and could not have been familiar with Herberstein, though he noted many of the same institutions. He, like Chancellor, was an admirer of Muscovite monarchy, but he went much further than the Englishman in his praise. Paul was unwilling, however, to ascribe absolute power to the tsar. According to the Syrian cleric, Muscovy was a kind of paradisical theocracy in which the tsar was "like a waiting slave" to the patriarch.[75] Staden's account recapitulated some of Herberstein's view, but his general perspective is entirely independent of and different from the Habsburg ambassador's. A mercenary who had served Ivan IV for several years, Staden offered a fine-grained view of the life of the military elite in the era of the bloody *oprichnina* rather than an overview of Muscovite government. His personal experience with Ivan's terror told him that Russian absolutism was personal, not systemic. If "everything he [Ivan] orders is done," the subjects' obedience was due to Ivan's cruel tyranny and not to inborn servility.[76] Staden no doubt knew (as Herberstein had said) that highborn Russians called themselves slaves and identified the will of the tsar with that of God, but for him these facts had nothing to do with Ivan's madness or the regime that resulted from it. Similarly, the German adventurer's understanding of despotism was linked to Ivan's personal brutality, not the long-term patterns of Russian history. According to Staden, Ivan personally "deprived [disgraced servitors] of their estates, which were given to those [men] in the *oprichnina*."[77] Staden implied that Ivan's seizures were illegal, an accidental result of the disturbed tsar's arbitrary rule. Tanner and Neuville, like Staden, seem

[74] Chancellor (1553), 232.
[75] Aleppo (1655), 1:400–401, 2:230.
[76] Staden (1578), 55–56.
[77] Ibid., 18.

to have been largely ignorant of Herberstein's text. More important, they did not share Herberstein's purpose: whereas the Habsburg ambassador sought to provide a guide to Russian culture, Tanner and Neuville subordinated ethnography to history. They wanted to tell stories—Tanner of his embassy and Neuville of Sophia's rise and fall—and they dabbled in ethnography only as an afterthought. Tanner offered no general characterization of Russian government, though his account is full of interesting quotidian detail, and Neuville provided only cliches about the tsar's "tyranny" and his subjects' "slavery." [78]

Cosmographers and the editors of travel compendia repeated Herberstein's statements about Russian despotism with great frequency and fidelity. Unlike men who had been to Muscovy, cabinet-bound scholars did not have the luxury of direct observation. They borrowed information from whatever description was at hand, and more often than not this seems to have been *Notes on the Muscovites*. André Thevet, for example, simply transcribed the key "lives and property" passage of Herberstein's work in his *Universal Cosmography* of 1575.[79] The same description of the tsar's power may be found in Botero's *Universal Relations* of 1591 and Avity's *The World, or the General Description of its Four Parts* of 1637.[80] As the terms of Herberstein's account were appropriated and altered by later ethnographers, the influence of *Notes on the Muscovites* on cosmographers became increasingly indirect. Peter Heylyn, for example, received the despotic interpretation from Fletcher, who in turn was influenced by Herberstein.[81] The version of despotism found in Herman Conring's *Examination of the Great Commonwealths of the World* is more difficult to trace. In his treatment of Muscovy, Conring cited the two compendia of Moscovitica published in 1630, as well as Olearius. Yet his characterization was so general that it could have come from Herberstein, a Herbersteinian text, or common opinion: "The form of government is monarchical: it is plain tyranny and is of the same type of government that obtains in Persia, Turkey, and today in all of Asia." [82] Samuel Pufendorf's description of 1682 was equally indistinct and, as a result, difficult to trace: "The Form of Government here is an Absolute Monarchy; the Grand Duke, whom they call in their native Language Czar, being not tied up to any Laws or Rules, unto whom his Subjects are obliged to pay Obedience without reserve, so that they are no more than Slaves." [83] All that can be said with confidence is that the image of Muscovite government found in Conring and

---

[78] Neuville (1698), 50, 54, 57.

[79] Thevet (1575), 109–10.

[80] Botero (1591), 93; Avity (1637).

[81] Heylyn (1652), 522.

[82] Ibid., 440. The passage is very reminiscent of Fletcher (1591), 194. The text could have been transmitted to Conring via Boxhornius (1630) or *Russia seu Moscovia* (1630), both of which reprint Fletcher.

[83] Pufendorf (1682), 380.

Pufendorf is, if not drawn directly from Herberstein, perhaps Herberstein-ian in origin.

Conclusion

Would the European image of Russia have been different if the views of a less critical author had been memorialized in the first major printed account of Russia? The evidence suggests that it might well have been. For while *Notes on the Muscovites* was in fact a better description of Russian ways than any before it, it was not only the quality of Herberstein's eye that made his book the seminal text in European Moscovitica. The accident of good timing, the power of the printing press, and the pervasive habit of borrowing from "authoritative" texts all played a large role in ensuring that the views expressed in *Notes on the Muscovites* became in large measure the opinions of most educated Europeans. Had Milton's favorite, Chancellor, found his way to Russia a few years earlier, written a major description instead of a brief overview, published his observations in an elaborate Latin edition rather than an obscure booklet, and become the primary source of European intelligence on Russia, Europeans of the second half of the sixteenth century might have believed that Muscovy was ruled by an upright king instead of a tyrant. Nonetheless, one should not exaggerate the power of Herberstein's influence. Chancellor's image of Russian rule was at odds with what most European visitors actually observed in Russia. Thus one would imagine that even if the English navigator had written *Notes on the Muscovites,* his impression that Russia was governed by a just king would not have been received with great sympathy by later writers. The fact Herberstein wrote first definitely strengthened the impression his book made on the European understanding of Muscovite society, but so did the fact that his observations rang true for later ethnographers. From the point of view of men such as Fletcher, Olearius, and Reutenfels, the Habsburg ambassador was to be followed not only because he was an authority but also because he was right.

5

TYRANNIS SINE TYRANNO
Political Categories and the Origin of "Russian Tyranny"

> He uses his authority as much over ecclesiastics as laymen, and holds unlimited control over the lives and property of all his subjects.
>
> SIGISMUND VON HERBERSTEIN, 1549

> His authority (*or rather tyranny*) extends equally to both clergy and laymen and every sort of person, he freely and by his whim controls the lives and property of everyone.
>
> ALEXANDER GUAGNINI, 1578

> Because of its inhuman laws, all European nations with one voice call this illustrious tsardom a tyranny. And, in addition, they say that the tyranny here is not a common one, but the greatest.
>
> IURII KRIZHANICH, 1663

BOTH THE FRENCH mercenary Jacques Margeret and the Syrian archdeacon Paul of Aleppo had extensive experience in Muscovy, yet they conceived of Russian government in very different ways. Margeret believed that the Russian monarchy was "absolute": the tsar's powers were unbridled, his subjects were held in fearful subjection, and he treated the realm in large measure as his personal property.[1] For Paul, Muscovy was ruled by a laudable form of Caesaropapism. The tsar's authority was not unrestricted; he governed with the aid of magnates and high clerics, whom he greatly respected.[2] Russians did not fear their prince but revered him "nearly in the same light as they do the Messiah," for he was "the leader of the nation in religious observances." The grand prince did not capriciously confiscate the properties of his servitors, but instead they routinely bequeathed "all their

---

[1] Margeret (1607), 3, 27–28, 35–36.
[2] Aleppo (1655), 2:59; also see 1:259–60, 317.

property to the emperor, out of great love and veneration in which they hold their sovereign." If the Byzantine Greeks had maintained an enlightened regime such as he had observed in Muscovy, Paul reasoned wistfully, "they would have retained their empire to the present moment." [3]

Why were Margeret and Paul unable to agree on the character of Russian government? The primary reason is not found in contrasting experiences in Russia, though they were a contributing factor. Margeret's chief employer, Boris Godunov, brought a very different spirit to the Muscovite court than did Paul's host, Tsar Aleksei Mikhailovich. The former ruthlessly dealt with his rivals at court while the latter was renowned for his piety. Nonetheless, Boris and Aleksei were the leaders of a very conservative political system whose basic institutions changed little between 1600 (when Margeret arrived) and 1667 (the date of Paul's first departure). Further, Margeret's and Paul's disagreement probably did not result from differing literary influences, though they too played a role. It is true that Paul knew next to nothing of Herberstein and his tradition, so he was free to interpret Muscovite rule outside the strictures of the predominant European stereotype. But it appears that Margeret was also ignorant of Herberstein. One searches the pages of *The Russian Empire and the Grand Dutchy of Muscovy* in vain for citations of books on Muscovy or even tangible signs of unacknowledged borrowing. Margeret doubtless knew something of the Herbersteinian stereotype of Russia, but he was no more a slave to it than was Paul. At base, the contrast between Margeret's and Paul's Russia was cultural and conceptual. Paul was not a European, and thus he did not come to Russia with the same mental furniture as did men such as Margeret. The European travelers brought to Russia abstract political scientific ideas—"tyranny," "despotism," "absolute monarchy"—that they used, consciously or unconsciously, to conceptualize Muscovite monarchy. Margeret, for example, may well have absorbed the notion of absolute monarchy from Jean Bodin.[4] Paul was unlikely to have been familiar with any such political scientific text. The two visitors, in essence, saw the same thing, but they interpreted it through different conceptual lenses.

As we will see, political concepts had a significant impact on the way Europeans conceived of early Russian government. The ethnographers of the sixteenth and seventeenth centuries were by and large well-bred, highly educated, and politically aware gentlemen. Their general knowledge of political theory and practical experience at court taught them well the difference between a well-proportioned monarchy and a tyranny. Throughout the sixteenth century, European visitors applied this rough distinction to Russian government and acclaimed that the Russian tsar—particularly Ivan IV—was a tyrant, a rogue prince who had temporarily transgressed the bounds

[3] Ibid., 1:400–401, 2:32, 265.
[4] See Dunning's introduction to Margeret (1607), xxv–xxvi.

of well-ordered monarchical power. Seventeenth-century travelers, however, were confronted with a conceptual paradox: unlike their predecessors, the Romanovs were not tyrants, though the system they ruled manifested every mark of tyranny. The most theoretically astute ethnographers solved the problem of tyranny without a tyrant by classifying Russian government as a "despotism," a state in which the prince was permanently the master of "natural" slaves.

The Ethnographer as Renaissance Gentleman

Who were the foreigners and how did their identities shape the way they viewed Russia? In many ways, they were a very diverse group, as Table 11

Table 11. Biographical data on major eyewitness ethnographers of Russia, 1517–1700

Author/text	Vital dates	Nationality	Faith	Occupation
Herberstein (1517–49)	1486–1566	Imperial	Catholic	Diplomat
Chancellor (1553)	d.1556	English	Protestant	Navigator
Jenkinson (1557)	1530–1611	English	Protestant	Merchant
Barberino (1565)	1532–82	Italian	Catholic	Merchant
Taube and Kruse (1571)	fl. 1571	Livonian	Catholic	Diplomats, nobles in Muscovite service
Schlichting (1571a)	fl. 1571	German	Protestant?	Translator in Muscovite service
Staden (1578)	1542?–?	German	Catholic?	Mercenary
Printz (1578)	1546–1608	Imperial	Catholic	Diplomat
Ulfeldt (1579)	d. 1593	Danish	Protestant?	Diplomat
Horsey (1584–1621)	1573–1627	English	Protestant	Diplomat, merchant
Possevino (1586)	1533/34–1611	Papal	Catholic	Diplomat
Fletcher (1591)	1546–1611	English	Protestant	Diplomat
Peyerle (1606)	fl. 1606	German	Catholic?	Merchant
Margeret (1607)	1565?–1619	French	Protestant?	Mercenary in Muscovite service
Petreius (1608)	1570–1622	Swedish	Protestant	Diplomat
Massa (1610)	1587–1643	Dutch	Protestant	Merchant
Bussow (1611)	?–1617	German	Protestant	Mercenary in Muscovite service
Maskiewicz (1611)	fl. 1580–1632	Polish	Catholic	Diplomat, officer
Paul of Aleppo (1653)	fl. 1636–6	Syrian	Orthodox	Archdeacon of Aleppo
Olearius (1656)	1603–71	Holsteinian	Protestant	Diplomat
Collins (1667)	1619–70	English	Protestant	Doctor in Muscovite service
Meyerberg (1661)	1612–88	Imperial	Catholic	Diplomat
Reutenfels (1671)	fl. 1671	Polish	Catholic	Agent?
Wickhart (1675)	fl. 1675	Imperial	Catholic	Diplomat
Tanner (1678)	fl. 1678	Polish	Catholic	Diplomat
Neuville (1698)	fl. 1698	French	Catholic?	Polish agent?
Korb (1700)	1670–1741	Austrian	Catholic	Diplomat

suggests. Each of the characteristics described in Table 11—the timing of their visit, their nationality, their faith, and their mission—had a distinct effect on the way the ethnographers viewed Muscovy. The importance of timing can be seen in the contrast between Richard Chancellor's depiction of Russian rule and those of later sixteenth- and seventeenth-century ethnographers. Chancellor praised the authority of Ivan IV over his men, whereas nearly all later accounts, written under the influence of Herberstein and with the horrific events of Ivan IV's reign in mind, offered a much more critical assessment of the tsar.[5] National and political allegiances also played a role in molding the foreigners' opinions. Anthony Jenkinson, whose queen had just been granted extensive trading privileges in Russia, had a rather favorable opinion of Ivan IV, while Taube and Kruse, whose native Livonia had recently been decimated by the Russians, took a rather different view of the man they called the "terrible tyrant of Moscow."[6] Religion also divided the observers. Samuel Collins, a Protestant, believed the Muscovites were idolaters for worshiping "a painted piece of board."[7] Catholics such as Possevino understood Russian Orthodoxy, like all Orthodoxy, to be apostate. "Muscovites adopted their Schism from the Greeks," wrote the Italian cleric, "who were themselves schismatics, but they subsequently became separated from the Greeks as well."[8] Typically, Johann Korb, a Catholic, disagreed with Collins on the subject of icon worship, writing that "the signal honor which the Russians unanimously pay to saints and their images is not to be censured."[9] Profession exercised a subtle influence on the travelers' ethnographic imaginations. Diplomats, who were generally well-educated men who spent but little time in Muscovy, tended to offer abstract overviews, as can be seen in Giles Fletcher's schema of Russian society.[10] Mercenaries and resident specialists—that is, men who often lived for extended periods in Muscovy—generally provided detailed, bottom-up representations. Heinrich von Staden, for example, a soldier with over twelve years' experience in the service of Ivan IV, described "how one lives and behaves" in Russia as an insider.[11]

Despite the various factors dividing the ethnographers, they shared an identity that clearly distinguished them as a group from the Muscovites. They were all in some sense Renaissance gentlemen—well-bred, literate, politically savvy notables whose lives and mentalities had been shaped by the major cultural currents that had swept Europe in the sixteenth and seven-

---

[5] Chancellor (1553), 232.

[6] Jenkinson (1557), 438–39; Taube and Kruse (1571), 30.

[7] Collins (1667), 89–92.

[8] Possevino (1586), 28.

[9] Korb (1700), 1:286. Some Catholics, however, thought the Russians were too enthusiastic in their worship of icons. Barbarino wrote: "They are very superstitious with Saints' images, and they adore Saint Nicholas almost without mentioning any other God" ([1565] 1:15).

[10] Fletcher (1591), 171. See Table 5 in Chapter 2 above.

[11] Staden (1578), 6.

teenth centuries. Their Russian counterparts, as the foreigners never failed to point out, were cut from very different cultural cloth. Indeed, it is in the visitors' observations on this cultural difference that we can see the specificity of their collective European identity. By and large, the foreigners were men educated in the Humanist tradition, as is witnessed by the very fact that they wrote ethnographies, an archetypal Renaissance scientific pursuit. The Russians they met—magnates, clergymen, and commoners alike—knew little or nothing of the liberal arts and sciences, a fact that clearly shocked the foreigners.[12] Isaac Massa, for example, told his readers that there was "good reason to be astounded at the ability, finesse, and boldness Boris [Godunov] showed in his career," particularly because "he could neither read nor write."[13] Further, as children of the Reformation, the ethnographers believed a literate understanding of the holy texts to be necessary for a true Christian, regardless of sect. The foreigners—Protestant and Catholic—often observed that neither Russian commoners nor clerics understood the first thing about true Christian doctrine but instead held fast to "superstitions" without any biblical foundation.[14] The Russians refused to be corrected, the foreigners noted, because they believed they were the "only true Christians."[15] Even if Russians had the inclination to return afresh to the holy books, they could not, for almost no one in Muscovy (high clerics included) could read Greek or Latin.[16] "Thus it cannot be doubted that their faith, or the substance of their belief," concluded Olearius, "is Christian; but . . . the way they express this belief is questionable, and it turns out, in fact, to be very poor."[17] A final collective difference between the visitors and their Russian hosts was this: the ethnographers were schooled in the "courteous" man-

[12] On the lack of learning among the Muscovites, see Ulfeldt (1575), 19; Printz (1578), 29–30; Possevino (1586), 28; Fletcher (1591), 226–27; Margeret (1607), 21–22; Maskiewicz (1611), 55–56; Massa (1614), 71, 111, 143; Olearius (1656), 130–31, 141, 269; Meyerberg (1661), 35, 85, 96, 103–4, 112; Collins (1667), 2–3; Reutenfels (1671), 73–74, 97–99, 156–60; Wickhart (1675), 244–45; Tanner (1678), 105; Milton (1682), 341; Neuville (1698), 54, 61; Korb (1700), 2:162–63, 194.

[13] Massa (1614), 36.

[14] Gabriele Scheidegger, *Perverses Abendland—barbarisches Russland*, 223–58. On Russians' ignorance of religious doctrine, see Chancellor (1553), 236; Adams/Chancellor (1553), 266; Jenkinson (1557), 442, 443; Ulfeldt (1575), 17, 19; Possevino (1586), 58; Fletcher (1591), 269, 270; Margeret (1607), 21–22; Maskiewicz (1611), 27–28; Olearius (1656), 236–37; Meyerberg (1661), 96, 103–4; Collins (1667), 2–3, 91–92; Reutenfels (1671), 115–16, 138; Wickhart (1675), 228–29, 247; Tanner (1678), 104–6; Korb (1700), 2:163, 173–74.

[15] On the Russians' belief that they were the "only true Christians," see Chancellor (1553), 236; Adams/Chancellor (1553), 268; Staden (1578), 114; Possevino (1586), 25, 27, 79; Fletcher (1591), 290; Bussow (1611), 83, 123, 158; Maskiewicz (1611), 48–49; Massa (1614), 61, 132; Meyerberg (1661), 103–4; Reutenfels (1671), 171–75.

[16] On Russians' ignorance of Classical languages, see Chancellor (1553), 236; Adams/Chancellor (1553), 266; Ulfeldt (1575), 19; Staden (1578), 94; Printz (1578), 32; Possevino (1586), 12, 52, 53, 58; Margeret (1607), 21–22; Maskiewicz (1611), 55–56; Petreius (1615), 142–43; Olearius (1656), 239; Meyerberg (1661), 87–88, 112; Reutenfels (1671), 97–99, 156–60; Wickhart (1675), 244–45; Neuville (1698), 24, 61; Gordon (1699), 54.

[17] Olearius (1656), 234.

ners characteristic of elite Italianate society; the Russians manifestly were not. The Muscovites knew little of European decorum before the end of the seventeenth century, and thus the foreigners uniformly reported that most Russians were dirty, smelly, and without manners, particularly at table.[18] Jacob Ulfeldt, for instance, was disgusted by the "vile and undignified" table manners of even the tsar: "One has never seen anyone, regardless of situation or station, who is so uncivilized at table as the highly praised tsar."[19]

It is clear that the foreigners self-servingly exaggerated their differences with the Russians so as to cast themselves in the best light. Though the Muscovites knew little of Humanism, Russian churchmen knew more than a little about Byzantine Greek thought; though it is true that most Russian notables could not read the Bible, their faith can hardly be called "superstitious" on that account; and though Russian courtiers did not practice the niceties of Renaissance courtesy, they certainly observed a highly mannered style of politeness that was (apparently) lost on most Europeans. Yet despite the inflated faultfinding of the foreigners' descriptions of Russian learning, religion, and manners, the Europeans did register a very real cultural difference. They were Renaissance gentlemen observing men who were not, however learned, pious, and polite their hosts might be in a Muscovite sense. And, as we will presently see, this difference powerfully affected the way the foreigners conceptualized Russian government.

The Political Categories of Renaissance Gentlemen

Just as the gentlemen-ethnographers shared certain historically and culturally specific assumptions about the education, faith, and manners of "civilized" persons, so too they had in common an understanding of "politic" government; that is, the proper constitution of legitimate political power. To be sure, we find a diversity of political opinion among the foreigners. The absolutist Margeret held a certain admiration for "the good order and civil administration" he found in Russia, whereas the civic Humanist Fletcher had nothing but disdain for the "intollerable servitude" he believed was the hallmark of Muscovite government.[20] Their particular political proclivities aside,

---

[18] Scheidegger, *Perverses Abendland—barbarisches Russland*, 41–132. Examples are too numerous to cite exhaustively. On Russians' dirtiness, see Olearius (1656), 155; Meyerberg (1661), 35–36, 49, 67–69, 171; Reutenfels (1671), 147–48; Tanner (1678), 34, 38; Neuville (1698), 57, 59; Gordon (1699), 43, 44. On stench, see Meyerberg (1661), 35–37; Tanner (1671), 38. On intemperance, see Olearius (1656), 116, 143, 143, 198, 283; Reutenfels (1671), 141–42; 145–46; Wickhart (1675), 257–59; Tanner (1678), 69, 71, 109; Korb (1700), 2:146–47; Perry (1716), 227–29. On poor table manners, see Olearius (1656), 141; Meyerberg (1661), 35–37; Reutenfels (1671), 147–48. For general descriptions of "the Muscovite character," see Olearius (1656), 133; Wickhart (1675), 248; Tanner (1678), 109; Neuville (1698), 57.
[19] Ulfeldt (1575), 31–32.
[20] Margeret (1607), 3; Fletcher (1591), 190.

the fact that they all shared the cultural background of Renaissance gentlemen and that they all viewed Russian government in a strikingly similar fashion strongly suggest that the ethnographers indeed held certain basic political principles in common. Their political beliefs may be reasonably inferred
from two sources, Classical political texts and contemporary political philosophy, both of which enjoyed wide currency among Renaissance elites. Of
the former, Aristotle's *Politics* was far and away the most important work.
First made available to European readers in William of Moerbeke's Latin
translation of 1260, it was by the sixteenth century certainly among the most
widely available Classical political texts.[21] Before 1500, there were sixteen
printings of some or all of the *Politics* in three languages and in six cities.[22] In
the sixteenth century the *Politics* was disseminated much more widely: 110
editions including some or all of the book were pressed in sixteen cities and
six languages (Latin, Greek, French, Italian, Spanish, and English) over the
course of the century.[23] The *Politics* was widely read, commented upon, and
taught in universities.[24] For example, Richard Hakluyt, the editor of the best
early modern collection of European voyages to Muscovy, lectured on the *Politics* at Christ's Church, Oxford, from 1581 to 1583.[25] The ethnographers
almost never cited Aristotle by name: only Olearius did so.[26] Neither did
they often tacitly borrow passages verbatim from the *Politics:* only Fletcher
did so.[27] Nonetheless, the ethnographers, particularly those with a Humanist education, knew Aristotle's political thought and were influenced by it.

The visitors also would have been conversant with the most important political doctrines of their own time. Many of the envoys and residents were
intimately involved with high politics, both professionally, as courtiers and
royal servants, and scientifically, as practitioners of ethnographic science, an
integral part of which was the description of the form of a commonwealth.
Only rarely did the ethnographers indicate their familiarity with contemporary political theory by venturing into the realm of positive political philosophy. Antonio Possevino, to offer a singular example, penned a commentary
on Bodin, Morney, and Machiavelli.[28] More often traces of contemporary
political theories can be obliquely seen in the Europeans' descriptions of

[21] On the reception of the *Politics* in the late Middle Ages, see Quentin Skinner, *Foundations of Modern Political Thought*, 2:349. Also see F. Edward Cranz, "Aristotelianism in Medieval Political Theory."

[22] Miroslav Flodr, *Incunabula classicorum*, 30.

[23] F. Edward Cranz, *Bibliography of Aristotle Editions*, 216–18.

[24] James Bass Mullinger, *University of Cambridge*, 3:135–36; Charles B. Schmitt, *John Case and Aristotelianism in Renaissance England*, 41; William T. Costello, *Scholastic Curriculum at Seventeenth-Century Cambridge*, 7–11.

[25] Lawrence V. Ryan, "Richard Hakluyt's Voyage into Aristotle."

[26] Olearius (1656), 151, 173.

[27] Fletcher borrowed his "Sophismata of secretes" from Aristotle. See Fletcher (1591), 194, and *Politics*, V.1313a.39–b.30

[28] Antonio Possevino, *Iudicium . . . Joannis Bodini, Philippi Mornaei et Nicolai Machiavelli quibusdam scriptis.*

Russia: Fletcher may have modeled his work on Sir Thomas Smith's *Of the English Commonwealth;* Margeret may have been influenced by Bodin's doctrine of absolutism; Neuville mentioned Machiavelli's *Prince.*[29] Like Aristotle, contemporary political philosophy exercised an ambient influence on the ethnographies.

What, then, did the ethnographers learn from the *Politics* and contemporary political philosophy? Aristotle, first of all, offered the fundamental definition of a commonwealth. Unlike the family or the household, the commonwealth is a natural alliance of freemen in pursuit of the highest end, which Aristotle called the "good life" or "civic virtue."[30] Forms of government that allow the pursuit of the "good life" seek what Aristotle called the "common advantage" and "are rightly framed"; those that do not seek instead "the rulers' own advantage" and are "faulty." Aristotle incorporated this fundamental distinction between "rightly framed" and "faulty" polities in his classification of constitutions, which might be considered his second major contribution to Renaissance political mentalities. Sovereignty, Aristotle argued, may either be held by one, by some, or by all. If the sovereign authority seeks the "common advantage," then these constitutions are designated, respectively, monarchy (or "kingship"), aristocracy, or "political." If the sovereign authority rather seeks some personal or partial advantage, then they are called, respectively, tyranny, oligarchy, and democracy.[31]

The issue of the impact of Renaissance political doctrine on the ethnographers is much more complex. Civic Humanism, resistance theory, absolutism, divine right theory, constitutionalism, and contractualism all differed among themselves, and one might imagine that each of these doctrines exercised a different sort of influence on the ethnographers. Nonetheless, smoothing the edges of all these theories, one can see a single thread working through the entire corpus of sixteenth- and seventeenth-century European political thought. Generally speaking, Renaissance political thinkers accepted Aristotle's premise that legitimate governments should seek the common good and not some sectarian interest. The Stagerite's "good life," however, proved much too abstract for the specific intellectual and political context of Renaissance Europe. First, Aristotle's doctrine of the state took no account of Christian "natural law" (*lex naturalis* or *ius naturale*)—the divinely imprinted sense, usually understood as "reason,"[32] that enabled men to determine what was just and thereby to create commonwealths consistent with the divine order.[33] The fact that such a moral sense existed below divine law (*lex*

---

[29] See Richard Pipes's introduction to Giles Fletcher, *Of the Russe Commonwealth;* Chester Dunning's introduction to Margeret (1607), xxv–xxvi; Neuville (1698), 47.

[30] Aristotle, *Politics,* I.1.1–2; also see III.5.10–15, III.4.3.

[31] Ibid., III.5.2–4.

[32] Locke wrote typically: "The State of Nature has a Law of Nature to govern it, which obliges every one: And Reason . . . is that Law" (*Two Treatises of Government,* 289).

[33] Skinner, *Foundations of Modern Political Thought,* 2:148–49.

divina) and above positive human laws (*lex humana, lex civilis,* or *ius positivum*) was taken for granted by virtually every Renaissance scholar. Further, Aristotle's "good life" was not sufficiently attuned to the basic constitutional question of the age of Renaissance princes and absolutist monarchs: What would be the limits of sovereign authority in postfeudal Europe? Opinions varied, and therein lies much of the history of early modern political thought. But on one principle most thinkers agreed: whatever the form of the commonwealth, natural law dictated that its sovereign power should preserve the liberty and property of each and every subject. The most widespread argument in favor of limiting the state's ability to attach person and property was this: men were born reasonable and free; realizing that life outside political society (in the "state of nature") was insecure, they reasonably (by the operation of the "law of nature") surrendered some of their freedom to a sovereign power and entered into civil society; this transfer of autonomy from subject to sovereign was designed solely to save some measure of liberty and property from the misfortunes of extrasocial life. Thus legitimate governments (monarchies, aristocracies, and "political" regimes) preserved liberty and property, while defective governments (tyrannies, oligarchies, and ochlocracies) did not.

The thesis that natural law required states to safeguard individual liberty and property may be seen in the most diverse political theories throughout the sixteenth and seventeenth centuries. Jean Bodin, writing in the 1570s, assured his readers that before the advent of society "nature hath given unto every one to live at his owne pleasure, bound within no lawes." This fundamental freedom, however, proved to be unsustainable: "Force, violence, ambition, covetousness, and desire of revenge" drove the weak into positions of dependence on the strong. As a result, "that full and entire libertie by nature given to every man" was lost and sovereignty emerged. Yet the institution of political rule did not entail the complete loss of the prepolitical freedoms, for under any legitimate constitution "the law of nature . . . reserveth unto everie man his libertie, and the soveraigntie over his owne goods." [34] About eighty years after Bodin, Thomas Hobbes rehearsed similar arguments. Men were born free by "the right of nature." Hobbes agreed, however, that original liberty could not be sustained, for all men abused their natural liberty and thus began the war "of every man against every man." Happily, though, men proved reasonable and, according to "the laws of nature," transferred their original rights to a sovereign power, thereby preserving some measure of liberty. The end of legitimate government, then, was to maintain some share of original liberty by preventing anarchy. [35] Finally, near the end of the seventeenth century, John Locke reiterated the natural law argument for the preservation of liberty and property with unmatched vigor. Men were born in a

[34] Jean Bodin, *Six Bookes of a Commonweale,* 14, 47, 203.
[35] Thomas Hobbes, *Leviathan,* 86, 85, 159, 153.

"State of perfect Freedom." This original liberty, however, was "very uncertain, and constantly exposed to the Invasion of others." Uncertainty, Locke proposed, made men "willing to joyn in Society with others who are already united, or have a mind to unite for the mutual Preservation of their Lives, Liberties and Estates, which I call by the general Name, Property." For Locke, the state's power extended no further than its mandate, "the Preservation of [subjects'] Property." [36]

For both Aristotle and the Classical political philosophers, the name for illegitimate monarchy was of course "tyranny" (*tyrannis*). It followed from Aristotle's "common interest" criterion of political legitimacy that tyranny was "monarchy ruling in the interest of the monarch." According to Aristotle, the tyrant willfully confused two distinct social units, each with its own goal: the household (*oikos*), which the master (*despotes*) owns and uses for his personal profit, and the kingdom (*basileia*), which the king (*basileus*) governs for the benefit of his subjects. The tyrant wrongfully asserts the power of the master over the kingdom, or, as the Stagerite himself put it, exerts "despotic power over the political community," where "despotic" means rule in the interest of the king *cum* master. In Aristotle, "tyranny" was rather a quality of a rogue prince than an attribute of a political system. The tyrant personally created a state of tyranny by ruling in an oppressive fashion, and it was to be expected that in the normal course of events the tyrant would be deposed and another form of government instituted. Regimes, Aristotle proposed, shifted in regular cycles: monarchies become aristocracies, aristocracies become oligarchies, oligarchies become tyrannies, tyrannies become democracies, and so on. [37] Moreover, the rule of tyrants was particularly prone to instability because rogue kings, having violated the public trust, did not enjoy the support of the population.

In accord with their emphasis on natural laws protecting liberty and property, Renaissance theorists altered Aristotle's definition of tyranny, emphasizing its "despotic" side. [38] For them, the tyrant was guilty first and foremost of "domesticating" the persons and properties of his subjects. This shift in stress is clear in Bodin's definition of "tyrannicall Monarchie," according to which the tyrant is a prince who, "contemning the lawes of nature and nations, imperiously abuseth the persons of his free borne subjects, and their goods as his owne." [39] Hobbes sarcastically dismissed the word "tyranny" as a slur used by those "that are discontented under monarchy"; but Locke's definition was much more characteristic of his age: a tyrant is a ruler whose

---

[36] Locke, *Two Treatises*, 287, 386, 368–69.

[37] *Politics* III.5.4, 5, 10.

[38] On the history of the ideas of tyranny and despotism, see Richard Koebner, "Despot and Despotism"; Melvin Richter, "Despotism"; Johannes Winckelmann, "Despotie, Despotismus"; Hella Mandt, "Tyrannis, Despotie."

[39] Bodin, *Six Bookes*, 200. Also see the formulation on 210: "Tirannicall Monarchie is that where one man treading under foot the lawes of God and nature, abuseth his free borne subjects as his slaves: and other mens goods as his owne."

"Actions are not directed to the preservation of the Properties of his People, but the satisfaction of his own Ambition, Revenge, Covetousness, or any other irregular Passion."[40] Despite the natural law emendation of Aristotle's concept, "tyranny" remained for most the fragile, temporary creation of a rogue prince, not a kind of society. Roman history (which all gentlemen read), practical experience (particularly for citizens of city-states), and the teachings of the Classical theorists provided ample evidence that evil monarchs personally lapsed into tyranny. Bodin's tyrant, for example, is a self-serving usurper, "which without the consent of the people, had by force of fraud possessed himselfe to the state; and of a companion made himselfe their master."[41] Students of politics from Machiavelli to Montesquieu followed Classical thinkers (particularly Polybius)[42] in arguing that tyrannies were impermanent because all regimes moved through regular cycles. Bodin, for instance, offered an extended digression on the "six perfect conversions or changes of Commonweales." Finally, most theorists agreed that tyrannies were particularly subject to the winds of change precisely because they lacked legitimacy in the eyes of free subjects. Bodin told his readers that "tyrannicall states and governments [are] soone to fall, and many tyrants in short time slain." Why? Because "men free borne, and lords of their owne goods in a royall Monarchie, if one would make them slaves, or take from them that theirs is, they would not take it, but easily rebell, bearing noble harts, nourished in libertie, and not abastardised with servitude."[43]

"Tyranny" in the sense of rogue kingship was not the only concept for overmighty monarchy in the Classical-Renaissance canon. Aristotle also conceived of a sort of monarchy that was in essence a stable tyranny, which he called "despotic rule" (*arkhe despotike*). Ordinary tyrannies were unstable because they aroused resentment among once free subjects. Not all men, however, were free. Early in the *Politics* Aristotle had defended the notion that some men were "natural slaves," men who "are capable of belonging to another . . . and who participate in reason so far as to apprehend it but not to possess it." Without reason, the natural slave is incapable of pursuing the good life and must, for his own benefit, place himself or be forcibly placed under the domination of a despot. Like the tyrant, the despot controlled the life and property of his subjects. But the despot ruled "legally," for his domestication of the *res publica* and *res privata* were in accordance with the customs of the realm, and permanently, for natural slaves would not rebel against tyrannical governance. Aristotle noted that examples of despotic rule were to be found "among some of the barbarians," for they "are more servile in their nature than the Greeks, and the Asiatics than the Europeans."[44]

---

[40] Hobbes, *Leviathan*, 105; Locke, *Two Treatises*, 416–17.
[41] Bodin, *Six Bookes*, 210.
[42] Polybius, *Histories of Polybius*.
[43] Bodin, *Six Bookes*, 204.
[44] Aristotle, *Politics*, I.2.13, III.9.3.

Resting on the stable base of natural, Asiatic slavery, despotic monarchy was removed from the throes of the natural cycle of polities.

Renaissance theorists interpreted despotic rule, like tyranny, through the prism of natural law. Thus they had to discard "natural slavery" as a basis for despotism because, according to most natural law theorists, all men were born free. There was no natural slavery, only legal and illegal slavery. The effect of this conceptual shift can be clearly seen in Bodin's redefinition of Aristotle's despotic monarchy, which the French theorist termed "lordly monarchie." Despotic rule, Bodin argues, is legitimate only in instances of victory in just war; natural servitude cannot serve as its basis, for there is no such thing. The repudiation of the idea of inbred servility enabled Bodin to distinguish "lordly monarchie" from "tyranny": in the former, the vanquished are rightfully enslaved, while in the latter, freemen are made slaves "against the laws of nature." [45] Like Bodin, Hobbes defined despotic monarchy and the slavery it entailed as the consequence of war: "Dominion acquired by conquest, or victory in war, is that which some writers call *despotical,* from *despotes,* which signifieth a lord or master, and is the dominion of the master over his servant." [46] Locke did the same, arguing that "Captives, taken in a just and lawful War, and such only, are subject to Despotical power," for the vanquished forfeited their natural rights by entering into an unjust war. [47]

Though European theorists tended to move away from the idea of natural slavery in defining despotic monarchy, the Aristotelian notion that this form of government was deeply rooted in the soil of Asian servility survived. Bodin, for example, believed that "the people of Europe, [being] more couragious, and better soldiers than the people of Africke or Asia, could never endure the lordly Monarques." For this reason, despotic monarchies were more prevalent in Asia, as was confirmed by evidence found in ancient texts, sacred and secular: "And in the whole course of the Bible, the Scripture speaking of the subjects of the kings of Assiria and Egipt, calleth them alwaies slaves: and not the holie scripture onley, but the Greeks also, who alwayes in their writings terme them selves free, and the Barbarians slaves; meaning by the Barbarians the people of Asia and Egipt." Because they ruled over populations reduced to a servile state, the Asian monarchies were removed from the cycle of polities and were more stable than tyrannies, a fact also demonstrated by Scripture: "the seigneure-like states, and namely the Lordly Monarchies have been of great and of long continuance, as the auntient Monarchies of the Assirians, the Medes, Persians, and AEgyptians." [48]

In sum, two concepts of deformed kingship were probably current among the gentleman-ethnographers of the sixteenth and seventeenth centuries. The

---

[45] Bodin, *Six Bookes,* 32–48, 200, 203. Aristotle of course discussed slavery resulting from conquest (*Politics,* I.2.16).

[46] Hobbes, *Leviathan,* 110.

[47] Locke, *Two Treatises,* 401.

[48] Bodin, *Six Bookes,* 202, 204.

first concept was that of the tyrant as rogue prince. The rogue prince was guilty of domesticating the *res publica* and *red privata* for his own benefit. He and he alone was responsible for the imposition of tyranny. Since the rogue prince's subjects were by nature free, his reign was temporary. After a time the downtrodden would rise up and overthrow him, pushing Aristotle's cycle of regimes forward. The second concept was that of the tyrant as despot. Like the rogue prince, the despot appropriated the *res publica* and *res privata*. He was not, however, the author of tyranny. Rather, he was made a tyrant by the character of his subjects, who were servile and therefore required despotic rule. Since the despot's people were natural slaves, his regime was secure: no one would question the despot, for all were content in their subjection.

"Ivan the Tyrant"

The first attempts to classify Russian government in terms of the general typology of regimes were made by the armchair ethnographers and cosmographers of the first half of the sixteenth century. By and large, these men seem to have understood Muscovy to be a principality not radically different from the ones they knew in Europe. In their accounts, the ruler of Muscovy was ordinarily referred to simply as "the duke," "the prince," or "the grand prince," and generally nothing unusual was noted about the way he governed. There were, however, early exceptions to this rule. Enraged by what they perceived to be Muscovite aggression, Christian Bomhover and Jacob Piso openly referred to the Russian ruler as a "tyrant" and complained of his "tyranny."[49] In their writings "tyranny" is a term of reproach rather than a technical definition of Russian rule: neither man suggested that the grand prince was the master of slaves. Other authors, however, had the learned definition of "tyranny" in mind even if they were too cautious to use the term itself: in 1518 Francesco Da Collo called the grand prince the master of slaves; in 1524, Alberto Campensé noted that Vasilii III ruled his subjects like a master; in 1529, Willibald Pirckheimer argued that the Muscovites were "subject to extreme servitude" and that the tsar owned all property.[50] Interestingly, Sebastian Franck repeated Pirckheimer's characterization and added the word that was obviously missing—"tyranny."[51]

If scholars of the first half of the sixteenth century had been hesitant to write that the Muscovite prince was a "tyrant," their successors were only too willing to apply the term to Ivan IV. The Englishmen Chancellor and Jenk-

---

[49] Bomhover (1508), 121; Piso (1514), n.p.
[50] Dzhuzeppe D'Amato, *Sochineniia ital'iantsev o Rossii kontsa XV–XVI vv.*, 62; Campensé (1524), 32; Pirckheimer, (1530), 105.
[51] Franck (1530), 30v.

inson represent early exceptions. They had seen nothing unusual in Ivan's behavior, nor, as agents of the Muscovy Company, were they particularly inclined to risk damaging their commercial enterprise by revealing the grand prince in a negative light. In 1557 Jenkinson offered a glowing characterization of Ivan IV to English readers: "And as this Emperor which is now Ivan Vasilivich, doeth exceede his predecessors in name, that is, from Duke to Emperour, even so much by report he doeth exceede them in stoutness of courage and valiantnesse, and a great deale more: for he is no more afraid of his enemies which are not few, then the Hobbie of the larks."[52] As we saw in Chapter 4, Ivan's image began to change in the 1560s as Europeans learned of Russian outrages committed in the Livonian War and of Ivan's attack on his own people during the *oprichnina*. By the early 1570s Ivan had come to be seen in Europe as a tyrant. The epithet proved to be permanent: every major ethnographer after Chancellor and Jenkinson had occasion to call Ivan a "tyrant" and mention his "tyrannical" practices.[53] In fact, a peculiar linguistic confusion made Ivan not just "a tyrant" but rather "the tyrant." Perhaps even during his reign, Ivan was popularly referred to as "Ivan Groznyi," an epithet that may be translated as "the fearsome" or "the terrible." With Ivan's oppression and European categories in mind, the foreigners interpreted *groznyi* to mean "tyrant," and began to tell their readers that the cruel tsar's name was Ivan the Tyrant. Margeret said that Ivan was "surnamed the Tyrant"; Meyerberg observed that unlike his father, Ivan "was called 'the tyrant'"; similarly, Collins explained that Ivan "is called the Tyrant"; and Neuville wrote that though "the present tsar's ancestor was called Ivan Vasil'evich," he is "known as the Tyrant."[54]

In describing Ivan's tyranny, the ethnographers often reached for biblical and Classical analogies they knew would be meaningful to their learned and well-read public. This expectation is clear in George Turberville's doggerel verse about Ivan:

> But all of custom doth unto the prince redound,
> And all the whole revenue comes unto the king his crown.
> Good faith, I see thee muse at what I tell thee now,
> But true it is; no choice, but all at prince's pleasure bow.
> So Tarquin ruled Rome, as thou rememb'rest well,
> And what his fortune was at last I know thyself canst tell.[55]

[52] Jenkinson (1557), 438.

[53] For Ivan IV as a tyrant, see Taube and Kruse (1571), 29; Schlichting (1571a), 213; Printz (1578), 19; Staden (1578), 5; Guagnini (1578), 27; Horsey (1584–1611), 271; Fletcher (1591), 190; Margeret (1607), 65–66; Peyerle (1608), 153; Petreius (1608), 76; Maskiewicz (1611), 55–56; Bussow (1611), 14; Massa (1614), 5; Olearius (1656), 181; Meyerberg (1661), 107; Collins (1667), 46–47; Reutenfels (1671), 60; Wickhart (1675), 177; Tanner (1678), 60; Neuville (1698), 65; Crull (1698), 23; Korb (1700), 2:42–43.

[54] Margeret (1607), 16, 23, 65–66; Collins (1667), 46–47; Meyerberg (1661), 109; Neuville (1698), 65.

[55] Turberville (1568), 442.

Turberville was sure that his public would recognize L. Tarquinius Superbus as the Roman tyrant who, after savaging his people for twenty-four years, was banished in 510 B.C. Others perpetuated this Classical-Russian trope: Albert Schlichting said that Ivan's "savagery is greater than Nero's"; Alexander Guagnini wrote that Ivan's cruelty exceeded all tyrants "before and after Christ," including "Nero, Valerius, Dionysius, Decius, Maximus, and Julianus"; Jerome Horsey called Ivan "this Heliogabalus"; Paul Oderborn compared Ivan to Nero, Caligula, and Domitianus; Jacob Ulfeldt thanked God that he had been delivered at last from the "true Pharoah, the Muscovite tsar, the greatest enemy of the German people"; Hans Georg Peyerle observed that Ivan "exceeded Nero in cruelty and tyranny, Caligula in evil-doing, and Heliogabalus in obscene behavior." [56] Once Ivan began to be mentioned in the same breath as the mythic tyrants of biblical and Classical times, the tsar himself assumed mythic status. In the minds of Europeans, the idea of "Ivan the Tyrant" became detached from the historical figure Ivan Vasil'evich. In the ethnographic literature an imaginary Ivan the Tyrant began to perpetrate the crimes of a perfect tyrant, crimes Ivan Vasil'evich definitely could not have committed. In short, within ethnographic discourse a European folklore concerning the wicked deeds of the persona Ivan the Tyrant evolved having everything to do with the idea of tyranny and little to do with Ivan Vasil'evich, the ruler of Russia.

The strongest and most distinctive element in this folkloric tradition is what might be called the "tsar-Dracula" story. In the second half of the fifteenth century, German publicists drafted a cycle of tales about the Wallachian prince Vlad Tsepes, or Dracula. Though some of the stories may be traced to actual events, the original episodes were all wildly embellished if not entirely made up by their German authors. The Germans used a peculiar literary formula to demonstrate Dracula's cunning and even witty tyranny. In a typical Dracula tale, Vlad Tsepes observes some transgression (of law, custom, his will) and devises an appropriate punishment, followed by an ironic statement of some kind. The story of the impertinent ambassador provides a ready example:

> Once several Wahlen were sent to him. When they came to him, they bowed and took off their hats and under them they had brown and red berets or caps, which they did not take off. So he asked them why they had not taken off their caps or berets. They said: "Lord, it is not our custom. We never take them off before our ruler." He said: "Well, I wish to strengthen you in your custom." And as they thanked his grace, he had them take good strong nails and had them nailed around the caps into the head, so that they could not take them off. In this way he strengthened them in their custom. [57]

[56] Schlichting (1571a), 213; Guagnini (1578), 28; Horsey (1584–1611), 304; Oderborn (1585), 224; Ulfeldt (1575), 54; Peyerle (1608), 153.
[57] Radu Florescu and Raymond T. McNally, *Complete Dracula*, 129–30. The text was composed ca. 1500. For a description, see Dieter Harmening, *Der Anfang von Dracula*, 82.

By about 1500, approximately thirty such stories were circulating in eastern and central Europe. Apparently Fedor Kurytsin, Muscovite ambassador to the Habsburgs, brought a number of Dracula tales to Russia in 1486, and they began to circulate within Muscovy.[58] By the mid–sixteenth century, Dracula stood as a Europe-wide symbol of tyrannical rule. Books of didactic examples, for instance, commonly included Dracula tales to illustrate tyranny, cruelty, and evil.[59] With time, the stories themselves assumed a kind of independence of Vlad Tsepes. They became pure scenarios in which any ruler, not necessarily Dracula, could be the title character. Ivan IV, already famous for his tyranny at mid-century, was an obvious candidate for inclusion in the abstracted Dracula scenarios. The Swedish cleric Olaus Magnus was the first European to substitute a Russian ruler for Dracula.[60] He had Ivan IV nail a hat to the head of an Italian ambassador.

> Moreover Albertus Cranztius, a famous German Historian, affirms in his *Vandalia,* that an embassadour of Italie was most miserably murthered, because he did not uncover his head when he was to deliver his message before the Prince of *Moscovia.* For when the Embassadour alleadged the custome of his Country (so that no majesty nor power could be supposed to be offended for the Embassadour's head being uncovered) the cruell Prince scoffing, said, That his hat should be nailed to his head with an iron pin; and that he would not violate such a custome but confirm it the more.[61]

In the era of Ivan IV, the tsar-Dracula stories enjoyed considerable currency in both European and Russian circles. Schlichting, for example, recorded more than a dozen tales in which the tsar is seen cleverly destroying his real and imagined enemies.[62] Guagnini borrowed and published all of Schlichting's tales, thereby transmitting them to later authors, including Oderborn, Olearius, and Reutenfels. The genre was productive: the number of tales expanded as authors recorded or invented new ones.[63] By the end of the seven-

---

[58] Iakov S. Lur'e, ed., *Povest' o Drakule.*

[59] Harmening, *Der Anfang von Dracula,* 41–52. For an example, see Theodor Zwinger, *Theatrum Vitae Humanae.*

[60] In the literature, Schlichting (1571a) is usually identified as the first to place Ivan IV in a Dracula vignette. See, for example, S. K. Rosovetskii, "Ustnaia proza ob Ivane Groznom"; Maureen Perrie, *Image of Ivan the Terrible in Russian Folklore,* 96.

[61] Magnus (1555), bk. 11, chap. 10. Magnus claimed he found the story in Krantz (1519), suggesting that the prince he had in mind was Vasilii III. But as John Grunlung points out, nothing of the sort is found in Krantz's book ("Kommentar," in Olaus Magnus, *Historia om de Norska Folken,* 4:394). Incidentally, Elena A. Savel'eva, *Olaus Magnus i ego "Istoriia severnykh narodov,"* 84, cites Granlung, yet she nonetheless affirms Magnus's attribution. It seems likely that Magnus simply made a mistake and had Ivan IV in mind.

[62] See Appendix.

[63] The origins of the tales are for the most part obscure. In most instances it is very difficult to determine whether an author saw a given episode and embellished it, heard of it from Russian or European informants, or simply made it up. Rosovetskii is the only researcher to discuss the question in any depth. In general he believes the stories about Ivan's terror were of indigenous origin and arose in response to internal political events. In his view they were the prod-

teenth century, the catalog of tsar-Dracula tales had grown to more than thirty distinct scenarios distributed in nineteen accounts. In European folklore, Ivan the Tyrant had truly become legendary.

Despotism: Tyranny without a Tyrant

The ethnographers recognized that the Classical definition of tyranny fitted Ivan IV's regime nicely. Almost all the commentators of Ivan IV's era (at least after 1565) agreed that Ivan was a rogue prince who had unjustly made Russia his private estate and its inhabitants his slaves. As Fletcher put it, the terrible tsar "reduce[d] his government into a more strickt forme" by making his people "not onely his vassals, but his *Kolophey,* that is his very villains or bondsmen." [64] Though Ivan had succeeded in creating tyranny, the ethnographers uniformly concurred that he was unpopular and that his regime was, as a consequence, unstable. Under the banner "How His Subjects Regard Him," Schlichting wrote that the "only people who have any use for the tyrant are the *oprichniki.* If the Muscovites could find anyone to guarantee their safety," he continued, "they would probably overthrow him." [65] Taube and Kruse noted that Ivan had "destroyed his country and people, diminished his treasury and, as a result of his unheard of tyranny, the people are not true to him and desire some other authority." [66] Staden openly wondered how long Ivan's oppressive regime could continue. After all, the German mercenary explained, "the grand prince has been such a grim and horrid tyrant that neither layman nor clerics favor him." [67] Fletcher predicted that the effects of Ivan's excess would not end with his death: "[His] wicked pollicy and tyrannous practise (though now it be ceassed) hath so troubled that countrey, and filled it so full of grudge and mortall hatred ever since, that it wil not be quenched (as it seemeth now) till it burne againe into a civill flame." According to Fletcher, Russia's condition was so dire after Ivan's passing that "the people of the most part . . . wishe for some forreine invasion, which they suppose to bee the onely meanes, to rid them of the heavy yoke of this tyrannous government." [68]

Yet there was also a sense in which the Aristotelian definitions of tyranny did not accord with what ethnographers observed. The theory of the rogue prince suggested that the tyrant was the primary author of tyrannical government. But as any ethnographer who had read the accounts of the first half

---

ucts of Russian authors and environments, and were passed on to foreigners, the earliest of whom he believed was Schlichting. See Rostovetskii, "Ustnaia proza ob Ivane Groznom," 82–84.

[64] Fletcher (1591), 199.
[65] Schlichting (1571b), 272.
[66] Taube and Kruse (1571), 56.
[67] Staden (1578), 55–56, 91.
[68] Fletcher (1591), 201, 210.

of the sixteenth century would have known, Ivan IV was not the originator of Russian tyranny. Several authors of the first half of the century, including Herberstein himself, had written or implied that Ivan III and Vasilii III were universal proprietors whose subjects were slaves. Further, though most ethnographers agreed that Ivan's successors were not tyrants, they continued to insist that Muscovite *government* was tyrannical. Two years after Ivan's death, in the reign of the feeble Fedor Ivanovich and his protector, Boris Godunov, Fletcher wrote that "the State and forme of [Russian] government" was tyrannical.[69] Olearius explained that Tsars Mikhail and Aleksei did not emulate "the former tyrants, who violently assaulted their subjects and their subjects' property." Yet, the Holsteinian legate insisted, their regime was tyrannical: "If one keeps in mind the basic distinction between a legitimate and tyrannical order, that the first subserves the welfare of the subjects and the second the personal wants of the sovereign, then the Russian government must be considered closely related to tyranny."[70] Similarly, Reutenfels observed that Tsar Aleksei was "most unlike" Ivan IV. But he was sure that Aleksei, though no tyrant, had complete control over the "life and death of his subjects and their property."[71] At the end of the century Korb told his readers that Peter was no more a tyrant than his father had been. But, like Ivan IV, Peter I used "his native country and its inhabitants as if power absolute, unbounded, uncircumscribed by any law, lay openly with him to dispose as freely of the property of private individuals, as if nature had produced everything for his sake alone."[72] Clearly, the standard notion of tyranny was well suited only to the reign of Ivan IV, for he was acknowledged to be a rogue prince and to have created a tyrannical form of rule. In contrast, the model of the rogue prince could not account for the existence of tyrannical government in the pre- and post-Ivan periods, for the monarchs of these eras were not tyrants, though they ruled tyrannical regimes. Paradoxically, Russia seemed to be a tyranny without a tyrant, a state in which the people were content in their servitude and the monarch, though not necessarily evil, held awesome powers.

By and large, the ethnographers failed to offer a conceptually satisfying solution to the puzzle presented by Russian monarchy. In their attempts to explain the stability of Russian tyranny, they habitually fell back on explanations that derived from conventional notions of good and evil monarchy. Everyone knew that righteous kings were made secure by the love and respect of their people. Might it not be the case, then, that Muscovite princes enjoyed the love and respect of their subjects even though they were oppressed by a tyrannical system? Indeed, there was some evidence that Russians felt a deep and uncoerced fealty to their ruler. As we saw earlier, the foreigners of-

---

[69] Ibid., 194.
[70] Olearius (1656), 175, 173.
[71] Reutenfels (1671), 61, 101.
[72] Korb (1700), 2:126, 129, 193–94.

ten observed with astonishment that the Russians spoke of their sovereign as a god, called themselves as his slaves, and prostrated themselves before him like humble servants. Naturally, an admirer like Paul of Aleppo would think that these displays suggested an abiding love. "As for the emperor," Paul wrote, "it is impossible to conceive the love that is borne to him, both by great and small." [73] But even men such as Olearius, who clearly believed the tsar's rule (if not the tsar) was tyrannical, said that the Russians "greatly love and respect their rulers." [74] Similarly, Reutenfels explained that it did not matter to the Russians that they lived "under the yoke of a cruel government," for Russian subjects held that "to calmly suffer a tyrant is honorable and in accordance with their faith." [75] More commonly the visitors adopted a less charitable point of view. Just as it was assumed that good kings ruled by love, so it was understood that tyrannical kings ruled by fear. Might it not be the case, then, that Muscovite princes were feared by their subjects, even though they were in some sense not tyrants? Again, there was evidence to support this proposition; indeed, the same evidence that suggests that the Russians loved the tsar—ritual praise, self-deprecation, prostration. These acts could indicate fear of the tsar if they were interpreted cynically. It is perhaps understandable that Possevino would be skeptical of the praise showered on the tyrant Ivan IV by his fearful courtiers. [76] Yet men who wrote after the passing of Ivan IV also suspected that fear motivated the Russians' marked tendency to praise the tsar and bend to his will. Margeret, for example, stated that "the absolute power of the prince in his state makes him feared and dreaded by his subjects." [77] Even Olearius, who admired Aleksei Mikhailovich, wrote that Russians "fear him exceedingly, even more than God." [78] Reutenfels also praised Aleksei, but affirmed that the Russians "are strongly subjected to a feeling of fear, which is their constant companion, as a result of the stern law of obedience." [79] Korb, a great fan of Peter I, agreed that "absolute power" such as that held by the Russian tsar "renders [a prince] more feared than revered." [80]

Within the confines of the "tyranny without a tyrant" paradox and on the basis of the ambiguous evidence at hand, it was plainly impossible for the

---

[73] Aleppo (1655), 1:287.

[74] Olearius (1656), 74.

[75] Reutenfels (1671), 142–43. For other examples of obedience through love, honor, and respect, see Fabri (1536), 297–99; Adams/Chancellor (1553), 260; Jenkinson (1557), 438–39; Maskiewicz (1611), 53; Bussow (1611), 11; Petreius (1615), 303; Aleppo (1655), 1:287, 2:401; Olearius (1656), 74; Reutenfels (1671), 142–43; Tanner (1678), 39.

[76] Possevino (1586), 11.

[77] Margeret (1607), 3.

[78] Olearius (1656), 174.

[79] Reutenfels (1671), 141–42.

[80] Korb (1700), 1:244. For further examples of the obedience-through-fear theory, see Jenkinson (1557), 438–39; Printz (1578), 29–30; Barberino (1565), 2:8, 21; Possevino (1586), 8, 35, 49, 50, 73; Fletcher (1591), 169–70; Margeret (1607), 3, 69–70; Massa (1614), 143; Olearius (1656), 147, 174; Meyerberg (1661), 55, 116–17; Tanner (1678), 40; Korb (1700), 1:136–37, 244, 262–63.

visitors to determine whether love or fear served as the fundament of Muscovite monarchy. It is not surprising that both explanations can be found
throughout the ethnographic literature, often in the same text, as in the cases
of Olearius and Reutenfels, or even in the same sentence, as in Chancellor's
seemingly contradictory pronouncement that "no prince in Christendome is
more feared of his owne then he is, nor yet better beloved." [81] But not all of
the ethnographers were stymied by the love-fear theory of political stability.
A third explanatory strain in the literature, suggested by Aristotle's concept
of despotic monarchy, transcended the limitations of the traditional categories. The conventional theory of monarchy assumed, as we have seen, that
the character of a regime was determined by the behavior of the prince: if he
were good, he would be loved and his government stable; if he were bad,
then he would be loathed and his reign would be short. Aristotle's idea reversed this causality: in despotic monarchies, the character of the people determined that of the prince. Natural slaves needed and rightfully received a
despot as ruler. Since natural slavery was a permanent condition, despotisms
were immobile. If it were assumed that the Russians were natural slaves, then
the question of love or fear became moot: whether they respected the tsar or
feared him was of no consequence—their very state of being required that
they submit to him completely.

None of the ethnographers offered an extended analysis of Muscovite tyranny in terms of natural slavery. Very occasionally one finds a phrase in the
ethnographies suggesting that the Muscovites were "born for slavery," but
this meant rather (as Reutenfels explicitly said) that Russians were condemned to a life of oppression by virtue of being born under the tsar.[82] Possevino agreed that it seemed "the Muscovites were a people more born to
slavery than to achievement." But this was an illusion: the Russians, he said,
were not natural slaves, for they "fully realize the nature of their servitude
and know that if they should flee the country their children would be killed
on the spot and all their property confiscated." [83] Despite their hesitance to
explicitly endorse the notion of natural slavery, the ethnographers were presented with evidence of inborn servility that they simply could not ignore.

The first of these data was the Muscovite practice of self-sale into slavery.
In 1517 Herberstein noted with curiosity that "persons on the point of death
very often manumit some of their serfs, but they immediately sell themselves
for money to other families. The people," he concluded, "enjoy slavery more
than freedom." [84] Well over a century later, Olearius observed that "when,
as a consequence of the death or generosity of their master, the slaves and
servants of some lord receive their freedom, they soon sell themselves again."

[81] Jenkinson (1557), 438–39.
[82] Reutenfels (1671), 176–78; Korb (1700), 2:155, 193–94.
[83] Possevino (1586), 11.
[84] Herberstein (1517–49), 1:95.

This behavior demonstrated that the Russians, like the Asians singled out by Aristotle,

> neither value freedom nor know how to use it. Their nature is such that, as the wise Aristotle said of the barbarians, "they cannot and shall not live other than in slavery." To them applies also what Aristotle said of the peoples of Asia Minor, who are called Ionians because they derived from the Greeks: "They are miserable in freedom and comfortable in slavery." [85]

At the end of the century, Korb told his readers that if Muscovite slaves "be manumitted by their dying masters, so accustomed are they to slavery, that they make themselves over as slaves to other masters, or bind themselves as slaves for a sum of money." For Korb, as for Herberstein and Olearius, the fact of self-sale indicated that "the nation itself has such a dislike of liberty." [86]

The ethnographers found further evidence of Russians' preference for bondage in the fact that Muscovites seemed to understand beating as a sign of affection. Herberstein was the first to note this dubious custom. Russian servants, he wrote, "think that they have displeased their masters, and that it is a sign of his anger if they are not beaten." The same, he said, was true of wives: if they were not beaten regularly by their husbands, they believed they were not loved. [87] This notion was not without its critics: both Olearius and Korb agreed that it was a fable. [88] Nonetheless, the more general idea that Russians understood beatings as a mark of fondness enjoyed wide support. According to the foreigners, Muscovites regularly thanked the tsar for punishing them. "When he [the tsar] himself punishes someone," Meyerberg observed, "or by his order someone is beaten with a rod, or whip, the person punished thanks him for it." [89] Reutenfels concurred: "They have a cere-monial custom by which they call the punishment, however terrible it may be, the grace of the tsar, and, having suffered it, they thank the tsar, the judge, and lord for it, bowing to the ground." [90] For the foreigners, the readiness of Russians to interpret punishment as devotion was perfectly consistent with the idea that they were somehow natively servile, or, as Olearius said when he observed this custom, that "they are all serfs and slaves." [91]

Finally, the ethnographers' uncharitable belief that Russians were by na-ture "rude and barbarous" led them to the conclusion that Muscovites were fit for despotic governance and in fact required it. By and large, the ethnog-raphers held a very low opinion of the Russian character, which they gener-

---

[85] Olearius (1656), 151.
[86] Korb (1700), 2:200–202.
[87] Herberstein (1517–49), 1:106–7, 93–95.
[88] Olearius (1656), 147, 170; Korb (1700), 2:209.
[89] Meyerberg (1661), 116–17.
[90] Reutenfels (1671), 117–19.
[91] Olearius (1656), 147.

ally understood to be wild and uncivilized.[92] The reason for Muscovites' incivility had been pondered since Herberstein asked "whether the brutality of the people has made the prince a tyrant, or whether the people themselves have become thus brutal and cruel through the tyranny of their prince."[93] Fletcher and others offered a resounding affirmation of the latter proposition, pointing out that the government intentionally kept the people from all learning "that they may be fitter for the servile condition, wherein now they are, and have neither reason, nor valure to attempt innovation."[94] Yet others answered that that ineradicable Russian rudeness produced despotism: Massa speculated that Russia must live under tyranny, "otherwise, she is lost"; Olearius wrote that since the Russians are naturally "fit only for slavery, they must constantly be kept under a cruel and harsh yoke"; Meyerberg believed that the Russians had to be kept in fear because otherwise they would surely run wild; Reutenfels argued that one could not "blame the rulers [of Russia] for the extraordinary rigidity of the laws, because the laws must suit the spirit of the people."[95] Perhaps under the influence of recently published reports of Oriental despotism, Reutenfels hinted that the Russians were suited for despotic government because they partook more of "Asiatic unruliness than European refinement."[96] The Russians had Asian manners because they were, despite appearances to the contrary, in fact Asians: "The color of their faces is like that of Europeans, because of the cold climate which changes the original dark, Asian color."[97]

Conclusion

The European ethnographers did not travel to Russia without preconceptions. They arrived with a set of culturally specific concepts that they employed in interpreting the government they observed. The most important of these ideas was tyranny, for nearly all the Europeans agreed that the Russian system of government was in fact premised on the notion that the tsar was the master of enslaved subjects. Several of the ethnographers noted, however, that the operation of Russian tyranny was at odds with the Aristotelian

[92] Ulfeldt (1575), 33; Margeret (1607), 86; Bussow (1611), 36; Petreius (1615), 136, 311; Olearius (1656), 133; Wickhart (1675), 248; Tanner (1678), 109; and Neuville (1698), 57.

[93] Herberstein (1517–49), 1:32.

[94] Fletcher (1591), 226–27. For similar arguments, see Adams/Chancellor (1553), 266; Bussow (1611), 14; Petreius (1615), 156; Meyerberg (1661), 95–96, 111–12; Reutenfels (1671), 171–75; Wickhart (1675), 228–29.

[95] Massa (1614), 185; Olearius (1656), 147; Meyerberg (1661), 116–17; Reutenfels (1671), 116–17.

[96] Reutenfels (1671), 146–47. Reutenfels frequently identified Russian customs as Asian; see 85, 89–90, 145–48. On late seventeenth-century European reports on China, Mogul India, and Persia (for example, Olearius [1656]) and their influence on the genesis of the idea of Oriental despotism, see Lawrence Krader, *Asiatic Mode of Production*, 19–29.

[97] Reutenfels (1671), 140.

ideal type. Tyrannies were supposed to be short-lived, momentary phenomena created by rogue princes, but Russian tyranny seemed to be a permanent fixture ruled by men who were (with the exception of Ivan IV) manifestly not tyrants, at least by choice. How was one to understand a permanent tyranny? Why didn't the Muscovites rise up and throw off their oppressive government? Some said the Russians were peculiarly quiescent because they were in a permanent state of fear, while others guessed that somehow the Russians loved their prince and therefore were happy in their servitude. Still others, having observed with astonishment the oddly servile manners of the Muscovites, groped after a third possibility, that the Russians were somehow "natural slaves" or "fit for servitude." Aristotle and his early modern followers had indeed described a regime in which a ruler rightfully and permanently held despotic powers over slavish subjects, and it may be the case that some of the most theoretically informed ethnographers were influenced by this idea. Olearius, for one, certainly was:

> The Russian system of government . . . is what the political thinkers call "a dominating and despotic monarchy." After he inherits the crown, the tsar, or grand prince, alone rules the whole country; all his subjects, the noblemen and princes as well as the common people, townsmen, and the peasants, are his serfs and slaves, whom he treats as the master of the house does his servants. This mode of rule is very like that which Aristotle describes in the following words: "There is also another kind of monarchy, found in the kingdoms of some barbarian peoples, which stands closest of all to tyranny." [98]

In theoretical sophistication and insight Olearius was unique among the travelers, for most of them puzzled in vain over the paradox of an immobile tyranny without a tyrant. Their conceptual framework simply offered no evident solution to this contradiction in terms.

---

[98] Olearius (1656), 173. Also see Crull (1698), 169.

6

SIMPLEX DOMINATUS
Russian Government in European Political Science

It is time to seek the true origin of the right of slavery. It should be founded on the nature of things; let us see if there are cases where it does derive from it. In every despotic government, it is very easy to sell oneself; there political slavery more or less annihilates civil liberty. Mr. Perry says that the Muscovites sell themselves easily: I know the reason well; it is because their liberty is worth nothing.

MONTESQUIEU, 1748

AT ONE POINT in *The Prince,* Machiavelli draws a sharp distinction between two kinds of monarchy. In one type, the king rules together with "barons who hold that rank by hereditary right, not through the favor of the ruler." In the other, the prince governs with the aid of his "servants, acting as ministers through his grace and favor." Machiavelli was a practical political philosopher, and thus he bolstered his analysis with two examples. "The king of France," he asserted, "is placed amidst a great number of hereditary lords, recognized in that state by their own subjects, who are devoted to them. The whole Turkish kingdom," in contrast, "is governed by one ruler, the others all being his servants; and his kingdom is divided into sanjaks, to which he sends various administrators, whom he changes and moves as he pleases." [1] Some sixty years after *The Prince* was written, Jean Bodin offered a somewhat broader discussion of types of governments. The French theorist asked how many sorts of monarchies existed, and answered that there were three, "for he hath the soveraigntie, is either lord of all: or else a king, or a tyrant." The tyrant is of course an unlawful transgressor of "the lawes of nature and nations." The other two forms of government, however, are lawful, and in Bodin's definitions of them one notes a similarity to Machiavelli's

---

[1] All citations to Machiavelli in this paragraph are to *The Prince,* 15.

168

twofold distinction: in "royall Monarchie," the king rules together with the nobility, whereas in "lordly Monarchie" the prince governs "as the master of a familie doth his slaves." Like Machiavelli, Bodin provided his readers with living instances of "royall" and "lordly" monarchy. "Northern" monarchies were, he said, by and large "royall." Bodin followed Machiavelli in pointing to Turkey as an example of "lordly monarchie."[2] Yet Bodin was able to provide a further example of despotic monarchy in Europe, one unavailable to Machiavelli in 1513—the Russians. The Muscovite monarchy must be "lordly," for, as Bodin had read in Herberstein's *Notes on the Muscovites,* the Russians "call themselves *chlopes,* that is to say, servants, which wee corruptly call slaves."[3]

Bodin's citation of Muscovy as an instance of archetypal despotism is indicative of the effect the ethnographies of Russia had on European political thought. Political theorists had no difficulty understanding what kind of place Muscovy was on the basis of what they found in the accounts of mid-sixteenth-century Russia. Long before Muscovy was known to Europeans, Classical theorists had described a kind of regime, called "tyranny" or "despotic rule," in which the prince was in essence the master of slaves. Beginning in the last quarter of the fifteenth century, printed descriptions of Ottoman Turkey provided Europeans with their first glimpse of what seemed to be a despotic regime. The imposition of this abstract type on Turkey can be seen in Machiavelli's stereotyped image of Ottoman government, in which it is difficult to tell where the ideal type stops and the empirical example begins. When the first detailed descriptions of Muscovy appeared in Europe in the mid-sixteenth century, theorists such as Bodin immediately recognized another example of tyrannical or despotic rule, and Muscovy was made to fit the theoretical mold. The task was not difficult because the ethnographers who supplied theorists with their "data" had the ideas of tyranny and despotism in mind when they first conceptualized what they had seen in Muscovy. As we will presently see, this cycle of reference helped produce a robust stereotype of Muscovite despotism.

Jean Bodin: The Beginnings of the Theory of Muscovite Despotism

Jean Bodin was the first political thinker to make extensive use of the burgeoning sixteenth-century ethnographic literature on Russia for theoretical purposes.[4] It is not difficult to understand why he took this pioneering step. In *Method for the Easy Comprehension of History* (1566), Bodin attempted

---

[2] All citations to Bodin in this paragraph are to *Six Bookes,* 199–202.

[3] Herberstein (1517–49), 1:95.

[4] For a brief biography of Bodin, about whom surprisingly little is known, see Kenneth D. McRae, "Bodin's Career," in Bodin, *Six Bookes,* A3–13.

to outline the logic of a positive science of society. One of his primary suggestions was that, like students of nature, scholars of history should collect large amounts of empirical data. He believed that political scientists "should bring together and compare the legal framework of all states, or of the most famous states." Thanks to men such as Herberstein, for the first time in history good descriptions of "the legal framework of all states" (or at least many of them) were readily available. In *Method,* Bodin took it upon himself to provide a preliminary guide to the available literature. In the course of his exposition he cited Persian, Greek, Egyptian, Roman, Hebrew, Spanish, British, Italian, and German sources, and regretted that Turkish law was unavailable. In the tenth chapter, "The Order and Collection of Historians," he listed approximately three hundred historical and ethnographic accounts, all neatly categorized by area of coverage ("Universal History," "Histories of Pagan Superstition," etc.).[5]

Bodin analyzed this treasury of data in *Six Books of a Commonwealth,* his summa of empirically informed political science, and it is here that we find Bodin using information drawn from ethnographic descriptions of Russia. Though the vast majority of the information about Russia in *Six Books* is drawn from Herberstein, Bodin used several other sources on Muscovy as well.[6] As early as 1565, he knew the works of both Miechowa and Giovio, for both are mentioned in the section of *Method* titled "Historians of the Tatars and Muscovites" (where, incidentally, *Notes on the Muscovites* is not found).[7] Nevertheless, Bodin did not use either source directly in *Six Books:* neither is cited nor does one find any indication of direct borrowing.[8] Information indirectly derived from Maciej z Miechowa, however, is found in *Six Books.* In a discussion of the sovereign's ability to deny citizens the right to leave their countries, Bodin noted that in "countries as wherein tyrants rule, . . . not only the citizens, but even the strangers also are oftentimes by the princes of such places prohibited to depart, as in Moscovia."[9] Bodin probably took this fact from Münster's *Cosmography,* which he cited by name twice.[10] Münster's source, in turn, was Maciej, though Bodin did not know it.[11] In addition to Münster, Bodin employed Magnus's *History of Northern People* (1555), from which he seems to have borrowed the story of Ivan driving a nail into the head of an Italian ambassador. Further, there is some evidence that Bodin used the popular press of his day as a source of intelligence about Russia. For example, writing about the innate cruelty of northern peo-

[5] Bodin, *Method for the Easy Comprehension of History,* 2, 3, 365–80.
[6] Bodin rarely cited his sources on Russia, but of the thirty-five statements about Muscovy in *Six Bookes,* twenty-two can be traced to *Notes on the Muscovites.*
[7] Bodin, *Method,* 378.
[8] Maciej is never mentioned. Giovio is cited in connection with the Ethiopians, Turks, and Venetians, but never in connection with Russia (*Six Bookes,* 11, 147, 204, 416, 668, 711).
[9] Ibid., 60.
[10] Ibid., 557, 567.
[11] Maciej (1517), 115.

ples, Bodin noted that the Tatars "force them that are condemned, to breake their own neckes, or else to whip and torment them: Which makes men to thinke, that the cruelties of the king of Moscovie published and printed, are verie likely." [12] Just what he had in mind by the "cruelties of the king of Moscovie published and printed" is not entirely clear. In his review of Muscovite judicial practice, Herberstein had described a variety of harsh punishments. [13] Nonetheless, it seems just as likely that Bodin was referring to recently published pamphlets detailing atrocities committed by Russians against Livonian civilians during the ongoing Baltic conflict. [14] Though he does not cite them by name, these items circulated throughout Europe and would have been available to Bodin. [15] Finally, quite a few facts adduced about Muscovy in *Six Books* cannot be traced to any known source. [16]

Given Bodin's politics, Herberstein was not an ideal source for intelligence about Russia. Bodin was convinced that strong monarchy was the best and indeed natural form of government. [17] In *Six Books,* the French theorist tried mightily to convince his divided countrymen that undivided sovereignty under a legitimate king would bring peace and order to the realm. To be sure, in the pages of Herberstein Bodin found a united government perhaps worthy of emulation. Unfortunately, Herberstein clearly identified Russian rule as tyrannical. He depicted Vasilii III as a cruel usurper who drove a once free nobility into submission. The system Vasilii created matched the Aristotelian definition of tyranny exactly, for he had appropriated the persons and properties of his subjects, who were little but slaves. [18] Obviously, if Bodin was to hold Muscovy up as a model of a well-maintained absolute monarchy, Herberstein's "data" would have to be creatively reinterpreted. Bodin was up to the task. In *Six Books,* Vasilii was transformed from tyrant into hero. Bodin wrote approvingly that the Russian monarch liberated the Muscovites from the "Tatar Yoke" and made himself equal to or greater than "the greatest kings his neighbors, excepting the kings of the Turkes." [19] And Muscovy was not a tyranny, but rather a "lordly monarchie"—a legal form of government in which "a soveraigne prince having in good and lawfull warre vanquished his enemies, should make himselfe lord of their goods and persons by the law of arms, governing them now his subjects, as doth the good householder his servants or slaves: as we see it a thing received by the manner and custome of almost all nations." [20] Bodin's recategorization of Russian government solved

---

[12] Bodin, *Six Bookes,* 636, 555.

[13] Herberstein (1517–49), 1:101.

[14] On these pamphlets see Andreas Kappeler, *Ivan Groznyi im Spiegel der ausländischen Druckschriften seiner Zeit.*

[15] For other possible citations of the press, see Bodin, *Six Bookes,* 44, 152, 617, 632.

[16] Ibid., 66, 118, 479, 484, 548, 550, 734, 751.

[17] Ibid., 718ff.

[18] Herberstein (1517–49), 1:32, 95.

[19] Bodin, *Six Bookes,* 149. Bodin's source is Herberstein (1517–49), 1:30–34 and 2:67ff.

[20] Bodin, *Six Bookes,* 201.

one difficulty insofar as it allowed him to label the Muscovite regime as legitimate. But it also raised an insoluble complication. A lordly monarch rightly
controlled the lives and properties of his subjects because he had conquered
them in a just war. But where was the just war that brought Vasilii and his
successors into possession of the persons and goods of the formerly free Russian princes? Bodin offered no answer, probably because none could be wrung
out of the pages of Herberstein.

Bodin's trouble with Muscovy did not end there. Not only was he unable
to point to the just conquest that made the grand prince's overwhelming authority legitimate, but neither could he explain why Muscovy was a despotism in terms of his climatic theory of regimes. Following his Classical masters, Bodin believed that the "forme of a commonwealth" should naturally
fit "the diversity of men's humors," these being determined by the climate in
which they lived.[21] The nations of the north, Bodin claimed, "being fierce
and warlike, trusting in their force and strength, desire Popular estates, or at
the least elective Monarchies"; southern nations, being deft in reason and
spiritual by nature, are best ruled by sacred authority; and the middling nations, being "more reasonable and lesse strong," prefer the rule of law. As
should be apparent, Muscovy could not easily be made to fit this schema.
The Russians were doubtless a northern people, for they have "flaxen haire
and . . . greene eyes; as Plutarch, Tacitus, Iuvenal, and in our times the Baron
of Herbestein have observed."[22] And indeed they exhibit some of the characteristics of northern peoples: they are formidable in battle; they are cruel
because they lack "reason and iudgement"; they are so misogynistic that "as
the Baron of Herberstein doth write . . . They never see their wives (saith he)
until the day of their marriage"; and they are disloyal as "the Baron of He-
berstein saith in their historie." But by no account could it be said—by
Bodin or anyone else who had read Herberstein—that Muscovite monarchy
was "popular" or "elective." Russian government was, as Bodin himself
stressed, the very opposite of "popular," for the prince ruled Russia as a
master does his household. Bodin realized this contradiction. Commenting
on royal majesty, he noted at one point that northerners are of "greater courage" than those of the south and "are not able to endure such a servitude
and slaverie." Yet he was compelled to admit that "the kings of England, Sweden, Denmarke, and Polonia, who are situat toward the North [are] much
better to maintaine the maiestie of their estates with their subiects, than doe
the kings of Fraunce, or the princes of Italie; and the kings of Moscovia yet
better than all the rest, and yet are not therefore the lesse, but well the more
of their subiects obeyed." Bodin never attempted to resolve the paradox of
lordly Muscovite monarchy among the putatively warlike, freedom-loving

---

[21] Ibid., 545. Incidentally, the ethnographers generally avoided climatic theory. For an exception, see Reutenfels (1671), 141–42.

[22] Bodin, *Six Bookes*, 559–60, 548. Herberstein does not say this, but rather speaks of the
"dark color of the people" (1:3).

people of the north. He did hint at a potential solution, noting that in some cases "the government of every Citie is of great force in the alteration of the peoples natures and dispositions."[23] Could the tyrannical nature of Vasilii's rule, as Herberstein himself had suggested, have imprinted itself on the naturally free character of the Russians, making them at once barbarous and servile?[24] Perhaps, but Bodin never made this argument.

Once he had turned Herberstein's interpretation of Muscovy on its head, Bodin was free to praise a whole host of Russian policies. It is true that one finds occasional censure of Russia in *Six Books*. Ambassadors, Bodin argued, must be treated well, something the Muscovites (particularly Ivan IV) failed to do.[25] Inequality of punishments for equal offenses is harmful for a commonwealth, yet in Muscovy a "base fellow's" life is worth less than a "gentleman's."[26] Much more commonly, however, the customs of the Muscovites are singled out as examples of good government. In a well-ordered commonwealth, fathers have the right of life and death over their children, and so in Muscovy "it is lawfull for the Father to sell his sonne foure times, after which if he shall redeeme himselfe he is for ever free."[27] Subjects should be required to gain the permission of the prince to leave his country, and in some cases foreigners also, "as in Moscovia, Tartaria, and AEthiopians."[28] Trial by combat is sometimes useful as a means of solving disputes among subjects, as may be seen in the Russian case.[29] Religious discussion should be forbidden because it causes faction, so the prince of the Muscovites "forbad them uppon paine of death any more to preach or dispute of religion."[30] Fortifications give subjects the opportunity to rebel and therefore should generally be avoided, a rule "which is more strictly observed in Moscovie."[31] It is no dishonor to submit to an opponent in time of necessity, about which "we have an example of the great Knez [prince] of Moscovie."[32] In fact, Bodin's zeal to present Muscovy as a place of enlightened monarchical policy seems to have led him to fabricate evidence where none was available. The French theorist said that "long experience and tract of time confirmed" that offices should be perpetual, and he cited Russia as an example.[33] Herberstein, however, had written that the Russian prince granted only temporary tenures.[34] Further, Bodin argued that the election of clerical officials was

[23] Bodin, *Six Bookes*, 550, 555, 557, 567, 507, 567.

[24] Herberstein (1517–49), 1:32.

[25] Bodin, *Six Bookes*, 635v, 636. Bodin's sources are Herberstein (1517–49), 1:10, and Magnus (1555), bk. 11, chap. 10.

[26] Bodin, *Six Bookes*, 779. Bodin's source is Herberstein (1517–49), 1:102–4.

[27] Bodin, *Six Bookes*, 23. Bodin's source is Herberstein (1517–49), 1:95.

[28] Bodin, *Six Bookes*, 60. Bodin's sources is Münster (1544), 1031.

[29] Bodin, *Six Bookes*, 528. Bodin's source is Herberstein (1517–49), 1:104.

[30] Bodin, *Six Bookes*, 536. Bodin's source is Herberstein (1517–49), 1:83.

[31] Bodin, *Six Bookes*, 598; also see 605. Bodin's source is Herberstein (1517–49), 1:30.

[32] Bodin, *Six Bookes*, 614. Bodin's source is Herberstein (1517–49), 1:30.

[33] Bodin, *Six Bookes*, 484.

[34] Herberstein (1517–49), 1:30–31.

dangerous because it caused faction, "for which cause also the bishops and abbats in Moscovie, are drawne by lot." [35] Herberstein contradicted this assertion: metropolitans and bishops had at one time been chosen "at an assembly of all the archbishops, bishops, abbots, and priors of monasteries," but by the time of the Imperial ambassador's visit, the grand prince filled clerical offices himself. [36]

In sum, Bodin used Russian ethnography to pursue two conflicting agendas. On the one hand, Bodin was an empirical political scientist, dedicated to the accurate analysis of information he found in the growing body of ethnographic literature. On the other hand, the French theorist was an absolutist, committed to the proposition that a powerful central authority could solve the woes he saw all around him in France. When these two agendas came into conflict, politics won out, at least in his depiction of Russian government. Given his allegiance to powerful monarchy and his desire to hold up an empirically verified exemplar of lordly monarchy, Bodin could not interpret the information he found in *Notes on the Muscovites* objectively. A neutral analysis of Herberstein would have indicated that Russian rule was tyrannical, and this conclusion was unacceptable to Bodin because it cast absolutist policies in a bad light and deprived him of a living example of a well-ordered absolutism in Europe. Better, Bodin must have thought, to reinterpret Herberstein in such as way as to make Russian government lordly and therefore legitimate.

Sir Walter Raleigh: The Rules of Russian Tyranny

Though *Six Books* was doubtless a major contribution to political theory, it could not have been of much use to the active statesmen of the day. Given the demands of high office, who had time to plow through the complex arguments, obscure examples, and detailed proofs that men such as Bodin so carefully crafted in their massive tomes? Harried statesman required not oceans of political philosophy but rather pearls of practical wisdom—maxims, sentences, commonplaces, apothegms, and aphorisms. [37] The collection of sentences from Classical authors and their arrangement in commonplace books was one of the standard techniques of fifteenth- and sixteenth-century Humanist research, and it remained the stock in trade of "politique thinkers" thereafter. Sir Walter Raleigh's *The Prince, or Maxims of State* provides an excellent example. Raleigh, unlike Bodin, was a man of action. This work, now better known as *Maxims of State,* was Raleigh's attempt to provide a rough-and-ready guide to politics. In a section titled "Of Policy," Raleigh attempted to set out systematically the "art of government of a common-

[35] Bodin, *Six Bookes,* 734.
[36] Herberstein (1517–49), 1:54–55.
[37] A. H. Charney, "English Maxim to 1756," 40–43, 45.

wealth." He began, following Aristotle, with standard definitions of the types of commonwealths. Political authority, he wrote, rests in the hands of "1. One; monarchy or kingdom; 2. Some few chief men for virtue and wisdom, called aristocracy; 3. Many, called a free state, or popular state. These three sorts of government have respect to the common good, and therefore are just and lawful states." Each of the just forms corresponded to a "degenerate" type of government in which the ruler or rulers "all respect their own, and not the public good, and therefore are called bastard governments." They are, of course, "1. Monarchy into tyranny; 2. Aristocracy into oligarchy; 3. Popular estate into commonwealth or government of all the common and baser sort, and therefore called a commonwealth by an usurpt nickname." [38]

If these dry logical forms were to be made valuable, examples would have to be given. As we might expect, when Raleigh turned to an exposition of the ways and means of tyranny, he cited the Muscovite instance. "Tyranny," he wrote,

> is the swerving or distorting of a monarchy, or the government of one tending not to the public good, but the private benefit of himself and his followers. As in the Russen and Turkish government, where the state and wealth of other orders are employed only to the upholding of the greatness of the king or emperor. This is the worst of all the bastard regimen, to wit, of a monarchy, which resembleth the sovereign government of God himself. [39]

Following Aristotle still further, Raleigh divided tyrannies into "two sorts": "1. Barbarous and professed, which is proper to those that have got head, and have power sufficient of themselves, without others' help"; and "2. Sophistical and dissembled; as in some states that are reputed for good and lawful monarchies, but inclining to tyrannies; proper to those which are not yet settled, nor have power sufficient of themselves but must use the power and help of others, and so are forced of be politic sophisters." [40] Raleigh had no difficulty identifying the "Russe government" (together with that of the Turk) as an archetypal example of a "barbarous and professed tyranny," for the outrages of Ivan IV and his predecessors were common knowledge in Raleigh's day. [41]

Raleigh, however, knew much more than this about both professed tyranny and Russia. Aristotle had detailed a list of policies used by the professed tyrant to maintain his state in the face of opposition by downtrodden subjects. [42]

---

[38] Raleigh, *Maxims of State*, 8:1–2.
[39] Ibid., 3–4. His definition is Aristotelian. See *Politics*, III.7.1279b.
[40] Raleigh, *Maxims of State*, 8:21–22. For the distinction in Aristotle, see *Politics*, V.9.1313a.34–b.11.
[41] Raleigh, *Maxims of State*, 8:21.
[42] Aristotle, *Politics*, V.8–9.1313a.34–14a.29.

The tyrant must lop off those who are too high, he must put to death men
of spirit; he must not allow common meals, clubs, education, and the like;
he must be on his guard against anything which is likely to inspire either courage or confidence among his subjects; he must prohibit schools . . . ; he must
prevent people from knowing one another . . . ; a tyrant . . . should employ
spies; . . . the tyrant is to sow quarrels among the citizens . . . ; also he should
impoverish his subjects . . . ; another practice is to multiply taxes . . . ; [he
should] make war in order that his subjects may have something to do and
be always in want of a leader.[43]

Raleigh thought this list useful and provided his readers with a version of it
under the heading "Sophisms of a barbarous and professed tyrant." And in
order to make his register of abstract rules for tyranny more tangible, he offered examples from contemporary history. Remarkably, Raleigh noted that
one could see almost all of Aristotle's "sophisms" in the practices of the Muscovites. The professed tyrant forbids learning, allows only "base occupations
and mechanical arts," and encourages drinking, as "the Russe emperor with
his Russe people"; he should reward cronies to maintain allegiance among
the military elite, as the "Russe his boyarens"; the barbarous tyrant must
disarm the populace and tax them, "as is the common practice of the Russe
and the Turk"; he should attempt to be at war at all times so a leader is needed,
"as the Russe doth yearly against the Tatar, Polonian, and Sweden, &c."; he
must oppress the wealthy and skilled and retain all offices as his own, "as the
Turk his bashaws, and the Russe his russes"; he should forbid all manner of
private association, which is "the Russe's practice"; he must divide his subjects against one another, "so the Russe made the faction of the Zemsky and
the Oppressiony."[44]

How did Raleigh come to believe that Russian practice matched the tyrannical policy imagined by Aristotle? His primary source (which he does not
identify), Fletcher's *Of the Russe Commonwealth*, told him so. Like Raleigh,
Fletcher was well read in Classical political theory, particularly in Aristotle.
As a student at Eton and King's College he no doubt had occasion to study
the *Politics*; later, as a lecturer in Greek and a royal servant, he surely read
the book.[45] It was only natural for Fletcher to use the models, figures, and
forms he found sketched in the *Politics* when he sat down to write his treatises on Muscovite government. And indeed, the influence of Aristotle can be
seen throughout *Of the Russe Commonwealth*. Aristotle had written that
the tyrant pursued his own interest rather than the public good. Fletcher described Muscovite monarchy in exactly these terms. Aristotle had insisted
that tyrants illegally appropriated the persons and properties of their subjects, making them slaves. Fletcher claimed Ivan IV had done precisely that.[46]

[43] Ibid., 1313a.39–b.30.
[44] Raleigh, *Maxims of State*, 22–23.
[45] Lloyd E. Berry, "Life of Giles Fletcher, the Elder."
[46] Aristotle, *Politics*, III.5.1279b.7–8; Fletcher (1591), 194, 199.

And, as we just saw, Aristotle drafted a list of policies that a tyrant should follow to maintain his cruel regime. Fletcher found that the Russians followed an Aristotelian "Sophismata of secretes" as if they had read the Stagerite himself.[47] Aristotle wrote that a tyrant must dispatch the leadership of the nation, so Ivan IV destroyed his nobility, bringing "it downe to a lesser proportion: till in the end he made them not onely his vassals, but his Kolophey, that is his very villains or bondsmen"; the tyrant should prohibit education, so Ivan forbade any "kinde of common arte, much lesse in any learning, or litteral kinde of knowledge" among the populace; the tyrant sows dissent among his people, so Ivan IV "divided his subjiects into two partes," the "Oppressini" and the "Zemskey," and set them against each other; the tyrant should impoverish his subjects, so Ivan IV's men "rack and spoile them [the people] without all regard of iustice, or conscience"; and the tyrant must tax and tax again, so Ivan IV's fiscal policy was guided by the belief that "his people were like to his beard: the oftner shaven, the thicker it would grow."[48]

Both Bodin and Raleigh began with Aristotelian concepts and used "data" they found in the Russian ethnographies to flesh them out. But where Bodin was compelled to force Herberstein's image of Muscovy into the mold of lordly monarchy, Raleigh must have been shocked at the remarkable correspondence between Aristotle's manual of tyranny and the practices Fletcher described. From our vantage point, the identity of the Stagerite's register of tyrannical policies and the practices of Ivan IV's government as represented in *Of the Russe Commonwealth* is unsurprising, for Fletcher had Aristotle in mind when he set about describing Ivan's regime. Though it would perhaps be too much to say that Fletcher imposed Aristotle's ideas concerning the maintenance of tyranny on Muscovy, it is clear that the way he conceived of Ivan's various policies was guided by the wisdom of the *Politics*. In this sense, *Of the Russe Commonwealth* was ready made for Aristotelian political analysis such as that found in *Maxims of State*.

Herman Conring: Russian Tyranny and the Discipline of Ethnography

Neither Bodin nor Raleigh were academics, at least in the institutional sense. Bodin was a renowned scholar when he drafted *Six Books*, but he held no seminars and delivered no lectures on his ruthlessly inductive political science. Raleigh was a well-known statesman when he wrote *Maxims of State*, but he did not intend his work to be part of a university curriculum. It was only in the 1660s that the theory of Russian tyranny began to be taught in an organized scholastic setting. Herman Conring and his colleagues in the Empire are to be credited with this development. Conring was a true poly-

---

[47] For the "Sophismata of secretes," see Fletcher (1591), 194–96.
[48] Ibid., 199, 226, 200, 208, 218.

math. At various times in his life he served as a medical doctor, a natural philosopher, a professor of political studies, and a councilor to great princes.[49] The German scholar believed that reading Classical histories or studying abstract political theory was insufficient preparation for the duties of a statesmen. Modern leaders needed an understanding of modern polities, for, as Conring had it, "one cannot properly conduct political activity without knowledge of contemporary states." Similarly, knowledge of one's own country was insufficient:

> It can be said that it is sufficient to know well the state one rules, such that it is unimportant to study other states. To which [proposition] I answer: it is required of anyone who would govern a state to know all about it, however it is also necessary that one be knowledgeable of the states with which one's own state has relations. Indeed one can neither enter into a treaty nor an alliance, nor begin a war, if one does not possess an exact knowledge of these [neighboring] states. Otherwise severe mistakes will be made.[50]

To help rulers avoid such mistakes, Conring sought to create a formal science of political ethnography and make out of it a full-fledged academic discipline. On November 20, 1660, Conring, in his capacity as professor of politics, began a series of lectures at Helmstedt designed to give students a complete understanding of the structures of the major European states.[51] The knowledge imparted was quite explicitly "unscientific" insofar as Conring intended to render *discriptio singularis rerum publicarum aevi nostri.*[52] This was, epistemologically speaking, *cognito singularium,* and thus could only be *prudentia; cognitio universalium* (as Bodin said) alone could be classed as *scientia,* as in the case of *scientia civilis,* an abstract political science aiming at universals.[53]

Insofar as Conring was building a self-consciously empirical, descriptive discipline, he paid special attention to sources that might provide data.[54] Though the professor agreed that personal experience was always the best source, he realized that few scientists would have the opportunity to travel to distant lands for ethnographic exploration. *Notitia rerum publicarum,* therefore, had to rely on the oral and written testimony of those who had firsthand experience in the states being analyzed. Conring stressed that interviews with seasoned statesmen and diplomats were to be given pride of place. Nonetheless, the bulk of the data on which his *notitia* was to be based

---

[49] On Conring's biography, see Dietmar Willoweit, "Herman Conring."

[50] Herman Conring, "De autoribus politicis," 20–21.

[51] For sources on Conring's career, see the literature cited in Marshall T. Poe, *Foreign Descriptions of Muscovy,* 166–67.

[52] Hermann Conring, "Prooemium."

[53] Arno Seifert, "Staatenkunde."

[54] Vincenz John, *Geschichte der Statistik,* 62–64; Ferdinand Felsing, *Die Statistik als Methode der politische Ökonomie,* 52–57.

would come from manuscript and printed sources, including official materials such as the highly esteemed Venetian *relazioni* and printed ethnographies or cosmographical compendia.[55] In the introduction to his own synoptic description of great states, *Examen rerum publicarum potiorum totis orbis,* Conring cited a variety of models and sources. Among them are found the Classical geographers Strabo and Ptolemy, and of course Conring could not fail to mention Aristotle and his famous collection of constitutions. But Conring clearly understood that a modern science of ethnography could not rely on Classical texts, no matter how esteemed they might be. He duly noted that "there have been certain [writers] of our day who have studied all the states of the world, as Aristotle did in his own time."[56] Therefore, in addition to the ancient fathers of his new discipline, he cited modern collections of ethnographic vignettes such as those by Francesco Sansovino, Giovanni Botero, and, naturally, the famous Elsevierian Republics, a series of over thirty Latinized ethnographies printed in the first half of the seventeenth century.[57] Indeed, Conring seems to have been acquainted with one of the chief editors of the Republics, the political scientist Joannes de Laet.[58] Further evidence of *notitia*'s reliance on the accumulated literature of ethnography is found in the individual entries in *Examen.*[59] In his exploration of Russian statecraft, Conring cited an impressive array of ethnographic sources; for example, the pertinent volume from the Elsevierian series (as well as a clone), various unnamed Polish sources, Herberstein, Possevino, Oderborn, Olearius, various unnamed Swedish sources, and the relevant sections from the compendia of Giovanni Botero, Nicolai Belli, and others.[60]

In Conring's program, the raw information drawn from interviews, diplomatic reports, and ethnographies was to be sorted, categorized, and arrayed according to a strict theoretical protocol. He constructed a general profile of a state by means of four categories, each built by metaphorical association with Aristotle's natural causes: *causa materialis,* the economic basis of a state's power (i.e., its population, production, and physical plant); the *causa*

[55] On the use of official materials (*constitutioner, sive conventioner, sive quae aliae tabulae*), see Herman Conring, "Exercitio Historica-Politica de Notitia singularis alicujus Respublicae." On the *relazioni* in particular, see Conring (1660s), 56.

[56] Conring (1660s), 56–57.

[57] Francesco Sansovino, *Del governo dei regni et delle respubliche,* and Giovannii Botero, *Relationi universali.* For a general treatment of the Elsevierian Republics, see David W. Davies, *World of the Elseviers,* 58–62.

[58] On de Laet, see Davies, *World of the Elseviers,* 143; "Laet (Johannes de)," in *Biographisch Woordenboek der Nederlanden,* ed. Abraham J. van der Aa, 4:8–9; and Cornelis C. Goslinga, *Dutch in the Caribbean and on the Wild Coast,* 25–31. On Conring's relation to de Laet, see Willoweit, "Herman Conring," 131.

[59] Each entry contains a "review of the literature" of sorts. The Elseverian Republics and a host of other ethnographies were in his library. See Paul Raabe, "Der Biblioteka Conringiana," 427.

[60] Conring (1660s), 433–35. Conring cited *Russia seu Moscovia* (1630); Boxhornius (1630); Herberstein (1517–49); Possevino (1586); Paul Oderborn, *Ioannis Basilidis Magni Moscoviae Ducis vita;* Olearius (1656); Botero, *Relationi universali;* and Nicolai Belli, *Philippi Honorii Thesaurus politicus.*

formalis, the constitutional and administrative form of the state in principle; the *causa efficiens,* the executive and administrative arms of the state in actuality; and the *causa finalis,* the ultimate purpose or goal of supreme power.[61] Conring's description of Russia demonstrated how his Aristotelian schema worked in practice. After a brief passage treating available sources, Conring launched into Muscovy's *causa materialis.*[62] This section is typical of the chorographies provided in the first parts of most ethnographies. Conring described the borders, major rivers, flora, and fauna of Russia. The professor then proceeded to what might be called human geography. He rendered a description of the *ingenio Russarum* based in large measure on Olearius's unflattering portrayal.[63] Russians, Conring wrote, are stupid, intemperate, lustful, untrustworthy, superstitious, and so on. From Conring's perspective, and that of ethnographic science, the Russian people were not considered very good material for state-building. Their saving grace in this regard was their servility, which prevented them from protesting the work of the other *causae.* Conring's human geography of Russia concluded with a brief treatment of the Muscovite economy and trade. He then moved on to the description of the Russian state per se. Pursuant to his plan, he began with the *causa finalis.* "The end of this republic," Conring wrote, "is the benefit of the lord alone, and only by accident seeks the benefit of the people." Perhaps following Olearius, Conring described the absolute authority of the tsar over both the nobility and commons. About the *modo regiminis* of the Russians there was no doubt: "The form of government is monarchical: it is plainly tyranny [*simplex Dominatus*] of the same species of regime that obtains in Persia, in Turkey, and in our own time in all of Asia."[64] The Muscovite *causa formalis* reflects the subservience of all to the grand prince. All official duties and powers are concentrated in the hands of the tsar, who delegates them in small allotments and for short periods to his noblemen *cum* servitors. The constitution is amorphous, for the Russians have little written law.[65] As concerns the Russian *causa efficiens,* the matter is simple. In a despotic state, the despot is the mover of all things; thus Conring gave this section over to a description of the character of the Romanovs.[66]

Over the course of the second half of the seventeenth and the eighteenth centuries, Conring's twin program for the collection and analysis of ethno-

---

[61] On Conring's descriptive schema, see John, *Geschichte der Statistik,* 58–59; Zehrfeld, *Herman Conring,* 29–35; Felsing, *Die Statistik als Methode,* 21–27. The pertinent passages in Conring are in the "Prooemium" to Conring (1660s), 50–54.

[62] Conring (1660s), 435.

[63] Olearius (1656), 126–54.

[64] Conring (1660s), 440. Also see Conring, "Exercitatio," 29, where he cites Aristotle and describes Muscovy as one of several Asian despotisms. In Conring (1660s) the section covering "De rebuspublicis asiaticis" follows directly after "De republica Muscovitica."

[65] Conring (1660s), 441: "Qui jus dicunt, non utuntur legibus scriptis, quas in toto Rusia non habent, sed jus dicitur. . . . " The passage is very reminiscent of Fletcher (1591), 169.

[66] Conring (1660s), 443–45.

graphic data grew into a fully institutionalized discipline, *Statistik*.[67] Practitioners focused attention on gathering ethnographic data: proposals for reform of ethnographic writing were issued, scholarly journals reviewed travel books, and scientific societies published instructions for travelers.[68] The eighteenth-century lights of *Universitätstatistik*—Gottfried Achenwall, Johann Gatterer, and August Schlözer—never failed to mention the value of travel and travel literature for their discipline.[69] Schlözer deserves special mention in this regard, as he created what he termed a *Reisekollegium* at Göttingen, a course of study designed to introduce students to the arts of travel and ethnography.[70] It is probably also worth mentioning the *Gelehrte Reise,* a sort of academic exchange aimed at allowing scholars to meet their peers and collect information.[71] Even more striking than the organization of data-collection within the context of *Universitätstatistik* was the increasing sophistication of analytic schemas. Over the course of the later seventeenth and eighteenth centuries, each new textbook of *Statistik* seemed to offer readers a more complex array of analytic categories than the last: states were thus refracted into hundreds of subunits.[72] Perhaps the ultimate expression of this tendency toward schematization was so-called *Tabellenstatistik*.[73] Works in this subgenre described states by means of tables of characteristics—qualitatively and quantitatively expressed—that permitted the reader to make what were in theory completely parallel comparisons of particular traits. With the benefit of such a table, for example, one could synoptically view the various types of governments of European states.[74] Not only did Conring's humble *notia rerum publicarum* blossom into a developed discipline, his figuration of Muscovite governance as a "plain tyranny" proved to be of lasting importance. *Statistische* treatises of the later seventeenth and eighteenth centuries described the tsar's rule in almost exactly the same terms as had the founder of the discipline.[75]

Krizhanich: The Paradox of Autocracy

Iurii Krizhanich was not a Muscovite, but he might well be considered the only man ever to construct a Muscovite political theory in the European

---

[67] John, *Geschichte der Statistik,* passim.
[68] William E. Stewart, *Die Reisebeschreibung und ihre Theorie,* 48–62.
[69] Gottfried Achenwall, *Abriß der neuesten Staatswissenschaft.*
[70] August L. Schlözer, *Entwurf zu einem Reise-Collegio* and *Vorlesung über Land- und Seereisen.* On the *Reisekollegium,* see Justin Stagl, "Methodizing of Travel in the Sixteenth Century."
[71] On the *gelehrte Reise,* see Schlözer, *Vorlesungen über Land- und Seereisen,* 12.
[72] See, for example, the incredibly fine divisions proposed for the description of states in Johann G. Meusel's *Lehrbuch der Statistik,* 3–5.
[73] John, *Geschichte der Statistik,* 88–95.
[74] See, for example, Johann P. Anchersen, *Descriptio statuum cultiovum in tabulis.*
[75] Harm Klueting, "Russland in den Werken deutscher Statistiker," 252–53.

sense. Written largely while he was in exile in Tobol'sk, between 1663 and
1666, the Croatian scholar's *Politika* represents an analysis of Russian government unlike anything written within the confines of the Russian empire
before the eighteenth century.[76] Just how he came to write the treatise is a
story unto itself.[77] Krizhanich was born in Croatia in 1618, a time in which
the faiths and political fortunes of the Balkans were in a sorry state. The
"infidel" Turks dominated almost the entire Balkan peninsula and its Christian populations, and there seemed to be little reason to believe that the Catholic powers of Central Europe, engulfed as they were in the conflagration of
Protestant religious dissent, would rush to their aid. It was in this context
that Krizhanich first discovered the two passions that would dominate his
life and thought—the dream of uniting Orthodoxy and Catholicism against
the heretical Muslims and Protestants and that of gathering the Slavic nations
under the aegis of Muscovy in order to protect Slavdom against the Turks
and Germans. Krizhanich attended the Jesuit gymnasium in Zagreb in 1636,
received a master's degree at the Collegium Croatorum at Graz in 1638, and
then began to study law and theology at the University of Bologna. While in
Italy, Krizhanich read Possevino's account of his mission to Muscovy and apparently decided to follow in the Italian cleric's footsteps.[78] He took the highly
unusual step of entering the Collegium Graecum in Rome, an institution
whose chief mission was the preparation of missionaries to the Orthodox.
Though Latin clerics were normally not granted admittance, Krizhanich impressed the authorities with his desire to work among the Orthodox Slavs.
Significantly, in 1641 the Croatian submitted a plan to the Congregatio de
Propaganda Fide to enter Muscovy, gain the confidence of the tsar, and convince him of the necessity of reuniting the Eastern and Western churches.[79]

After his ordination in 1642, Krizhanich held a series of offices in his native
Croatia. In 1644 he requested an assignment in Smolensk, then in Polish-
Lithuanian hands, but at least closer to Moscow than Zagreb. In 1647 his
efforts to enter Russia were met with success when he accompanied a Polish
embassy to the capital.[80] While in Moscow, he attempted to repeat the experience of Possevino and discuss the possibility of ecclesiastical union with the
tsar. Alas, his requests for an audience went unanswered. For the next decade Krizhanich traveled throughout Europe on various ecclesiastical and

---

[76] The only possible exception is Gregorii Kotoshikhin's *O Rossii v tsarstvovanie Alekseia Mikhailovicha*. Kotoshikhin's book, however, is rather a description of Muscovite society than a critical analysis of Muscovite government. Morever, Kotoshikhin—like all Muscovites of his era—was completely ignorant of contemporary European political theory and the Classical concepts on which it rested. In addition, *O Rossii* was written not in Muscovy but in Sweden after Kotoshikhin had fled Russia.

[77] For a brief treatment of Krizhanich's life and the origins of *Razgowori ob Wladetelystwu*, see Josip Bozicevič, "Krizhanich, Yurii."

[78] Anté Kadič, "Krizhanich and Possevino."

[79] Anté Kadič, "Krizhanich's Memorandum."

[80] Sergei A. Belokurov, *Iurii Krizhanich v Rossii.*

diplomatic missions, but he never forgot his higher obligation to Slavic Christendom or his dream that Russia would be its savior. Without the blessing of Rome, Krizhanich took it upon himself in 1659 to travel to Muscovy once again. A change of identity would be necessary, for Krizhanich knew that Catholics—particularly Catholic missionaries—were not permitted to cross the Muscovite frontier. He disguised himself as a Serbian scholar and petitioned to enter the tsar's service. The Muscovite authorities were apparently impressed with the credentials of "Iurii Ivanov Bilish (Serbianin)," for he was quickly given a post in the important Ambassadorial Chancellery. During his sixteen months there he succeeded in passing a petition to Tsar Aleksei Mikhailovich requesting permission to write a history of Russia, complete a Slavic grammar, and translate books on a variety of subjects for the tsar's benefit. But events turned against him. In January 1661 he was exiled to Siberia for, as he put it, "one foolish word." More likely, his true identity and religious convictions were discovered. In distant Tobol'sk, far from the circles of power where Krizhanich believed his message would be received and acted upon, the Croatian expatriate was compelled to confine himself to scholarly activities.

He pursued them with a diligence befitting his ambitious though, it must be said, quixotic dreams. While in Siberia Krizhanich wrote much, but his crowning achievement and most ambitious work was *Politika*. The Croatian cleric intended the book to be no less than a plan for the reform of the entire Russian realm. His general understanding of the nature of Russian society reflects his dual identity as European thinker and Russian patriot. On the one hand, though he mercilessly castigated the opinions of "German" ethnographers about Russia (all of whom he read), he had in many ways assimilated their view that Russia lagged far behind Europe: Muscovy's economy was undeveloped, its people were rude and uneducated, and its political system was oppressive and corrupt. At the same time, he recognized that Russia had great potential: Muscovy was in many ways rich, its people lived a simple, pious, obedient life, and so much power was concentrated in the hands of the tsar that all Russia's difficulties could be easily remedied. Krizhanich's work was an attempt to provide the analysis necessary to unlock Russia's riches and enable the beleaguered nation to become a truly European power, one capable of protecting the Uniate faith from Protestantism and the downtrodden Slavic peoples from the hated "Germans."

Krizhanich believed that all political wisdom rested on two principles: "Know thyself" and "Do not trust foreigners." Since the king and the body politic were inseparable, self-knowledge for a monarch was the same as knowledge of his realm. Therefore, the monarch and his advisers must attempt to learn all they could about the people and country they ruled. Russia's basic problem, Krizhanich suggested, was that previous sovereigns had not invested sufficient energy in this sort of intelligence. They had therefore ruled badly and thereby led their people into rudeness and barbarity. The sad state of the Russian realm, in turn, had caused Russia's rulers to violate the second principle of political wisdom. Having made their realm weak through lack of "self-knowledge," the Russian elite allowed "more cunning nations"—always European and especially German—to ridicule and dominate them. The Russians, he claimed, had in fact developed a kind of national pathology—"xenomania," the self-defeating belief that they were so imperfect that only Europeans could save them.[81] The purpose of Krizhanich's council was clear: he wanted to use political science to allow Aleksei Mikhailovich to understand his nation and thereby enable him to throw off "German" domination.

How was this goal to be reached? First, the Russians needed to take a sober account of their advantages and disadvantages vis-à-vis other nations; that is, they had to discover themselves. Though he was a patriot and he believed the foreign ethnographers had exaggerated Muscovite faults, Krizhanich took a balanced and sometimes openly critical view of the abilities and customs of Russians. Russians were not among the most intelligent people in the world, so they should reserve confrontations for weaker peoples (such as Siberians and Tatars) and exercise great caution when dealing with "more cunning" nations (Germans). Their language, which was rude and undeveloped, might be corrected and improved, but it would never be suitable for the study of higher science (only Latin and Greek were appropriate here). Their clothes were undignified and should be reformed along European lines. In addition to cultural difficulties, the Russians were beset by a variety of what might be called natural disadvantages, including a lack of natural resources, long winters, evil neighbors and merchants (Crimean Tatars, Swedes, Greeks, Germans), and a scanty population. Yet the Russians also had significant advantages over their neighbors—safe frontiers, some good friends (Persians, Poles, Lithuanians), potential for large-scale trade, favorable conditions for shipping, and valuable domestic products.[82]

The most important advantage enjoyed by the Russians, however, was their form of government, which Krizhanich called "absolute autocracy." Why? Krizhanich offered a variety of arguments drawn from Classical, biblical, patristic, and modern sources suggesting that autocracy was the best form of government: it ensured justice; it created the greatest peace and tranquillity for the populace; it provided the greatest protection against disaster; and, of course, it most resembled God's authority in heaven. Two particular factors made autocracy most suitable for the Russian case. As Krizhanich repeatedly said, under autocracy "it is easy to correct all mistakes, shortcomings, and perversions and to introduce all kinds of beneficial laws." In governments whose "king does not enjoy full authority, or where many rulers exist, once errors have become part of the law, they remain uncorrected forever." Not

---

[81] Krizhanich (1663–66), 461, 463, 497–99.
[82] Ibid., 465–75, 481–83.

so under autocracy, "because whatever the autocrat orders is accomplished without delay." This was particularly the case in Russia because of the pliant nature of the Russian people: "Our people are not ambitious," Krizhanich asserted, "they do not yearn for power and therefore readily submit themselves to anyone who knows their nature, who can thus easily force them to hard work, to military labors, and to deadly danger." [83] The combination of autocracy and the meekness of the Russian nation should, the Croation cleric suggested, enable Aleksei Mikhailovich to reform Russian society along the lines he proposed in *Politika*.

Yet if the state was to fulfill this program, Krizhanich noted, it would first have to reform itself, for decades of oppressive rule had ruined Russian society. In explaining how Russian government became corrupt, Krizhanich offered an interesting historical excursus. The "tyrant" Ivan IV was ultimately responsible for introducing a particularly rapacious form of autocracy, embodied in an oath that Krizhanich claimed required Russian officials to fleece the Muscovite population: "Among the vicious tyrannical laws of Tsar Ivan the first and most important was that which compelled all officials and servants to take an oath to the sovereign tsar. . . : "'I [name], on every possible occasion, by every means at my disposal, will seek profit for the sovereign's treasury and will not let any opportunity pass to increase it.'" Such an ill-considered law and so damning an oath inevitably caused great evil, because "officials, in the tsar's name, and for their own and the tsar's benefit, used every conceivable means, torture, and torment to pillage unfortunate subjects and let pass no opportunity to plunder them." Ivan's oath was "illegal" because it was based on the assumption that the tsar was the absolute owner of his subjects' property and that he could thus do what he would with them. But this idea was erroneous—no one has the ultimate right over property, for God is the master of all. All men, including kings, are but guardians of God's creation and are charged with its proper care. In a word, Krizhanich said, "kingdoms were not created for kings, but kings for kingdoms." [84] Ivan did not understand this, and neither did Boris Godunov and False Dmitrii, both of whom were tyrants. [85] The Romanovs, though they were well intentioned, proved unable to alter the predatory nature of Russian autocracy. Thus what was a momentary innovation introduced by a horrible tyrant became a pathological national custom. The corrupt system, Krizhanich said, outlived its creator and took hold of his successors, making them unwilling tyrants. [86]

Furthermore, Krizhanich argued, decades of exploitive rule had transformed the mild, obedient Russian people into brutes.

[83] Ibid., 548, 482, 548, 539.
[84] Ibid., 583–84, 569–75.
[85] On Godunov and Dmitrii, see ibid., 522, 580–81, 594.
[86] On the distinction between a ruler and the system of government, see ibid., 576–77.

> As a result [of oppressive government], so many revolting habits have arisen among this nation that other nations consider the Russians cheaters, traitors, merciless plunderers and killers, foul mouths, and slovens. What causes this? The fact that taverns, monopolies, prohibitions, tax farmers, sworn-in deputies, tax collectors, toll collectors, and secret informers are everywhere, so that people are everywhere and always constrained, and cannot do what they would like and cannot freely enjoy what they have acquired with their work and sweat.[87]

Immoderate government, then, was ultimately responsible for the rudeness that marked Russian culture. But, Krizhanich continued, Russian customs could be altered. The European ethnographers were wrong in suggesting that "Russians have brutish and mulish dispositions and they can accomplish nothing of any worth if they are not forced to do it with sticks and whips." [88] Olearius and the "Germans" made the mistake of essentializing a quality—servility—that was really a secondary result of cruel government. The Russians were not natural slaves, as comparative analysis demonstrates.

> The Russians have the same language, belong to the same family, and have the same habits as other Slavs—Poles, Ukrainians, Croats, and others who do not possess these mulish features, but have other, more refined characteristics. If at present many Russians do nothing out of respect, and everything only because of fear of punishment, then the cause of this is harsh government, which has made their lives repulsive and without honor.[89]

All that was needed was a brave sovereign to use the extensive powers of autocracy to reform the government, and the barbarous customs of the Russians would be reformed accordingly.

Krizhanich, of course, had a blueprint for accomplishing this feat. The sovereign must bridle autocracy by granting "good laws" to the entire nation and "proper privileges" to each of its classes.[90] Krizhanich knew the Russians would object to the limitation of the tsar's power. To refute these criticisms, he constructed a dialogue between "Boris," a typical Russian, and "Khrevoi," a figure that clearly represented the Croatian scholar himself. Boris, of course, rejected the notion that autocratic power should be fettered. "Autocracy is the best form of government. Moreover, where subjects have no privileges, autocracy is firmly maintained. Conversely, where subjects enjoy privileges, autocracy is destroyed. This means that it is improper to grant privileges to subjects." Khrevoi agreed that "autocracy is the best form of government," but counterargued that "it is not true that autocracy would

---

[87] Ibid., 587.
[88] Ibid., 586.
[89] Ibid., 587.
[90] Ibid., 591.

perish from appropriate privileges." Good laws and privileges in fact preserve autocracy by placing a "bridle" on

> [royal] servitors, so that they cannot easily indulge in their vicious desires and
> drive the people to despair. This is the only means by which subjects can pro-
> tect themselves against the evildoing of [royal] servants. This is also the only
> way to safeguard justice in the realm. If there are no privileges, then no restric-
> tions and no punishments by the king can cause [his] servants to renounce
> their evildoing, and high-placed advisers [to renounce] their godless, inhu-
> man council.[91]

The unhappy fate of Ivan IV, Boris Godunov, and False Dmitrii demonstrated
that God would not suffer a tyrant: because of Ivan's tyranny, his dynasty
was destroyed by Providence; Godunov's failure to improve the government
caused God to send a rival—Dmitrii—to eliminate his line; and Dmitrii, the
defrocked monk, by the will of the Creator died a horrible death. Neither
would the oppressed live under a rogue prince. The tyrannies of Ivan, Godunov, and Dmitrii produced the greatest crisis Russia had ever known (the
Time of Troubles), and the continuation of their brutal system culminated in
"three upheavals of our own times, one in Pskov [1650] and two in Moscow
[1648 and 1662], and three treasons, the Ukrainian [1657], Bashkir [1662],
and Berezovo [1663]."[92]

Krizhanich cast his plan for the reform of the Russian government in the
form of a "hypothetical address" to be delivered to the nation by the tsar or
one of his ministers. Oddly, Krizhanich, the virulent Russian chauvinist and
xenophobe, had the tsar turn to "foreign" manners for instruction on how
to reform his realm. "In a word," the tsar is made to say, "we have examined
and investigated the legislation of various kingdoms—Greek, French, Spanish, German, and Polish—and those laws which we have considered to be
good, appropriate, and necessary for our kingdom we wish to grant generously to you." What the exiled scholar arrived at through this liberal survey
of foreign customs was a kind of autocratic *Ständestaat*. The estates are to
be granted privileges of various sorts: noblemen will be exempt from taxation, will have exclusive right to own landed properties, will be called by dignified names (not "slave"), and will be exempt from corporal punishment
and from the requirement of prostration before the tsar; the clergy will be
exempt from taxation and freed from the jurisdiction of secular courts; urban residents will have the right to expel unwanted foreigners, elect city councils, and judge minor cases; officials will be freed from Ivan IV's exploitive
oath and given an enlightened one. In general, the government will promise
to act as the guardian, not the owner, of the lives and property of the realm's

---

[91] Ibid., 592.
[92] Ibid., 578–79, 581.

subjects. Nonetheless, all the privileges granted by the tsar will be strictly conditional: the tsar and his successors are to be bound by an oath to up-hold estate privileges, but (as Krizhanich had the Russian prince say) "if in time you or your descendants of any estate exhibit disobedience—that is, if people, hiding behind some privilege, will not obey and fulfill our orders—in such a case we and our heirs are not obligated to preserve the privilege that resulted in disobedience, and we shall neither grant nor issue any such right." [93]

Krizhanich was torn between two worlds. In one sense, he was a man of Humanist Europe—Classically educated, literate, and concerned with re-finement and the "higher things" in life. Despite his belief that much of what the foreign ethnographers wrote about Russia was wrong, his background made it impossible for him to dissociate himself from the common European opinion that Russia was a barbaric place. In another sense, however, Krizha-nich was more Russian than the Russians. *Politika* is full of vitriolic attacks on foreigners and hopeful paeans to the glorious future of the downtrodden Muscovite people. He loved the simplicity, piety, and humility of common Russians. Krizhanich's two worlds, European and Russian, collided with par-ticular force in his treatment of Muscovite autocracy. Russian government was, as the foreigners said, tyrannical and desperately in need of moderation along European lines. But the awesome authority of the tsar was the very in-strument that would allow Russia to become civilized and assume its proper place among the European kingdoms. This was a paradox that Krizhanich could not solve—autocracy had to be limited to reform Russia, but in order to reform Russia, it would have to remain, at least for a time, unlimited.

Montesquieu: The Science of Despotism

There is a sense in which Bodin, Raleigh, Conring, and Krizhanich were practitioners of "political science." It is likely that all of them would have seconded Francis Bacon, the great champion of empirical methodology, who believed that too much effort had been expended on "delicate learning" or "vain affectations" by Classical-minded scholars who studied "words and not matter." [94] What was needed for the advancement of "civil philosophy" was not abstract speculation but the empirical study of hard data—in this instance the data provided by European travelers—and careful general-ization. Yet each of them was careful to distinguish the kind of knowledge produced by his inductive method from high science, that is, absolutely sure knowledge of universals. In this they followed Aristotle. The Stagerite clas-

[93] Ibid., 597, 599–614, 601.
[94] Francis Bacon, "Advancement of Learning," 114–15.

sified disciplines according to the ends they pursued and the level of generality they could attain: "theoretical" disciplines, such as mathematics, sought the universal; "practical" disciplines, such as economics, sought general understanding useful in policy formation; and "poetical" disciplines, such as rhetoric, sought technical knowledge aimed at making artifacts.[95] For Aristotle, politics was first and foremost a practical discipline concerned with "what kind of government is adapted to particular states." The ideal form of polity, he maintained, "is often unattainable, and therefore the true legislator and statesman ought to be acquainted, not only with that which is best in the abstract, but also that which is best relative to circumstances."[96] This was precisely the goal of most sixteenth- and seventeenth-century political scientists—an understanding of what sort of government best fitted the conditions of particular states.

The traditional Aristotelian understanding of the nature of prudential political science, however, was changing in the later seventeenth and early eighteenth centuries. Not everyone was convinced that the empirical disciplines could not be raised to the level of theoretical science. For one thing, inductive logic tended to erase the firm line that Aristotle had drawn between higher and lower disciplines. Probability made it possible for practical political scientists to claim they were concerned with the discovery of regularities of human and social behavior, just as natural philosophers such as Newton discovered the regularities of motion. Perhaps the ultimate expression of this tendency is found in Montesquieu, whose world picture is mechanistic and whose science, as a consequence, is strikingly positivistic. *The Spirit of the Laws* opens with a startling claim, typical of the Enlightenment's faith that even the most complex "systems" could be reduced to "laws" by the power of human reason: "Laws, taken in the broadest meaning, are the necessary relations deriving from the nature of things; and in this sense, all beings have their laws: the divinity has its laws, the material world has its laws, the intelligences superior to man have their laws, the beasts have their laws and man has his." Montesquieu conceived that social laws existed and that he, like Newton in physics, was capable of discovering them. "I have set down the principles," he wrote, "and I have seen particular cases conform to them as if by themselves, the histories of all nations being but their consequences, and each particular law connecting with another or dependent on a more general one." These "principles," he claims, were not drawn "from my prejudices but from the nature of things." Once Montesquieu had revealed the logic of the "nature of things," the social world appeared to him like a "watch," with distinctive "wheels," "gears," and "springs."[97]

---

[95] See, among others, Aristotle, *Topics*, 145a.15–18; *Metaphysics*, 1025b.19–27; and *Nicomachean Ethics*, 1180b.16 and 1112b.1–8.

[96] Aristotle, *Politics*, IV.1.1288b.22–29.

[97] Montesquieu, *Spirit of the Laws*, 3, xliii, xli.

Not only did Montesquieu amend Aristotle's epistemology of the human sciences; he also (and perhaps more significantly) reformed the Stagerite's typology of political regimes. The traditional Aristotelian theory of governments was built on a numerical analysis of the distributions of sovereignty (rule by one, the few, and the many) and the tendency of the various distributions to devolve into degenerate forms ("tyranny," "oligarchy," and "democracy") and to cycle from one form to another. In contrast, Montesquieu focused on the ways in which different regimes interact with human passions to produce characteristic laws, mores, and customs within society. He partially abandoned the old typology premised on the numeric principle and substituted a typology of political cultures built on the observation of "natural" affinities between what he termed the "nature" and "principle" of actual governments. Montesquieu's "nature" is superficially similar to Aristotle's definition of a regime in that both relied on distributive criteria. But the baron de La Brède's investigation of extant governments led him to add an element never considered by Aristotle—intermediary bodies such as social classes, courts, and laws. These "mediate channels through which power flows" served as a brake on the authority of the sovereign.[98] The addition of intermediary bodies was important because it allowed Montesquieu to alter the composition of Aristotle's regime typology. Aristotle's distinction between aristocracy and democracy became moot, for according to Montesquieu, any regime governed by some or all of the people necessarily entailed an intermediary element insofar as the rulers were both sovereign and the executors of sovereignty. Self-governing regimes were self-limiting. Moreover, a distinction appeared between two types of Aristotle's "rule of one," depending on the presence or absence of intermediary elements. Monarchies have them, despotisms do not. Thus Montesquieu arrived at a threefold typology of regimes that united Aristotle's numeric principle and the novel idea of "nature": "Republican government is that in which the people as a body, or only part of the people, have sovereign power; monarchical government is that in which one alone governs, but by fixed and established laws; whereas, in despotic government, one alone, without law and without rule, draws everything along by his will and his caprice." In addition to a distinct "nature," regimes possessed signature "principles." The baron explained the difference between the two in this way: "its nature is that which makes it what it is, and its principle, that which makes it act. The one is its particular structure, and the other is the human passions that set it in motion." He believed that social principles "derive naturally" from social natures. In popular government (aristocracy or democracy), without the force of the law or the threat of the despot, the motive principle is virtue or "love of the homeland, that is, love of equality"; in monarchy, moderated by intermediary bodies, "honor" or "the prejudice of each person and each condition" is the spring;

---

[98] Ibid., 18.

in despotism, without any check on the caprice of the prince, "fear" is the spring.[99]

Though Montesquieu was careful to point out that each form of government possesses a measure of each kind of spring, the whole aim of his analysis was to show that empirical observation of actual states suggested that only a limited number of combinations of nature and principle occur, that certain natures and certain principles have a kind of lawlike affinity.[100] One does not find, for example, aristocracy or democracy moved by the spring of honor, or monarchy enlivened by virtue. The laws of Montesquieu's social physics disallowed these combinations. Having discovered three distinct regimes, Montesquieu then proposed that the nature and principle of each—its political culture—should have a determinative effect on laws. The demonstration of this thesis is found in Books 4 through 8 of the *Spirit of the Laws,* which deal respectively with the "the laws of education," positive laws, criminal law, sumptuary laws, and the "corruption of the principles of the three governments." The remainder of the *Spirit of the Laws* explore how the three regimes, in accordance with their natures and principles, deal with the necessities of rule. Thus Part 2 treats defense, Part 3 treats climate and the humors associated with it, Part 4 treats trade and commerce, and Part 5 treats religion.

Montesquieu argued that his social physics was the product of careful observation of humankind as it was represented in numerous ancient and modern sources.[101] He did not impose his theory on the evidence, but rather discovered it within the data. And when he explored the instance of Muscovy, he uncovered despotism.[102] Throughout *Spirit of the Laws,* Montesquieu cited Muscovite customs as evidence of the lawlike uniformity of all despotisms. For example, Montesquieu proposed that "honor is not the principle of despotic states" because "men in them are all slaves"; thus, Montesquieu argued, honor is unknown in Muscovy. It is in the nature of despotic government that no laws can fetter the will of the sovereign, not even fundamental laws governing the inheritance of the crown; thus, "according to the constitutions of Muscovy, the tsar can choose whomever he wants as his successor, either from within his family or from outside it." In despotic regimes, "one is so unhappy that one fears death more than one cherishes life; therefore, punishments should be more severe there"; thus, in Muscovy "the penalty for robbery is the same as for murder." In despotic countries, a lord "who can be stripped of his lands and his slaves at any moment" has no interest in preserving his serfs; thus the Russian despot Peter I required each

---

[99] Ibid., xli, 10, 21–30.

[100] Ibid., preface and 30.

[101] Montesquieu cited more than 300 sources in *Spirit of the Laws.*

[102] On Montesquieu's figuration of Muscovy, see Albert Lortholary, *Le Mirage russe en France au XVIIIe siècle;* Georges Chklaver, "Montesquieu et la Russie"; and Fedor V. Taranovskii, "Montesk'iu i Rossiia."

magnate to collect taxes from his serfs so that it would be in their "interest not to harass his peasants." Despotism allows no liberty, but has the virtue of imposing modest taxes; thus "in Russia, taxes are of medium size [and] they have been increased since despotism has become more moderate." The political slavery of despotic governments destroys civic liberty, making it "very easy to sell oneself"; thus "the Muscovites sell themselves easily." Despotic governments hinder international commerce because no exchange can be established; thus no exchange can be founded in Muscovy.[103]

How did Montesquieu come to view Russia as a despotism? The baron was a keen reader of ethnographic literature.[104] As had his theoretical predecessors, he used a variety of travel accounts as sources of evidence on Russia and the Eurasian north.[105] His main source, however, and the one that stands in the background of his general image of Russia, was John Perry's *State of Russia under the Present Czar* (1716).[106] Perry was a naval engineer who had been recruited by Peter the Great during the tsar's stay in England in 1698. He was a close associate of Peter's and worked on several important projects, notably a canal linking the Don and Volga rivers, the drydocks at Voronezh, and a survey of the waterways of St. Petersburg.[107] Perry returned to England in 1712, after having been held in virtual captivity by Peter for several years.[108] Perry's patron, of course, was Russia's great reforming tsar, and the English engineer witnessed tremendous changes in Russia over the course of his stay. Perry's very purpose in writing *The State of Russia* was to inform the English public of the "several improvements which the czar has made among his people."[109] Much of *The State of Russia* is given over to a comparison of what Perry called "the old methods of Russia" with Peter's plans for their "reformation" and the results of his attempts.[110] Perry

---

[103] Montesquieu, *Spirit of the Laws,* 27–28, 62, 82, 216, 221, 251, 416–17.

[104] On Montequieu's use of the literature of ethnography, see Muriel Dodds, *Les Récits de voyages.*

[105] Montesquieu cited several sources on Russia and the Eurasian north drawn from Jean Fédéric Bernard, ed., *Recueil de voyages au Nord.* In addition, Montesquieu used Samuel Pufendorf, *Histoire de Suède* (cited erroneously as *Introduction à l'histoire générale et politique de l'universe*). Montesquieu often did not cite the source of his intelligence on Muscovy. See, for example, *Spirit of the Laws,* 60, 62, 111, 137, 147, 154, 216, 233, 280–81, 287, 315–16, 416–17, 517, where facts are adduced but no sources referenced. There is some evidence that Montesquieu knew Neuville's *Relation curieuse, et nouvelle de Moscovie,* though he did not cite it. In the *Persian Letters* he wrote that the tsar was "the absolute master of the lives and property of his subjects, all of whom are slaves except for four families" (letter 51). This passage is similar to one in *Relation curieuse,* 57.

[106] Though Perry is cited by name only four times in *Spirit of the Laws* (28, 92, 209, 251), much of the information on Russia in the book is certainly drawn from *State of Russia under the Present Czar.* The intelligence concerning Russia cited on 154, 216, 233, 280–81, and 315–16 of *Spirit of the Laws* can be traced to Perry with confidence.

[107] Perry (1716), preface (n.p.).

[108] See ibid., 19ff., where Perry describes his arduous attempts to gain his arrears and leave the country.

[109] Ibid., preface (n.p.).

[110] For "old methods," see ibid., 261.

was sympathetic to Peter's cause, for he clearly understood the "old methods" to be barbaric: he described the Russians at some length as idolatrous drunkards, wanting in all learning, honor, and honesty.[111] He reviewed in detail Peter's attempts to reform the state administration, cultural practices (beards, clothing, marriage, the keeping of servants), religion, education, and the armed forces.[112] For example, he noted that Peter issued an edict banning the age-old practice of calling oneself the tsar's slave. Perry was not at all sanguine, however, about the prospect for a successful reformation of Muscovy or the wayward customs of its people. To be sure, Peter had made improvements: "There are a great many other Things which his Majesty has done to reform and convince his people of the Folly of being bigoted to their old Ways and Customs, and that there was no real Evil in changing them for new, that are either more reasonable, or more becoming and decent." But all hinged on the reformer-tsar, and Perry feared his reforms would perish with him: "And this is certain, that if the present Czar should happen to die, without the greatest part of his present old Boyars go off before him, the generality of Things wherein he had taken so much Pains to reform his Country, will for the most part revolve into their old Form." And in any case, Peter's alterations were largely cosmetic, for while Russians might no longer call themselves slaves, "they are," he concluded, "Slaves still." Peter was attempting to reform despotism by means of despotism. His government, like that of his benighted Muscovite ancestors, remained cruel and (in Perry's terminology) "arbitrary." As in "old" Russia, so under Peter, "all the common People, or Peasants of Russia (who dress and till the Land &c.) are slaves, either directly to the *Czar* himself, to the *Boyars,* to the Monasteries or to the Gentlemen of the Country." Indeed, Perry believed that "Slavery [was] hereditary to them." Having reviewed Peter's regime and the results of his reforms, the English engineer concluded with words that could have been borrowed from Fletcher: "I believe I have said enough to let the Reader see the Happiness of living in a free Country." [113]

Montesquieu's figuration of Muscovy was, as is apparent, heavily reliant on Perry. Like Perry, Montesquieu viewed Muscovy as a despotism in transition. In contrast to the peoples of "the East," whose characters made them fit for permanent slavery, the Russians were a nation of the north—strong, courageous, and freedom-loving.[114] He believed despotism was "foreign to the climate" of Russia and thought that the regime must have been "carried [to Muscovy] by the mixture of nations and by conquests," though he never

---

[111] Ibid., 177–78, 223 (superstition and idolatry), 227–29 (drunkenness and general misbehavior), 209ff. (ignorance), 216–18 (dishonor and dishonesty).

[112] Ibid., 187–95 (state administration), 195–203 (beards, clothing, marriage, servants), 205–8 (religion), 209–21 (education), 270–80 (armed forces).

[113] Perry (1716), 236–38, 261, 237, 241, 258, 260, 267.

[114] On the immutability of the "East," see Montesquieu, *Spirit of the Laws,* 235. On the nations of the "north," see ibid., 231–34, 278.

specified what nations or which conquests. "Although the Muscovite nobility was reduced to servitude by one of its princes," Montesquieu wrote, "one will always see there marks of impatience that the southern climates do not produce." [115] In reforming Russia, Peter was simply giving "the mores and manners of Europe to a European nation." [116]

> I beg you to observe with what industry the Muscovite government seeks
> to escape the despotism which weighs on the government even more than it
> does on the peoples. Great bodies of troops have been disbanded; penalties for
> crimes have been lessened; tribunals have been established; some men have be-
> gun to be versed in the laws; the peoples have been instructed. [117]

Though Montesquieu believed Peter was making great strides, he was no more optimistic than Perry about the prospects for a successful transition to monarchy in Russia. After reviewing recent improvements, Montesquieu warned that "there are particular causes that perhaps [will] return it to a misfortune it had wanted to flee." [118]

Montesquieu was perhaps the first European to devise a political sociology in the modern sense. Unlike his predecessors, he was not satisfied to repeat the old prudential maxims about the rule of one, the few, and the many, or their cyclical evolution. His aim was a theoretical knowledge of the basic dynamics of political cultures. Within this positivistic framework, the political scientific image of Muscovy changed. To be sure, Muscovy remained a tyrannical state in which the ruler was the master of slave-subjects. This was the basic message of nearly every European ethnography of Russia, including Perry, and Montesquieu accepted it completely. Yet the baron's understanding of Muscovite government was novel in that he offered a political-cultural explanation of the stability of Russian despotism. Montesquieu imagined that in the distant past, Russia had been reduced to despotism by a foreign nation, a force that ruled through fear. Over time, the naturally freedom-loving habits of a northern people were extinguished, only to be replaced by a kind of fawning servility. Once the "nature" of the government—rule by one without law—came into alignment with the now habitual "principle"—fear—Russian society was in essence fixed by the mutual attraction of these elements. Even the strenuous efforts of Peter I (which themselves smacked of despotism) could not break the hold of the social physics that bound Russia to endless servitude. "Muscovy had tried to leave its despotism," Montesquieu concluded, but "it cannot." [119]

---

[115] Ibid., 316, 280–81. Montesquieu does not cite his source, but he could be referring to Perry (1716), 187ff., where Peter's program for reform of the state is described.
[116] Montesquieu, *Spirit of the Laws*, 316.
[117] Ibid., 60.
[118] Ibid.
[119] Ibid., 416.

Conclusion: The Cycle of Reference

Bodin, Raleigh, Conring, Krizhanich, and Montesquieu all agreed with Aristotle that a despotic or tyrannical polity was one in which the ruler was master and his subjects were slaves. As empirically minded scientists, they investigated the pages of European ethnography in search of actual instances of this theoretical type. Each of them "found" examples of archetypal tyranny in (respectively) Herberstein, Fletcher, Olearius, Petreius, and Perry. Nonetheless, there is an obvious sense in which their discovery of despotism in the ethnographic literature was preordained. The European ethnographers were part of the same intellectual and conceptual world as the European political theorists. Herberstein and his successors, too, had read Aristotle and were familiar with his notions of tyranny and despotism. Naturally, the travelers relied on Aristotle's familiar concepts to provide a descriptive language that their contemporaries would understand. When one reads that the tsar is a tyrant or despot, that he controls the lives and properties of his people, and that his subjects are in fact nothing but slaves, this is a good indication that the ethnographers were consciously or unconsciously translating what they experienced in Muscovy into the Aristotelian lingua franca of educated Europe. The political scientists, in turn, read the travelers' accounts with these same notions in mind. They searched the ethnographic descriptions and found Muscovite tyranny in them, for the concept itself was a constituent part of the foreign accounts. The visitors began with Aristotle, and the theorists ended with him.

✦ 7

WAS MUSCOVY A DESPOTISM?

And Samuel told all the words of the LORD unto his people that asked of him a king. And he said, This will be the manner of the king that shall reign over you: He will take your sons, and appoint them for himself, for his chariots, and to be his horsemen; and some shall run before his chariots. And he will appoint him captains over thousands, and captains over fifties; and will set them to ear his ground, and to reap his harvest, and to make his instruments of war, and instruments of his chariots. And he will take your daughters to be confectioneries, and to be cooks, and to be bakers. And he will take your fields, and your vineyards, and your oliveyards, even the best of them, and give them to his servants. And he will take the tenth of your seed, and of your vineyards, and give to his officers, and to his servants. And he will take your menservants, and your maidservants, and your goodliest young men, and your asses, and put them to work. He will take the tenth of your sheep: and ye shall be his servants.

1 SAMUEL 8:10−17[1]

IN HIS MONUMENTAL *Politika,* the Croatian expatriate Iurii Krizhanich reported having a rather revealing conversation on July 26, 1663, with a "deceitful German" resident of Muscovy. The unnamed European told Krizhanich:

It appears that all principal Russian boyars carry poison with them so that they can take it when they learn that the tsar is angry with them. A boyar who was near Kamenets, they say, took poison in Kiev. And another one, who investi-

---

[1] In the first complete Slavonic printed Bible, the *Ostrozhskaia biblia* of 1580, the word the editors of the King James version translated as "servant" is rendered *rab,* meaning "servant" or "slave." For the passage, see 1 Kings 8:14, 15, and 17 in the *Ostrozhskaia biblia.* Note that in the Slavonic Bible the two books of Samuel are included with the two books of Kings. All four books are called "Kings."

gated the pilfering of the treasury in the Ukraine, showed him this poison saying: "Look how slavishly we live."[2]

According to Krizhanich, such stories were common among foreigners within
Russia and without, for most Europeans held that the tsar was a kind of despot and his servitors—even his magnates—were servile creatures living in
fear of their prince's capricious wrath. To demonstrate the depth of this opinion among Europeans, Krizhanich quoted extensively from the works of Ulfeldt, Olearius, and Petreius on the topic of Russian despotism and barbarism,
and he mentioned the printed accounts of a host of other European ethnographers of Russia, including Giovio, Herberstein, Heidenstein, Henning, and
Oderborn.[3] And though he too felt that Russian government was unbalanced,
Krizhanich was convinced that what he called the "German slander" was part
of a misguided, spiteful campaign—which he associated erroneously with
Protestantism[4]—to blacken the good name of Russia. The pages of the European descriptions of Muscovy, he wrote, were full of "venomous, offensive, insulting words and false stories" that brought unearned shame on the
Slavs. Not only were the foreigners prejudiced, they were often simply wrong
because they were unable to comprehend Muscovite life. At one point in *Politika,* Krizhanich had the archetypal Russian "Boris" ask the wise Croatian
"Khrevoi" to explain "what the reasons are behind the judgments and accu-
sations against us by foreigners." Khrevoi, who is of course Krizhanich himself, responds that the Europeans have simply failed to penetrate the surface
of Russian life: "Foreigners judge us by superficial, external things, . . . our
appearance, our language, our clothes and customs, and the way we build
our houses and make our tools." It is true, Khrevoi conceded, that the Russians are inferior to the Europeans in many ways, but their inadequacy had
been exaggerated by confused visitors who were at once unwilling and incapable of seeing the significant advantages enjoyed by the Muscovites.[5]

In many ways, it is hard not to sympathize with Krizhanich's dual attack
on European ethnography of Russia, for it is certain that some visitors were
both biased against and ignorant of Russian ways, and so could not paint a
true picture of what they encountered in Muscovy. Many of the itinerant envoys visited Russia for only a short period of time and probably never gained
sufficient experience to understand in depth the workings of Russian politics

---

[2] Krizhanich (1663–66), 586.

[3] Ibid., 484–92.

[4] In his "answer to foreign slander," Krizhanich argued (ibid., 487–92) that works by Catholics of the sixteenth century were somehow more fair than treatments by Protestants in the seventeenth century. Thus he concluded that Protestant ("German") religious hostility to Orthodoxy stood behind the "slanders" found in the writings of Olearius et al. Having read all the
accounts, he knew this allegation to be false, for the depictions of Russia offered by both
Catholics and Protestants are, if not uniformly negative, then predominantly critical. Clearly Krizhanich projected his own Catholicism and hatred of Protestantism on the travelers' writings.

[5] Ibid., 488, 478, 548.

or administration. Residents remained longer and knew more, but, as Krizhanich would surely have pointed out, as Europeans they were biased against what they reflexively perceived as "barbarous" Russian customs. Though Krizhanich does not mention it, the Europeans' habit of liberally borrowing text from outdated books about Russia and of using native European categories to describe Russian reality casts further doubt on the veracity of the foreigners' accounts.

Yet, Krizhanich's criticism notwithstanding, it should not be concluded that simply because there were forces impeding the visitors' investigation and comprehension of Russia, everything they related is dubious, tainted, or incorrect. Each individual statement found in the European accounts must be carefully investigated if the truth or falsehood of their testimony is to be found out.[6] Scholars must ask whether a foreigner could have seen what he reported, whether he had plagiarized earlier treatises, or whether he was forcefully projecting some European category on a Russian phenomenon that might be better understood in another way. This important work should properly be left to specialists investigating narrowly defined topics in Muscovite history. It would seem to be appropriate, however, to conclude this book by exploring the veracity of foreign testimony concerning the nature of Russian government. The question at hand might be put in this way: Once the effects of Russian suspicion, borrowing, and conceptual imposition have been stripped away, what is left of the foreigners' thesis that Muscovite government was a tyranny or despotism, that is, a type of regime in which the king was the master of all political power and property and his subjects were servitors or even slaves? An attempt to answer this query will, it is hoped, shed some light on the troublesome problem of the specificity of Russian government in comparison with early modern European regimes generally.

Observation, Influence, and Conceptualization

One might imagine the impressions of the Europeans as signals that have passed from their point of origin—Russian reality—through a variety of filters, each of which modulated the original transmission in a particular way. Such filters are of course many, but we have identified three that perhaps had the greatest impact on the observations and subsequent writings of European visitors. The first is Russian suspicion. The Russian government took active measures to sequester foreigners in diplomatic quarters or foreign ghettos and presented visiting Europeans with an idealized picture of Russian power relations. Thus many travelers may not have been able to gather all the information relevant to their topics, and what they did collect was not

---

[6] For some suggestions on how this task might be approached, see Marshall T. Poe, "Use of Foreign Descriptions of Russia as Sources for Muscovite History."

perhaps a true reflection of Russian reality. The second filter is borrowing. Foreigners commonly read accounts of Muscovy before their journeys to Russia and used older descriptions as sources of information when they themselves described the little-known northern kingdom. Thus many visitors did not observe everything they reported, but rather borrowed information, sometimes uncritically, from earlier accounts. The third filter is conceptual. When the visitors arrived in Muscovy they carried with them various sorts of specifically European mental baggage, the most important of which for our purposes were concepts and attitudes about well-formed and ill-formed government. In the process of describing Russian rule, the Europeans were compelled to use these alien notions, and they may have forced them on Muscovite institutions without regard for what they had truly observed.

To what extent did these filters distort the signal emanating from Russian reality through the foreign ethnographers and into their accounts? Let us begin with the impact of Russian suspicion. The Muscovite government was relatively successful in preventing visiting ambassadors from actively investigating its affairs, at least in certain areas. Surrounded by officials and held in closed apartments, ambassadorial parties generally had little opportunity to familiarize themselves with much beyond the confines of the court and state offices. Envoys such as Herberstein, Possevino, Olearius, and Korb were able to provide accurate though only very general observations about political power and government in Moscow. About the operation of the state in the provinces, the life of the provincial gentry, and the condition of the peasantry, the Moscow-bound envoys were able to learn little. The impact of propagandistic Russian stagecraft on the visiting legates was negligible. The ambassadors were all seasoned observers of court ceremonies and were therefore well aware that Muscovite officials were putting on a kind of show during their various "entertainments" in Russia. Most of them were not fooled. As for the residents, it seems clear the government enjoyed little success in preventing them from investigating its affairs. Though the court may have wished to isolate foreign residents in special settlements, most of those who worked in Muscovy did not reside in any "German" ghetto. Indeed, men such as Staden, Margeret, Bussow, and Collins moved in the shadow of the court, worked in state offices, and lived among the Russians for many years. As a result, only the most intimate details of Russian civic life generally escaped their grasp. And their knowledge was not confined to the capital: as employees of the crown and estate holders, many of the residents were able to provide detailed intelligence about the gentry and peasantry of the provinces. Having observed Russian government from the inside, the residents were no more likely than their ambassadorial counterparts to be tricked by Russian propaganda or stagecraft.

There is little doubt that the most popular ethnographies of Russia exercised considerable influence over early modern descriptions of Muscovite government generally. The most important account in this regard was of course Herberstein's *Notes on the Muscovites,* which was both very widely available and particularly harsh in its censure of Russian civic life. Beginning almost immediately after its first publication in 1549, author after author turned to this seminal work for guidance as to the nature of Russian government. By the turn of the century, Herberstein's opinion that the grand prince was a tyrant had become a fundamental part of the European image of Muscovy. The popularity of Possevino and Olearius, both of whom owed much to Herberstein, served to spread the Habsburg diplomat's message of Russian tyranny. Though the evidence of influence is reasonably clear, an important caveat is in order. Herberstein understood that political relations in Russia had changed rather dramatically in the second half of the fifteenth century. The once independent princes and free servitors of northeastern Russia had been brought to heel by the grand princes of Moscow, the most important of them Ivan III and Vasilii III. The Habsburg legate wrote correctly that the fallen elite was in a state of dependence on the Muscovite prince, and he called this condition tyranny. Later authors, many of whom had read Herberstein, said nearly the same thing. Textual correspondence, however, does not conclusively prove borrowing. The record contains several instances in which authors—for example, Margeret, Collins, and Neuville—offered Herbersteinian descriptions of Russian rule even though they may not have been familiar with *Notes on the Muscovites* or a text dependent on it. Certainly these ethnographers could have been subject to the atmospheric influence of Herberstein's ideas. This could not be the case, however, with Paul of Aleppo. The itinerant Arab-speaking cleric knew neither the European literature of Muscovy nor European opinions about Russian government, but he nevertheless described Muscovite rule as a kind of despotism, albeit a benign one. Paul did not *plagiarize* Herberstein and those who agreed with him; rather he independently *corroborated* their testimony. Moreover, even where it is clear that a later author was influenced by an earlier one, the repeated bit of information is not necessarily erroneous. Many Europeans, particularly residents, had ample opportunity to observe the workings of Russian government. They did not need to rely on Herberstein or any other author for information of this sort. If they chose to characterize Russian rule in words borrowed from Herberstein, it might well indicate that the situation they observed was nearly identical to that described in *Notes on the Muscovites.* And the foreigners were also capable of reading Herberstein critically. Olearius, for example, rejected his esteemed predecessor's claim that Russian wives understood beating as a sign of affection. Nonetheless, his investigation of Russian government relations apparently gave him no reason to depart significantly from Herberstein's characterization, so he did not.

Finally, the ethnographers had no choice but to conceptualize Muscovite rule in European terms that could not completely capture the specificity of Russian government. Thus *tsaria* became "kings," *boiare* became "magnates," *dvoriane* became "gentry," and, more generally, Muscovite *samoder-*

zhavie was made to fit the mold of what Europeans understood as "tyran-nical" or "despotic" government. Yet the degree to which this process of imperfect translation distorted the image of Russian rule should not be ex-aggerated. Though European and Muscovite political cultures were surely as different as all the ethnographers said they were, in a broader perspective they were fundamentally similar. Muscovy was, despite its peculiarities, a monarchy of the common early modern type: Russia was ruled by a king, who was simultaneously the head of a dynastic family, the chief prince of a central court, and the titular lord of a large territorial state; Russia had a rec-ognizable governing class composed of princes, untitled servitors, and a large provincial gentry; the Russian governing class worked in institutions that were similar to those all over Europe—a court, central chancelleries, a judi-ciary, a provincial administration, and, most important, an army. European travelers may have been at a loss to understand the political organizations they encountered in the New World or even in the hinterlands of Europe (Ireland, Lapland, the northern Urals, and the Eurasian steppe), but they im-mediately and intuitively comprehended the basic structures of Russian rule precisely because they were roughly similar to their own governmental forms. Thus, when they arrived in Muscovy, the visitors had a ready set of concepts that could, with some adjustment, be made to fit Russian government quite easily. And some (though by no means all) European ethnographers were both willing and able to make the necessary categorical adjustments when they learned that their perceptions were at odds with preexisting political and governmental concepts. For example, the ethnographers—and one might include Krizhanich here as well—were troubled by the fact that seventeenth-century tsars held tyrannical powers but were not themselves tyrants in the received sense. Some of them demonstrated considerable inventiveness and flexibility in altering the idea of tyranny to capture what they believed to be a paradoxically stable system of despotic rule.

Binary Categories, Comparative Continua, and the Power of Russian Rule

To sum up, Russian suspicion, literary influence, and the use of European concepts seem to have produced only marginal distortion of the signals per-ceived and recorded by the European ethnographers, or at the very least the best of them—Herberstein, Possevino, Margeret, and Olearius. Nonethe-less, though the most sensitive of the European visitors do not seem to have fallen prey to the three pitfalls examined above, they all evidenced a marked tendency to exaggerate the power of the tsar and the servility of his subjects. One need not embark on an extensive comparison of foreign opinion and the findings of modern historical science to demonstrate that this is the case, for the ethnographers often couched their descriptions of Russian government in plainly fantastic terms. It was not at all uncommon for the ethnographers to write that the tsar's power was completely unlimited, that all property was entirely in his control, and that all his subjects were nothing but slaves, or words to that effect. Such a state of affairs is, as numerous modern critics have pointed out, quite literally impossible: no early modern king held unlimited power, for every prince had to rely on agents of the court to do his bidding, and these persons were often jealous, corrupt, and hostile to royal incursions; no early modern king could control all the property in his realm, for, even with an unimaginably effective royal fisc, there was an inexorable tendency for even the most conditional benefices to be appropriated by their holders; finally, no early modern king could treat his subjects literally as slaves, for every monarch depended on a privileged nobility to administer his "estate."

The origin of the ethnographers' predilection for exaggerating the authority of the Muscovite monarch is to be found in their fondness for sharp binary distinctions, and behind that fondness, a deep-seated psychic desire for a self-affirming counterconcept to idealized European liberty. Three such binary oppositions were operative, to a greater or lesser degree, in all the foreigners' accounts: limited vs. unlimited power, private vs. public ownership, and freedom vs. slavery. To be sure, as experienced men, the ethnographers understood that everywhere political power was in actual fact more or less fettered, that property was more or less conditional, and that liberty was more or less protected. And if they understood this, then they comprehended that a just monarchy—a regime in which royal power was perfectly limited, private ownership was perfectly protected, freedom was perfectly preserved—and its logical opposite, absolute tyranny,—a regime in which royal power was untrammeled, all property was the king's, and subjects were royal slaves—were but dreams that occupied the extremes of a long and variegated continuum between liberty and slavery. These ideal forms lived in the imaginations of European gentlemen, in the works of abstract political philosophers, and nowhere else. Nonetheless, some of the things the ethnographers observed in Muscovy seemed to be at odds with the distinction between actual and ideal polities. The Europeans were amazed to learn that the Russians themselves said that the tsar's authority was unfettered, that he was a universal proprietor, and that they were but his lowly slaves. It is important to bear in mind that the ethnographers had seen much in the course of their investigations that contradicted each of these improbable claims. Nearly all the foreigners dutifully recorded that the tsar was surrounded by powerful lords who served in a royal council, that magnates owned estates seemingly out of the purview of the fisc, and that in many ways these lords did not act at all like slaves, despite their odd habit of self-deprecation. Yet when it came time to offer general characterizations of the tsar's authority, the conceptual clarity and psychic attraction offered by ideologically laden binary oppositions often proved to be too much for the ethnographers. The recalcitrant evidence was conveniently forgotten, and the tsar's rule was made to fit the mold of a counterconcept. As Fletcher put it, our king is limited, theirs is not; our property is secure, theirs is not; our freedom is maintained, theirs is not.

The ethnographers' fantastic claims about the tsar's "universal" powers, like the numerous folkloric tales about Ivan IV that circulated throughout the corpus of foreign Moscovitica, should rightly be classified as European mythology, for they have much less to do with Russian reality than with the dynamics of early modern European political consciousness. Nonetheless, for the historian of Muscovy proper, they are not without value. If properly understood, these statements, together with the much more numerous subtle characterizations found in the European accounts, can be used to identify the specificity of Muscovite rule within the context of early modern European government generally. The most problematic part of the ethnographers' characterization of Russian governance is not the simple thesis that royal authority in Muscovy was different than it was in Europe, but that it was in some fundamental sense typologically distinct. There is little reason to believe that this was the case, because (as I argued a moment ago) the Muscovite and European kingdoms were, in a broader perspective, both members of the genus "early modern European monarchy," and because the ethnographers were impelled by deep-rooted beliefs to exaggerate the differences between the Russians and themselves. If, however, we replace the ethnographers' ill-suited categories of distinct types of monarchy with the continuum of royal power that actually stands behind it, then the European characterizations may be properly used to compare the Muscovite monarchy with its European counterparts.

And here the ethnographers spoke with one voice: royal authority was far more extensive in Russia than anywhere else in Europe. The ethnographers arrived at this conclusion through implicit or, more rarely, explicit comparison of various indices of royal power that they had formulated in their own personal experience in Europe and brought with them to Russia. The first of these indices was the relative strength of institutions that might stay the monarch's hand—royal councils, national estates, laws, and the courts that adjudicated them. All of the ethnographers knew that such institutions were operative in Europe; many of them had personally served in them. As a general rule, they observed that the Boyar Council was a weak consultative institution with little or no independent authority, that Russian national representative bodies were nonexistent or very irregularly convened, and that neither law nor court restrained the will of the tsar. A second common measure investigated by the ethnographers was the security of private property. The ethnographers were especially keen to explore this topic because they themselves were estate holders in their home countries. As a rule, the foreigners believed that the tsar did not respect private property, and in more extreme cases that he was in fact a universal landholder. Finally, the third index of the extent of royal authority was the degree to which the Russian monarch could demand services of various sorts from the population, particularly from the nobility and gentry. When the foreigners wrote, knight service was a faint memory in Europe, but the European visitors were probably aware that at some time in their not too distant past the king could extract aid from his men, and that even in their day he held the right to request financial if not personal assistance from communities of the realm. The ethnographers were surprised to learn that the Russian monarch could demand extensive military and civil services from the Muscovite nobility and gentry, and that in fact all of the other "estates" were obliged to support him in whatever way he required. Having explored these three indices, the ethnographers logically concluded that the tsar's authority was much broader than that enjoyed by his European counterparts, though they misleadingly cast this judgment in wildly exaggerated binary terms.

Tyranny, Despotism, and the Discourse of Deference in Muscovy

As we saw earlier, for many Europeans the Russian monarchy presented a conceptual paradox. It was tyranny insofar as the tsar treated his subjects like servants. Yet it was not tyranny insofar as those subjects did not rise up to liberate themselves, as Aristotle predicted and experience suggested they should. Several of the ethnographers attempted to solve the puzzle of immobile tyranny by claiming that the Russians must be natural slaves and therefore fit for despotism. Among the foreign commentators there were two schools of thought concerning the genesis of Russian natural slavery. On the one hand, foreigners such as Reutenfels showed a marked willingness to admit the possibility that Russians were simply rude and servile by nature. On the other hand, men such as Krizhanich believed that cruel government had reduced the Muscovites to a condition of habitual (thought not natural) servility.

From the point of view of the modern historian, the idea of inborn servility can be dismissed out of hand as an artifact of early modern European racial, ethnic, and class consciousness. Like the foreigners' statements about the absolute power of the tsar, the theory of natural slavery is a part of European mythology, a reflex not only of the need to explain the peculiar stability of Russian tyranny but also a response to a psychic desire to build a self-affirming counterconcept to an imagined European freedom. Krizhanich's thesis, however, is much more plausible, and if properly reinterpreted might be of some value to historians attempting to understand the mysteries of Muscovite political culture. There is a historical sense in which Krizhanich was doubtless correct, though he did not know it. Though the record is far from clear, the despotic character of Muscovite government and the menu of servile behaviors that went with it were not ur-Russian characteristics (as they appear in most of the ethnographies), but rather inventions of the later fifteenth and early sixteenth centuries. As Herberstein knew, in the mid–

fifteenth century northern Russia was dominated by a collection of independent principalities and two republican city-states, Pskov and Novgorod. It is known that these entities were served on a contractual basis by free princes and their warriors, men who were far from slaves and who in fact reserved the right to swear fealty to whomever they wished, at least in theory. In the reign of Ivan III, however, the relatively liberal political culture of northeastern Russia underwent a dramatic and (in hindsight) irreversible revolution: the major independent principalities and city-states were conquered by Moscow, the once free princes and servitors were compelled to serve the grand prince, and the so-called right of departure was revoked. Moscow had captured northeastern Russia and Muscovy was born.

In the course of its effort to conquer Russia and build a centralized autocracy, the Muscovite magnates gradually developed a novel ceremonial persona reflecting what they hoped would be their new status as lords of "all Russia." The best-known alterations in this campaign are of course Ivan III's adoption of the title "tsar" (likely a translation from the Byzantine *basileius*) and the imperial double-headed eagle (borrowed from the Habsburg crest), both of which served to enhance the Muscovites' international prestige. Interestingly, however, the court simultaneously developed a ceremonial discourse perhaps based on the master-slave metaphor. The grand prince came to be called *gospodar'* or *gosudar'*, a title meaning "lord," "master," or "owner," particularly of slaves.[7] This term was first used with reference to the Muscovite prince around 1450.[8] Early examples from the 1450s and 1460s are scattered, a fact that suggests the terms were not sanctioned in official communications. Most researchers believe that *gospodar'/gosudar'* probably became a part of the grand prince's title in the 1470s.[9] It is difficult to tell exactly when *gosudar'* entered Muscovite administrative discourse because no serial records survive before the last quarter of the fifteenth century. Beginning in 1474, diplomatic documents appear in which *gosudar'* is indeed attested. In that year, Russian ambassadors to the Crimean Tatars were

[7] Documentary sources are for all practical purposes nonexistent for northeastern Russia before the fourteenth century, so any attempt to reconstruct the meaning of *gospodar'* or *gosudar'* is problematic. The best evidence is legal codes that indicate norms and uses. An examination of these codes indicates that *gospodar'* and *gosudar'* in general indicated "lord," and in more specific contexts meant master of slaves, employer of laborers, and owner of inanimate objects. See *gospodar'* and *gosudar'* in the indexes and texts of Daniel H. Kaiser, trans. and ed., *Laws of Rus'*; Boris D. Grekov, ed., *Sudebniki XV–XVI vekov*; and Richard Hellie, trans. and ed., *Muscovite Law Code (Ulozhenie) of 1649*.

[8] Stepan G. Barkhudarov et al., eds., *Slovar' russkogo iazyka XI–XVII vv.* (hereafter SRIa), 4:100; Izmail I. Sreznevskii, *Materialy dlia slovaria drevne-russkogo iazyka*, 1:563; Gunter Stökl, "Die Begriffe Reich, Herrschaft und Staat bei den orthodoxen Slawen," 115; Marc Szeftel, "Title of the Muscovite Monarch Up to the End of the Seventeenth Century," 62, 64; Gustav Alef, "Political Significance of the Inscriptions on Muscovite Coinage," 11, and "Origins of Muscovite Autocracy," 77.

[9] Sreznevskii, *Materialy*, 1:571; Stökl, "Begriffe Reich," 114; Szeftel, "Title of the Muscovite Monarch," 63; Joel Raba, "Authority of the Muscovite Ruler at the Dawn of the Modern Era," 322.

instructed to refer to Ivan III as *gosudar' moi* ("my master"), a practice followed thereafter in diplomatic protocols. *Velikii ospodar' Russki zemli* ("great master of the Russian land") is found in a royal missive of 1484. And the term appears in what must have been a standard administrative missive (*gramota*) among diplomatic documents written in 1489.[10] The regalian salutation "To the *gosudar'* . . ." is found in each subsequent document inscribed in the Crimean diplomatic registers after that date.[11] *Gosudar'* was also used with reference to the grand prince in a variety of other administrative charters in the last quarter of the fifteenth century.[12] The title is ubiquitous in sources of the sixteenth and seventeenth centuries and was a mandated element in the salutations of *chelobitnye* (petitions) and *otpiski* (official dispatches).[13] If the tsar was to be master, then his men logically had to be *kholopy*, or slaves. From the earliest time *kholop* was the official term for "slave," and it continued to be used in this capacity into the seventeenth century.[14] Some researchers suggest that *kholop tvoi* (your slave) had become a sanctioned part of the Muscovite regalian salutation by the late 1480s.[15] Because documentation is lacking, it is impossible to determine exactly when the phrase gained currency. It does not appear as a self-address in administrative documents until 1489.[16] Thereafter it is commonly found: *kholop tvoi* is universal in sixteenth- and seventeenth-century dispatches and petitions addressed to the tsar. Finally, if royal servants were slaves, then it was only fitting for them to bow down before their master. It is not known when Russians began to prostrate themselves before the grand prince, but it is possible to trace the origins of the official term for this act, *bit' chelom,* literally to "strike one's head" and figuratively to "humbly greet."[17] The phrase first appears in Russian sources in the early fourteenth century.[18] A corresponding noun, *chelobit'e* (a petition), appeared shortly thereafter.[19] *Bit' chelom* was probably borrowed from the Mongol administrative lexicon. The phrase is a calque of the Turkic *bas ur-,* which in turn is a derivative of the Chinese

---

[10] Gennadii F. Karpov, ed., "Pamiatniki diplomaticheskikh snoshenii Moskovskogo gosudarstva s Krimskim," 3, 41, 81.

[11] Ibid., 110, 118, 133, 148, and so on.

[12] See the documents in Lev V. Cherepnin, ed., *Akty sotsial'no-ekonomicheskoi istorii severo-vostochnoi Rusi.* Also see the numerous references in Georgii E. Kochin, *Materialy dlia terminologicheskogo slovaria Drevnei Rossii,* 69.

[13] Mikhail N. Tikhomirov, "Prikaznoe deloproizvodstvo v XVII v.," 364–65, 369.

[14] See the many references in Kaiser, *Laws of Rus',* and Hellie, *Muscovite Law Code.*

[15] Alef, "Origins of Muscovite Autocracy," 75.

[16] Karpov, *Pamiatniki,* 81.

[17] Sreznevskii, *Materialy,* 3:1490; SRIa, 1:188. The phrase also took on the meaning of "to request" or "to bring a complaint against." See Sreznevskii, *Materialy,* 3:1490; SRIa, 1:188; and the examples in Cherepnin, *Akty,* 3: no. 5 (1391), no. 6 (1392 or 1404), no. 7 (1397). Also see the numerous citations in Kochin, *Materialy dlia terminologicheskogo slovaria,* 28.

[18] SRIa, 1:188; Sreznevskii, *Materialy,* 3:1488; Sviatoslav S. Volkov, "Iz istorii russkoi leksiki," 48, and *Leksika russkikh chelobitnykh XVII veka,* 36; Horace Dewey, "Russia's Debt to the Mongols in Suretyship and Collective Responsibility," 268.

[19] Sreznevskii, *Materialy,* 3:1490; Volkov, "Iz istorii russkoi leksiki," 49.

koutou, both of which mean literally "to hit the head" and figuratively "to make obeisance."[20] As in the case of *gosudar',* it is difficult to tell exactly when *bit' chelom* became the official manner in which one greeted the grand prince. The first official missive to the Russian prince with *bit' chelom* in the sense of "to humbly greet" is dated 1489.[21] The phrase appears in every subsequent charter in the diplomatic protocols and was a standard element of administrative communications throughout the sixteenth and seventeenth centuries. In short, it appears reasonably certain that the menu of "servile" behavior that the foreigners habitually adduced as evidence of native Muscovite slavery was in fact introduced in the later fifteenth century as part of a court-sponsored campaign to transform the Muscovite prince from a *primus inter pares* into the "lord" of ritually subservient "slaves." The court of Ivan III in some fashion imposed this novel identity on its men, and in this sense Krizhanich was correct in asserting that the government was ultimately responsible for this particular emanation of Muscovite "barbarity."

Yet what the foreigners, Krizhanich included, did not seem to comprehend was that in the course of the sixteenth century, the new and strange vocabulary of imperial subservience became the familiar common coin of everyday official and polite interaction, a manner of speaking that—to native Russians if not to foreign observers—was largely bereft of consciously registered servile connotations. For Russians of the second half of the sixteenth and entire seventeenth century, *gosudar'* when used to address the tsar did not necessarily mean "the universal master of slave subjects," but rather simply "sovereign." This meaning, in fact, may have been the primary one intended by the men who introduced it into the grand prince's title in the last quarter of the fifteenth century, for they knew that the term was being used in the sense of "sovereign" by a variety of neighboring powers: it had been part of the title of the rulers of Lithuania (*gospodar'*) and Moldavia (*hospodar*) since the fourteenth century;[22] it was used in the title of Novgorod;[23] and it was the Slavic translation of a part of the title of the Byzantine emperor—*despotes.*[24] Even if *gosudar'* was originally intended to mean "master of slaves," there is evidence that it may not have been understood in this way in the later sixteenth and seventeenth centuries, at least on a conscious level. First, *gosudar'* was always accompanied in written correspondence addressed to the grand prince by the titles *tsar'* and *velikii kniaz'.* Thus the formulaic regalian salutation *tsariu gosudariu i velikomu kniaziu* ("To the tsar, sover-

[20] Peter B. Golden, "Turkic Calques in Medieval Eastern Slavic," 109–10. Also see Donald Ostrowski, "Mongol Origins of Muscovite Political Institutions," 534. For the use of *bit' chelom* in Mongol-Turkic diplomatics, see Mirkasym A. Usmanov, *Zhalovannye akty Dzhuchieva Ulusa XIV–XVI vv.,* 194–95.
[21] Karpov, *Pamiatniki,* 81.
[22] Stökl, "Begriffe Reich," 114–15.
[23] Sreznevskii, *Materialy,* 1:571–72; SRIa, 4:109.
[24] Szeftel, "Title of the Muscovite Monarch," 63. See Aleksandr P. Kazhdan et al., eds., *Oxford Dictionary of Byzantium,* s.v. "despotes."

eign, and grand prince") was a semantic unit indicating the Russian ruler.[25] In this context *gosudar'*, referring only to the grand prince, could have easily been understood as "sovereign." Second, "slaveholder" was not the only meaning of *gosudar'*—it was also a polite form of address indicating little about the addressee's status. For example, by the seventeenth century it had become common to address the recipients of letters (*gramotki*) as *gosudar'*.[26] Finally, perhaps because *gosudar'* had come to be a polite form of address, the official term for slaveholder—which had been *gosudar'* for centuries—was replaced by *boiarin* (boyar), as can be seen in the Council Law Code of 1649.[27] It seems likely, then, that for Russians of the later sixteenth and seventeenth centuries, *gosudar'*, when used in reference to the tsar, meant "sovereign" primarily and "slaveholder" only in a metaphorical sense.

Similarly, it is not at all clear that the original use of *kholop* by Russian servitors was meant to connote "slave" with all the negative connotations that the term entailed in common speech. If the late fifteenth-century adoption of *kholop* is placed in a wider context, it takes on a slightly different meaning. The use of "slave" as a designation for elite servitors was well established in the Tatar-Turkic world, and it is possible that Muscovite authorities borrowed it from that esteemed source.[28] It is more likely, however, that *kholop tvoi* ("your slave") was appropriated from Byzantine diplomatics.[29] Long before *kholop tvoi* is attested in Muscovite sources, an analogous term of self-identification—"slave of God" (*rab bozhii*)—is found in early Russian charters: "In the name of the Father, Son, and Holy Spirit, lo, I, evil, sinful slave of God, Ivan, . . ."[30] This biblical trope was taken from Greek practice.[31] In late Byzantine terminology, subjects were called "slaves of the emperor" (*dulos tes basileias*), a phrase that was apparently understood to signify humility and fidelity, not servility.[32] Hence this seemingly undignified title was considered honorable among Byzantine elites, a symbol of their status as servitors of the most powerful ruler in the world.[33] Thus, when it was originally adopted by the court of Ivan III, "slave" may have connoted, para-

[25] For many examples, see Sergei I. Kotkov, ed., *Pamiatniki delovoi pis'mennosti XVII veka*, 149–220.

[26] See, for example, ibid., 249. Also see the numerous examples in S. I. Kotkov, ed., *Gramotki XVII–nachala XVIII v.* The editors of SRIa note this usage (4:109).

[27] Hellie, *Muscovite Law Code*, chap. 10, art. 134, and many others. On this usage, see Vasilii I. Sergeevich, *Drevnosti russkogo prava*, 1:437, and SRIa, 1:308.

[28] See Hamilton A. R. Gibb, ed., *Encyclopedia of Islam*, s.v. "kul" and "ghulam."

[29] Alef, "Origins of Muscovite Autocracy," 89; Ostrowski, "Mongol Origins," 537, n. 52.

[30] Lev V. Cherepnin, ed., *Dukhovnye i dogovornye gramoty velikikh i udel'nykh kniazei XIV–XVI vv.*, nos. 1, 3, 4, and so on.

[31] Aleksandr Kazhdan, "Concept of Freedom (*eleutheria*) and Slavery (*douleia*) in Byzantium," 219.

[32] Kazhdan et al., *Oxford Dictionary of Byzantium*, s.v. "doulos." Also see Kazhdan, "Concept of Freedom," 219–20, and Helga Köpstein, *Zur Sklaverei im ausgehenden Byzanz*, 33ff.

[33] Kazhdan, "Concept of Freedom," 219–20; Köpstein, *Zur Sklaverei im ausgehenden Byzanz*, 33ff.

doxically, both fealty and dignity rather than simple submission. The term certainly designated both in the later sixteenth and seventeenth centuries. *Kholop tvoi* was the official petitionary designation for the highest rung of Russian society. According to Muscovite protocol, service people (*sluzhilye liudi*) addressing the grand prince were to refer to themselves as "your slave" (*kholop tvoi*), taxpayers "your orphan" (*sirota tvoia*), and clerics "your pilgrim" (*bogomolets tvoi*).[34] All this is described in some detail by Grigorii Kotoshikhin and was well known to Meyerberg.[35] Seen in this context, *kholop tvoi* designated both submission and relative honor.[36] Krizhanich made this explicit. He understood the Bible to say that all subjects, especially military servitors, were "slaves" of the prince.[37] Thus he distinguished this sort of political dependence from economic bondage, which he condemned.[38] Of political slavery he wrote: "To be tsar is to serve God, but to be the slave of the tsar of one's own people, this is honorable and is actually a kind of freedom."[39] This honorable sense of *kholop* is reflected in the passage of the term into epistolary discourse, where it seems to have been used by servants of any sort writing to their superiors.[40] It is true that Krizhanich called on wellborn Muscovites to stop calling themselves slaves, but this was part of his effort to raise the image of Russians in the eyes of Europeans.[41] He knew the foreigners would not understand the more subtle, honorable sense of "slave," and in this he was right.[42]

Finally, there is reason to believe that Russians did not ordinarily associate extreme servility with the act of ritual prostration or with the analogous verbal formula (*bit' chelom*). Since at least the fourteenth century, the Russians had observed their Tatar-Turkic neighbors greeting each other and paying obeisance to their betters with deep bows. Given that they had very little contact with other forms of civility in this early period, it is entirely possible that the Muscovites simply understood profound bows and prostration to be *the* polite form of address toward those of a higher station. Krizhanich and the other Europeans may have seen the act as undignified, but they understood it from the perspective of European manners. The Muscovites knew little or nothing about "refined" European customs before the early sixteenth

---

[34] Kotkov, *Pamiatniki delovoi pis'mennosti XVII veka*, 149–220.

[35] Grigorii Kotoshikhin, *O Rossii v tsarstvovanie Alekseia Mikhailovicha*, fols. 186–88. See Meyerberg (1661), 116–17.

[36] For a similar interpretation, see Valerie Kivelson, "Merciful Father, Impersonal State," 650.

[37] Lev M. Mordukhovich, "Iz rukopisnogo nasledstva Iu. Krizhanicha," 185.

[38] Lev M. Mordukhovich, "Iurii Krizhanich o 'rabstve.'"

[39] Mordukhovich, "Iz rukopisnogo nasledstva Iu. Krizhanicha," 185. Also see Krizhanich (1663–66), 552–54.

[40] Many examples are reprinted in Kotkov, *Pamiatniki delovoi pis'mennosti XVII veka* and *Gramotki XVII–nachala XVIII veka;* and Aleksei I. Iakovlev, ed., *Akty khoziaistva Boiarina B. I. Morozova.*

[41] Krizhanich (1663–66), 603.

[42] Krizhanich mentioned that Europeans singled out the use of "the sovereign's slaves" for particular censure (ibid., 546–47).

century, long after "striking one's head" had become the "traditional" form of upward address throughout Russian society. Moreover, the phrase *bit' chelom* as used in written formulas may not have reminded sixteenth- and seventeenth-century Russians of the act it had originally designated.[43] In that later period, the typical word for a deep bow seems to have been not *bit' chelom* but rather *poklonit'sia*.[44] For example, the mid-sixteenth-century domestic manual *Domostroi* describes in some detail how Christians should "bow" (*pokloniatisia*) in religious settings, but does not mention *bit' chelom*.[45] In the mid–seventeenth century Kotoshikhin did not use *bit' chelom* to designate the act of bowing in diplomatic rituals: his word is *poklonitisiia*.[46] Further, both of the original meanings of *bit' chelom*—to greet humbly and to request—underwent further development in the sixteenth and seventeenth centuries that blanched them of inordinately servile connotations. The former became the standard polite mode for written greetings, not only for the grand prince but for people of any rank.[47] Seventeenth-century letter writers *bil chelom* ("humbly greeted") the people they were addressing.[48] The evolution of *bit' chelom* in the sense of "request" was stimulated by the formation of the Petition Chancellery (*chelobitnyi prikaz*) in the 1550s.[49] *Bit' chelom* came to mean "an official request or complaint addressed to the tsar." It is used in this sense in post-1549 Muscovite legal codes.[50] Following this meaning, the terms *chelobitnaia* ("a petition") and *chelobitchik* ("a petitioner") entered the Muscovite legal lexicon.[51] In short, Muscovites did not necessarily understand *bit' chelom* to mean "to strike one's forehead in submission."[52] The phrase also meant "to humbly greet" or "petition."

In analyzing the evidence of Russian servility, then, the European visitors tended to commit three rather uncharitable errors. First, men such as Reutenfels "naturalized" the fawning behavior they observed throughout Russian society. Freedom-loving people, they believed, would naturally rebel against tyrannical authority. But the Muscovites did not rise up, at least to destroy autocracy. Therefore, some Europeans concluded that Russians were natural slaves. But this was obviously not so: as the evidence of resistance to what the *Russians themselves* perceived as unjust rule suggests, Muscovites had the same capacity for conceiving of and acting against governmental oppres-

---

[43] The editors of SRIa are unsure, translating the term as *klaniat'sia* or *privetstvovat'* (1:188).

[44] Ibid., 16:158.

[45] Vladimir V. Kolesov, ed., *Domostroi*, 41.

[46] Kotoshikhin, *O Rossii v tsarstvovanie Alekseia Mikhailovicha*, fol. 72.

[47] Volkov, *Leksika russkikh chelobitnykh XVII veka*, 36.

[48] See, for example, Kotkov, *Pamiatniki delovoi pis'mennosti*, 249.

[49] Segurt O. Shmidt, "Chelobitennyi prikaz v seredine XVI stoletiia."

[50] *Sudebnik* of 1550, arts. 7, 8, 24, 70, 72, 78, 79, 85, and 100, in Grekov, *Sudebniki XV–XVI vekov.*

[51] Volkov, "Iz istorii russkoi leksiki," 53, 57.

[52] Volkov, *Leksika russkikh chelobitnykh XVII veka*, 36, argues that *chelo* lost the meaning *golova* and *lob* in the course of the fifteenth and sixteenth centuries. If this is so, Muscovites could not have parsed *bit' chelom* and understood it literally.

sion as any other peoples. Just as Europeans rebelled against what they understood as tyrannical government in the Dutch Revolt, the Fronde, and the English Civil War, some Muscovites stood their ground during the *oprichnina,* the Time of Troubles, the urban riots of 1648, the Copper revolt of 1662, Razin's rebellion in 1669–71, the Solovetskii Monastery rising of 1668–76, and the revolt of the *strel'tsy* in 1682—all of which, incidentally, were recorded by the foreigners and forgotten when they discussed inbred servility. There was, of course, a crucial difference between these Muscovite protestations and, for example, the English Civil War: none of the Russian revolts aimed at fundamental constitutional change. This fact, however, would seem to be evidence that the Russians accepted the basic precepts of autocratic government, rather than that they were possessed by some sort of inborn servility.

Other Europeans offered the more sensible thesis that the Russians had been taught their distinctive habit of deference by the government itself. In some sense, as we have seen, this is true, for it seems reasonably clear that Ivan III was responsible for at least codifying the master-slave idiom that characterized Russian political behavior. Yet even those foreigners who presented this milder hypothesis concerning the origins of Russian servility were guilty of a second misstep, for they routinely interpreted the vocabulary of deference literally when the evidence suggests it should be comprehended metaphorically. Once Ivan III's strange innovations became a routine part of the Russian language of deference, the everyday meanings of *gosudar',* *kholop,* and *bit' chelom*—"slavemaster," "slave," and "prostration"—were joined by more polite significations used by respectable people throughout Muscovite society—"lord," "servant," and "humble greetings." Once this is understood, the semantic similarity between the Muscovite and European vocabularies of deference is immediately obvious, for Europeans used almost the same terminology for polite address—"my lord," "your servant," and "humble greetings." It would be a mistake, however, to dismiss the ethnographers' gloss entirely because they correctly (if clumsily) realized that the Muscovite and European customs of deference were not identical. For all their similarity, the two lexicons subsisted in different social worlds, and for that reason they took on different significations. In the context of the European *Ständestaat,* with its limitations on monarchical power, powerful nobilities, and right-embodied legal orders, the discourse of deference was not linked by any but the most tenuous metaphorical associations with a truly servile condition. When a European gentleman called his king "lord" and himself "servant," it never occurred to him that the king held despotic powers over his person and property. In the Muscovite autocracy, with its overwhelming monarchical authority, its service-bound elite, and its hierarchy of subject classes, the language of deference retained powerful metaphorical links with actual institutions of subservience. When a Muscovite servitor called the tsar his *gosudar'* and himself the tsar's *kholop,* he was perhaps reminded both of the tsar's actual power over him and the actual institution of slavery that flourished in Muscovy until the later seventeenth century.[53] As the foreigners pointed out, the tsar could treat his subjects as slaves, beating them, seizing their property, and even executing them. To be sure, such harsh treatment was exceptional, but it was doubtless never far from the minds of Muscovite servitors, particularly when they were addressing their "master" and calling themselves his "slaves."

A final difficulty with the foreigners' interpretation of Russian deference is that it was based on a peculiarly simplistic understanding of slavery. Though the foreigners did not offer any extended meditations on the idea itself, it seems reasonably clear from their writings that they believed political slavery to be a state of absolute dependence. In their view, the tsar held all power and his subjects held none. This, of course, is both an unrealistic understanding of the actual institution of slavery and, more important, of the metaphorical slavery that characterized political discourse in early modern Russia: slaves have power and Muscovite subjects acting in the role of slaves had even more. What the foreigners failed to realize was that the master-slave metaphor implied reciprocal obligations on the part of the tsar and his people. Though the exact parameters of the tsar's duties are difficult to interpret in the absence of programmatic texts, Muscovite official ideology stressed that the grand prince himself was the slave of God just as his subjects were slaves to him.[54] The Lord gave the tsar great power over men, but required him to care for His earthly creatures, "to preserve the whole realm from injury and to its flock unharmed from wolves."[55] As one mid-sixteenth-century text had it, "Though an emperor in body be like all men, in the power of his worthy office he is like a god, who rules over all; for he has no man on earth who is higher than he; he is inaccessible to man because of the loftiness of his earthly empire, yet he receives suppliants by reason of the heavenly power."[56] Though this exhortation to "receive suppliants" and, more generally, to protect and show mercy to royal subjects is ultimately of Greek origin, it had special resonance in Muscovy.[57] Unlike European principalities

[53] On Muscovite slavery, see Richard Hellie, *Slavery in Russia*.

[54] The obligation of the tsar to protect his charges, both spiritually and physically, has been widely discussed in works on Muscovite political thought. See, for example, Daniel Rowland, "Problem of Advice in Muscovite Tales about the Time of Troubles" and "Did Muscovite Literary Ideology Place Any Limits on the Power of the Tsar?"; Valerie A. Kivelson, "The Devil Stole His Mind." For an older view stressing limits on the tsar's authority, see Vladimir Val'denberg, *Drevnerusskiia ucheniia o predelakh tsarskoi vlasti.*

[55] Elpidifor V. Barsov, ed., "Drevne-russkie pamiatniki sviashchennogo venchaniia tsarei na tsarstvo," 58. This quotation is taken from Metropolitan Makarii's benediction at Ivan IV's coronation on Jan. 16, 1547. It is not of Russian origin, but was rather borrowed from the sixth-century Byzantine deacon Agapetus's benediction of Emperor Justinian. For an analysis, see David B. Miller, "Coronation of Ivan IV of Moscow." On the origin of the text in Agapetus, see Ihor Shevchenko, "A Neglected Byzantine Source of Muscovite Political Ideology."

[56] *Polnoe sobranie russkikh letopisei,* 21:609–11.

[57] This passage was borrowed, probably by Ivan IV's confessor, Afanasii, from the sixth-century Byzantine deacon Agapetus and placed in the "Book of Degrees of the Imperial Ge-

that recognized autonomous spheres within society, the tsar's court seemed to conceive of Russia as a unified liturgical state in which all classes were bound to serve the tsar or to serve those who served the tsar.[58] Evidence of this mentality is found in all manner of Muscovite documentation dedicated to recording services required of and rendered by various classes, the intrusive nature of Muscovite legislation, and, finally, the plain fact that Muscovy knew no right-embodied, incorporated estates, corporations, or guilds of the European variety.[59] The foreigners, of course, clearly saw the liturgical nature of the Russian state. What they did not see was that, having required service from all classes, the court simultaneously obligated itself to afford universal protection to these same classes, at least in principle. Russian political "slavery" was not, as the foreigners implied, a relation of the powerful to the powerless but rather a relationship of mutual responsibility—Russian "slaves" served their "master," while the "master" protected his "slaves." Evidence that common Russian servitors conceived of their relation to royal authority in this way is not far to seek. Indeed, it is recorded in the constant hum of complaints that were registered literally daily in thousands of petitions for relief from servitors throughout Russia. These documents begin with a ritual of debasement in which the petitioner humbles himself as the tsar's "slave," "orphan," or "pilgrim." What followed this formula looks to be the pleadings of a humiliated servant. If the petitioner wanted a salary increase or promotion, he would stress his long history of quiet sacrifice to the tsar; if he wanted retirement from service, he would focus on his age, infirmity, and injuries; if the supplicant wished to complain about a corrupt official, he would cite his community's suffering at the man's hands.[60] The petitions end, as one might expect, with a plea for mercy. But the underlying rhetoric of the petitions was not of servility but rather of entitlement. The petitioners were in essence saying, "We have suffered as required for you. Now, if you please, protect us." The tsar was, of course, not obliged to do anything of the sort: Muscovite political culture was not contractarian.[61] But in the

---

nealogy" in the mid–sixteenth century. On the sources, see Shevchenko, "Neglected Byzantine Source," 161–63.

[58] Nancy S. Kollmann, "Concepts of Society and Social Identity in Early Modern Russia."

[59] On service registry, see Marshall T. Poe, "Elite Service Registry in Muscovy, 1500–1700." On the Council Law Code of 1649, see Hellie, *Muscovite Law Code*. On the question of estates, see Günter Stökl, "Gab es im Moskauer Staat 'Stände'?" and Hans-Joachim Torke, *Die staatsbedingte Gesellschaft im Moskauer Reich*, 268–98.

[60] For numerous examples, see Kotkov, *Pamiatniki delovoi pis'mennosti XVII veka*. On complaints against officials, see Valerie A. Kivelson, *Autocracy in the Provinces*, 124–53.

[61] George Weickhardt has argued that Muscovites (particularly the framers of the *Ulozhenie* of 1649, Kotoshikhin, Simeon Polotskoi, and Krizhanich) believed that "the ruler and the laws derived their legitimacy from a contract or from popular consent." He even sees similarities between these "Russian" ideas and the thought of Locke. See Weickhardt, "Political Thought in Seventeenth-Century Russia," 337. Leaving aside the question as to whether Kotoshikhin, Simeon, and Krizhanich could be considered representative of *Muscovite* political thought, it seems that Weickhardt's thesis overreaches the evidence. There was certainly some sense in which all Muscovites believed the ruler was beholden to the people. But to speak of a "contract" is to

course of everyday affairs it was to be expected that mercy would be shown, if not because God's commandments required it of the tsar, then because from the point of view of imperial administrators, it seemed both equitable and efficient to keep one's "slaves" satisfied.[62]

Political Mentalities, Functionality, and
the Stability of Russian Political Culture

By the mid–sixteenth century at the latest, many Muscovites were surely aware that Europeans believed their common manner of deference was undignified. There is some evidence that they learned of this European disdain directly from printed ethnographies. In 1581, for example, the Polish king Stefan Batory dispatched a copy of Guagnini to Ivan IV so that he would "know what the world thought of him."[63] In 1653, a Polish translation of Guagnini was purchased by order of the tsar, and sometime between 1653 and 1690 the tome was translated into Russian.[64] Meyerberg noted that the Russians took umbrage at unnamed "Polish books" about Muscovy and demanded that the works be withdrawn from publication.[65] Krizhanich reported that foreigners in Moscow owned copies of Petreius and "value it because it describes in detail and at length the violent rule of [False Dmitrii]."[66] While in Russia, Gordon cited unnamed works about "Tzaar Johannes Basilides" that might well have been provided to him by residents of the foreign suburb.[67] More commonly, the Muscovites became acquainted with European opinions about them directly from foreigners. Reutenfels heard that Ivan IV "ordered a certain German, living in Moscow, to tell him what foreign rulers thought of him"; the man responded, "You have a reputation as a tyrant among all foreigners."[68] Krizhanich told all who would listen that Russia was "the laughingstock of the entire world." The Croatian scholar said it was common "at negotiations and frontier meetings" for the Poles to praise "their licentious freedom and belittle us and our state. Both the Poles

---

ignore the informal framework of Muscovite political culture and, more important, the indisputable fact that no *Muscovite* ever composed a contractarian political philosophy that explicitly bound the activities of the tsar to the will of the people.

[62] Kivelson, "Merciful Father, Impersonal State," 652.

[63] Quoted in Hugh F. Graham, "Guagnini, Alessandro," 174. On translations of European literature in Muscovy, see Aleksei I. Sobolevskii, *Zapadnoe vlianie na literaturu Moskovskoi Rusi XV–XVII vekov.*

[64] The book in question was *Kronika Sármacyey europskiey* (Cracow, 1611). The Russian translation by Marcin Pashkovskii is in the "Sbornik Kurbskogo," found in the Russkii Gosudarstvennyi Arkhiv Drevnykh Aktov, fond 181, nos. 60–61, fols. 271–322. The manuscript is described in Iakov S. Lur'e and Dmitrii S. Likhachev, eds., *Poslaniia Ivana Groznogo*, 547. Also see Il'ia A. Shliapkin, *Sv. Dimitrii Rostovskii i ego vremia*, 56, 72, 83.

[65] Meyerberg (1661), 4–5.

[66] Krizhanich (1663–66), 488.

[67] Gordon (1699), 44.

[68] Reutenfels (1671), 116–17.

and the Lithuanians glorify their chaotic, tyrannical system," while "they heap a great deal of evil slander on our autocratic government." Krizhanich was afraid that the Russians would become "infected by this Polish illness," and suggested that "it would be wise to explain to [common Russians] in detail why Russian autocracy is so much more dignified than the chaotic rule of Poland." [69] European theorist and Slavic patriot that he was, Krizhanich took it upon himself to provide a point-by-point critique of the "Polish illness" and an apologia of autocracy.

The Muscovite authorities, though they may have been offended by foreign criticism, were neither as threatened nor as theoretically adept as their Croatian visitor, for they never composed or issued any programmatic defense of their "undignified" governmental system. Why, they may have asked, was such a defense necessary when there was no sustained opposition to the tsar's rule among his subjects? On the contrary, aside from the simple fact that, so far as is known, no Muscovite ever raised his voice against autocracy as a form of government,[70] there is some—albeit slight—positive evidence that Russian servitors were quite proud of their submission to the tsar, that they were at ease with the seemingly oppressive master-slave metaphor that was the fulcrum of their political idiom. Krizhanich not only reported that the Poles and other foreign ambassadors attacked "Russian slavery," but he also noted that Muscovites sometimes rose to the defense of their governmental system. According to his testimony, one Russian ambassador responded to Polish insults with the following speech:

> Forgive me for saying so, but in my view you [Polish magnates] resemble pigs running to a trough full of forage, every [pig] climbing into the trough with all four legs and trying to push all others away from the trough with his snout so that he can remain in it. Thus they fight until they turn over the trough and lose the lot. Similarly, because of vain rivalry, you upset all national authority. You don't see your own disgrace. You say that every one of you is worthy of the throne, yet you do not want to bow to any of your kinsmen. Instead you bow deeply to foreigners. In this way you reveal your own lies and, in essence, confirm that none of you is worthy of the throne.[71]

The passage is certainly suspect. One wonders where Krizhanich could have heard it, if a Muscovite could have said such an impertinent thing at a diplo-

---

[69] Krizhanich (1663–66), 498, 511, 547, 549.

[70] The single exception may be Kurbskii's writings to and about Ivan IV. See John L. I. Fennell, ed. and trans., *Correspondence between Prince A. M. Kurbsky and Tsar Ivan of Russia* and *Prince A. M. Kurbsky's History of Ivan IV.* Two provisos, however, are in order. First, the provenance of Kurbskii's letters is by no means clear, and they may well be products of the seventeenth century. On the possibility that the letters are forgeries, see Edward L. Keenan, *Kurbskii-Groznyi Aprocrypha.* Keenan's work is the subject of much debate. For a review of the literature and assessment of the argument, see Charles J. Halperin, "Edward Keenan and the Kurbskii-Groznyi Correspondence in Hindsight." Second, even if Kurbskii's writings are genuine, the object of his attack is not the institution of autocracy but rather the tyranny of Ivan IV.

[71] Krizhanich (1663–66), 511.

matic meeting, and why the Russian would have included a reference to Krizhanich's hobbyhorse, the dreaded foreign rule of Slavic nations. There is
some reason, however, to believe that such confrontations actually took
place. In a remarkable passage in the diary of Samuel Maskiewicz, the Polish
magnate described how, while in negotiations with the Muscovites in 1611,
he praised Polish liberty and advised the Russians "to unite with the Polish
people and obtain freedom." One of his Russian interlocutors answered as
follows:

> Your way is freedom, while ours is bondage. You do not have will, but rather
> simple caprice: the strong plunder the weak; they can seize another's property
> and very life. . . . In contrast, among us even an esteemed boyar does not have
> the authority to offend the least simple person: upon the first complaint, the
> tsar brings justice and right. If the sovereign proceeds unjustly, it is within his
> authority. Like God, the tsar punishes and pardons. It is easier for us to suffer
> offenses from the tsar than from our brother, because he is the ruler of all the
> world.[72]

Again, one suspects that Maskiewicz, as a Polish officer and partisan of Polish freedoms, did not report the Russian's speech with perfect accuracy.
Nonetheless, it must be admitted that the words of this unnamed Russian
magnate are representative of what may have been a common reaction among
Muscovite servitors faced with criticism of their "servitude," and therefore
a reflection of their own political attitudes. Maskiewicz's Russian in essence
reversed the evaluative polarity of freedom and slavery. Where Maskiewicz
and his European counterparts viewed freedom as the fundamental virtue
of a political system, the Muscovites saw it as a vice that corrupted a polity.
Rather than freedom, what just government required was the firm hand of a
sovereign who would bring order to society by punishing those who strayed
from the true path. For this reason, bondage was far more honorable than
any freedom. Interestingly, the few surviving programmatic statements concerning the tsar's authority, such as Iosif Volotskii's "Discourse No. 16" in
Prosvetitel' or Makarius's benediction offered at Ivan IV's coronation ceremony, emphasize the God-granted power of the tsar and the necessity of obedience on the part of all his subjects.[73]

Behind these contrasting opinions concerning the relative value of freedom and servitude stood two distinct universes of assumptions about political life. The European political worldview was informed by what might be
called the cultural mythology of liberty. At least since the Renaissance, Europeans had believed that though men might be born in sin, they were capable of achieving a certain degree of self-perfection, be it material (wealth),

---

[72] Maskiewicz (1611), 56. See Krizhanich (1663–66), 491–92, 511, 546–49, for similar
exchanges.
[73] Iosif Volotskii, *Prosvetitel' ili oblochenie eresi zhidovstvuiushchikh, slovo* 16.

spiritual (salvation), or political (justice). It was to this end that God had granted men natural freedom, for freedom was necessary if the divine plan for self-improvement was to be properly pursued. In the course of their quest, men discovered that authority was necessary to check the willful tendencies of human nature. But God had foreseen this and (depending on whether one was a divine-right theorist or a republican) created political authority himself or provided men with the rational capacities ("Natural Law, which is reason") to create it themselves. In both the divine-right and republican mythologies, political authority was forged by the transfer of some measure of divinely granted liberty to another for the purposes of protection, which in turn allowed further self-perfection. In the case of divine-right kingship, God granted the prince a measure of His people's liberty; in the case of republican government, the people explicitly lent a portion of their freedom to the prince. In either instance, the transfer was conditional: the prince was to ensure that justice prevailed among the people and that he did not transgress the dictates of natural law by unjustly appropriating their freedom. Both divine-right theorists and republicans agreed that all subjects could not be perfectly equal in a well-ordered political society. Some would retain a greater measure of freedom and would be more honorable while others would retain less and therefore have less dignity.

If we may judge by the de facto support given the government by Muscovite servitors, their apparent willingness to act in a "demeaning" fashion before the tsar, the occasional statements concerning the importance of humble service to the crown, and the few positive statements concerning the God-granted authority of the tsar, it would seem that the Muscovites understood the metaphysics of political life very differently from their European counterparts. The Russian political worldview—after the innovations of Ivan III and before it was infected by Krizhanich's "Polish illness" in Petrine times—was founded in the cultural mythology of submission. Their view of human nature was rooted in Old Testamentary pessimism, which is understandable given that the Bible was the primary source of literate "philosophical" doctrine in Muscovite Russia. Fallen man, the Muscovites believed, was born in sin and, given the slightest opportunity, would stray from the true path into lust, greed, avarice, and so on. In the Muscovite conception, then, freedom was not a vehicle for self-perfection (a belief that smacked of the greatest sin, pride) but a capricious condition that allowed man to descend deeper into depravity and further away from salvation. God had, of course, foreseen that humankind would be incapable of self-governance, and loving His creation, He had provided men with kings. Their purpose was to restrain the wayward tendencies of human nature such that men might live in relative peace in "this vale of tears." One mid-sixteenth-century Russian cleric, quoting the words of the Byzantine cleric Agapetus, provided an apt metaphor for the duty of the tsar to care for the souls of his people: "As the eye is rooted in the body, so too is the emperor established in the world, sent by God to render benefits to provide for man as for himself that he remains virtuous and does not stumble into evil."[74] God not only bound the tsar to guide his subjects toward salvation, He also instructed subjects to remain submissive. As both the Old and New Testaments record, God made it the duty of men to serve their temporal rulers as "slaves," with the same measure of submission as they accorded God and Christ.[75] Such submission did not, as the Europeans protested, bring disgrace to subjects, but rather added "luster to the doctrine of God our Savior."[76] With the European divine-right theorists, the Russians believed that God had transferred the liberty of his people to kings. But, in contrast to European thinkers, the Muscovites seem to have held that this transfer was conditional in the limited sense that the tsar was required to protect his subjects from oppression and sin. For this requirement he was beholden to God, not to man. Thus, as the holy books plainly explained, men were compelled by divine law to submit completely, even to the point of suffering tyrants:

> Let every soul be subject unto the higher power. For there is no power but of God: the powers that be are ordained of God. Whosoever therefore resisteth the power, resisteth the ordinance of God: and they that resist shall receive to themselves damnation. For rulers are not a terror to good works, but to the evil. Wilst thou then not be afraid of the power? do that which is good, and thou shalt have praise of the same.[77]

In the early sixteenth century, no less a writer than Iosif Volotskii could quote Scripture to demonstrate that evil rulers must be resisted. But, given the behavior of Russian courtiers during Ivan's reign of terror, we have some reason to believe that Iosif's Caesaropapism rang truer to Muscovites.[78] Finally, like the European ethnographers, the Russians accepted that classes would exist in political society. But their understanding of estate distinctions differed in two major respects from the common European conception. First, all subjects, regardless of station, were equally subject to the tsar, just as all men, regardless of station, were identically subject to God. Second, status differences were determined not by the degree of freedom one maintained after the hypothetical transfer of liberty, but rather by the dignity and power of one's master. The Muscovite magnates and gentry served the tsar directly, thus they retained the exclusive right to be called the sovereign's slaves.

If one takes into account these background assumptions of Russian political mentalities, the deferential style of Muscovite political culture becomes

---

[74] *Polnoe sobranie russkikh letopisei*, 21, chap. 2, 609–11.
[75] For the duty to serve as "slaves," see 1 Sam. 8:18; Eph. 6:5–8; Titus 2:9–10; and 1 Tim. 6:1–2.
[76] Titus 2:9–10.
[77] Rom. 13:1–3.
[78] Volotskii, *Prosvetitel' ili oblochenie eresi zhidovstvuiushchikh*, slova 7, 16.

much more comprehensible. The large set of Russian sayings concerning the authority of the tsar that were so carefully recorded by the ethnographers was a popular reflection of a deep attitude about the divinity of royal authority. For the Muscovites "the will of the prince was the will of God," as the Russian proverb had it and the Bible itself authorized.[79] When Russians called the tsar *gosudar'*, they were reminded that he was the master of Russia just as God (*Gospod*) was master of all men. As Russians humiliated themselves with terms such as "slave," another habit authorized by the Bible, they likely recalled the dependence of men on God and the dependence of all subjects on His vicar, the tsar.[80] Bowing low to the ground before their ruler, as the Scripture instructed, they were no doubt cognizant of the similarity of prostration before the tsar and ritual veneration before icons.[81] The ceremonial repetition of these acts served to reflect and reinforce the notion that the tsar was the instrument of God, the divinely granted master of humble slaves. In fact, the biblical character of Muscovite political beliefs suggests a potential explanation for perhaps the most bizarre behavior noted by the ethnographers—the Russian habit of thanking secular authorities for punishments. If the Muscovites believed that earthly punishments were, in fact, divine retribution for sins seen and unseen, and therefore guidance toward the true path, might they not have understood the tsar's wrath—itself a tool in God's hands—as divine retribution and direction? And didn't one customarily thank God for His mercy and kindness, particularly when He showed man his evil ways?

The fact that Russians believed on some level that the tsar was the divinely ordained master of willful, sinful slaves goes some distance toward accounting for the character of Russian political culture. It does not, however, provide a complete explanation for the stability of the Muscovite regime over almost two centuries. In order to persist over long periods of time, political belief systems not only have to be seen as legitimate by their members, they also must provide a means of solving the mundane problems that face any political organization: Who will rule? Who will pay? Who will serve? Who will decide? The truth of this commonplace is provided by the fate of any number of fanciful though (at least to the participants) legitimate political projects, from the radical Protestant community of Thomas Münster to the early Communist utopia of the Bolsheviks. By almost any standard, Muscovite political culture proved to be quite durable, lasting in its pristine form for almost two centuries and, according to the opinions of some continuity theorists, well into modern times under one guise or another.[82] It seems ob-

---

[79] Rom. 13:1–3; Eccles. 8:2–4.

[80] 1 Sam. 8:18; Eph. 6:5–8; Titus 2:9–10; 1 Tim. 6:1–2.

[81] 1 Sam. 25:41; 2 Sam. 9:6, 8; 1 Kings 1:16, 23, 31, 47; Matt. 27:29.

[82] Continuity theories of Russian history are numerous, and most are very poorly conceived. For two stimulating exceptions, see Richard Hellie, "Structure of Modern Russian History," and Edward L. Keenan, "Muscovite Political Folkways."

vious, then, that the Muscovite elite somehow solved the basic problems of politics and government. What makes this remarkable is the fact that they did so in a singularly inopportune environment. From nearly the moment of the birth of the Muscovite state in the era of Ivan III, the Russian royal family and its tiny boyar elite were faced with the unenviable task of knitting together an expansive, poor, sparsely populated region of far northeastern Europe and mobilizing it for constant defense against a host of aggressive neighbors—Tatars, Cossacks, Lithuanians, Poles, Teutonic Knights, and Swedes. Moreover, not only did the Russians survive, they prospered, creating in the span of a bit over a century an empire that stretched from Archangelsk to Kiev and from Smolensk to Kamchatka. It would hardly be an exaggeration to claim that no other early modern state succeeded so well against such stubborn obstacles as did the Muscovites. How did they do it? Obviously this is no place to attempt a complete answer to this important and complex query, but it seems clear that the nature of their political culture had much to do with the stability and success of the Muscovite enterprise. As repulsive as this form of government was to the visiting Europeans who observed it in action, despotism—or what we should perhaps neutrally call a patrimonial state—in fact provided the Russian elite with a remarkably economical way to stabilize, unify, and mobilize their subject peoples and far-flung territories.[83] It did so by solving or at least ameliorating four problems that faced every early modern kingdom—the problem of faction, the problem of wealth, the problem of mobilization, and the problem of conflict resolution.

By formally concentrating all political power in the hands of one legitimate ruling dynasty, the Muscovites largely avoided a difficulty that plagued early modern European monarchies—division among the upper elite, and particularly division between a centralizing king and his magnates. The history of European absolutism is in essence the history of this or that monarch's struggle to coordinate a divisive nobility into the courts, offices, and armies of an expanded postfeudal state. The king's work was made difficult by the nature of European mentalities and institutions. The nobility believed that it had the right to share power with the monarch, a right that was deeply rooted in the compacts, contracts, and accords of the feudal past. Moreover, the governing class was often entrenched in institutions—national estates,

---

[83] On the patrimonial state, see Max Weber, *Economy and Society*, 3:1006–69. Treatments of Muscovy as a patrimonial state include Richard Pipes, *Russia under the Old Regime*, 1–110, and Nancy S. Kollmann, *Kinship and Politics*, 3. Richard Hellie has suggested the term "garrison" or "service" state, emphasizing the importance of military pressure on the genesis of Muscovite government. The underlying idea seems similar to Weber's. See Hellie, "Structure of Modern Russian History," 3. Since Marx, various social theorists and historians have proposed that Muscovy was a species of Oriental despotism or the Asiatic mode of production, stressing the similarity of early modern Russian government to those of premodern Asia. See, for example, Karl A. Wittfogel, *Oriental Despotism*, 174–77, and Samuel H. Baron, "Feudalism or the Asiatic Mode of Production." Again the underlying concepts are similar to Weber's.

courts, local councils—that were sufficiently powerful to enable it to resist reforms aimed at expanding the monarchy's authority. In short, the nobility wanted a hand in ruling the state and had the power to fight for it. In some places, the absolutist state-builders succeeded in overcoming nobles' resistance (France and Prussia) and in others they did not (England and the Netherlands). But everywhere there was conflict over the fundamental issue of the day, the extent of royal political authority. In contrast, the patrimonial character of Muscovite political mentalities and institutions enabled the Russian elite to avoid much of this infighting and get on with the business of empire-building. After the reign of Ivan III, the question of who would rule was made moot by the understanding that all political power—at least in principle—rested in the hands of the God-ordained tsar. Moreover, even if the Russian elite wanted to oppose autocracy, it possessed no powerful, European-style institutions that might be used as levers against tsarist authority. The Russian magnates, then, did not lay claim to political power, nor were they likely to have been able to seize political authority had they desired it.[84] As we've seen, several of the European ethnographers interpreted the political passivity of the Muscovite elite as a sign that it had been forcibly reduced to slavery. It is true that in the era of Ivan III the rights of once free servitors were annulled by the crown, and there was perhaps some early resistance to patrimonialism that has not survived in the record. After Ivan III's reign, however, there is little or no positive evidence of any significant political resistance on the part of the elite to the *institution* of patrimonial autocracy. To be sure, the Muscovite state was not monolithic. Modern historians have identified clan-based factions that fought among themselves in both the sixteenth and seventeenth centuries.[85] But these groups were struggling for power at court, not over the extent of the royal prerogative. Even the most serious division of the upper elite—over the question of Władysław's candidacy for the throne in 1611—was not so much about the form of political power as about who would hold it. Moreover, the ethnographers' "reduction" interpretation sells the magnates short, in two senses. First, it naively assumes that the Muscovites could not truly have believed that they were in some sense the tsar's slaves. But the fact of the matter is that they consistently proclaimed their slavery over the course of two centuries. Perhaps more important, the ethnographers' thesis fails to take into consideration the benefit that the magnates derived from surrendering political power to the tsar. It is not hard to imagine that they willingly embraced an authoritative ruler as a means of keeping peace among the major clans. From the magnates' perspective, open warfare with either the royal or other elite families was a risky, expensive, and wasteful proposition. It was simply more profitable (not to men-

---

[84] On the question of elite opposition in Muscovy or the lack of it, see Hartmut Rüss, *Adel und Adelsoppositionen in Moskauer Staat.*

[85] Kollmann, *Kinship and Politics;* Robert O. Crummey, *Aristocrats and Servitors.*

tion in accordance with the dictates of the Scriptures) to agree that the tsar would rule absolutely. He was, after all, one of them and would ensure that their interests would be served.[86]

A second advantage afforded the Muscovites by the patrimonial state was the ability to extract resources from the population almost at will. In the course of building absolutist states, European monarchs were compelled to request subsidies from organized social groups—estates, corporate towns, and provincial elites—that controlled much of the commonwealth. Again, the king's task was made difficult by European political mentalities and institutions. Most Europeans believed that natural and divine law protected their properties from undue incursions by the royal fisc. To be sure, they were also obliged to contribute to the maintenance of the king's estate, but there were limits. These limits were given force by the existence of various constitutional bodies—national estates, courts of law, and provincial councils—that could be used to stave off the affronts of overreaching princes. It is little wonder that much of the political conflict that beset early modern European states can be attributed to the king's need for cash and his subjects' reluctance to provide it. In contrast, the assumptions and institutions of the Muscovite patrimonial state made it much easier for the tsar to collect resources from his subjects. Muscovites accepted that the tsar, while not the universal proprietor imagined by European ethnographers, was at the very least the titular owner of the realm and rightfully had a claim to part of what was in private hands. Furthermore, even if Muscovites wanted to protest royal taxation, they lacked the strong political and social institutions that might have provided a permanent brake on the incursions of the fisc. The ethnographers assumed that the tsar had violently imposed despotic authority over the property of his subjects. To some degree they were correct, for on several occasions—particularly in the mid–seventeenth century—the urban classes rose in revolt against high taxes. Yet, by and large, the record contains comparatively little indication of positive resistance to royal imposts and no organized resistance at all to the right of the tsar to distribute and seize prebendal estates. The ethnographers' interpretation of the powers of the tsar over property is at once naive and one-sided. It excludes the possibility that Muscovites truly felt that everything they owned was in some way within the discretion of the tsar, despite the fact that Russians themselves openly stated this was the case. And it ignores the underlying interest calculus that may have led Russians to embrace the principle of titular universal proprietorship. For reasons having to do with their own political beliefs, the Europeans imagined that property in a regime of universal royal ownership would be insecure. After all, what was given by the king could just as easily be taken away. The Russians, in contrast, may have felt that nominal universal pro-

---

[86] This thesis was first suggested in Keenan, "Muscovite Political Folkways," and is elaborated in Kollmann, *Kinship and Politics*.

prietorship secured property if only in a fictitious or psychological sense. Private property had to be defended by its owners, who would be all but powerless against the tangible and imagined threats that inhabited the violent Russian world. Titular tsarist property, however, was protected by the most powerful ruler in the world. In this way, "all that is mine is God's and the tsar's" could be understood not only as a sign of servile submission to an overmighty authority but equally as a threat issued to possible felons.

The patrimonial state also allowed the Muscovite court to demand extensive personal services from its subjects. The European monarchs of the sixteenth and seventeenth centuries required not only money to build their absolutist states but also men to work in them. And here they faced a singular difficulty, a difficulty imposed upon them, again, by the character of European political beliefs and the nature of the European estate structure. After the end of knight service, princes could not simply order their highborn subjects into royal offices. One of the rights generally reserved by the postfeudal nobility was free service: privileged men might have to pay dues, but they were at liberty to pursue their own careers in the professions, in the clergy, in business, or perhaps in royal service. What is more, the European nobility and gentry had the institutional power necessary to defend this right. It is little wonder that European monarchs commonly opted to bypass their once dependent nobilities and hire commoners to staff the administration and army. In contrast, the mentalities and institutions of the Muscovite patrimonial state made it much easier for the tsar to extract services from his subjects. Muscovites believed that all men, regardless of station, were bound to serve the tsar in some capacity. Moreover, even if they wanted to avoid service, the Russian estates did not possess the institutional power necessary to create and preserve an extensive sphere of personal autonomy. Many of the ethnographers believed that universal service had been violently imposed on Muscovite society by a tyrannical authority. Indeed, the requirement that all landholders aid the tsar by serving in the army personally or by providing troops was probably the work of Ivan IV. But the record contains no evidence of sustained, organized opposition to the requirement of knight service. As in the case of their interpretation of the tsar's political and fiscal authority, the foreigners' understanding of knight service rests on misguided assumptions about the veracity of Muscovite claims and the utility of universal service. Most Europeans simply could not believe that the Russians possessed an ethos in which service to the tsar was the honorable obligation of every subject, no matter how many times it was explained to them. Moreover, the ethnographers could not understand the cultural logic behind the ethos of service. The Europeans believed that obligatory service was a dangerous and undignified institution. If men were deprived of their natural liberty, they would have no way to protect themselves or their honor against the harsh realities of the world. For the Muscovites, royal service was precisely the condition that preserved their freedom and dignity. In their eyes, a man without a master was a poor creature indeed, for he was subject to the violence and insults that predatory humans were so wont to inflict on their fellow men. But a man in service—particularly in service to the tsar—was protected by the strength of his master and shared in his lord's dignity.

Finally, the patrimonial state provided the court with a mechanism through which disputes over politics, taxation, and service requirements could be peacefully resolved. In their effort to build absolutist states, European monarchs often faced crises of legitimacy. As any student of European thought knows, the early modern period was host to a great variety of political ideologies. Though the most important of these creeds possessed certain common elements that distinguish them from Muscovite beliefs, they were distinctive enough to provide various autonomous social groups with political ideas that put them seriously at odds with centralizing monarchies. In this way, the common discourse of monarchical legitimacy broke down in early modern Europe, often with frightful consequences for kings and their subjects alike, as in the Dutch Revolt, the Thirty Years' War, and the English Civil War. In marked contrast, both the hegemonic character of Muscovite political discourse and the absence of independent social groups within which oppositional ideologies might take root enabled the Russian state, at least in most cases, to efficiently diffuse disputes enlivened by the requirements of state-building. Though a host of scholars (particularly Soviet historians) have searched for anti-autocratic thought in sixteenth- and seventeenth-century Russia, it seems clear that what Father George Florovsky called the "silence of Muscovy" held sway in the arena of political thought, for no oppositional political philosophies per se have been found in the small corpus of Muscovite political writing.[87] Recalling that Russian autocracy had no real political theorist on the order of Bodin, James I, or Hobbes, one might even go further and suggest that the ideological hegemony of tsarism was so profound that even its basic precepts did not require explication. The only person in Muscovite times to propose that the metaphysics of autocracy should be systematically expostulated was Krizhanich, a Croatian.[88] Interestingly, he argued that a theory of autocracy was needed not to combat *Russian* political opposition but to fight *European* arguments against tsarism, arguments that, so far as is known, had no currency in Russia. Moreover, even if some Russians, having become infected with what Krizhanich termed the "Polish illness," were to have formulated some anti-autocratic credo, it seems unlikely that it could have provided a basis for any political movement. In aggressively coordinating all groups within its structure, the Russian government did its best to make sure that there would be no fertile seedbed for contrarian ideas. Occasionally, distinct sodalities within the Muscovite state spoke out—peasants and cossacks in the Bolotnikov and Razin rebellions,

[87] George Florovsky, "Problem of Old Russian Culture."
[88] Krizhanich (1663–66), 549.

the service gentry in petition campaigns, the urban classes in the riots of the mid–seventeenth century, the Solovetskii monks, and the *strel'tsy*. Nonetheless, none of these groups ever broke out of the basic paradigm of Muscovite political legitimacy, that is, the idea that a merciful tsar (not necessarily the reigning one, but the "true" one) should show mercy to his humble, suffering subjects. The European visitors, of course, interpreted the "silence" of Muscovy as a politically inspired hatred of learning and the discourse of deference as undignified servility. It seems more sensible, however, to understand Russian political muteness as the product of a kind of state-secured (not state-created) consensus. To be sure, the Muscovites took active and often violent measures to ferret out political heresy, as in "word and deed" cases. But it seems that by and large their work was not difficult, for there was no principled opposition to the institution of autocracy. Further, the discourse of deference was not so much evidence of the government's power and its subjects' servility as it was *the* conventional means of pleading one's case before the authorities. It is true that the state required petitioners to follow the protocol of humility and prosecuted those who did not, such as those who omitted a part of the tsar's title from the royal salutation.[89] But again, very little prosecution of this type seems to have been necessary, for it was both ideally and practically in the interest of servitors to follow the formulas of deference.

Conclusion

Was Muscovy a despotism or, as we have neutrally termed it, a patrimonial state? The European ethnographers certainly thought so, and we have some reason to believe them. Their vision was in some small measure clouded by Muscovite suspicion, but they succeeded in observing much of Russian civic life. They were indeed influenced by the accounts of other European travelers, but they read critically and generally did not blindly follow even their most esteemed predecessors. They conceptualized Muscovite governance within European categories, but the concepts they employed were to a considerable degree well fitted to Muscovite circumstances. To be sure, the ethnographers exaggerated the authority of the tsar by unreasonably juxtaposing idealized images of a servile Muscovy to free Europe. If, however, their fantastic binary oppositions are reconfigured as comparative continua, then it is possible to agree with them that the authority of the Muscovite monarchy was far more extensive than that of any European monarch.

Their most sophisticated explanation of the basis for this overwhelming authority—natural slavery—must be found wanting, for Muscovites were

[89] The formulas of petitions were legislated, albeit erratically. See *Polnoe sobranie zakonov Rossiiskoi imperii*, 2: nos. 677, 709, 715, 820, 964.

certainly capable of protestation. Moreover, the foreigners interpreted the Muscovite discourse of deference literally, when it seems more appropriate to view it metaphorically. The Russian tsar was not the master of slaves. Rather, the language of mastery and servitude was a habitual part of everyday Muscovite political expression, a means of polite interaction. Finally, the foreigners misunderstood the meaning of this discourse by imposing an idealized concept of slavery on it. To them the master was all-powerful and the slave powerless. Yet for the Muscovites the language of servitude implied mutual obligations: the "master" protected the "slave" and the latter served the former.

The underpinnings of Muscovite autocracy, then, are to be found not in natural slavery but rather in the deep structure of the Muscovite worldview and the practical utility of a patrimonial state. Unlike the Europeans, who believed government should be limited so that men could perfect themselves, Muscovites held that the rule of the tsar had to be nearly untrammeled if the sinful ways of men were to be checked. But the fit of this model to the Muscovite worldview was not the only anchor of Russian political culture. The patrimonial state also provided the Muscovite elite with an effective means of maintaining and expanding their realm. It allowed the Russian court to avoid dangerous political infighting, to extract fiscal resources from the tsar's subjects, to mobilize the manpower necessary to staff the administration and army, and to resolve conflicts involved in state-building. In the end, Muscovite rule was not, as the foreigners thought, a faulty, deviant, or illegitimate form of government imposed by a ruthless king, but rather a logical adaptive strategy that permitted the Muscovite elite to build an empire under the most trying of conditions.

APPENDIX
Folkloric Stories about Ivan IV in European Ethnographies, 1555–1700

THIS APPENDIX PRESENTS a catalog of folkloric stories about the tyranny of Ivan IV found in European accounts of Russia from 1555 to 1700. It is not complete, though it represents the largest collection of stories available in the literature.

Table A1 presents an overview of the dissemination of the stories. In the first column of the table, the scenarios are arranged in alphabetical order. In the second column, the conformity of the scenario to a German or Russian Dracula story of the later fifteenth or early sixteenth century is indicated. "G 30" indicates "German story number 30" cataloged in Radu Florescu and Raymond McNally, *The Complete Dracula;* "R 5 indicates "Russian story number 5" described in the same source. The third column traces the dissemination of the scenario in European treatments of Muscovy. The accounts in the third column are arranged in chronological order. Succession does not necessarily indicate influence.

Table A2 describes the stories found in each sixteenth- and seventeenth-century author's work. The authors are arranged chronologically, beginning with Magnus (1555) and ending with Korb (1700). After the short title of the story is given, its location in the text is provided. For example, "The Tsar's Harem" is rehearsed in Taube and Kruse (1571), 41–42. After the citation, the possible source ("Source") of the story is indicated, if it appears to have been borrowed from a preceding text. "Subject" refers to the protagonist of the story. Ivan IV is usually the protagonist, but in several instances earlier grand princes (particularly Ivan III and Vasilii III) were originally the subjects of stories that later featured Ivan IV. Finally, the stories themselves are outlined under "Scenario." A brief synopsis is rendered after the first occurrence of a story. Thereafter, unless there is a major variant, reference is made to the outline provided in the first occurrence. For example, Magnus (1555) was the first to offer "The Impertinent Ambassador," so the story is described in his entry. The later instances of the story (Danckaert [1611], Heylyn [1621], Collins [1667], Reutenfels [1671]) refer back to Magnus.

The Dracula stories are analyzed in Chapter 5.

Table A1. Synoptic distribution of folkloric stories

Story	Dracula story	Author/text
Afraid No Longer		Schlichting (1571a), Guagnini (1578)
Alms for the Poor	G 30, R 5	Horsey (1584)
Blinding the Builder	G 25	Horsey (1584), Fletcher (1591), Olearius (1656), Wickhart (1575)
Chasing the Chickens		Taube and Kruse (1571), Staden (1578)
Dressed Like a Goose		Fletcher (1591), Collins (1667)
Drinking the Tsar's Health		Schlichting (1571a), Guagnini (1578)
Drunktown ("Naleika")		Reutenfels (1671)
Gifts to the Sultan		Massa (1610)
He Made No Attempt to Live		Schlichting (1571a), Guagnini (1578)
Horse as a Wife		Schlichting (1571a), Guagnini (1578), Olearius (1656), Reutenfels (1671)
How Pleasantly You Sing!		Massa (1610)
How to Defend a Fortress		Schlichting (1571a), Guagnini (1578)
No Quarter		Collins (1667)
Picking Up Peas		Collins (1667)
The Abdication		Schlichting (1571a), Guagnini (1578), Oderborn (1585)
The Bald Men		Collins (1667)
The Bear Hunt		Schlichting (1571a), Guagnini (1578)
The Blind Horse		Schlichting (1571a), Guagnini (1578)
The Devils in the Volkhov		Schlichting (1571a), Guagnini (1578), Olearius (1656)
The Hurtful Present		Schlichting (1571a), Guagnini (1578), Oderborn (1585)
The Impertinent Ambassador	G 32, R 1	Magnus (1555), Bodin (1576), Danckaert (1611), Heylyn (1621), Collins (1667), Reutenfels (1671)
The Kneeling Elephant		Oderborn (1585), Reutenfels (1671)
The Load of Cedar		Collins (1667)
The Mark of Honor		Massa (1610)
The Measure of Fleas		Fletcher (1591), Collins (1667)
The Royal Bride Selection		Taube and Kruse (1571), Printz (1578)
The Severed Head		Schlichting (1571a), Guagnini (1578)
The Bast Shoes		Collins (1667)
The Small Fish		Schlichting (1571a), Guagnini (1578)
The Tatar and the Knife		Horsey (1585), Fletcher (1591)
The Tsar among Thieves		Collins (1667), Reutenfels (1671)
The Tsar's Harem		Taube and Kruse (1571), Schlichting (1571a), Guagnini (1578), Printz (1578), Staden (1578), Horsey (1585), Massa (1610), Collins (1667), Reutenfels (1671)
Wounds in the Back	R 2	Staden (1578)
33 stories		73 instances

Table A2. Distribution of folkloric stories (chronological)

Magnus (1555)

Story: The Impertinent Ambassador: bk. 11, chap. 10.
Source: Very similar to German 32 and Russian 1. Magnus claimed to have found this
   story in Albert Krantz's *Vandalia* (1519), a book the author cited extensively. However, as John Granlung has pointed out ("Kommentar," 4:394), the tale is not found
   in Krantz's book.
Subject: Ivan III or Ivan IV?
Scenario: A foreign ambassador (Italian) refuses to doff his cap before Ivan because it
   is not the custom of his country. The tsar nails the Italian's hat to his head so that his
   native custom may be better observed.

Taube and Kruse (1571)

Story: The Tsar's Harem: 41–42.
Source: Unknown.
Subject: Ivan IV.
Scenario: Ivan orders his henchmen to gather women in his harem, some of whom are in
   turn distributed to his courtiers.

Story: Chasing the Chickens: 42.
Source: Unknown.
Subject: Ivan IV.
Scenario: Ivan orders girls and women to be stripped naked and to catch chickens for his
   amusement.

Story: The Royal Bride Selection: 55.
Source: Unknown. Herberstein (1549), 1:50, was the first to report a bride selection, but it
   was of a milder character and concerned Vasilii III. The institution is reported in a num-
   ber of treatises, but without any hint of sexual abuse. See Horsey (1584), 277; Collins
   (1667), 11–12; Reutenfels (1671), 81–82; Neuville (1698), 50; Korb (1700), 2:131.
Subject: Ivan IV.
Scenario: Desiring a wife, Ivan orders beautiful virgins brought to the capital from all over
   Russia. He then sexually abuses them and distributes them to his courtiers.

Schlichting (1571a)

Story: Drinking the Tsar's Health: 214–15.
Source: Unknown.
Subject: Ivan IV.
Scenario: Ivan orders Dmitrii Ovchinin to a banquet and orders the man to drink his health
   until he vomits. He then sends him to the wine cellar for more, where he is killed.

Story: The Severed Head: 221.
Source: Unknown.
Subject: Ivan IV.
Scenario: Ivan decapitates the "Prince of Rostov" and has a short discussion with his head.

Story: The Abdication: 223–24.
Source: Unknown.
Subject: Ivan IV.
Scenario: Ivan "abdicates" in favor of Ivan Petrovich Fedorov-Cheliadnin, genuflects before
   him, then murders him on the throne.

Story: Horse as Wife: 235–36.
Source: Unknown.
Subject: Ivan IV.
Scenario: Ivan orders the archbishop of Novgorod tied to a mare and paraded about. The tsar explains that the horse is his wife.

Story: Devils in the Volkhov: 236–37.
Source: Unknown.
Subject: Ivan IV.
Scenario: Ivan throws an official into the Volkhov River, pulls him out, and asks him what he saw at the bottom. The man replies that he saw devils, devils who would soon come to get Ivan. Ivan murders him.

Story: The Blind Horse: 244.
Source: Unknown.
Subject: Ivan IV.
Scenario: Ivan binds Vasilii Dmitr'evich Danilov, accused of treason, to a cart drawn by a blind horse. The horse pulls the cart into a river and Ivan exhorts Vasilii to use the vehicle to flee to Poland.

Story: The Tsar's Harem: 247
Source: Unknown.
Subject: Ivan IV.
Scenario: See Taube and Kruse.

Story: The Hurtful Present: 247–48.
Source: Unknown.
Subject: Ivan IV.
Scenario: Ivan offers to bestow royal favor on Boris Titov. He cuts Titov's ear off, hands it to him, and tells him to be thankful for the gift because he may receive finer ones in the future.

Story: The Bear Hunt: 249.
Source: Unknown.
Subject: Ivan IV.
Scenario: For his amusement, the tsar orders his courtiers to dress in bearskins and then sics dogs on them.

Story: The Small Fish: 250.
Source: Unknown.
Subject: Ivan IV.
Scenario: An official is accused of stealing only large fish from Ivan's preserves. Ivan drowns him, exhorting the official not to neglect the small fish.

Story: How to Defend a Fortress: 250–51.
Source: Unknown.
Subject: Ivan IV.
Scenario: Ivan says he will teach his defeated commanders how to defend a fortress. He ties them to a stake and shoots them with arrows.

Story: He Made No Attempt to Live: 254.
Source: Unknown.
Subject: Ivan IV.
Scenario: Ivan wounds a courtier, then regrets it and orders doctors to attend him. The man dies, but the tsar dismisses him, saying he made no attempt to live.

Story: Afraid No Longer: 257–58.
Source: Unknown.
Subject: Ivan IV.

Scenario: Ivan asks a guard why he fled at the sight of him. The guard answers that he was afraid. The tsar says he will ensure that the guard will be afraid no longer and kills him.

Ulfeldt (1575)

Story: The Tsar's Harem: 38.
Source: Unknown.
Subject: Ivan IV.
Scenario: See Taube and Kruse.

Bodin (1576)

Story: The Impertinent Ambassador: 636.
Source: Magnus.
Subject: Ivan III or Ivan IV.
Scenario: See Magnus.

Guagnini (1578)

Story: The Tsar's Harem
Source: Schlichting.
Subject: Ivan IV.
Scenario: See Taube and Kruse.

Story: Drinking the Tsar's Health: 28.
Source: Schlichting.
Subject: Ivan IV.
Scenario: See Schlichting.

Story: The Severed Head: 29.
Source: Schlichting.
Subject: Ivan IV.
Scenario: See Schlichting.

Story: The Abdication: 30.
Source: Schlichting.
Subject: Ivan IV.
Scenario: See Schlichting.

Story: He Made No Attempt to Live: 31–32.
Source: Schlichting.
Subject: Ivan IV.
Scenario: See Schlichting.

Story: The Hurtful Present: 32.
Source: Schlichting.
Subject: Ivan IV.
Scenario: See Schlichting.

Story: Horse as Wife: 35.
Source: Schlichting.
Subject: Ivan IV.
Scenario: See Schlichting.

Story: Devils in the Volkhov: 35
Source: Unknown.

Subject: Ivan IV.
Scenario: See Schlichting.

Story: The Blind Horse: 38.
Source: Schlichting.
Subject: Ivan IV.
Scenario: See Schlichting.

Story: The Bear Hunt: 39.
Source: Schlichting.
Subject: Ivan IV
Scenario: See Schlichting.

Story: Afraid No Longer: 42.
Source: Schlichting.
Subject: Ivan IV.
Scenario: See Schlichting.

Story: The Small Fish: 46.
Source: Schlichting.
Subject: Ivan IV.
Scenario: See Schlichting.
Story: How to Defend a Fortress: 46.
Source: Schlichting.
Subject: Ivan IV.
Scenario: See Schlichting.

Printz (1578)

Story: The Royal Bride Selection: 28.
Source: Unknown.
Subject: Ivan IV.
Scenario: See Taube and Kruse.

Story: The Tsar's Harem: 62.
Source: Unknown.
Subject: Ivan IV.
Scenario: See Taube and Kruse.

Staden (1578)

Story: Chasing the Chickens: 21.
Source: Unknown.
Subject: Ivan IV.
Scenario: See Taube and Kruse.

Story: The Tsar's Harem: 32–33.
Source: Unknown.
Subject: Ivan IV.
Scenario: See Taube and Kruse.

Story: Wounds in the Back: 55.
Source: Unknown. Identical to Russian 2.
Subject: Ivan IV.
Scenario: Ivan orders that those warriors with wounds in the back be punished, while those with wounds in the front be rewarded.

Horsey (1584)

Story: Blinding the Builder: 266.
Source: Similar to German 25. Immediate source unknown.
Subject: Ivan IV.
Scenario: Ivan IV orders the fortress of Ivangorod constructed and then blinds the architect so another building of equal strength cannot be built. Horsey is confused. Ivangorod was built in 1492 by Ivan III.

Story: The Tsar's Harem: 300 and 304.
Source: Unknown.
Subject: Ivan IV.
Scenario: See Taube and Kruse.

Story: The Tatar and the Knife: 313.
Source: Unknown.
Subject: Ivan IV.
Scenario: After the destruction of Moscow by the Tatars in 1571, the khan sends a knife to Ivan IV and suggests that he kill himself. Note that Taube and Kruse (1571), 54, report that the khan sent Ivan a knife as a mark of respect.

Story: Alms for the Poor: 313.
Source: Very similar to German 30 and Russian 5. The immediate source is unknown.
Subject: Ivan IV.
Scenario: During a famine Ivan invites the poor to receive alms at his table. They arrive and he throws them in the river so that they may eat fish. They drown.

Oderborn (1585)

Story: The Hurtful Present: 235.
Source: Guagnini?
Subject: Ivan IV.
Scenario: See Schlichting.

Story: The Abdication: 228.
Source: Guagnini?
Subject: Ivan IV.
Scenario: See Schlichting.

Story: The Kneeling Elephant: 261.
Source: Unknown.
Subject: Ivan IV.
Scenario: Ivan receives an elephant from the shah of Persia. The tsar is so prideful that he orders it to be taught to kneel before him. Staden (1578), 29, reports an elephant but does not mention kneeling.

Fletcher (1591)

Story: Dressed Like a Goose: 219.
Source: Unknown.
Subject: Ivan IV.
Scenario: Ivan discovers that an official has been stealing money by hiding coins in dressed geese. He orders his executioners to dress the official like a goose.

Story: The Load of Cedar: 223.
Source: Unknown.

Subject: Ivan IV.
Scenario: Ivan orders the people of Perm to cut cedar for him, knowing full well that no cedar grows in Perm. He imposes a huge fine on them.

Story: The Measure of Fleas: 223.
Source: Unknown.
Subject: Ivan IV.
Scenario: Ivan orders the city of Moscow to provide him with a measure of live fleas, knowing that the task is impossible. He fines them.

Story: Blinding the Builder: 243.
Source: Horsey?
Subject: Ivan III.
Scenario: See Horsey. Note that Fletcher correctly attributes the building of Ivangorod to Ivan III, whereas Horsey had mistakenly claimed Ivan IV built it.

Story: The Tatar and the Knife: 247.
Source: Horsey?
Subject: Ivan IV.
Scenario: See Horsey.

Massa (1610)

Story: How Pleasantly You Sing!: 15.
Source: Unknown.
Subject: Ivan IV.
Scenario: Ivan tortures his subjects, all the while exclaiming, "How pleasantly you sing!"

Story: The Mark of Honor: 15–16.
Source: Unknown.
Subject: Ivan IV.
Scenario: A noble claims that no member of his family has never been whipped. Ivan explains it is a mark of honor and whips the man.

Story: Gifts to the Sultan: 17 and 123–24.
Source: Unknown.
Subject: Ivan IV.
Scenario: Ivan is insulted by the Turkish sultan. He sends him a present of a rat skin for a robe and a shaven fox skin for a hat, each with peculiar meanings.

Story: The Tsar's Harem: 20–21.
Source: Unknown.
Subject: Ivan IV.
Scenario: See Taube and Kruse.

Danckaert (1611)

Story: The Impertinent Ambassador.
Source: Magnus?
Subject: Ivan IV.
Scenario: See Magnus.

Heylyn (1621)

Story: The Impertinent Ambassador: 346.
Source: Magnus?

Subject: Ivan IV.
Scenario: See Magnus. A very brief reference.

Olearius (1656)

Story: Horse as a Wife: 92.
Source: Guagnini.
Subject: Ivan IV.
Scenario: See Schlichting. Olearius himself ascribed the story to Guagnini.

Story: Devils in the Volkhov: 92.
Source: Guagnini.
Subject: Ivan IV and Fedor Dmitrievich Syrkov.
Scenario: See Schlichting. Olearius himself ascribed the story to Guagnini.

Story: Blinding the Builder: 114.
Source: Unknown.
Subject: Ivan IV.
Scenario: See Horsey. Olearius provides a significant variation on the story originally
   supplied by Horsey and Fletcher. In their accounts, Ivan (IV in Horsey; III in Fletcher)
   blinded the architect of Ivangorod. In Olearius, Ivan IV blinds the architect of the Church
   of the Holy Trinity.

Collins (1667)

Story: The Measure of Fleas: 48.
Source: Fletcher?
Subject: Ivan IV.
Scenario: See Fletcher. Collins's rendition is very similar to Fletcher's, but where Fletcher has
   Ivan order Moscow to provide the fleas, Collins has Ivan order Vologda to do the same.

Story: Picking Up Peas: 48.
Source: Unclear.
Subject: Ivan IV.
Scenario: Some foreign women laugh at Ivan. He strips them naked and orders them to
   pick up a bushel of peas he has thrown on the floor before him. Note that this scenario
   shows a certain similarity to "Chasing the Chickens," found in Taube and Kruse (1571)
   and Staden (1578).

Story: The Bald Men: 48–49.
Source: Unknown.
Subject: Ivan IV.
Scenario: An official misunderstands an order from Ivan and sends him "eighty or ninety"
   bald men. Ivan discovers the mistake, makes merry with the bald men, and sends them
   home.

Story: Dressed Like a Goose: 49.
Source: Fletcher?
Subject: Ivan IV.
Scenario: See Fletcher. Collins's version is very similar to Fletcher's, but where Fletcher has
   a provincial *diack* as the perpetrator, Collins has a *voevod*.

Story: The Impertinent Ambassador: 49–51.
Source: Magnus, Danckaert?
Subject: Ivan IV.
Scenario: See Magnus. In Collins's version, the ambassador is French.

Story: The Bast Shoes: 49–51.
Source: Unknown.
Subject: Ivan IV.
Scenario: A shoemaker presents Ivan with a pair of bast shoes and a great turnip. Ivan orders all his men to buy similar shoes and the man becomes rich. Another man attempts to win favor by giving the tsar a fine horse, but he receives only a turnip in return.

Story: No Quarter: 52.
Source: Unclear.
Subject: Ivan IV.
Scenario: Ivan goes incognito through a village asking for help. Only a poor man gives him quarter. He rewards the poor man and burns the village, telling the villagers that they should know what it is like to live out of doors.

Story: The Tsar among Thieves: 52–53
Source: Unclear.
Subject: Ivan IV.
Scenario: Ivan incognito joins a band of thieves to rob the exchequer. One of the thieves refuses, saying that the tsar is good and should not be robbed. He is richly rewarded by Ivan.

Story: The Tsar's Harem: 102.
Source: Unclear.
Subject: Ivan IV.
Scenario: See Taube and Kruse.

Reutenfels (1671)

Story: Horse as Wife: 61.
Source: Guagnini.
Subject: Ivan IV.
Scenario: See Schlichting. Reutenfels relates only that Ivan IV forces a *posadnik* (not the archbishop) of Novgorod to marry a horse.

Story: Drunktown ("Naleika"): 61.
Source: Olearius?
Subject: Vasilii III or Ivan IV.
Scenario: Ivan builds a suburb of Moscow called Naleika, from the verb *nalivat'* ("to pour"), so named to signify that his henchmen can drink freely there. Reutenfels (1671), 94, however, attributes the building of the suburb to Vasilii III. The story appeared many places, but the builder is always Vasilii III, not Ivan IV. See Herberstein (1549), 4; Thevet (1575), 16; Fletcher (1591), 186; Olearius (1656), 116; and Tanner (1678), 69.

Story: The Kneeling Elephant: 64.
Source: Oderborn?
Subject: Ivan IV.
Scenario: See Oderborn.

Story: The Tsar's Harem: 64.
Source: Unknown.
Subject: Ivan IV.
Scenario: See Taube and Kruse.

Story: The Impertinent Ambassador: 105.
Source: Magnus, Danckaert, Collins?
Subject: Ivan IV.
Scenario: See Magnus. In Reutenfels's version, the ambassador is Tatar.

Story: The Tsar among Thieves: 123–24.
Source: Unclear.
Subject: Ivan IV.
Scenario: Reutenfels's version differs from Collins's. Ivan incognito joins a band of thieves. One of them tells a joke at the tsar's expense and a thief slaps him. The thieves are arrested, but the tsar's defender is rewarded and thereafter called Dolgorukii (Longarm).

Wickhart (1675)

Story: Blinding the Builder: 177.
Source: Olearius?
Subject: Ivan IV.
Scenario: See Horsey. This version differs from those found in Horsey, Fletcher, and Olearius. Here Ivan IV blinds the architect of the "Church of Jerusalem."

Tanner (1678)

Story: Blinding the Builder: 60.
Source: Unknown.
Subject: Ivan IV.
Scenario: See Horsey. Tanner explains the discrepancy between Olearius's and Wickhart's versions of the story: resident Germans call the church built by Ivan IV Jerusalem whereas Russians call it Holy Trinity.

Crull (1698)

Story: Blinding the Builder: 9–10.
Source: Olearius?
Subject: Ivan IV builds Jerusalem or Holy Trinity.
Scenario: See Horsey.

BIBLIOGRAPHY 1
Primary Sources: Foreign Accounts of Russia, 1476–1700

THIS BIBLIOGRAPHY LISTS the ninety-seven ethnographic, cosmographical, and historical accounts, and compendia of accounts cited in the notes to this book. In the column on the left, the accounts are listed in abbreviated form beginning with the name of the author and followed by the approximate year(s) in which the item was written. In the column on the right, full bibliographic information on the account is offered in the following form: (a) the full name of the author or authors; (b) basic biographical data about the author or authors; (c) bibliographic information on the first edition, if the account was published in the sixteenth or seventeenth century; (d) a note giving the date in which the account was composed, if it is significantly different from the date of publication or if the account was not published in the sixteenth or seventeenth century; (e) data on the edition cited in the notes.

Abbreviation

Hakluyt (1969) Richard Hakluyt, ed. *The Principal navigations, voiages, traffiques and discoveries of the English Nation.* 12 vols. Glasgow: James MacLehose & Sons, 1903–5. Rpt. New York: Augustus M. Kelly, 1969.

Authors/Texts

Adams/Chancellor (1553) Clement Adams (1519–87; English author; never in Muscovy) and Richard Chancellor (d. 1556; English navigator). "The newe Navigation and discoverie of the kingdome of Moscovia, by the Northeast, in the yeere 1553: Enterprised by Sir Hugh Willoughbie knight, and perfourmed by Richard Chancelor Pilot major of the voyage: Written in Latine by Clement Adams." In *The Principall navigations, voiages and discoveries of the English nation,* comp. Richard Hakluyt, 280–92. London: G. Bishop and R. Newberie, 1589. Written 1553. Cited text: Hakluyt (1969) 2:239–70.

Aleppo (1655)   Macarius (fl. 1636–66; patriarch of Antioch) and Paul of Aleppo (archbishop of Aleppo). No title: Travels to Muscovy, 1653. Written 1653. Cited text: *The Travels of Macarius Patriarch of Antioch. Written by His Attendant Archdeacon, Paul of Aleppo, in Arabic.* Trans. Francis C. Belfour. 2 vols. London: Oriental Translation Committee, 1829–36.

Avity (1613)   Pierre d'Avity (1572–1635; French cosmographer; never in Muscovy). *Les Estates, empires et principautez du monde.* Paris: Olivier de Varenes, 1613. Cited text: *The estates, empires and principalities of the world,* trans. Edward Gramstone. London: A. Islip, 1615.

Avril (1691)   Philippe Avril (1654–98; Jesuit missionary). *Voyage en divers états d'Europe et d'Asie.* Paris, 1691. Cited text: original.

Barbaro   Josaphat Barbaro (d. 1494; Venetian diplomat, merchant). "Viag-
(1488–89)   gio alla Tana." In *Viaggi fatti da Vinetia, alla Tana, in Persia, in India, et Constantinopoli,* ed. Antonio Manuzio. Venice: Nelle Case de Figlivoli di Aldo, 1543. Written 1488–89. Cited text: *Travels to Tana and Persia by Josefa Barbaro and Ambrogio Contarini,* trans. William Thomas and S. A. Roy, esq. London: Hakluyt Society, 1873.

Barberino   Raffaelle Barberino (1532–82; Italian merchant). "Relazione di
(1565)   Moscovia." In *Viaggi di Moscovia de gli anni 1633, 1634, 1635 e 1636.* Viterbo: s.n., 1658. Cited text: "Puteshestvie v Moskoviiu Rafaelia Berberini," ed. and trans. Vasilii I. Liubich-Romanovich. *Syn otechestva* (1842), no. 6: 3–16 and no. 7: 3–50.

Belleforest   François de Belleforest (1530–83; French historian; never in Mus-
(1575)   covy). *La Cosmographie universelle de tout le monde . . . Auteur en partie Munster.* Paris: M. Sonnius, 1575. Cited text: original.

Boch (1578)   Johann Boch (1555–1609; Dutch poet, traveler). *Ioannis Bochii. S.P.Q. Psalmorum Davidis parodia heroica. Eiusdem variae in Psalmos Observationes, physicae, ethnicae, politicae, et historicae.* 2 vols. Antwerp: Ex officina Plantiniana, apud Ioannem Moretum, 1608. Written 1578. Cited text: "Johann Boch in Moscow," trans. Hugh Graham. *Russian History/Histoire Russe* 13 (1986): 93–110.

Boemus (1520)   Joannes Boemus (fl. 1500; German geographer; never in Muscovy). *Omnium gentium mores leges et ritus ex multus clarissimis rerum scriptoribus.* Augsburg: Excusa in officina Sigismundi Grim medici, ac Marci Vuirsung, 1520. Cited text: *The Manners, Lawes, and Customes of All Nations,* trans. E. Aston. London: George Eld, 1611.

Bomhover   Christian Bomhover (before 1469–1518; Livonian official; never
(1508)   in Muscovy?). *Eynne schonne hystorie van vnderlyken gescheffthen der heren tho lyfflanth myth den Rüssen unde tataren.* Cologne?, 1508. Cited text: "Eynne Schonne hystorie," ed. Carl. C. G. Schirren. *Archiv für die Geschichte Liv-, Est-, Curlands* 8 (1861): 113–265.

Botero (1591)
:   Giovanni Botero (1544–1617; Italian cosmographer; never in Muscovy). *Relationi Universali.* Rome, 1591. Cited text: *The Travellers breviat, or an historicall description of the most famous kingdoms.* London: Edmund Bollifant, 1601; facs. ed., Amsterdam: Da Capo, 1969.

Bowes (1583)
:   Jerome Bowes (d. 1616; English ambassador). "The discourse of the Ambassage of Sir Jerome Bowes, to the foresayd Emperour." In *The Principall navigations, voiages and discoveries of the English nation,* comp. Richard Hakluyt, 491–500. London: G. Bishop and R. Newberie, 1589. Written 1583. Cited text: Hakluyt (1969) 3:315–29.

Boxhornius (1630)
:   Marc-Zuérius Boxhornius, ed. (1612–53; Dutch scholar; never in Muscovy). *Respublica Moscoviae et Urbes. Accedunt quaedam latinè nunquam antehac edita.* Leiden: Ioannis Maire, 1630. Cited text: original.

Bussow (1611)
:   Konrad Bussow (German mercenary). *Verwirrter Zustand des Russischen Reichs.* Written 1611. Cited text: *The Disturbed State of the Russian Realm,* trans. G. Edward Orchard. Montreal: McGill–Queen's University Press, 1994.

Campensé (1524)
:   Alberto Campensé [Albertus Pighius Campensis] (ca. 1490–1542; papal official; never in Muscovy). *Lettera d'Alberto Campense che scrivo al beatissimo Padre Clemente VII intorno alle cose di Moscovia.* Venice, 1543. Written 1524. Cited text: "Pis'mo Al'berta Kampenze." In *Biblioteka inostrannykh pisatelei o Rossii,* ed. Vladimir Semenov. 2 vols. St. Petersburg: V tip. III Otd-niia Sobstvennoi E. I. V., 1836. Folio 3: 9–55.

Chamberlayne (1612)
:   Thomas Chamberlayne (English mercenary). "Propositione of the Muscovits to render them subiects to the Kinge of England." Written 1612. Cited text: "A Project for the Acquisition of Russia by James I," ed. Inna I. Liubimenko. *English Historical Review* 29 (1914): 246–56.

Chamberlayne (1631)
:   Thomas Chamberlayne (fl. 1650; English mercenary), "A Relation of the Empire and State of Russia." Written 1631. Cited text: "Thomas Chamberlayne's Description of Russia, 1631," ed. Serge Konovalov. *Oxford Slavonic Papers* 5 (1954): 107–16.

Chancellor (1553)
:   Richard Chancellor (d. 1556; English diplomat). "The Booke of the Great and Mighty Emperor of Russia, the Duke of Moscovia, and of the Dominions, Orders, and Commodities Thereunto Belonging: drawn by Richard Chancelour." In *The Principall navigations, voiages and discoveries of the English nation,* comp. Richard Hakluyt, 280–311. London: G. Bishop and R. Newberie, 1589. Written 1553. Cited text: Hakluyt (1969), 2:224–38.

Chytraeus (1586)
:   David Chytraeus (1530–1600; Livonian historian; never in Muscovy?). *Vandaliae & Saxoniae Alberti Cranzii continuatio. Ab anno Christi 1500.* Wittenberg: Typis haeredum Johannis Cretonis, 1586. Cited text: original.

Collins (1667)   Samuel Collins (1619–70; English doctor). *The present State of Russia.* London: John Winter, 1667. Cited text: original.

Conring   Herman Conring (1606–81; German political theorist; never in
(1660s)   Muscovy). "Examen rerum publicarum Potiorum totius Orbis." Written 1660s. Cited text: "Examen rerum publicarum Potiorum totius Orbis." In *Opera,* ed. Johann W. Gobel, 4:47–548. 7 vols. Braunschweig, 1730; rpt. Aalen: Scientia Verlag, 1970–.

Contarini   Ambrogio Contarini (d. 1499; Venetian envoy). *Questo e el Viazo*
(1476)   *de misier Ambrosio Contarini.* Venice: H. Foxius, 1487. Written 1476. Cited text: *Travels to Tana and Persia by Josefa Barbaro and Ambrogio Contarini,* trans. William Thomas and S. A. Roy, esq. London: Hakluyt Society, 1873.

Crull (1698)   Jodocus Crull (d. 1713?; English doctor). *The Ancient and Present State of Muscovy.* London: A. Roper and A. Bosville, 1698. Cited text: original.

Cuningham   William Cuningham (English writer; never in Muscovy). *The cos-*
(1559)   *mographical glasse, conteinyng the pleasant principles of cosmographie.* London: In officina Ioan. Day typographi, 1559. Cited text: original.

Da Collo   Francesco da Collo (ca. 1430–1571; Imperial diplomat). *Tratta-*
(1518)   *mento di Pace trà il serenissimo Sigismondo Rè di Polonia, et Gran Basilio principe de Moscovia.* . . . Padua, 1603. Written 1518.

Danckaert   Jan Peter Danckaert (Dutch diplomat). *Beschrijvinge van Mosco-*
(1611)   *vien ofte Ruslandt.* Amsterdam: s.n., 1615. Written 1611. Cited text: original.

Eden (1555)   Richard Eden, ed. (1521–76; English translator; never in Muscovy). *The decades of the newe worlde or west India.* London: Guilhelmi Powell, 1555. Cited text in *The First Three English Books on America,* ed. Edward Arber, 281–334. Birmingham: Turnbull & Spears, 1885; rpt. New York: Kraus Reprint, 1971.

Fabri (1526)   Johann Fabri (1478–1541; papal official; never in Muscovy). *Ad serenissimum principem Ferdinandum archiducem Austriae, Moscovitarum iuxta mare glaciale religio, a D. Iaonne Fabri aedita.* Basel: Ioannem Bebelium, 1526. Cited text: "Donesenie d. Ioanna Fabri ego vysochestvu Ferdinandy." *Otechestvennye zapiski* 25 (1826): 285–327 and 27 (1826): 47–67.

Fabritius   Ludwig Fabritius (1648–1729; mercenary). No title: Autobiogra-
(1688)   phy (concerning Razin). Written 1688. Cited text: "Ludvig Fabrius's Account of the Razin Rebellion," trans. Serge Konovalov. *Oxford Slavonic Papers* 6 (1955): 76–94.

Fabritius   Ludwig Fabritius (1648–1729; mercenary), "Kurtze Relation von
(1700)   meinen drei gethane Reisen." Written 1700. Cited text: "Ludvig Fabrius's Account of the Razin Rebellion," ed. and trans. Serge Konovalov. *Oxford Slavonic Papers* 6 (1955): 95–101.

Fletcher (1591)   Giles Fletcher (1546–1611; English diplomat). *Of the Russe Commonwealth.* London: Printed by T. D. for Thomas Charde, 1591.

Cited text: "Of the Russe Commonwealth." In *The English Works of Giles Fletcher, the Elder*, ed. Lloyd E. Berry, 135–308. Madison: University of Wisconsin Press, 1964.

Franck (1534)

Sebastian Franck (1499–1542/43; German mystic, cosmographer; never in Muscovy). *Weltbuch: Spiegel und Bildnisz des gantzen Erdbodens, von Sebastiano Franco Wordensi in vier Bücher, nemlich in Asiam, Aphricam, Europam und Americam gestelt und abteilt.* Cited text: original.

Giovio (1525)

Paolo Giovio (1483–1552; Italian humanist, papal official; never in Muscovy). *Pauli Iovii Novocomensis libellus de legatione Basilij magni principis Moscoviae ad Clementem VII.* Rome: Ex Aedibus Francisci Minitii Calui, 1525. Cited text: "Kniga o posol'stve, otpravlennom Vasiliem Ioannovichom k Pape Klimentu VII." In *Biblioteka inostrannykh pisatelei o Rossii*, ed. Vladimir Semenov, folio 4: 11–55. 2 vols. St. Petersburg: V tip. III Otd-niia Sobstvennoi E. I. V., 1836.

Gordon (1661–99)

Patrick Gordon (1639–99; Scottish mercenary). No title: Diary. Russian portion written 1661–99. Cited text: *Passages from the Diary of General Patrick Gordon of Auchleuchries in the Years 1635–99.* Aberdeen: Printed for the Spalding Club 1859; rpt. New York: Da Capo, 1968.

Guagnini (1578)

Alexander Guagnini [Aleksander Gwagnin], ed. (1538?–1614; Italian mercenary in Polish service). *Sarmatiae Evropeae descriptio, quae regnum Poloniae, Lituaniam, Samogitiam, Rusiam, Mazoviam, Prusiam, Pomeraniam, Livoniam, et Moschoviae, Tartariaeque partem camplectitur.* Cracow: Matthiae Wirzbietae, 1578. Cited text: "Omnium regionum Moschoviae descriptio." In *Historiae Ruthenicae Scriptores Exteri Saeculi XVI*, ed. Wojciech Starczewski, vol. 1, sec. 7, pp. 3–48. 2 vols. Berlin and St. Petersburg: Berolini, 1841–42.

Hebdon (1671)

Thomas Hebdon (English merchant). No title: Letter to Richard Daniel dated 6 June 1671 on Razin's rebellion. Cited text: "Razin's Execution: Two Contemporary Documents," ed. Serge Konovalov. *Oxford Slavonic Papers* 12 (1965): 97–98.

Henning (1590)

Salomon Henning (1528–89; Livonian statesman; never in Muscovy). *Lifflendische churlendische Chronica; was sich von Jahr Christi bis auff 1590 in den langwiergen moscowiterischen und andern Kriegen . . . gedenckwirdiges zugetragen.* Rostock, 1590. Cited text: original.

Herberstein (1517–49)

Sigismund von Herberstein (1486–1566; Imperial diplomat). *Rerum moscoviticarum commentarii.* Vienna: Egydius Aquila, 1549. Basic text written 1517–49. Cited text: *Notes upon Russia*, trans. R. H. Major, 1851–52. 2 vols. London: Hakluyt Society; rpt. New York: B. Franklin, 1963?

Heylyn (1621)

Peter Heylyn (1599–1662; English author; never in Muscovy). *Microcosmus. A Little Description of the Great World.* Oxford: John Lichfield and James Short, 1621. Cited text: London, 1629 ed.

Heylyn (1652)   Peter Heylyn (1599–1662; English author; never in Muscovy), *Cosmographie in Four Books: Containing the chorographie and history of the whole world*. London: Printed for Henry Seile, 1652. Cited text: London, 1657 ed.

Horsey   Jerome Horsey (1573–1627; English merchant). "Travels." Writ-
(1584–1621)   ten 1584–1621. Cited text: "Travels." In *Rude and Barbarous Kingdom. Russia in Accounts of the Sixteenth-Century English Voyagers*, ed. Lloyd E. Berry and Robert O. Crummey, 262–372. Madison: University of Wisconsin Press, 1968.

Hutichius   Johannus Hutichius [Johann Huttich], ed. (1480–1544; German;
(1532)   never in Muscovy). *Novus Orbis regionum et insularum veterubus incognitarum una cum tabula cosmographica et aliquot aliis consimilis argumenti libellis*. Paris: Apud Ioannem Paruum, 1532. Cited text: original.

Jenkinson   Anthony Jenkinson (1530–1611; English navigator). "The voyage
(1557)   of M. Anthony Jenkinson into Russia, wherein Osep Napea, first Ambassador from the Emperour of Moscovia to Queene Mary, was transported into his Countrey, Anno 1557." In *The Principall navigations, voiages and discoveries of the English nation, comp*. Richard Hakluyt, 333–47. London: G. Bishop and R. Newberie, 1589. Written 1557. Cited Text: Hakluyt (1969), 2:413–49.

Juusten   Paul Juusten (1516–76; Swedish diplomat). "Acta Legationis
(1569–72)   Moscoviticae per Paulum Juusten Episcopum Aboënsem, breviter comprehensa. 1569–72." Written 1569–72. Cited text: "Paul Juusten's Mission to Muscovy," trans. Hugh Graham. *Russian History/Histoire Russe* 13 (1986): 41–92.

Kilburger   Johann Philip Kilburger (d. 1721; Swedish diplomat). No title:
(1674)   Report on trade. Written 1674. Cited text: *Sochinenie Kil'burgera o russkoi torgovle v tsarstvovanie Alekseia Mikhailovicha*, ed. Boris G. Kurts. Kiev: Tip. I. I. Chokolova, 1915.

Koblenzl   Hans Koblenzl (Imperial diplomat). "Herrn Hanss Kobenzl's von
(1576)   Prosseg Teutschordens-Ritters und Herrn Daniel Prinzens allerunderthenigste Relation uber ihre getragene Legation bey dem Grossfürsten in der Mosca, mit Beylagen ab A usque Z inclusive, sambt Et und 9, anno 1576." Written 1576. Cited text: "Doneseniia I. Kobentselia." In *Materialy k istorii Moskovskogo gosudarstva*, ed. Teodor Wierzbowski (aka Fedor Verzhbovskii), 4:1–68. 5 vols. Warsaw, 1896–1903.

Koblenzl   Hans Koblenzl (Imperial diplomat). *Philipi Pernisteri Relatio de
(1579)   Magno Moscoviae Principe*. Frankfurt, 1579. Cited text: "Account of the Most Excellent Signor Don Felippo Prenestain, Imperial Ambassador of His Caesarean Majesty to Grand Prince of Muscovy, 1579." In "The Sixteenth-Century 'Account of Muscovy' attributed to Don Felippo Prenestein," ed. and trans. B. Mitchell and Russell Zguta. *Russian History/Histoire Russe* 8 (1981): 390–412.

Korb (1700)   Johann Georg Korb (1670–1741; Austrian diplomat). *Diarium itineris in Moscoviam.* Vienna: Typis Leopoldi Voigt, 1700 or 1701. Cited text: *Diary of an Austrian Secretary of Legation at the Court of Czar Peter the Great,* trans. and ed. Count MacDonnell. London: Bradbury & Evans, 1863; rpt. London: Cass, 1968.

Koyett (1675)   B. Koyett? (Dutch diplomat). *Historisch Verhael of Beschryving van de Voyagie gedaan onder de Suite van den Heere Koenraad van Klenck.* Amsterdam: By Jan Claesz. ten Hoorn, boeckverkooper tegen over 't oude Heeren Logement, 1677. Cited text: *Posol'stvo Konraada fan Klenka k tsariam Alekseiu Mikhailovichu i Fedoru Alekseevichu,* trans. Aleksandr M. Loviagin. St. Petersburg: Tip. Glav. upr. udelov, 1900.

Krantz (1504)   Albert Krantz (1448–1517; German cleric, scholar, Hansa official; never in Muscovy?). *Wandalia in qua de Wandalorum populis, et eorum patrio solo, ax in italiam, galliam, hispanias, aphricam, et dalmatiam, migratione: et de eorum regibus, ac bellis domi, foris que gestis.* Cologne: Ioannes Soter alias Heil, 1519. Written 1504. Cited text: original.

Krizhanich   Iurii Krizhanich (1618?–83; Croatian cleric, political thinker).
(1663–66)   "Rozgowori ob Wladetelystwu." Written 1663–66. Cited text: *Politika,* trans. Aleksandr L. Gol'dberg. Moscow: Nauka, 1965.

Lane (1560)   Henry Lane (English merchant). "The maner of Justice by lots in Russia, written by Master Henrie Lane, and executed in a controversie betweene him and one Sheray Costromitskey in Mosco. 1560." Written 1560. In *The Principall navigations, voiages, traffiques and discoveries of the English nation,* comp. Richard Hakluyt, 1:309. 3 vols. London: G. Bishop and R. Newberie, 1598–1600. Cited text: Hakluyt (1969), 2:411–12.

Łasicki (1582)   Jan Łasicki, ed. (1534–1600; Polish Protestant; never in Muscovy?). *De Russorum, Moscovitarum et Tartorum religione, sacrificiis, nuptiarum et funerum ritu e diversis scriptoribus.* Speyer: Barnardus d'Albinus, 1582. Cited text: original.

Maciej   Maciej z Miechowa (ca. 1457–1523; Polish scholar; never in Muscovy). *Tractatus de duabus Sarmatiis asiatiana et europiana et de contentis in eis.* Cracow: Opera & impensis prouidi viri d[omi]ni Ioannis Haller, 1517. Cited text: *Traktat o dvukh Sarmatiiakh,* ed. and trans. Sergei A. Anninskii. Moscow and Leningrad: Izd. Akademii nauk SSSR, 1936.
(1517)

Magnus (1539)   Olaus Magnus (1490–1557; archbishop of Uppsala; never in Muscovy). *Carta marina et descriptio septentrionalium terrarum diligentissimo elaboratat anno Domini 1539.* Venice, 1539.

Magnus (1555)   Olaus Magnus (1490–1557; archbishop of Uppsala; never in Muscovy). *Historia de gentibus septentrionalibus.* Rome: Joannes Maria de Viottis, 1555. Cited text: *A Compendious History of the Goths, Svvedes, and Vandals, and Other Northern Nations.* London: J. Streater, 1658.

Manuzio
(1541)

Antonio Manuzio, comp. (Italian; never in Muscovy). *Viaggi fatti da Vinetia, alla Tana, in Persia, in India, et in Constantinopoli.* Venice: Nelle Case de Figlivoli di Aldo, 1541. Cited text: original.

Margeret
(1607)

Jacques Margeret (1565?–1619; French mercenary). *Estat de l'Empire de Russie et Grand Duché de Muscovie.* Paris: Mathieu Guillemot, 1607. Cited text: *The Russian Empire and the Grand Duchy of Muscovy,* trans. and ed. Chester S. L. Dunning. Pittsburgh: University of Pittsburgh Press, 1983.

Maskiewicz
(1611)

Samuel Maskiewicz (ca. 1580–1632; Polish statesman, diarist). "Dyaryusz Samuela Maskiewicza." Relevant passages written 1611. Cited text: "Dnevnik Maskevicha." In *Skazaniia sovremennikov o Dmitrii Samozvantse,* ed. and trans. Nikolai G. Ustrialov, 2:13–124. 2 vols. St. Petersburg: Tip. I. Akademii nauk, 1859.

Massa (1610)

Isaac Massa (1587–1643; Dutch merchant). "Een coort verhael van beginn oospronck deser tegenwoordige troeblen in Moscovia, totten jare 1610 int cort overlopen ondert gouvernenment van diverse vorsten aldaer." Written 1610. Cited text: *A Short History of the Beginnings and Present Origins of these Present Wars in Moscow under the Reign of Various Sovereigns down to the Year 1610,* trans. and ed. G. Edward Orchard. Toronto: University of Toronto Press, 1982.

Meyerberg
(1661)

Augustin Freiherr von Meyerberg (1612–88; Imperial diplomat). *Iter in Moschoviam . . . ad Tsarem et Magnum Ducem Alexium Mihalowicz, Anno M.DC.LXI.* Cologne?: s.n., 1679? Written 1661. Cited text: "Puteshestvie v Moskoviiu Barona Avgustina Maierberga," trans. A. N. Shemiakin. In *Chteniia v Imperatorskom obshchestve istorii i drevnostei rossiiskikh pri Moskovskom universitete* (1873), bks. 3 (1–104), 4 (105–68), 5 (169–216).

Milton (1648)

John Milton (1608–74; English author; never in Muscovy). *A Brief History of Muscovy.* London, 1682. Written 1648. Cited text: *The Works of John Milton,* ed. Frank A. Patterson et al., 10:327–82. 18 vols. New York: Columbia University Press, 1931–.

Mniszek
(1607)

Abraham Rozniatowski? (member of Maryna Mniszek's party). No title: Diary of Maryna Mniszek. Part 1. Text cited: "Dnevnik Mariny Mnisheka i polskikh poslov." Written 1607. In *Skazaniia sovremennikov o Dmitrii Samozvantse,* ed. and trans. Nikolai G. Ustrialov, 2:129–98. 2 vols. St. Petersburg: Tip. I. Akademii nauk, 1859.

Münster
(1530)

Sebastian Münster (1488–1552; German cosmographer; never in Muscovy). *Germaniae atque aliarum regionum, quae ad imperium usque constantinopolitanu protenduntur, descriptio.* Basel: A. Cratander, 1530. Cited text: original.

Münster
(1534)

Sebastian Münster (1488–1552; German cosmographer; never in Muscovy). *Mappa Europae.* Frankfurt: Christian Egenolff, 1534. Cited text: *Mappa Europae.* Basel, 1536; rpt. Wiesbaden: G. Pressler, 1965.

Münster
(1544)

Sebastian Münster (1488–1552; German geographer; never in Muscovy). *Cosmographia. Beschreibung aller Lender durch Sebastianum Munsterum in welcher begriffen Aller völker Herrschafften, Stetten, und namhafftiger flecken herkommen.* Basel: Henrichum Petri, 1544. Cited text: *Cosmographei,* ed. Ruthardt Oehme. Basel, 1550; rpt. Amsterdam: Theatrum Orbis Terrarum, 1968.

Neander
(1586)

Michael Neander (1525–95; German scholar). *Orbis Terrae partium succincta expilicatio.* Leipzig: G. Defnerus imprimebat, 1586.

Neuville (1698)

"De La Neuville" [pseudonym]. *Relation curieuse, et nouvelle de Moscovie.* Paris: Pierre Aubouyn, 1698. Cited text: *A Curious and New Account of Muscovy in the Year 1689,* ed. Lindsey Hughes, trans. J. A. Cutshall. Occasional Papers no. 23 (London: School of Slavonic and East European Studies, 1994).

Oderborn
(1585)

Paul Oderborn (1555?–1604; Livonian pastor; never in Muscovy?). *Ioannis Basilidis Magni Moscoviae Ducis vita.* Wittenberg, 1585. Cited text: original.

Olearius
(1656)

Adam Olearius (1603–71; Holsteinian diplomat). *Ausführliche Beschreibung der kundbaren Reyss nach Muscow und Persien.* Schleswig: Gedruckt in der Furstl. Druckerey, durch Johan Holwein, 1647. 2d updated ed. 1656. Cited text: *The Travels of Olearius in Seventeenth Century Russia,* trans. and ed. Samuel H. Baron. Stanford: Stanford University Press, 1967.

Oleśnicki
(1606)

Mikołaj Oleśnicki (Polish diplomat) and Alexander Gąsiewski (d. 1639; Polish diplomat). "Dyariusz dziejów Moskiewskich i legacyi J. J. M. M. p. p. Posłów, P. Mikołaja Oleśnickiego z Oleśnicy, Kasztelana Małachowskiego i Pana Alexandra Korwina Gąsiewskiego Starosty Wieleńskiego, Sekretarza J. K. Mości. Spisany w roku MDCVI w Moskwie." Written 1660. Cited text: "Dnevnik pol'skikh poslov." In *Skazaniia sovremennikov o Dmitrii Samozvantse,* ed. and trans. Nikolai G. Ustrialov, 2:199–262. 2 vols. St. Petersburg: Tip. I. Akademii nauk, 1859.

Ortelius (1570)

Abraham Ortelius (1527–93; German geographer; never in Muscovy). *Theatrum orbis terrarum.* Antwerp: Apud Aegid. Coppenium Diesth, 1570. Cited text: *Theatrum orbis terrarum.* Antwerp, 1570; facs. ed. Amsterdam: N. Israel, 1964.

Perry (1716)

John Perry (1670–1732: English engineer). *The state of Russia under the present Czar.* London: B. Tooke, 1716. Cited text: original.

Petreius (1608)

Petrus Petreius [Peer Peerson] (1570–1622; Swedish diplomat). *Een wiss och sanfärdigh Berättelse, om nagra Förandringar som j thesse framledne ahr, uthi Storfurstendömet Muskow akedde äre.* Stockholm, 1608. Cited text: *Reliatsiia Petra Petreia o Rossii,* trans. Iurii A. Limonov and Viktor I Buganov. Moscow: In-t istorii SSSR AN SSR, 1976.

Petreius (1615)

Petrus Petreius [Peer Peerson] (1570–1622; Swedish diplomat). *Regni Muschowitici sciographia. Thet är: Een wiss och egentelich*

Beskriffing om Rysland. Stockholm: Tryckt hoos I. Meurer, 1614–15. Cited text: "Historien und Bericht von dem Grossfürstentumb Muschkow." [Leipzig, 1620.] In *Rerum rossicarum scriptores exteri,* 1:137–382. 2 vols. St. Petersburg, Tip. Eduarda Pratsa, 1851.

Peyerle (1606)   Hans Georg Peyerle (German merchant). "Beschreibung der Moscovitterischen Rayss, welche Ich Hanns Geörg Peyerle, von Augspurg, mit herrn Andreasen Nathan, und Matheo Brenhardt Manlichen dem Jüngern, Ady 19 Marty Ao. 1606 von Crachaw aus, angefangen." Cited text: "Zapiski Georga Paerle, o puteshestvii ego iz Krakova v Moskvu i obratno." Written 1606. In *Skazaniia sovremennikov o Dmitrii Samozvantse,* ed. and trans. Nikolai G. Ustrialov 1:153–234. 2 vols. St. Petersburg: Tip. I. Akademii nauk, 1859.

Pirckheimer (1530)   Willibald Pirckheimer (1470–1530; German scholar; never in Muscovy). *Germaniae ex variis scriptoribus perbrevis explicatio.* Nuremberg: Apud I. Petreium, 1530. Cited text: "Germaniae." In *Opera politica, historica, philologica et epistolica.* Frankfurt, 1610; rpt. Hildesheim, New York, and Olms, 1969.

Piso (1515)   Jacob Piso (papal legate; never in Muscovy). "Epistola Pisonis ad Ioannem Coritium, de conflictu Polonorum et Lituanorum cum Moscovitis." In Ianus Damianus, *Iani Damiani Senensis ad Leonem X. Pont. Max. de expeditione in Turcas Elegia.* Basel: Ioannes Frobenius, 1515. Cited text: original.

Possevino (1586)   Antonio Possevino (1533/34–1611; papal diplomat). *Moscovia, s. de rebus Moscviticis et acta in conuentu legatorum regis Poloniae et Magni Ducis Moscouiae anno 1581.* Vilna: Apud Ioannem Velicensem, 1586. Cited text: *The Moscovia of Antonio Possivino, S.J.,* trans. Hugh Graham. Pittsburgh: University of Pittsburgh Press, 1977.

Printz (1578)   Daniel Printz von Buchau (1546–1608; Imperial diplomat). *Moscoviae ortus progressus.* Neisse in Schlesian: Typis Ignatij Constant. Schubart, 1668. Written 1578. Cited text: "Nachalo i Vozvyshenie Moscovii." *Chteniia v Imperatorskom obshchestve istorii i drevnostei rossiiskikh pri Moskovskom universitete* (1876), bks. 3 (1–46) and 4 (47–73).

Pufendorf (1682)   Samuel Pufendorf (1632–94; German historian; never in Muscovy). *Einleitung zu der Historie der vornehmsten Reiche und Staaten so itziger Zeit in Europa sich befinden.* Frankfurt: In Verlegung F. Knochens, 1682. Cited text: *An Introduction to the History of the Principal Kingdoms and States of Europe.* 9th ed. London: Printed for J. Knapton et al., 1728.

Raleigh (1600)   Sir Walter Raleigh? (1554–1618; English statesman; never in Muscovy). *The Prince, or, Maxims of State.* London, 1641. Written ca. 1600. Cited text: "Maxims of State." In *The Works of Sir Walter Raleigh,* 8:1–34. 8 vols. Oxford: The University Press, 1829.

Ramusio (1550)   Giovanni Battista Ramusio, ed. (1485–1557; Italian publicist; never in Muscovy). *Delle navigationi et viaggi.* Venice: Appresso gli heredi di Lucantonio Giunti, 1550 (vol. 1), 1556 (vol. 3), 1559 (vol. 2); 2d ed. 1574. Cited text: *Navigationi et viaggi: Venice, 1563–1606,* introduced by R. A. Skelton and analysis by George B. Parks. 3 vols. Amsterdam: Theatrum Orbis Terrarum, 1967–70.

Randolfe (1568) Thomas Randolfe (1523–90; English diplomat). "The Ambassage of Thomas Randolfe Esquire from the Queenes Maiestie to the Emperour Russia." Written 1568. In *The Principall navigations, voiages and discoveries of the English nation,* comp. Richard Hakluyt, 399–402. London: G. Bishop and R. Newberie, 1589. Written 1568. Cited text: Hakluyt (1969), 3 : 102–7.

Rerum (1600) *Rerum Moscoviticarum auctores varii: unum in corpus nunc primum congesti.* Frankfurt: Apud haeredes Andreae Wecheli, Claud. Marnium, Ioan. Aubrium, 1600. Cited text: original.

Reutenfels (1671) Jacob Reutenfels (Polish agent). *De rebus Muschoviticis ad serenissimum Magnum Hetruriae Ducem Cosmum tertium.* Padua: Typis P. M. Frambotti, 1680. Written 1671. Cited text: "Skazanie sviatleishemu gertsogu toskanskomu Koz'me Tret'emu o Moskovii." *Chteniia v Imperatorskom obshchestve istorii i drevnostei rossiiskikh pri Moskovskom universitete* (1905), bk. 3: 1–137; (1906), bk. 3: 129–228.

Russia sue Moscovia (1630) *Russia seu Moscovia itemque Tartaria, commentario Topographico atque politico illustratae.* Leiden: Ex officina Elzeviriana, 1630. Text cited: original.

Schlichting (1571a) Albert Schlichting (German translator in Russian service). "De Moribus et Imperandi Crudelitate Basilij Moschoviae Tyranni Brevis Enarratio." Written 1571. Cited text: "'A Brief Account of the Character and Brutal Rule of Vasil'evich, Tyrant of Muscovy' (Albert Schlichting on Ivan Groznyi)," trans. Hugh Graham. *Canadian-American Slavic Studies* 9 (1975): 213–66.

Schlichting (1571b) Albert Schlichting (German mercenary). "Nova ex Moscovia per nobilem Albertum Schlichting allta de Principis Iwani vita et tyranide." Written 1571. Cited text: "'A Brief Account of the Character and Brutal Rule of Vasil'evich, Tyrant of Muscovy' (Albert Schlichting on Ivan Groznyi)," trans. Hugh Graham. *Canadian-American Slavic Studies* 9 (1975): 267–72.

Staden (1578) Heinrich von Staden (b. 1542?; German mercenary). "Aufzeichnungen über den Moskauer Staat." Written 1578. Cited text: *The Land and Government of Muscovy,* ed. and trans. Thomas Esper. Stanford: Stanford University Press, 1967.

Tanner (1678) Bernard Leopold Franz Tanner (Polish diplomat). *Legatio Polono-Lithuanica in Moscoviam.* Nuremberg: Sumptibus Johannis Ziegeri, 1680 or 1689? Written 1678. Cited text: "Opisanie puteshestvia pol'skogo posol'stva v Moskvu v 1678 g." *Chteniia v Imperatorskom obshchestve istorii i drevnostei rossiiskich pri Moskovskom universitete* (1891), bk. 3: 1–203.

Taube and
Kruse (1571)

Johann Taube and Elbert Kruse (German-Livonian nobles). *Erschreckliche greuliche und unerhorte Tyranney Iwan Wasilowictz jtzo regierenden Grossfürsten in der Muscow*. N.p., 1582. Written 1571. Cited text: "Poslanie Ioganna Taube i Elberta Kruze kak istoricheskii istochnik," ed. and trans. Mikhail G. Roginskii. *Russkii istoricheskii zhurnal* 8 (1922): 10–59.

Thevet (1575)

André Thevet (1502–92; French cosmographer; never in Muscovy). *Cosmographie universelle*. Paris: P. L'Huilier, 1575. Cited text: *Cosmographie Muscovite par André Thevet*, ed. Augustin Galitzin. Paris: J. Techener,1858.

Trakhaniot
(1486)

Iurii Trakhaniot (Muscovite diplomat). No title: Interview with Milanese officials. Written 1486. Cited text: "George Trakhaniot's Description of Russian in 1486," ed. and trans. Robert M. Crosky and E. C. Ronquist. *Russian History/Histoire Russe* 17 (1990): 55–64.

Turberville
(1568)

George Turberville (d. 1597?; English diplomat). "The Author being in Muscovy, wrytes to certaine his friends in Englande of the state of the place. . . . The three Epistles followe." In George Turberville, *Epitaphes and Sonnets*. London, 1576? Written 1568. Cited text: "The Author being in Muscovy . . ." In George Turberville, *Epitaphes, Epigrams, Songs and Sonets (1567) and Epitaphes and Sonnets (1576)*, introduced by Richard J. Panofsky, 424–44. Delmar, N.Y.: Scholars' Facsimiles & Reprints, 1977.

Ulfeldt (1579)

Jacob Ulfeldt (d. 1593: Danish diplomat). *Hodoeporicon Ruthenicum in quo de moscovitarum regione, moribus, religione, gubernatione, & Aula Imperatoria quo potuit compendio & eleganter exequitur*. Frankfurt: Typis M. Beckeri, impensis I. T. & I. I. de Bry, 1608. Written 1579. Cited text: "Puteshchestvie v Rossii datskogo poslanika Iakova Ul'fel'dta v 1575 g." *Chteniia v Imperatorskom obshchestve istorii i drevnostei rossiiskikh pri Moskovskom universitete* (1883), bk. 1, pt. 3: 1–16; bk. 2, pt. 3 (1883): 17–40; bk. 3, pt. 3: 40–61.

Wickhart
(1675)

Carl Valerius Wickhart (Imperial diplomat). *Moscowittische Reiß-Beschreibung*. Vienna: J. J. Kürner, 1677. Cited text: original.

BIBLIOGRAPHY 2
Other Primary Sources

ACHENWALL, GOTTFRIED. *Abriß der neusten Staatswissenschaft der vornehmsten europäischen Reiche und Republicken zum Gebrauch in seinen Academischen Vorlesungen.* Göttingen: Joh. Wilhelm Schmidt, 1749.

ANCHERSEN, JOHANN P. *Descriptio statuum cultiovum in tabulis.* Copenhagen and Leipzig, 1741.

ANON. *Avisi di diversi luoghi del Mondo.* Florence, 1572.

————. *Eigenliche Warhfftige Beschreibung.* Frankfurt, 1572.

————. *Kurtze glaubwürdige Zeitung.* Frankfurt, 1572.

————. *La légende de la vie et de la mort de Démétrius, dernier Grand-Duc de Moscovie.* Amsterdam, 1606.

————. *Warhaffige Newe Zeitung.* N.p., 1571.

————, ed. *Russia seu Moscovia, itemque Tartaria, commentario topographico atque politico illustratæ.* Leiden: Ex oficina Elzeviriana, 1630.

ARISTOTLE. *Metaphysics.* Trans. Hippocrates G. Apostle. Bloomington: Indiana University Press, 1966.

————. *Nicomachean Ethics.* Trans. Terence Irwin. Indianapolis: Hackett, 1985.

————. *The Politics.* Trans. Benjamin Jowett. Ed. Stephen Everson. Cambridge: Cambridge University Press, 1988.

————. *Topics.* Trans. Edward S. Forster. Cambridge: Harvard University Press, 1960.

BACON, FRANCIS. "The Advancement of Learning." In *Essays, Civil and Moral.* London: Ward Lock, 1910.

————. "Of Travaile." In *The Essayes or Counsels, Civil and Moral,* ed. Michael Kiernan, 55–57. Oxford: Clarendon, 1985.

BARSOV, ELPIDIFOR V., ed. "Drevne-russkie pamiatniki sviashchennogo venchaniia tsarei na tsarstvo." *Chteniia v Imperatorskom obshchestve istorii i drevnostei rossiiskikh pri Moskovskom universitete* 124 (1883): 1–160.

BELLI, NICOLAI. *Philippi Honorii Thesaurus politicus.* Cologne, 1617.

BERNARD, JEAN FÉDÉRIC, ed. *Recueil de voyages au Nord, contenant divers Mémoires très utiles au Commerce et à la Navigation.* 4 vols. Amsterdam: J. F. Bernard, 1715–18.

BIENEMANN, FRIEDRICH G., ed. *Briefe und Urkunden zur Geschichte Livlands in den Jahren 1558–1562.* 5 Vols. Riga: N. Kymmel, 1865–76.

BODIN, JEAN. *Method for the Easy Comprehension of History* [1566]. Trans. Beatrice Reynolds. New York: Columbia University Press, 1945.

——. *The Six Bookes of a Commonweale* [1576]. Trans. Richard Knolles. Cambridge: Harvard University Press, 1962.

BOEMUS, JOHANN. *The fardle of façions conteining the aunciente maners, customes, and Lawes, of peoples enhabiting the two partes of the earth, called Affrike and Asie.* London, 1555.

BOTERO, GIOVANNI. *Relationi universali.* Rome, 1591.

BUSSE, KARL H. VON, ed. "*Deutsche Reichtags-Verhandlungen über Livland vom Jahre 1559 und 1560.*" In *Monumenta Livoniae antiqua,* 5:706–48. Riga and Leipzig: E. Frantzen, 1847.

CHEREPNIN, LEV V., ed. *Akty sotsial'no-ekonomicheskoi istorii severovostochnoi Rusi kontsa XIV–nachala XVI v.* 3 vols. Moscow: Izd. Akademii nauk SSSR, 1952–64.

——, ed. *Dukhovnye i dogovornye gramoty velikikh i udel'nykh kniazei XIV–XVI vv.* Moscow and Leningrad: Izd. Akademii nauk SSSR, 1950.

CHURCHILL, AWNSHAM, and JOHN CHURCHILL, eds. *A Collection of Voyages and Travels.* 4 vols. London: A. Churchill and J. Churchill, 1704.

CONRING, HERMANN. "De autoribus politicis." In *Opera,* ed. Johann W. Gobel, vol. 3. 7 vols. Braunschweig, 1730; rpt. Aalen: Scientia, 1970.

——. "Exercitio Historica-Politica de Notitia singularis alicujus Respublicae." In *Opera,* ed. Johann W. Gobel, 4:1–43. 7 vols. Braunschweig, 1730; rpt. Aalen: Scientia, 1970–.

——. "Prooemium." In *Opera,* ed. Johann W. Gobel, 4:48–57. 7 vols. Braunschweig, 1730; rpt. Aalen: Scientia, 1970–.

DAMIANUS, IANUS. *Iani Damniani Senensis ad Leonem X. Pont. Max. de expeditione in Turcas elegia.* Basel: Ioannes Frobenius, 1515.

FENNELL, JOHN L. I., ed. and trans. *The Correspondence between Prince A. M. Kurbsky and Tsar Ivan of Russia, 1564–1579.* Cambridge: Cambridge University Press, 1963.

——, ed. and trans. *Prince A. M. Kurbsky's History of Ivan IV.* Cambridge: Cambridge University Press, 1965.

FORSTEN, GEORGII V., ed. *Akty i pis'ma k istorii Baltiskogo voprosa v XVI i XVII stoletiiakh.* St. Petersburg: Tip. I. N. Skorokhodova, 1889–1893.

GEORGIUS DE HUNGARIA. *Cronica, Abconterfayung und Entwerffung der Turckey: Mit yrem begyff, Inhalt, Provintzen, Volckern ankunfft, Kryegen, Sigen, nyderlgae, glauben, Religio Gesatzen, sitten, Regiment, Pollicey, reutterey, fromkeit und bossheit.* Trans. Sebastian Franck. Augsburg: Haynrich Stainer, 1530.

GREKOV, BORIS D., ed. *Sudebniki XV–XVI vekov.* Moscow and Leningrad: Izd. Akademii nauk SSSR, 1952.

HELLIE, RICHARD, trans. and ed. *The Muscovite Law Code (Ulozhenie) of 1649.* Irvine, Calif.: Charles Schlacks, 1988.

HESSUS, HELIUS E. *A profectione ad Des. Erasmum hodoeporican.* Erfurt: T. Martin, 1519.

HOBBES, THOMAS. *Leviathan, or Matter, Form, and Power of a Commonwealth Ecclesiastical and Civil* [1651]. Ed. Nelle Fuller. Chicago: Encyclopaedia Britannica, 1952.

HOWELL, JAMES. *Instructions for forreine travell* [1642]. London: English Reprints, 1869.

IAKOVLEV, ALEKSEI I., ed. *Akty khoziaistva Boiarina B. I. Morozova.* 2 vols. Moscow and Leningrad: Izd. Akademii nauk SSSR, 1940–45.

JOHNSON, ROBERT. *Essaies, or Rather Imperfect Offers* [1607]. Grainesville, Fla.: Scholars' Facsimiles & Reprints, 1955.

KAISER, DANIEL H., trans. and ed. *The Laws of Rus'—Tenth to Fifteenth Centuries.* Salt Lake City: Charles Schlacks, 1992.

KARAJAN, THEODOR G. VON, ed. *Selbstbiographie Sigmunds Freihern von Herberstein, 1486–1553.* Fontes Rerum Austriacarum, Abt. 1, Scriptores, Bd. 1. Vienna: Österreichische Akademie der Wissenschaften, 1855.

KARPOV, GENNADII F., ed. "Pamiatniki diplomaticheskikh snoshenii Moskovskogo gosudarstva s Krimskim i Nagaiskoiu ordami i s Turtsiei." *Sbornik imperatorskogo russkogo istoricheskogo obshchestva* 41 (1885): 1–558.

KENNAN, GEORGE F. *The Marquis de Custine and His Russia in 1839.* Princeton: Princeton University Press, 1971.

———. "Moscow Embassy Telegram no. 511, February 22, 1946." In *Containment: Documents on American Policy and Strategy,* ed. Thomas H. Etzold and John L. Gaddis, 50–63. New York: Columbia University Press, 1978.

——— ["X"]. "The Sources of Soviet Conduct." *Foreign Affairs* 25, no. 4 (July 1947): 566–82.

———. "The Soviet Union and the Noncommunist World in Historical Perspective." In *The Threat of Soviet Imperialism,* ed. C. Grove Haines, 3–19. Baltimore: Johns Hopkins University Press, 1954.

KLUCKHOHN, AUGUST, ed. *Briefe Friedrichs des Frommen, Kurfursten von der Pflaz mit verwandten Schriftstücken.* 2 vols. Braunschweig: C. A. Schwetschke und Sohn, 1868–72.

KOLESOV, VLADIMIR V., ed. *Domostroi* [1550s?]. Moscow: Sovetskaia Rossiia, 1990.

KOTKOV, SERGEI I., ed. *Gramotki XVII–nachala XVIII v.* Moscow: Nauka, 1969.

———, ed. *Pamiatniki delovoi pis'mennosti XVII veka: Vladimirskii krai.* Moscow: Nauka, 1984.

KOTOSHIKHIN, GRIGORII. *O Rossii v tsarstvovanie Alekseia Mikhailovicha.* Ed. Ann E. Pennington. Oxford: Oxford University Press, 1980.

LOCKE, JOHN. *Two Treatises of Government* [1690]. Ed. Peter Laslett. Cambridge: Cambridge University Press, 1970.

LUR'E, IAKOV S., ed. *Povest' o Drakule.* Moscow and Leningrad: Nauka, 1964.

LUR'E, IAKOV S., and DMITRII S. LIKHACHEV, eds. *Poslaniia Ivana Groznogo.* Moscow and Leningrad: Izd. Akademii nauk SSSR, 1951.

MACHIAVELLI, NICCOLÒ. *The Prince* [1513]. Ed. Quentin Skinner and Russell Prince. Cambridge and New York: Cambridge University Press, 1988.

MEUSEL, JOHANN G. *Lehrbuch der Statistik.* 3d ed. Leipzig: C. Fritsch, 1804.

MEYERBERG, AUGUSTIN, FREIHERR VON. *Al'bom Meierberga: Vidy i bytovye kartiny Rossii XVII veka.* Ed. Friedrich von Adelung and A. M. Loviagin. 2 vols. St. Petersburg: Izd. A. S. Suvorina, 1903.

MONTAIGNE, MICHEL DE. "Of Cannibals" [1570s]. In *The Complete Essays of Montaigne,* trans. Donald M. Frame, 150–58. Stanford: Stanford University Press, 1958.

MONTESQUIEU, CHARLES DE SECONDAT, BARON DE. *Persian Letters* [1721]. Trans. Christopher J. Betts. Harmondsworth: Penguin, 1973.

ODERBORN, PAUL. *Ioannis Basilidis Magni Moscoviae Ducis vita*. Wittenberg, 1585.

OLEARIUS, ADAM. *Vermehrte Newe Beschreibung der Muscowitischen und Persischen Reyse* [1656]. Facs. rpt. Tübingen: Niemeyer, 1971.

Ostrozhskaia biblia. Ostrog, 1580–81; facs. rpt. Moscow and Leningrad: Slovo-Art, 1988.

PISO, JACOB. *Die Schlacht von dem kunig Poln. und mit dem Moscowiter. gescheen am tag Marie gepurt*. N.p., 1514.

Polnoe sobranie russkikh letopisei. 41 vols. to date. St. Petersburg and Moscow, 1841–.

Polnoe sobranie zakonov Rossiiskoi imperii. 45 vols. St. Petersburg: Tip. otdeleniia Sobstvennoi E. I. V. Kantseliarii, 1830–84.

POLYBIUS. *The Histories of Polybius*. Trans. Evelyn S. Shuckburgh. 2 vols. Bloomington: Indiana University Press, 1962.

POSSEVINO, ANTONIO. *Iudicium ... Joannis Bodini, Philippi Mornaei et Nicolai Machiavelli quibusdam scriptis*. Lyons: Apud I. B. Buysson, 1593.

PUFENDORF, SAMUEL, FREIHERR VON. *Histoire de Suède*. Amsterdam: Z. Chatelain, 1743.

———. *Introduction à l'histoire générale et politique de l'univers*. Amsterdam: Par mr. Bruzen de la Martinière, 1748.

PYRCKMAIR, H. *Commentariolus de arte apodemica, seu vera peregrinandi ratione*. Ingolstadt: Ex officina D. Sartorij, 1577.

QUARLES, FRANCIS. *Enchiridon Miscellaneum*. Amsterdam: Stephan Swart, 1677.

SACRANUS, JOHANNES. *Errores atrocissimorum ruthenorum*. Cologne: Johann Landen, 1507.

SANSOVINO, FRANCESCO. *Del governo de regni et delle respubliche antiche et moderne*. Venice: Appresso F. Sansovino, 1561.

SCHIRREN, CARL C. G., ed. *Neue Quellen zur Geschichte des Untergangs livländischer Selbständigkeit: Aus dem dänischen geheimeh Archive zu Kopenhagen*, Bd. 1–3. In *Archiv für Geschichte Liv-, Est- und Curlands*, N.F. 9–11 (1883–85).

———, ed. *Quellen zur geschichte des Untergangs livländischer Selbständigkeit: Aus dem swedischen Reichsarchive zu Stockholm*. Reval: F. Kluge, 1861–79.

SCHLÖZER, AUGUST L. *Entwurf zu einem Reise-Collegio von A. L. S. Prof. in Göttingen nebst einer Anzeige seiner Zeitungs Collegii*. Göttingen: Vandenhoekschen Buchhandlung, 1777.

———. *Vorlesung über Land- und Seereisen* [1795–96]. Göttingen: Musterschmidt, 1964.

SHAKESPEARE, WILLIAM. *Love's Labour's Lost* [c. 1600] Ed. Alfred Harbage. Baltimore: Penguin, 1963.

VAISSIÈRE, PIERRE DE. *Charles de Marillac: Ambassadeur et homme politique sous les règne de François I, Henri II, et François II, 1510–1560*. Paris: H. Welter, 1896.

VOLOTSKII, IOSIF. *Prosvetitel', ili oblochenie eresi zhidovstvuiushchikh*. 3d ed. Kazan: Imp. Universitet, 1896.

ZWINGER, THEODOR. *Theatrum vitae humanae*. Basel: Ex officina Frobiana, 1571.

BIBLIOGRAPHY 3
Secondary Sources

Abbreviations

MERSH   *The Modern Encyclopedia of Russian and Soviet History,* ed. Joseph L. Wieczynski. 59 vols. Gulf Breeze, Fla.: Academic International Press, 1976–96.

Pferschy   Gerhard Pferschy, ed. *Siegmund von Herberstein, Kaiserlicher Gesandter und Begründer der Rußlandkunde und die europäische Diplomatie.* Graz: Akademische Druck- und Verlagstalt, 1989.

Authors/Texts

AA, ABRAHAM J. VAN DER, ed. *Biographisch Woordenboek der Nederlanden.* 21 vols. Haarlem: J. J. van Brederode, 1852–78; rpt. Amsterdam: B. M. Israel, 1969–70.

ABRUSOW, LEONID. "Die Beziehungen des Deutschen Ordens zum Ablasshandel seit dem 15. Jahrhundert." *Mitteilungen aus dem Gebiete der Geschichte Liv-, Est- und Kurlands* 20 (1910).

ADELUNG, FRIEDRICH VON. *Kritisch-literarische Übersicht der Reisenden in Russland bis 1700, deren Berichte bekannt sind.* 2 vols. St. Petersburg: Eggers, 1846.

ALEF, GUSTAV. "The Origins of Muscovite Autocracy." *Forschungen zur osteuropäischen Geschichte* 39 (1986): 7–331.

———. "The Political Significance of the Inscriptions on Muscovite Coinage in the Reign of Vasili II." *Speculum* 34 (1959): 1–19.

ALPATOV, MIKHAIL A. *Russkaia istoricheskaia mysl' i zapadnaia Evropa XII–XVII vv.* Moscow: Nauka, 1973.

ANGERMANN, NORBERT. "Kulturbeziehungen zwischen dem Hanseraum und den Moskauer Rußland um 1500." *Hansische Geschichtsblätter* 84 (1966): 20–48.

BAKHRUSHIN, SERGEI V., and SERGEI D. SKAZKIN. *Diplomatiia v novoe vremia (XVI–XVII veka)*. Vol. 1 of *Istoriia diplomatii,* ed. Vladimir P. Potemkin et al. Moscow: Gos. sotsial'no-ekon. izd., 1941.

BARBIERI, GINO. *Milano e Mosca nella politica del Rinascimento.* Bari: Adriatica, 1957.

BARKHUDAROV, STEPAN G., et al., eds. *Slovar' russkogo iazyka XI–XVII vv.* 17 vols. to date. Moscow: Akademiia nauk SSSR, Institut russkogo iazyka, 1975–.

BARON, SAMUEL H. "Feudalism or the Asiatic Mode of Production: Alternative Marxist Interpretations of Russian History." In Baron, *Muscovite Russia,* chap. 10. London: Variorum Reprints, 1980.

———. "Herberstein's Image of Russia and Its Transmission through Later Writers." In Pferschy, 245–72. Rpt. in Baron, *Explorations in Muscovite History,* chap. 13. Brookfield, Vt.: Gower, 1991.

———. "The Influence in Sixteenth-Century England of Herberstein's *Rerum moscoviticarum commentarii.*" In Baron, *Explorations in Muscovite History,* chap. 15. Brookfield, Vt.: Gower, 1991.

BEHRENS, B. "Treatises on the Ambassador Written in the Fifteenth and Early Sixteenth Centuries." *English Historical Review* 51 (1936): 616–27.

BELOKUROV, SERGEI A. *Adam Olearii o greko-latinskoi shkole Arseniia Greka v Moskve v XVII v.* Moscow: L. I. A., Snegirevy, 1888.

BENNINGHOVEN, FRIEDRICH. "Rußland im Spiegel der livändischen *Schonnen Hystorie* von 1508." *Zeitschrift für Ostforschung* 11 (1962): 601–25.

BERRY, LLOYD E. "Giles Fletcher the Elder and Milton's *A Brief History.*" *Review of English Studies* 11 (1960): 150–56.

BOZICEVIC, JOSIP. "Krizhanich, Yurii (1618?–83)." MERSH 18:81–84.

BRAUDO, A. I. "Poslanie Taube i Kruze k gertsogu Ketleru (bibliograficheskaia zametka)." *Zhurnal Ministerstva narodnogo prosvieshcheniia* 271 (October 1890): 386–95.

BUTLER, WALTER E. "Foreign Impressions of Russian Law to 1800: Some Reflections." In *Russian Law in Historical and Political Perspective,* ed. Walter E. Butler, 65–92. Leiden: A. W. Sijthoff, 1977.

CHARNEY, A. H. "The English Maxim to 1756." Ph.D. dissertation, University of California, Los Angeles, 1973.

CHEREPNIN, LEV V. *Obrazovanie russkogo tsentral'izovannogo gosudarstva v XIV–XV vekakh.* Moscow: Izd. sotsial'no-ekonomicheskoi literatury, 1960.

CHKLAVER, GEORGES. "Montesquieu et la Russie." *La vie des peuples* 8, no. 32 (1922): 1082–1110.

COSTELLO, WILLIAM T. *The Scholastic Curriculum at Seventeenth-Century Cambridge.* Cambridge: Harvard University Press, 1958.

CRANZ, F. EDWARD. "Aristotelianism in Medieval Political Theory: A Study of the Reception of the *Politics.*" Ph.D. dissertation, Harvard University, 1938.

———. *A Bibliography of Aristotle Editions, 1501–1600.* Ed. Charles B. Schmidt. Baden-Baden: V. Koerner, 1984.

CROSKEY, ROBERT M. "Byzantine Greeks in Late Fifteenth- and Early Sixteenth-Century Russia." In *The Byzantine Legacy in Eastern Europe,* ed. Lowell Clucas, 35–56. Boulder, Colo.: East European Monographs, 1988.

CRUMMEY, ROBERT O. *Aristocrats and Servitors: The Boyar Elite in Russia, 1613–1689.* Princeton: Princeton University Press, 1983.

D'AMATO, DZHUZEPPE. *Sochineniia ital'iantsev o Rossii kontsa XV–XVI vv.* 2d ed. Moscow: Russkoe slovo, 1995.

DAVIES, DAVID W. *The World of the Elseviers, 1580–1712.* The Hague: Martinus Nijoff, 1954.

DEMIDOVA, NATALIA F. *Sluzhilaia biurokratiia v Rossii XVII v. i ee rol' v formirovanii absoliutizma.* Moscow: Nauka, 1987.

DEWEY, HORACE. "Russia's Debt to the Mongols in Suretyship and Collective Responsibility." *Comparative Studies in Society and History* 30 (1988): 249–70.

DODDS, MURIEL. *Les Recits de voyages: Sources de 'L'Esprit des lois' de Montesquieu.* Paris: H. Champion, 1929.Donnert, Erich. *Die livländische Ordensritterstaat und Russland: Der livländische Krieg und die baltische Frage in der europäischen Politik, 1558–1583.* Berlin: Rutten & Loening, 1963.

DUNNING, CHESTER S. "Russia Company." MERSH 32:27–33.

ECKERT, WILLEHAD P., and CHRISTOPH VON IMHOFF. *Willibald Pirckheimer: Dürers Freund im Spiegel seines Lebens, seiner Werke und seiner Umwelt.* Cologne: Wienand, 1971.

FELSING, FERDINAND. *Die Statistik als Methode der politische Okonomie im 17. und 18. Jahrhundert.* Borna: R. Noske, 1930.

FLODR, MIROSLAV. *Incunabula classicorum.* Amsterdam: A. M. Hakkert, 1973.

FLORESCU, RADU, and RAYMOND T. MCNALLY. *The Complete Dracula.* Acton, Mass.: Copley, 1992.

FLOROVSKY, GEORGE. "The Problem of Old Russian Culture." *Slavic Review* 21 (1962): 1–15.

FRANKLIN, JULIAN H. *Jean Bodin and the Sixteenth-Century Revolution in the Methodology of Law and History.* New York: Columbia University Press, 1963.

FUHRMANN, JOSEPH T. *The Origins of Capitalism in Russia: Industry and Progress in the Sixteenth and Seventeenth Centuries.* Chicago: University of Chicago Press, 1972.

GIBB, HAMILTON A. R., ed. *Encyclopedia of Islam.* New ed. 9 vols. to date. Leiden: Brill, 1954–.

GLEASON, ABBOT. *Totalitarianism: The Inner History of the Cold War.* Oxford: Oxford University Press,1995.

GOLDEN, PETER B. "Turkic Calques in Medieval Eastern Slavic." *Journal of Turkish Studies* 8 (1984): 103–12.

GÖLLNER, CARL. *Turcica: Die europäischen Türkendürcke des XVI. Jahrhunderts.* 2 vols. Berlin: Akademie-Verlag, 1961.

GOSLINGA, CORNELIS C. *The Dutch in the Caribbean and on the Wild Coast, 1580–1680.* Gainesville: University of Florida Press, 1971.

GRAHAM, HUGH F. "Guagnini, Alessandro (1538?–1614)." MERSH 13: 173–76.

———. "Pomest'e." MERSH 29:29–33.

GRANLUNG, JOHN. "Kommentar." In Olaus Magnus, *Historia om de Nordiska Folken,* ed. Granlung. 4 vols. Stockholm: Gidlung, 1976.

GREENFELD, LIAH. "The Formation of Russian National Identity: The Role of Status Insecurity and *Ressentiment.*" *Comparative Studies in Society and History* 32 (1990): 549–91.

———. *Nationalism: Five Roads to Modernity.* Cambridge: Harvard University Press, 1992.

HAINES, C. GROVE. Foreword to *The Threat of Soviet Imperialism,* ed. Haines, v–vii. Baltimore: Johns Hopkins University Press, 1954.

HALPERIN, CHARLES J. "Edward Keenan and the Kurbskii-Groznyi Correspondence in Hindsight." *Jahrbücher für Geschichte Osteuropas* 46 (1998): 376–403.

HAMPTON, TIMOTHY. *The Rhetoric of Exemplarity in Renaissance Literature.* Ithaca: Cornell University Press, 1990.

HARDER–VON GERSDORFF, ELISABETH. "Die niedere Stände im Moskauer Reich in der Sicht deutscher Rußlandberichte des 16. Jahrhunderts." *Zeitschrift für Ostforschung* 11 (1962): 274–91.

HARMENING, DIETER. *Der Anfang von Dracula: Zur Geschichte von Geschichten.* Wurzburg: Königshausen & Neumann, 1983.

HARRAUER, CHRISTINE. "Beobachtungen zu Darstellungsweise und Wahrheitsanspurch in der 'Moscovia' Herbersteins." In *Landesbeschreibungen Mitteleuropas vom 15. bis 17. Jahrhundert,* ed. Hans-Bernd Harder. Cologne: Bohlau, 1983.

HELLIE, RICHARD. "Dvorianin." MERSH 10:77–79.

———. *Enserfment and Military Change in Muscovy.* Chicago: University of Chicago Press, 1971.

———. *Slavery in Russia, 1450–1725.* Chicago: University of Chicago Press, 1982.

———. "The Structure of Modern Russian History: Towards a Dynamic Model." *Russian History/Histoire Russe* 4 (1977): 1–22.

———. "Sudebniki." MERSH 38:15–21.

———. "Ulozhenie of 1649." MERSH 48:192–98.

———. "Zemskii sobor." MERSH 45:226–34.

HIXTON, WALTER L. *George F. Kennan: Cold War Iconoclast.* New York: Columbia University Press, 1989.

HODGEN, MARGARET T. *Early Anthropology in the Sixteenth and Seventeenth Centuries.* Philadelphia: University of Pennsylvania Press, 1964.

HOLBORN, HAJO. *Ulrich von Hutten and the German Reformation.* Trans. Roland H. Bainton. New Haven: Yale University Press, 1937.

HÖSCH, EDGAR. "Die Stellung Moskoviens in den Kreuzzugsplänen des Abendlands: Bemerkungen zur griechischen Emigration im Moskau des ausgehenden 15. und beginnenden 16. Jahrhunderts." *Jahrbücher für Geschichte Osteuropas* 15 (1967): 321–40.

HUGHES, LINDSEY. "Foreign Settlement." MERSH 11:216–18.

IUZEFOVICH, LEONID A. *Kak v posol'skikh obychaiakh vedetsia.* Moscow: Mezhdunarodnye otnosheniia, 1988.

———. "Russkii posol'skii obychai XVI veka." *Voprosy istorii* 9 (1977): 114–26.

JOHN, VINCENZ. *Geschichte der Statistik.* Pt. 1. *Von dem Ursprung der Statistik bis auf Quetelet.* Stuttgart: F. Enke, 1884.

KADIČ, ANTÉ. "Krizhanich and Possevino—Missionaries to Muscovy." In *Juraj Krizănič (1618–1683): Russophile and Ecumenic Visionary,* ed. Thomas Eekman and Anté Kadič, 73–90. The Hague: Mouton: 1976.

———. "Krizhanich's Memoradum." *Jahrbücher für Geschichte Osteuropas* 12, no. 3 (1964): 331–49.

KÄMPFER, FRANK. "Herbersteins nicht eingestandene Abhängigkeit von Johann Fabri aus Leutkirch." *Jahrbücher für Geschichte Osteuropas* 44 (1996): 1–27.

KAPPELER, ANDREAS. "Die deutschen Flugschriften über die Moskowiter und Iwan den Schrecklichen im Rahmen der Rußlandliteratur des 16. Jahrhunderts." In *Russen und Rußland aus deutscher Sicht 9.–17. Jahrhundert,* ed. Mechthild Keller, 150–82. Munich: W. Fink, 1987.

———. "Die deutschen Russlandschriften der Zeit Ivans der Schrecklichen." In *Reiseberichte von Deutschen über Russland und von Russen über Deutschland,* ed. Friedheim B. Kaiser and Bernhard Stasiewski, 1–23. Cologne: Bohlau, 1980.

———. *Ivan Groznyi im Spiegel der ausländischen Druckschriften seiner Zeit: Ein Beitrag zur Geschichte des westlichen Russlandbildes.* Bern: Herbert Land, 1972.

———. "Die letzen Oprichninajahre (1569–1571) im Lichte dreier zeitgenössischer deutscher Broschüren." *Jahrbücher für Geschichte Osteuropas* 19 (1971): 1–30.

KARAJAN, THEODOR G. VON. "Selbstbiographie Sigmunds Freiherrn von Herberstein, 1486–1553." *Fontes Rerum Austriacarum,* pt. 1, vol. 1, fol. 2 (1855): 67–396.

KAZHDAN, ALEKSANDR P. "The Concept of Freedom (*eleutheria*) and Slavery (*douleia*) in Byzantium." In *La Notion de liberté au Moyen âge.* Paris: Belles Lettres, 1985.

KAZHDAN, ALEKSANDR P., et al., eds. *Oxford Dictionary of Byzantium.* 3 vols. New York: Oxford University Press, 1991.

KEENAN, EDWARD L. *The Kurbskii-Groznyi Apocrypha.* Cambridge: Harvard University Press, 1971.

———. "Muscovite Political Folkways." *Russian Review* 45 (1986): 115–81.

KHOROSHKEVICH, ANNA L. "Die Quellen Herbersteins und die Moscovia als Quelle zur politischen, Sozial- und Wirtschaftsgeschichte der Rus im ersten Viertel des 16. Jahrhunderts." In Pferschy, 179–244.

———. "Sigizmund Gerbershtein i ego Zapiski o Moskovii." In Sigizmund von Gerbershtein, *Zapiski o Moskovii,* ed. Valentin L. Ianin et al., 9–15. Moscow: Izd. Moskovskogo univ., 1988.

KIVELSON, VALERIE A. *Autocracy in the Provinces: Russian Political Culture and the Gentry in the Seventeenth Century.* Stanford: Stanford University Press, 1997.

———. "The Devil Stole His Mind: The Tsar and the 1648 Moscow Uprising." *American Historical Review* 98 (1993): 733–56.

KLEIMOLA, ANN M. "The Duty to Denounce in Muscovite Russia." *Slavic Review* 31 (1972): 759–79.

KLUETING, HARM. *Die Lehre von der Macht der Staaten: Das aussenpolitische Machtproblem in der "politischen Wissenschaft" und in der praktischen Politik im 18. Jahrhundert.* Berlin: Duncker & Humbolt, 1986.

KLUG, EKKEHARD. "Das 'Asiatische' Rußland: Über die Entstehung eines europäischen Vorurteils." *Historische Zeitschrift* 245 (1987): 265–89.

KOCHIN, GEORGII E. *Materialy dlia terminologicheskogo slovaria Drevnei Rossii.* Moscow: Izd. Akademii nauk SSSR, 1937.

KOEBNER, RICHARD. "Despot and Despotism: Vicissitudes of a Political Term." *Journal of the Warburg and Courtland Institutes* 14 (1951): 275–302.

KOLLMANN, NANCY S. "Concepts of Society and Social Identity in Early Modern Russia." In *Religion and Culture in Early Modern Russia and Ukraine,* ed. Samuel H. Baron and Nancy S. Kollmann, 34–51. De Kalb: Northern Illinois University Press, 1997.

———. *Kinship and Politics: The Making of the Muscovite Political System, 1345–1547.* Stanford: Stanford University Press, 1987.

KÖPSTEIN, HELGA. *Zur Sklaverei im ausgehenden Byzanz.* Berlin: Akademie-Verlag, 1966.

KRADER, LAWRENCE. *The Asiatic Mode of Production: Sources, Development, and Critique in the Writings of Karl Marx.* Assen: Van Gorcum, 1975.

LEITSCH, WALTER. "Herberstein's Ergänzungen zur Moscovia in späteren Auflagen und die beiden zeitgenössischen Übersetzungen ins Deutsche." *Forschungen zur osteuropäischen Geschichte* 27 (1980): 177–94.

———. "Herberstein's Impact on the Reports about Muscovy in the Sixteenth and Seventeenth Centuries: Some Observations on the Technique of Borrowing." *Forschungen zur osteuropäischen Geschichte* 24 (1978): 163–77.

———. "Westeuropäische Reiseberichte über den Moskauer Staat." In *Reiseberichte als Quellen europäischen Kulturgeschichte,* ed. Hans J. Teuteberg, 153–76. Wolfenbütteler: Herzog August Bibliothek, 1982.

LEMBERG, HANS. "Zur Entstehung des Osteuropabegriffs im 19. Jahrhundert vom 'Norden' zum 'Osten' Europas." *Jahrbücher für Geschichte Osteuropas* 33 (1985): 48–91.

LINDEMANN, MARGOT. *Deutsche Presse bis 1815.* Berlin: Colloquium, 1969.

LOEWENSON, LEO. "The Work of Robert Boyle and 'The Present State of Russia' by Samuel Collins (1671)." *Slavonic and East European Review* 33 (1954–55): 470–85.

LORTHOLARY, ALBERT. *Le Mirage russe en France au XVIIIᵉ siècle.* Paris: Boivin, 1951.

LUR'E, IAKOV S. *Idologicheskaia bor'ba v russkoi publitsistike kontsa XV–nachala XVI veka.* Moscow and Leningrad: Izd. Akademii nauk SSSR, 1960.

LUR'E, IAKOV S., and DMITRII S. LIKHACHEV, eds. *Poslaniia Ivana Groznogo.* Moscow and Leningrad: Izd. Akademii nauk SSSR, 1951.

MANDT, HELLA. "Tyrannis, Despotie." In *Geschichtliche Grundbegriffe: Historisches Lexikon zur politisch-sozialer Sprache in Deutschland,* ed. Otto Brunner, Werner Conze, and Reinhart Koselleck, 6:651–706. 7 vols. to date. Stuttgart: E. Klett, 1971–97.

MATTINGLY, GARRETT. *Renaissance Diplomacy.* Boston: Houghton Mifflin, 1955.

MILLER, DAVID B. "The Coronation of Ivan IV of Moscow." *Jahrbücher für Geschichte Osteuropas* 15 (1967): 559–74.

MORDUKHOVICH, LEV M. "Iurii Krizhanich o 'rabstve.'" *Trudy Otdela drevnerusskoi literatury* 33 (1979): 142–55.

———. "Iz rukopisnogo nasledstva Iu. Krizhanicha." *Istoricheskii arkhiv,* no. 1 (1958): 185.

MULIUKIN, A. S. *Ocherki po istorii iuridicheskogo polozheniia inostrannykh kuptsov v Moskovskom gosudarstve.* Odessa: Tekhnik, 1912.

———. *Priezd inostrantsev v Moskovskoe gosudarstvo: Iz istorii russkogo prava XVI i XVII vv.* St. Petersburg: Trud, 1909.

MULLINGER, JAMES BASS. *The University of Cambridge.* 3 vols. Cambridge: Cambridge University Press, 1873–1919.

NAARDEN, BRUNO. "Marx and Russia." *History of European Ideas* 12 (1990): 783–97.

NOSOV, NIKOLAI E. *Stanovlenie soslovno-predstavitel'nykh uchrezhdenii v Rossii.* Leningrad: Nauka, 1969.

OSTROWSKI, DONALD. "The Mongol Origins of Muscovite Political Institutions." *Slavic Review* 49 (1990): 525–42.

PERRIE, MAUREEN. *The Image of Ivan the Terrible in Russian Folklore.* Cambridge: Cambridge University Press, 1987.

PICARD, BERTHOLD. *Das Gesandtschaftswesen Ostmitteleuropeas in der frühen Neuzeit: Beitrag zur Geschichte der Diplomatie in der ersten Hälfte des sechzehnten Jahrhunderts nach den Aufzeichnungen des Freiherrn Sigmund von Herberstein.* Wiener Archiv für Geschichte des Slaventums und Osteuropas 6. Graz: Bohlau, 1967.

PIPES, RICHARD. "Introduction." In Giles Fletcher, *Of the Russe Commonwealth,* ed. Richard Pipes and John Fine. Cambridge: Harvard University Press, 1965.

———. "Max Weber and Russia." In Pipes, *Russia Observed: Collected Essays on Russian and Soviet History,* 151–76. Boulder: Westview, 1989.

PLATZHOFF, WALTER. "Das erste Auftauchen Rußlands und der russischen Gefahr in der europäischen Politik." *Historische Zeitschrift* 115 (1915–16): 77–93.

PLAVSIČ, BORIVOJ. "Seventeenth-Century Chanceries and Their Staffs." In *Russian Officialdom: The Bureaucratization of Russian Society from the 17th to the 20th Century,* ed. Dan K. Rowney and Walter M. Pintner, 19–45. Chapel Hill: University of North Carolina Press, 1980.

POE, MARSHALL T. "Boyar Duma." Forthcoming in MERSH, 2d suppl.

———. *Foreign Descriptions of Muscovy: An Analytic Bibliography of Primary and Secondary Sources.* Columbus, Ohio: Slavica, 1993.

———. "The Use of Foreign Descriptions of Russia as Sources for Muscovite History." Forthcoming in *Forschungen zur osteuropäischen Geschichte.*

———. "What did Muscovites Mean When They Called Themselves 'Slaves of the Tsar'?" *Slavic Review* 57, no. 3 (1998): 585–608.

PRUTZ, ROBERT E. *Geschichte des deutschen Journalismus.* Pt. 1. Hanover: C. F. Kius, 1845; rpt. Göttingen: Vandenhoeck & Ruprecht, 1971.

QUELLER, DONALD E. "The Development of the Ambassadorial Relazioni." In *Renaissance Venice,* ed. John R. Hale. London: Faber & Faber, 1973.

———. *The Office of Ambassador in the Middle Ages.* Princeton: Princeton University Press, 1967.

RAABE, PAUL. "Der Biblioteka Conringiana: Beschreibung einer Gelehrtenbibliotek der 17. Jahrhunderts." In *Herman Conring (1606–1681): Beiträge zu Leben und Werk,* ed. Michael Stolleis, 413–37. Berlin: Duncker & Humbolt, 1983.

RABA, JOEL. "The Authority of the Muscovite Ruler at the Dawn of the Modern Era." *Jahrbücher für Geschichte Osteuropas* 24 (1976): 321–44.

REIMANN, EDUARD. "Das Verhalten des Reiches gegen Livland in den Jahren 1559–1561." *Historische Zeitschrift* 35 (1876): 346–80.

RIASANOVSKY, NICHOLAS V. *Russia and the West in the Teaching of the Slavophiles: A Study in Romantic Ideology.* Cambridge: Harvard University Press, 1952.

RICHTER, MELVIN. "Despotism." In *The Dictionary of the History of Ideas,* ed. Philip P. Wiener et al., 2:1–18. 5 vols. New York: Scribner, 1974.

ROSOVETSKII, S. K. "Ustnaia proza ob Ivane Groznom—'pravitele.'" *Russkii fol'klor* 20 (1981): 71–95.

ROWLAND, DANIEL. "Did Muscovite Literary Ideology Place Any Limits on the Power of the Tsar?" *Russian Review* 49 (1990): 125–56.

———. "The Problem of Advice in Muscovite Tales about the Time of Troubles." *Russian History/Histoire Russe* 6 (1979): 259–83.

RUFFMANN, KARL H. *Das Russlandbild im England Shakespeares.* Göttingen: Musterschmidt, 1952.

RUSHCHINSKII, LEV P. *Religioznyi byt russkikh po svedeniiam inostrannykh pisatelei XVI i XVII vv.* Moscow: Izd. Imperatorskogo ob-va istorii drevnostei rossiskikh pri Moskovskom universitete, 1873. Also in *Chteniia v imperatorskom obshchestve istorii i drevnostei rossiiskikh pri Moskovskom universitete* 78, no. 3 (1871): 1–338.

RÜSS, HARTMUT. *Adel und Adelsoppositionen in Moskauer Staat.* Wiesbaden: Steiner, 1975.

RYAN, LAWRENCE V. "Richard Hakluyt's Voyage into Aristotle." *Sixteenth Century Journal* 12 (1981): 73–83.

SAVEL'EVA, ELENA A. *Olaus Magnus i ego "Istoriia severnykh narodov."* Leningrad: Nauka, 1983.

SCHEIDEGGER, GABRIELE. *Perverses Abendland—barbarisches Russland: Begegnungen des 16. und 17. Jahrhunderts im Schatten kultureller Missverständnisse.* Zurich: Chronos, 1993.

SCHMITT, CHARLES B. *John Case and Aristotelianism in Renaissance England.* Kingston, Ont.: McGill–Queen's University Press, 1983.

SCHWOEBEL, ROBERT. *The Shadow of the Crescent: The Renaissance Image of the Turk, 1453–1517.* Nieukoop: B. de Graf, 1967.

SEIFERT, ARNO. "Staatenkunde: Eine neue Disziplin und ihr wissenschaftstheoretischer Ort." In *Statistik und Staatsbeschreibung in der Neuzeit, vornehmlich im 16.–18. Jahrhundert,* ed. Mohammed Rassem and Justin Stagl, 217–44. Paderborn: Schöningh, 1980.

SERGEEVICH, VASILII I. *Drevnosti russkogo prava.* 3 vols. St. Petersburg: M. M. Stasiulevicha, 1903–9.

SHAABER, MATTHIAS A. *Some Forerunners of the Newspaper in England, 1476–1622.* Philadelphia: University of Pennsylvania Press, 1929.

SHEVCHENKO, IHOR. "A Neglected Byzantine Source of Muscovite Political Ideology." *Harvard Slavic Studies* 2 (1954): 141–79.

SHLIAPKIN, IL'IA A. *Sv. Dmitrii Rostovskii i ego vremia (1651–1709 g.).* St. Petersburg: Transhel', 1891.

SHMIDT, SEGURT O. "Chelobitennyi prikaz v seredine XVI stoletiia." *Izvestiia Akademii nauk SSSR, Seriia istorii i filosofii* 8, no. 5 (1950): 445–58.

SKINNER, QUENTIN. *The Foundations of Modern Political Thought.* 2 vols. Cambridge: Cambridge University Press, 1978.

SKRYNNIKOV, RUSLAN G. *Oprichnyi terror.* Leningrad: Izd. Leningradskogo universiteta, 1969.

SKRZHINSKAIA, ELENA CH., ed. *Barbaro i Kontarini o Rossii: K istorii italoruskikh sviazei v XV v.* Leningrad: Nauka, 1971.

SOBOLEVSKII, ALEKSEI I. *Zapadnoe vlianie na literaturu Moskovskoi Rusi XV–XVII vekov.* The Hague: Europe, 1966.

SOMMERFELDT, GUSTAV. "Die Betrachtung über eine Kreuzzug gegen Russland und die Türkei zu gewährende Reichshilfe 1560–1561." *Historische Vierteljahrsschrift* 13 Jg. (1910): 191–201.

SREZNEVSKII, IZMAIL I. *Materialy dlia slovaria drevne-russkogo iazyka.* 3 vols. Moscow: Tip. Imp. Akademii nauk, 1893–1903.

STAGL, JUSTIN. "Die Apodemik oder 'Reisekunst' als Methodik der Sozielforschung vom Humanismus bis zur Aufklärung." In *Statistik und Staatsbeschreibung in der Neuzeit, vornehmlich im 16. und 18. Jahrhundert,* ed. Mohammed Rassem and Justin Stagl, 131–204. Paderborn: Schöningh, 1980.

———. "The Methodizing of Travel in the Sixteenth Century: A Tale of Three Cities." *History and Anthropology* 4 (1990): 303–38.

———. "Das Reisen als Kunst und als Wissenschaft (16.–18. Jahrhundert)." *Zeitschrift für Ethnologie* 108 (1983): 15–34.

———. "Der wohl unterwiesene Passagier, Reisekunst und Gessellschafts Beschreibung vom 16. bis zum 18. Jahrhundert." In *Reisen und Reisebeschreibungen im 18. und 19. Jahrhundert als Quellen der Kulturbeziehungsforschung,* ed. Boris I. Krasnobaev, 353–84. Berlin: U. Camen, 1980.

———, comp. *Apodemiken: Eine rèsonnierte Bibliographie der reisetheoretischen Literatur des 16., 17. und 18. Jahrhunderts.* Paderborn: F. Schöningh, 1983.

STÖKL, GÜNTER. "Die Begriffe Reich, Herrschaft und Staat bei den orthodoxen Slawen." *Saeculum* 5 (1954): 104–18.

———. "Gab es im Moskauer Staat 'Stände'?" *Jahrbücher für Geschichte Osteuropas* 11 (1963): 321–42.

STRAUSS, GERALD. *Sixteenth-Century Germany: Its Topography and Topographers.* Madison: University of Wisconsin Press, 1959.

SZEFTEL, MARC. "The Title of the Muscovite Monarch Up to the End of the Seventeenth Century." *Canadian-American Slavic Studies* 13 (1979): 59–81.

TARANOVSKII, FEDOR V. "Montesk'iu i Rossiia." *Trudy russkikh uchenykh za granitsei* 1 (1922): 178–223.

TIKHOMIROV, MIKHAIL N. "Ital'iantsy v Rossii XIV–XVI stoletii." In Tikhomirov, *Rossiiskoe gosudarstvo XV–XVII vekov.* Moscow: Nauka, 1973.

———. "Prikaznoe deloproizvodstvo v XVII v." In Tikhomirov, *Rossiiskoe gosudarstvo XV–XVII vekov.* Moscow: Nauka, 1973.

TORKE, HANS-JOACHIM. *Die staatsbedingte Gesellschaft im Moskauer Reich: Zar und Zemlja in der altrussischen Herrschaftsverfassung, 1613–1668.* Leiden: E. J. Brill, 1974.

TSVETAEV, DMITRII V. *Protestantstvo i protestanty v Rossii do epocky preobrazovanii.* Moscow: Universitetskaia tip., 1890.

UEBERSBERGER, HANS B. *Österreich und Russland seit dem Ende des 15. Jahrhunderts.* 2 vols. Vienna and Leipzig: E. Braumuller, 1906.

USMANOV, MIRKASYM A. *Zhalovannye akty Dzhuchieva Ulusa XIV–XVI vv.* Kazan: Izd. Kazanskogo universiteta, 1979.

VAL'DENBERG, VLADIMIR. *Drevnerusskiia ucheniia o predelakh tsarskoi vlasti.* Petrograd: A. Benke, 1916.

VESELOVSKII, STEPAN B. *Issledovaniia po istorii oprichniny.* Moscow: Izd. Akademii nauk SSSR, 1963.

VOLKOV, SVIATOSLAV S. "Iz istorii russkoi leksiki. II. Chelobitnaia." In *Russkaia istoricheskaia leksikologiia i leksikografiia,* ed. Sviatoslav S. Volkov. Leningrad: Izd. Leningradskogo universiteta, 1972.

————. *Leksika russkikh chelobitnykh XVII veka: Formuliar, traditsionnye etiketnye i stilevye sredstva.* Leningrad: Izd. Leningradskogo universiteta, 1974.

WEBER, MAX. *Economy and Society: An Outline of Interpretive Sociology.* Ed. Guenther Roth and Claus Wittich. 3 vols. New York: Bedminster Press, 1968.

WEICKHARDT, GEORGE G. "Due Process and Equal Justice in Muscovite Law." *Russian Review* 51 (1992): 463–80.

————. "Political Thought in Seventeenth-Century Russia." *Russian History/ Histoire Russe* 21 (1994): 316–38.

————. "The Pre-Petrine Law of Property." *Slavic Review* 52 (1993): 663–79.

WILLOWEIT, DIETMAR. "Hermann Conring." In *Hermann Conring (1606– 1681): Beiträge zu Leben und Werk,* ed. Michael Stolleis. Berlin: Duncker & Humbolt, 1983.

WINCKELMANN, JOHANNES. "Despotie, Despotismus." In *Historisches Wörterbuch der Philosophie,* ed. Joachim Ritter and Karlfried Gründer, 2:131– 46. 8 vols. to date. Basel and Stuttgart: Schwabe, 1971–.

WITTFOGEL, KARL A. *Oriental Despotism: A Comparative Study in Total Power.* New Haven: Yale University Press, 1957.

WOLFF, LARRY. *Inventing Eastern Europe: The Map of Civilization on the Mind of the Enlightenment.* Stanford: Stanford University Press, 1994.

ZEHRFELD, REINOLD. *Hermann Conrings (1606–1681) Staatenkunde.* Berlin: W. De Gruyter, 1926.

ZIMIN, ALEKSANDR A. *Formirovanie boiarskoi aristokratii v Rossii v vtoroi polovine XV–pervoi treti XVI v.* Moscow: Nauka, 1988.

————. *Oprichnina Ivana Groznogo.* Moscow: Mysl', 1963.

BIBLIOGRAPHY 4

Secondary Sources on European Authors

Abbreviations

ADB	*Allgemeine deutsche Biographie.* 56 vols. Leipzig: Duncker & Humblot, 1875–1912; rpt. Berlin: Duncker & Humblot, 1967–71.
Adelung	Friedrich von Adelung. *Kritisch-literarische Übersicht der Reisenden in Russland bis 1700, deren Berichte bekannt sind.* 2 vols. St. Petersburg: Eggers, 1846.
BBI	*British Biographical Index.* Ed. David Banks and Anthony Esporito. 4 vols. London: Saur, 1990. Index to *British Biographical Archive,* ed. Laureen Baille and Paul Sieveking. Munich: Saur, 1984.
Brokgauz-Efron	F. A. Brokgauz and I. A. Efron, eds. *Entsiklopedicheskii Slovar'.* 41 vols. St. Petersburg: Brokgauz i Efron, 1890–1904.
BU	*Biographie universelle, ancienne et moderne* Ed. Jacques F. Michaud and Louis G. Michaud. 85 vols. Paris: Michaud frères, 1811–62.
ChOIDR	*Chteniia v Imperatorskom obshchestve istorii i drevnostei rossiiskikh pri Moskovskom universitete.* 264 vols. Moscow, 1845–1918.
DBdI	*Dizionario biografico degli Italiani.* Ed. Alberto M. Ghisalberti. 45 vols. to date. Rome: Instituto della Enciclopedia italiana, 1960–.
DBI	*Deutscher biographischer Index.* Ed. Willi Gorzny, Hans-Albrecht Koch, Uwe Koch, and Angelika Koller. 4 vols. Munich: Saur, 1986. Index to *Deutsches biographisches Archiv: eine Kumulation aus 254 der wichtigsten biographischen Nachschlagewerke für den deutschen Bereich bis zum Ausgang des neunzehnten Jahrhunderts,* ed. Bernard Fabian and Willi Gorzny. Munich: Saur, 1982–87.

DNB   *Dictionary of National Biography.* Ed. Leslie Stephen and Sid-
                      ney Lee. 22 vols. New York: Macmillan; London: Smith, Elder,
                      1908–09.

Florovskii   Antonii V. Florovskii. *Chekhi i vostochnye slaviane.* Vol. 2.
                      Ocherki po istorii chekhsko-russkikh otnoshenii (X–XVIII vv.).
                      Prague: Orbis, 1947.

Hakluyt (1969)   Richard Hakluyt, ed. *The Principal navigations, voiages, traf-
                      fiques and discoveries of the English Nation.* 12 vols. Glasgow:
                      James MacLehose & Sons, 1903–05. Rpt. New York: Augus-
                      tus M. Kelly, 1969.

IBF   *Index biographique français.* Ed. Helen and Barry Dwyer. Lon-
                      don: Saur, 1993. Index to *Archives biographiques françaises,* ed.
                      Tommaso Nappo. London: Saur, 1993–96.

IBI   *Indice biografico italiano.* Ed. Tommaso Nappo and Paolo Noto.
                      4 vols. Munich: Saur, 1993. Index to *Archivio biografico italiano:
                      cumulativo di 321 repertori biografici fra i più importanti a par-
                      tire dal sec. XVII sino all'inizio del sec. XX,* ed. Tommaso Nappo
                      and Silvio Furlani. Munich: Saur 1988.

Jöcher   Carl G. Jöcher, ed. *Allgemeines Gelehrten-Lexikon.* 4 vols. Leip-
                      zig: Johann Friedrich Gleditschens Buchhandlung, 1751; rpt. Hil-
                      desheim: G. Olms, 1961.

Kappeler   Andreas Kappeler. *Ivan Groznyi im Spiegel der ausländischen
                      Druckschriften seiner Zeit: Ein Beitrag zur Geschichte des west-
                      lichen Russlandbildes.* Bern: Herbert Land, 1972.

Kordt   Veniamin Kordt. *Chuzozemni podorozhni po skhidnii Evropi
                      do 1700 r.* Zbirnyk Istorychno-filolohichnoho viddilu 38. Kiev,
                      1926.

Lankau   Jan Lankau. *Prasa staropolska na tle rozwoju prasy w Europie
                      1513–1729.* Cracow: Państwowe Wydawnictwo, Naukowe,
                      Oddział w Krakowie, 1960.

MERSH   *The Modern Encyclopedia of Russian and Soviet History.* Ed. Jo-
                      seph L. Wieczynski. 59 vols. Gulf Breeze, Fla.: Academic Inter-
                      national Press, 1976–.

NDB   *Neue deutsche Biographie.* 17 vols. to date. Berlin: Duncker &
                      Humbolt, 1953–.

Pferschy   Gerhard Pferschy, ed. *Siegmund von Herberstein, Kaiserlicher Ge-
                      sandter und Begründer der Rußlandkunde und die europäische
                      Diplomatie.* Graz: Akademische Druck- und Verlagstalt, 1989.

PSB   *Polski Słownik Biograficzny.* Ed. Władyslaw Konopczynski et al.
                      Wroclaw and Cracow: Sklad glowny w ksiegi Gebethnera i Wolffa,
                      1935–.

Recke and   Johann F. von Recke and Karl E. Napiersky. *Allgemeines Schrift-
  Napiersky   steller-und-Gelehrten-Lexikon der Provinzen Livland, Estland
                      und Kurland,* 5 vols. Mitau: J. F. Steffenhagen and Sohn, 1827–32.

Semenov   Vladimir Semenov, ed. *Biblioteka inostrannykh pisatelei o Rossii.*
(1836)   2 vols. St. Petersburg: V tip. III Otd-niia Sobstvennoi E. I. V., 1836.

Ustrialov   Nikolai G. Ustrialov, ed. and trans. *Skazaniia sovremennikov o*
(1858)   *Dmitrii Samozvantse.* 2 vols. St. Petersburg: Tip. I. Akademii
     nauk, 1859.

Secondary Sources on European Authors

BARBERINO, RAFFAELLE (1532–82; Italian merchant)
     Studies: Adelung 1:233–39; DBdI 2:179ff.; Kappeler, 94; Kordt, 37.
     TSCHARYKOW, N. "Le chevalier Raphael Barberini chez tsar Jean le Terrible,
        1564." *Revue d'histoire diplomatique* 18 (1904): 252–74.

BOEMUS, JOHANN (fl. 1500; German geographer; never in Muscovy)
     Studies: ADB 3:30; NDB 3:403.

BOMHOVER, CHRISTIAN (before 1469–1518; Livonian official; never in
     Muscovy?)
     Studies: Kappeler, 23.
     BENNINGHOVEN, FRIEDRICH. "Rußland im Spiegel der livändischen
        Schonnen Hystorie von 1508." *Zeitschrift für Ostforschung* 11 (1962): 601–25.

BUSSOW, KONRAD (German mercenary)
     Studies: Adelung 2:46–111.
     GRAHAM, HUGH. "Bussow, Konrad (?–1617)." MERSH 6: 51–54.
     GROT, IAKOV K. "Deistvitel'no li Martin Ber avtor Khroniki?" *Zhurnal Mini-*
        sterstva narodnogo prosvieshcheniia 12 (1849), no. 5.
     KUNIK, ARIST. *Aufklärung über Konrad Bussow und die verschiedenen Redak-*
        tionen seiner Moskowischen Chronik. St. Petersburg, 1851.
     MYL'NIKOV, ALEKSANDR S., and Wolfgang Milde. "Handschriftliche Slavica
        der Herzog-August-Bibliothek." *Wolfenbütteler Beiträge* 7 (1987): 79–98.
     SMIRNOV, IVAN I. "Konrad Bussov i ego Khronika." In Konrad Bussov, *Mos-*
        kovskaia khronika, 1584–1613, ed. and trans. Ivan I. Smirnov. Moscow: Izd.
        Akademii nauk SSSR, 1961. 5–56.

CAMPENSÉ, ALBERTO [Albertus Pighius Campensis] (ca. 1490–1542; papal of-
     ficial; never in Muscovy)
     Studies: Adelung 1:181–84; Kappeler, 25.

CHANCELLOR, RICHARD (d. 1556; English diplomat)
     Studies: Adelung 1:200–205; BBI 1:8 (Adams); DNB 1:94–95 (Adams); BBI
        1:351 (Chancellor); DNB 1:37–38 (Chancellor).
     IVANOV, I. "Sobranie svedenii o priezde Chanslera." *Arkhangel'skie gubernskie*
        vedomosti, 1869, no. 63.

COLLINS, SAMUEL (1619–1670; English doctor)
     Studies: Adelung 2:342–44; DNB 4:832; BBI 1:409.

LOEWENSON, L. "The Work of Robert Boyle and 'The Present State of Russia' by Samuel Collins." *Slavonic and East European Review* 33 (1954–55): 470–85.

CONTARINI, AMBROGIO (d. 1499; Venetian envoy)
   Studies: Adelung 1:146–49; Kappeler, 22; IBI 2:460.
   "Contarini, Ambrogio (?–1499)." MERSH 8:53.
   LENNA, N. DI. *Ambroggio Contarini, politico e viaggiatore nel sec. XV*. Padua, 1921.

DA COLLO, FRANCESCO (1480–1571; Imperial diplomat)
   Studies: Adelung 1:175–77; IBI 2:639.
   D'AMATO, DZHUZEPPE. *Sochineniia ital'iantsev o Rossii kontsa XV–XVI vv.* 2d ed. Moscow: Russkoe slovo, 1995.

FABRI, JOHANN (1478–1541; papal official; never in Muscovy)
   Studies: Adelung, 184–86; Kappeler, 25.
   HELBLING, LEO. *Dr. Johann Fabri. Generalvikar von Konstanz und Bischof von Wien. 1478–1541. Beitrag zu seiner Lebensgeschichte.* Reformationsgeschichte Studien und Texte, 67/68. Münster i. W., 1941.

FLETCHER, GILES (1546–1611; English diplomat)
   Studies: Adelung, 1:377–79; BBI 2:681; DNB 7:302–303.
   BARON, SAMUEL H. "Fletcher's Mission to Moscow and the Anthony Marsh Affair." *Forschungen zur Osteuropäischen Geschichte* 46 (1992): 107–30. Rpt. in Baron, *Explorations in Muscovite History*, chap. 3. Brookfield, Vt.: Gower, 1991.
   ———. "Ivan the Terrible, Giles Fletcher and the Muscovite Merchantry: A Reconsideration." *Slavonic and East European Review* 56 (1978): 563–85. Rpt. in Baron, *Muscovite Russia*, chap. 4. London: Variorum Reprints, 1980.
   BERRY, LLOYD E. "Giles Fletcher, the Elder, and Milton's *A Brief History*." *Review of English Studies* 11 (1960): 150–56.
   ———. "The Life of Giles Fletcher, the Elder." In *The English Works of Giles Fletcher, the Elder,* ed. Lloyd E. Berry, 3–49. Madison: University of Wisconsin Press, 1964.
   LEONARD, EMILY V. "Fletcher, Giles (1546–1611)." MERSH 14:187–88.
   ———. "Muscovy in the Sixteenth Century: The Accounts of Sigismund von Herberstein and Antonio Possevino." Ph.D. dissertation, Indiana University, 1966.
   LINDSAY, ROBERT O. "Richard Hakluyt and 'Of the Russe Commonwealth.'" *Papers of the Bibliographical Society of America* 57 (1963): 312–27.
   SEREDONIN, SERGEI M. *Sochinenie Dzhil'sa Fletchera "Of the Russe common wealth" kak istoricheskii istochnik.* St. Petersburg: Tip. I. N. Skorokhodova, 1891.
   VILENSKAIA, ELENA S. "K istorii russko-angliiskikh otnoshenii v XVI v. (Neizdannye zapiski Dzhil'sa Fletchera koroleve Elizavete)." *Istoricheskie zapiski* 29 (1949): 123–34.

FRANCK, SEBASTIAN (1499–1542/43; German mystic, cosmographer; never in Muscovy)
Studies: NDB 5:320–21; DBI 1:576; ADB 7:214–19.
BISCHOF, HERMANN. *Sebastian Franck und deutsche Geschichtsschreibung.* Tübingen: E. Reicker, 1857.
HAYDEN-ROY, PATRICK M. "The Inner Word and the Outer World: A Biography of Sebastian Frank." Ph.D. dissertation, Stanford University, 1988.
KACZEROWSKY, KLAUS, comp. *Sebastian Franck Bibliographie.* Wiesbaden: G. Pressler, 1976.
KINTNER, PHILIP L. "Studies in the Historical Writings of Sebastian Franck (1499–1542)." Ph.D. dissertation, Yale University, 1958.
PEUCKERT, WILL-ERICH. *Sebastian Franck: Ein deutscher Sucher.* Munich: Piper, 1943.

GIOVIO, PAOLO (1483–1552; Italian Humanist, papal official; never in Muscovy)
Studies: Adelung 1:187–91; Kappeler, 24.
KAZAKOVA, NATAL'IA A. "Dmitrii Gerasimov i russko-evropeiskie kul'turnye sviazi v pervoi treti XVI v." In *Problemy istorii mezhdunarodnykh otnoshenii (sbornik statei pamisti akademika E. V. Tarle),* ed. Nikolai E. Nosov et al., 248–66. Leningrad: Academiia Nauk SSSR, Institut Istorii, Leningradskoe otdelenie, 1972.

GORDON, PATRICK (1639–99; Scottish mercenary)
Studies: Adelung 2:364–65; BBI 2:770; DNB 8:222–24.
BOGOSLOVSKII, MIKHAIL M. *Petr I: Materialy dlia biografii.* 5 vols. Moscow: Ogiz, Gos. sotsial'no-ekon. izd., 1940–48.
BRUCKNER, ALEKSANDR. *Patrik Gordon i ego dnevnik.* St. Petersburg: V. S. Balashev, 1878.
LEONARD, EMILY V. "Gordon, Patrick (1635–99)." MERSH 13:49–50.

GUAGNINI, ALEXANDER [Aleksander Gwagnin] (1538?–1614; Italian mercenary in Polish service)
Studies: Adelung 1:226–30; Kappeler, 53–55; PSB 9:202–4.
CIPOLLA, CARLO C. "Un italiano nella Polonia e nella Svezia tra il XVIe e XVII secolo." *Miscelanea di Storia italiana* 2, no. 26 (1887): 549–657.
GRAHAM, HUGH. "Guagnini, Alessandro (1538?–1614)." MERSH 13:173–76.
"GUAGNINI." *Bibliografia polska: XV–XVI Stólecia,* ed. Karol Estreicher, 480–86. Cracow: Czionkami drukarini C. K. Uniwersytetu Jagiellonskiego, 1875.

HERBERSTEIN, SIGISMUND VON (1486–1566; Imperial diplomat)
Studies: ADB 12:35–39; DBI 2:855; Adelung 1:160–75; Kappeler, 26; NDB 8:579–80.
ADELUNG, FRIEDRICH VON. *Siegmund Freiherr von Herberstein: Mit besonderer Rücksicht auf seine Reisen in Rußland.* St. Petersburg: N. Gretsch, 1818.
BARON, SAMUEL H. "Herberstein and the English 'Discovery' of Muscovy." *Terrae Incognitae* 18 (1987): 43–54. Rpt. in Baron, *Explorations in Muscovite History,* chap. 14. Brookfield, Vt.: Gower, 1991.

————. "Herberstein's Image of Russia and Its Transmission through Later Writers." In Pferschy, 245–72. Rpt. in Baron, *Explorations in Muscovite History*, chap. 13. Brookfield, Vt.: Gower, 1991.

————. "The Influence in Sixteenth-Century England of Herberstein's *Rerum Moscoviticarum Commentarii.*" In Baron, *Explorations in Muscovite History*, chap. 15. Hampsh Brookfield, Vt.: Gower, 1991.

BILIARSKII, PETR S. "O pervom opyte perevoda Gerbershteina na russkii iazyk." *Zapiski imp. Akademii nauk* 4 (1864): 98–100.

BURKERT, GUNTER R. "Herberstein in der Politik der innerösterreichischen Stände." In Pferschy, 117–35.

DONNERT, ERICH. "Siegmund von Herberstein: Zur deutschen Rußlandkunde des 16. Jahrhunderts." *Wissenschaftliche Zeitschrift der Friedrich-Schiller-Universität Jena GSR (Gesellschafts- und sprachwissenschaftliche Reihe)* 7 (1957/58): 77–80.

ERIUKHIN, A. "Istoriko-geograficheskie izvestiia o severe Moskovskogo gosudarstva v 'Zapiski o Moskovii' Gerbershteina." In *Trudy Arkhangel'skogo statisticheskogo komiteta za 1890 god*. Archangel: Arkhangel'skii statisticheskii komitet, 1890.

FIEDLER, JOSEPH. "Aktenstücke zu Siegmund's Freiherrn von Herberstein zweiter Mission nach Rußland 1525–26." In *Slavische Bibliothek oder Beiträge zur slavischen Philologie und Geschichte*, ed. Franz Miklosich and Joseph Fielder, 1:63–93. Vienna: W. Braumuller, 1858.

FLOROVSKII, ANTONII V. "Kakim letopisnym tekstom pol'zovalsia Gerbershtein?" *Uchenye zapiski Vyshei shkoly g. Odessy, otdel gumanitarno-obshchestvennykh nauk* 2 (1922): 69–80.

GRAHAM, HUGH. "Herberstein, Sigismund Freiherr von (1486–1566)." MERSH 14:6–10.

GENNADI, GRIGORII. "Zapiski Gerbershteina na russkom iazyke." *Vremennik Imperatorskogo moskovskogo obshchestva istorii i drevnostei rossiskikh*, 1855, 9–12.

HARRAUER, CHRISTINE. "Beobachtungen zu Darstellungsweise und Wahrheitsanspurch in der 'Moscovia' Herbersteins." In *Landesbeschreibungen Mitteleuropas vom 15. bis 17. Jahrhundert*, ed. Hans-Bernd Harder. Cologne: Bohlau, 1983.

————. "Die zeitgenössischen lateinischen Drucke der Moscovia Herbersteins und ihre Entstehungsgeschichte (Ein Beitrag zur Editionstechnik im 16. Jahrhundert)." *Humanistica Lovaniensia: Journal of Neo-Latin Studies* 31 (1982): 141–63.

HÖFLECHNER, WALTER. "Zur Entwicklung der europäischen Bündnissysteme und des Gesandtschaftswesens bis zur Zeit Herbersteins." In Pferschy, 17–25.

ISACHENKO, ALEKSANDR V. "Herbersteiniana I: Sigmund von Herbersteins Rußlandbericht und die russische Sprache des XVI. Jahrhunderts." *Zeitschrift für Slavistik* 2 (1957): 321–46.

————. "Herbersteiniana II: Herbersteins Moskowiterbuch und seine Bedeutung für die russische historische Lexikographie." *Zeitschrift für Slavistik* 2 (1957): 493–512.

KÄMPFER, FRANK. "Herbersteins nicht eingestandene Abhängigkeit von Johann Fabri aus Leutkirch." *Jahrbücher für Geschichte Osteuropas* 44 (1996): 1–27.

————. "Siegmund von Herbersteins 'Rerum Moscoviticarum Commentarii' als religionsgeschichtliche Quelle." In Pferschy, 147–64.

KARAJAN, THEODOR G. VON. "Selbstbiographie Sigmunds Freiherrn von Herberstein, 1486–1553." *Fontes Rerum Austriacarum.* Pt. 1, vol. 1, folio 2 (1855): 67–396.

KHOROSHKEVICH, ANNA L. "Die Quellen Herbersteins und die Moscovia als Quelle zur politischen, Sozial- und Wirtschaftsgeschichte der Rus im ersten Viertel des 16. Jahrhunderts." In Pferschy, 179–244.

————. "Sigizmund Gerbershtein i ego Zapiski o Moskovii." In Sigizmund Gerbershtein, *Zapiski o Moskovii,* ed. Valentin L. Ianin et al., 9–15. Moscow: Izd. Moskovskogo universiteta, 1988.

KORELKIN, I., et al. "Sigizmund, baron Gerbershtein, ego zhizn' i znachenie kak pisatelia o Rossii." In *Sbornik, izdavaemyi studentami Peterburgskogo universiteta,* 1–102. St. Petersburg: Tip. II-ogo otd. sob. E.I.V. Kantseliarii, 1857.

KRONES, FRANZ X. "Sigmund von Herberstein: Ein Lebensbild, mit besonderer Rücksicht auf die Beziehungen Herbersteins zur Steiermark und seine Schriften." *Mitteilungen des Historischen Vereins für Steiermark* 19 (1871): 3–76.

LANZER, ANDREA. "Das Gesandtschaftswesen im Westen zu Beginn des 16. Jahrhunderts." In Pferschy, 63–78.

LEITSCH, WALTER. "Das erste Rußlandbuch im Westen—Sigismund Freiherr von Herberstein." In *Russen und Rußland aus deutscher Sicht 9.-17. Jahrhundert,* ed. Michthild Keller, 118–49. Munich: W. Fink, 1985.

————. "Herbersteiniana." *Jahrbücher für Geschichte Osteuropas* 38 (1990).

————. "Herberstein's Ergänzungen zur Moscovia in späteren Auflagen und die beiden zeitgenössischen Übersetzungen ins Deutsche." *Forschungen zur osteuropäischen Geschichte* 27 (1980): 177–94.

————. "Herberstein's Impact on the Reports about Muscovy in the Sixteenth and Seventeenth Centuries: Some Observations on the Technique of Borrowing." *Forschungen zur osteuropäischen Geschichte* 24 (1978): 163–77.

————. "Probleme bei der Edition von Herbersteins Moscovia." In Pferschy, 165–78.

————. "Russia-Rutheni und Moscovia-Mosci bei Herberstein." In *Geschichte Altrusslands in der Begriffswelt ihrer Quellen: Festschrift zum 70. Geburtstag von Günter Stökl,* ed. Uwe Halbach, Hans Hecker, and Andreas Kappeler, 113–23. Stuttgart: F. Steiner, 1986.

————. "Sigismund Freiherr zu Herberstein: Ein österreichischer Forscher und Diplomat der Epoche Karls V." *Alte und moderne Kunst* 3 (1958): 163–77.

LIMONOV, IURII A. "Gerbershtein i russkie letopisi." *Vspomogatel'nye istoricheskie distsipliny* 2 (1969): 214–29.

————. *Kul'turnye sviazi Rossii s evropeiskimi stranami v XV–XVII vv.,* 149–67. Leningrad: Nauka, 1978.

————. "Russkie izdaniia 'Zapisok o Moskovii' Sigizmunda Gerbershteina." In *Rukopisnye i redkie knigi v fondakh biblioteki Akademii nauk SSSR,* ed. Sergei P. Lupov and Ariadna A. Moiseeva, 110–18. Leningrad: BAN, 1976.

LOBOIKO, I. N. *O vazhneishikh izdaniiakh Gerbershteina "Zapisok o Rossii" s kriticheskim obozreniem ikh soderzhaniia.* St. Petersburg, 1818.

MARCH VON ULM, DANIEL. "Reisebegleiter des Rußlandentdeckers Sigmund von Herberstein, 1526–27." In *Mitteilungen des Vereins für Kunst und Altertum in Ulm und Oberschwaben,* 158–71. Donau: Dr. Karl Hohn, 1941.

MORITSCH, ANDREAS. "Geographisches in Herbersteins Moscovia." In Pferschy, 135–46.

NAHLIK, STANISLAW E. "Völkerrechtliche Aspekte der frühen Diplomatie." In Pferschy, 42–62.

NEHRING, ALFRED. "Einige Bemerkungen über Anton Weids 'Moscovia' und das dazugehörige Urusbild." *Globus* 71:85–89.

———. "Hirschvogels Bezeihung zu Herbersteins Werken." *Repertorium für Kunstwissenschaft* 20 (Berlin, Stuttgart, 1897): 121–29.

———. "Über die Herbersteinischen Abbildungen des Ur und des Bison." *Landwirtschaftliche Jahrbücher* 25 (1896): 915–33.

———. *Über Herberstein und Hirschvogel. Beiträge zur Kenntnis ihres Lebens und ihrer Werke.* Berlin: F. Dummler, 1897.

NEVINSON, JOHN L. "Siegmund von Herberstein: Notes on Sixteenth-Century Dress." *Waffen- und Kostumkunde* 1–2 (1959), 86–93.

PAPST, E. "Herbersteins Bericht über Livland." *Inland,* 1850, no. 15.

PEKARSKII, PETR P. "Dokladnaia zapiska ob izdanii Gerbershteina." *Zapiski imperatorskoi Akademii nauk* 4 (St. Petersburg, 1864): 80.

PFERSCHY, GERHARD, ed. *Siegmund von Herberstein, Kaiserlicher Gesandter und Begründer der Rußlandkunde und die europäische Diplomatie.* Graz: Akademische Druck- und Verlagstalt, 1989.

PICARD, BERTHOLD. *Das Gesandtschaftswesen Ostmitteleuropeas in der frühen Neuzeit: Beitrag zur Geschichte der Diplomatie in der ersten Hälfte des sechzehnten Jahrhunderts nach den Aufzeichnungen des Freiherrn Sigmund von Herberstein.* Wiener Archiv für Geschichte des Slaventums und Osteuropas 6. Graz: Bohlau, 1967.

———. "Herberstein als habsburgischer Diplomat." In Pferschy, 101–16.

PRAKHOV, M. "Ob izdanii Gerbershteina s russkim perevodom i obiasneniiami." *Zapiski imperatorskoi Akademii nauk* 4 (St. Petersburg, 1864): 245–64.

RENSING, E. "Sigismund von Herberstein, der Grenzlanddeutsche." *Mitteilungen der Akademie zur wissenschaftlichen Erforschung und Pflege des Deutschtums* 3 (1935): 464–87 and 4 (1935): 555–85.

STÖKL, GÜNTER. "Herbersteiniana." *Jahrbücher für Geschichte Osteuropas* 15 (1967).

———. "Das moskovitische Gesandtschaftswesen bis in die Zeit Herbersteins." In Pferschy, 79–88.

———. "Siegmund Freiherr von Herberstein: Diplomat und Humanist." *Ostdeutsche Wissenschaft* 7 (1960): 69–80.

STRAHL, K. "Rußlands älteste Gesandtschaften in Deutschland, deutsche Gesandtschaften in Rußland und erstes Freundschaftsbündnis zwischen Rußland und Österreich unter Friedrich III. und Maximilian I.: Aus deutschen und vorzüglich russischen Quellen." *Archiv der Gesellschaft für ältere deutsche Geschichtskunde* 6 (1838): 523–46.

THOMAS, CHRISTIANE. "Diplomatie im eigenen Haus: Geheime dynastiebezogene Vereinbarungen der Casa de Austria." In Pferschy, 27–42.

ZAHN, JOSEF VON. "Das Familienbuch Sigmunds von Herberstein." *Archiv für österreichische Geschichte* 39 (1866): 296–303.

ZAMYSLOVSKII, EGOR E. "Baron Sigizmund Gerbershtein i ego sochinenie o Rossii v XVI v." *Drevniaia i novaia Rossiia* (1875), nos. 9, 10, 12.

————. *Gerbershtein i ego istoriko-geograficheskie izvestiia o Rossii.* St. Petersburg: Tip. brat. Pateleevykh, 1884).

HORSEY, JEROME (1573–1627; English merchant)
    Studies: Adelung 1:352–54; DNB 9:1272–73.
CROSKEY, ROBERT M. "The Composition of Sir Jerome Horsey's 'Travels.'"
    Jahrbücher für Geschichte Osteuropas 26 (1978): 362–75.
KOLOBKOV, V. A. "Deiatel'nost' Dzheroma Gorseia v Rossii (1588–89)."
    Vestnik Leningradskogo universiteta, 2d ser., 2, no. 9 (1987): 81–85.
————. "Dzherom Gorsei i ego sochineniia o Rossii XVI veka." Abstract, candidate dissertation, Leningradskii gosudarstvennyi institut, 1988.
————. "Sochenenie Dzheroma Gorseia o Rossii XVI v. kak istoricheskii istochnik." In *Student i nauchno-tekhnicheskii progress,* 24–29. Novosibirsk, 1984.
LAYTON, DONALD L. "Horsey, Sir Jerome." MERSH 11:81–82.
LUR'E, IAKOV S. "Pis'ma Dzheroma Gorseia." *Uchenye zapiski Leningradskogo universiteta, Seriia istoricheskikh nauk,* pt. 8, no. 73 (1941).
PERRIE, MAUREEN. "Jerome Horsey's Account of the Events of May 1591."
    Oxford Slavonic Papers 13 (1980): 28–49.
SEVAST'IANOVA, ALLA A. "Sochineniia Dzeroma Gorseia kak istochnik po istorii Rossii XVI–nachala XVII veka." Candidate dissertation, Moskovskii gosudarstvenny universitet, 1974.
————. "Zapiski Dzheroma Gorseia o Rossii v kontse XVI–nachale XVII veka (Raznovremennye sloi istochnika i ikh khronologiia)." In *Voprosy istoriografii i istochnikovedeniia otechestvennoi istorii: Sbornik trudov,* ed. Vladimir B. Kobrin, 63–83. Moscow: MGPI, 1974.
————. "Zapiski o Moskovii Dzheroma Gorseia (K voprosu o printsipakh nauchnogo perevoda terminov pri publikatsii istochnikov)." *Arkheograficheskii ezhegodnik za 1976* (Moscow, 1978), 71–78.
SISSON, CHARLES H. "Englishmen in Shakespeare's Muscovy, or The Victims of Jerome Horsey." In *Mélanges en l'honneur de Jules Legras,* 232–46. Paris: Droz, 1939.
TOLSTOI, IURII V. "Poslednee posol'stvo korolevny Elizavety k tsariu Ivanu Vasil'evichu: Ser Eromei Gorsei." *Russkii vestnik* 36 (1861).
————. "Skazaniia anglichanina Gorseia o Rossii v iskhode XVI v." *Otechestvennye zapiski* 126, no. 9 (1859).

JENKINSON, ANTHONY (1530–1611; English navigator)
    Studies: Adelung 1:214–20; DNB 10:744–46.
BARON, SAMUEL H. "B. A. Rybakov on Jenkinson's Map of Russia." In *New Perspectives on Muscovite History,* ed. L. Hughes. London, 1993. 3–13. Rpt. in Baron, *Explorations in Muscovite History,* chap. 12. Brookfield, Vt.: Gower, 1991.
————. "The Lost Jenkinson Map of Russia (1562) Recovered, Redated and Retitled." *Terrae Incognitae* 25 (1993): 53–65.
————. "William Borough and the Jenkinson Map of Russia (1562)." *Cartographica* 26 (1989): 72–87. Rpt. in Baron, *Explorations in Muscovite History,* chap. 11. Brookfield, Vt.: Gower, 1991.
KEUNING, JOHANNES. "Jenkinson's Map of Russia." *Imago Mundi: A Review of Early Cartography* 10 (1953): 65–80.

MORTON, MARGARET B. G. *The Jenkinson Story.* Glasgow: W. MacLellan, 1962.

RYBAKOV, BORIS A. *Russkie karty Moskovii, XV–nachala XVI veka.* Moscow: Nauka, 1974.

KOBLENZL, HANS (Imperial diplomat)
Studies: Kappeler, 92; NDB 3:297.

BANTYSH-KAMENSKII, NIKOLAI N. *Obzor vneshhikh snoshenii Rossii (po 1800 god).* Vol. 1. Moscow: Izd. Kommissii Pechataniia Gos. Grammot i dogovorov pri Moskovskom Glavnom Arkhive Ministerstva Inostrannykh Del, 1896.

MITCHELL, BONNER, and RUSSELL ZGUTA, eds. and trans. "The Sixteenth-Century 'Account of Muscovy' Attributed to Don Felippo Prenestein." *Russian History / Histoire Russe* 8 (1981): 390–412.

SHMURLO, EVGENII F. "Otzyv o trude F. F. Verzhbovskogo . . ." *Zapiski Imperatorskoi akademii nauk,* 8th ser., 8 (1908): 181–217.

WIERZBOWSKI, TEODOR (aka Fedor Verzhbovskii), ed. *Donesenie Ioanna Kobentselia o Moskovii ot 1576 goda.* Warsaw: Tip. Varshavskogo uchebnogo okruga, 1901.

———. "Otchet IV kandidata stipendiata Imperatorskogo Varshavskogo Universiteta Fedora Verzhbovskogo o nauchnykh zaniatiiakh za granitseiu v techenie vtoroi poloviny 1877 goda." *Varshavskie universitetskie izvestiia* 3 (1878): 2–12.

———. "Posol'stvo Ioanna Kobentselia v Moskvu v 1575–76 gg." *Varshavskie universitetskie izvestiia* 7 (1896).

KORB, JOHANN GEORG (1670–1741; Austrian diplomat)
Studies: ADB 16:701–2; Adelung 2:398–400; DBI 2:1139.

ORCHARD, G. EDWARD. "Korb, Johann Georg." MERSH 17:174–75.

KRANTZ, ALBERT (1448–1517; German cleric, scholar, Hansa official; never in Muscovy?)
Studies:

GROBECKER, MANFRED. *Studien zur Geschichtsschreibung des Albert Krantz.* Hamburg, 1964.

NORDMAN, V. A. "Die Wandalia des Albert Krantz—eine Untersuchung." *Annales Academiae scientiarum Fennicae* 29 (1934): 1–294.

KRIZHANICH, IURII (1618?–83; Croatian cleric, political thinker). "Rozgowori ob Wladetelystwu." (Generally known as "Politika.")
Studies:

BOZICEVIČ, JOSIP. "Krizhanich, Yurii (1618?–83)." MERSH 18:81–84.

EEKMAN, THOMAS, and ANTÉ KADIČ, eds. *Juraj Križanič (1618–83): Russophile and Ecumenic Visionary.* The Hague: Mouton, 1976.

GOL'DBERG, ALEKSANDR L. "J. Krizhanich und Adam Olearius (Aus der Literarischen Polemik der 17. Jahrhunderts)." In *Studien zur Geschichte der russischen Literatur des 18. Jahrhunderts,* ed. Helmut Graßhoff and Günter Jarosch, 2:93–113, 390–94. Berlin: Akademie-Verlag, 1968.

———, comp. "Bibliografija o Jurju Krizanicu." In *Zivot i djelo Jurja Križaniča,* ed. Anté Pazanin, 259–77. Zagreb: Fakultet politickih nauka Sveucilista u Zagrebu; Izdavacki servis "Liber," 1974.

GOL'DBERG, ALEKSANDR L., and IVAN GOLUB, comps. "Bibliography." In *Juraj Križanič (1618–1683): Russophile and Ecumenic Visionary,* ed. Thomas Eekman and Anté Kadić, 329–52. The Hague, Mouton: 1976.

MACIEJ Z MIECHOWA (ca. 1457–1523; Polish scholar; never in Muscovy)
Studies: Adelung 1:179–81; Kappeler, 24; PSB 19:28–33.
BUCZEK, KAROL. *Maciej z Miechowa, 1457–1523.* Wrocław: Zakład Narodowy im. Ossolińskich, 1960.
LIMONOV, IURII A. *Kul'turnye sviazi Rossii s evropeiskimi stranami v XV–XVII vv.* Leningrad: Nauka, 1978.
ZANTUAN, KONSTANTY. "The Discovery of Modern Russia: *Tractatus de duabus Sarmatiis.*" *Russian Review* 27 (1968): 327–37.

MAGNUS, OLAUS (1490–1557; archbishop of Uppsala; never in Muscovy)
Studies:
GRANLUNG, JOHN. "Kommentar." In Olaus Magnus, *Historia om de Nordiska Folken,* ed. John Granlung. 4 vols. Stockholm: Gidlung, 1976.
JOHANNESSON, KURT. *The Renaissance of the Goths in Sixteenth-Century Sweden: Johannes and Olaus Magnus as Politicians and Historians.* Trans. James Larson. Berkeley: University of California Press, 1991.
KNAUER, ELFRIEDE R. *Die Carta Marina des Olaus Magnus von 1539.* Göttingen: Gratia, 1981.
SAVEL'EVA, ELENA A. *Olaus Magnus i ego "Istoriia severnykh narodov."* Leningrad: Nauka, 1983.

MARGERET, JACQUES (1565?–1619; French mercenary)
Studies: Adelung 2:18–46; IBF 3:1473.
DUNNING, CHESTER S. "Margeret, Jacques (1565?–1619)." MERSH 21:96–99.
———. "Quand un français redecouvrait la Russie." *Revue historique* 272 (1984): 331–51.
———. "The Use and Abuse of the First Printed French Account of Russia." *Russian History/Histoire Russe* 10 (1983): 357–80.

MASKIEWICZ, SAMUEL (ca. 1580–1632; Polish statesman, diarist)
Studies: Adelung 2:283–84; PSB 20:120–22.

MASSA, ISAAC (1587–1643; Dutch merchant)
Studies: Adelung 2:217–21.
KEUNING, JOHANNES. "Isaac Massa, 1586–1643." *Imago Mundi: A Review of Early Cartography* 10 (1953): 65–80.
LEERINK, J. A. "Een Nederlandsche cartograph in Rusland: Amsterdam–Moscou in de zeventiende eeuw." *Phoenix* 1 (1946).
LINDE, ANTONIUS VAN DER. *Isaac Massa van Haarlem: een historische studie.* Amsterdam, 1864.
MULLER, FREDRICK. *Essai d'une bibliographie neerlando–russe.* Amsterdam: N. Israel, 1859.
ORCHARD, G. EDWARD. "Massa, Isaac Abrahamson (1587–1643)." MERSH 21:133–63.

RIJKVOSEL, M. VAN. "Die beide portretten van Isaac Abrahamsz. Massa op de Frans Hals-tentoonstrelling." *Historia* 3 (1937).

SCHELTEMA, JACOBUS. *Rusland en de Nederlanden.* 4 vols. Amsterdam: H. Gartman, 1817.

MEYERBERG, AUGUSTIN FREIHERR VON (1612–88; Imperial diplomat)
Studies: Adelung 2:332–33; Jöcher 3:330; Napiersky 3:222–23.

ADELUNG, FRIEDRICH VON. *Augustin Freiherr Meyerberg und seine Reise nach Russland nebst einer von ihm auf dieser Reise veranstalteten Sammlung von Ansichten, Gebrauchen, Bildnissen u.s.w.* St. Petersburg: K. Kray, 1827.

———. *Baron Meierberg i ego puteshestvie po Rossii.* St. Petersburg: K. Kray, 1827.

LOVIAGIN, ALEKSANDR M. *Al'bom Meirberga: Vidy i bytovye kartiny Rossii XVII veka.* St. Petersburg: Izd. A. S. Suvorina, 1903.

MILTON, JOHN (1608–74; English author; never in Muscovy)
Studies: BBI 3:1288; DNB 8:471–88.

BERRY, LLOYD E. "Giles Fletcher, the Elder, and Milton's *A Brief History.*" *Review of English Studies* 11 (1960): 150–56.

CAWLEY, ROBERT R. "Brief History of Moscovia, A." In *A Milton Encyclopedia,* ed. William B. Hunter Jr., 1: 200–202. Lewisburg, Pa.: Bucknell University Press, 1978.

———. *Milton and the Literature of Travel.* Princeton: Princeton University Press, 1951.

———. *Milton's Literary Craftsmanship: A Study of "A Brief History of Moscovia."* Princeton: Princeton University Press, 1941.

GLEASON, JOHN B. "The Nature of Milton's *Moscovia.*" *Studies in Philology* 61 (1964): 640–91.

LIMONOV, IURII A. *Kul'turnye sviazi Rossii s evropeiskimi stranami v XV–XVII vv.,* 231–51.Leningrad: Nauka, 1978.

———. "Russkie istochniki 'Istorii Moskovii' Dzhona Mil'tona." In *Problemy istorii mezhdunarodnykh otnoshenii,* ed. Viktor I. Rutenberg, 243–47. Leningrad: Nauka, 1972.

PARKS, GEORGE B. "The Occasion of Milton's *Moscovia.*" *Studies in Philology* 40 (1943): 399–404.

PARKER, WILLIAM R. *Milton: A Biography.* 2 vols. Oxford: Clarendon, 1968.

POLUDENSKII, M. N. "Russkaia istoriia Mil'tona." *Russkie vesti,* 1860, no. 8: 533–45.

THOMPSON, ELBERT N. "Milton's Knowledge of Geography." *Studies in Philology* 16 (1919): 148–71.

MÜNSTER, SEBASTIAN (1488–1552; German cosmographer; never in Muscovy)
Studies: DBI 3:1429; ADB 23:31–33.

BURMEISTER, KARL H. "Neue Forschungen zu Sebastian Münster." *Beiträge zur Ingelheimer Geschichte* 21 (Ingelheim, 1971).

———. *Sebastian Münster: Versuch eines biographischen Gesamtbildes.* Basel and Stuttgart: Herbling & Lichtenhahn, 1963.

STRAUSS, GERALD. "A Sixteenth-Century Encyclopedia: Sebastian Münster's

Cosmography and Its Editions." In *From Renaissance to the Counter-Reformation: Essays in Honor of Garrett Mattingly,* ed. Charles H. Carter, 145–63. New York: Cape, 1965.

WEICHMANN-KADOW, A. "Sebastian Münsters *Cosmographie* 1537." *Archiv für die zeichnenden Künste* 1 (Leipzig, 1855).

"Neuville" [pseud.]

Studies: Adelung 2:379–81.

HUGHES, LINDSEY. "Russia in 1689: Court Politics in Foy de la Neuville's *Relation curieuse et nouvelle de Moscovie.*" In *New Perspectives in Muscovite History: Selected Papers from the Fourth World Congress for Soviet and East European Studies, Harrogate, 1990,* ed. Hughes, 177–87. New York: St. Martin's Press, 1993.

LAVROV, ALEKSANDR S. "'Zapiski' de la Nevillia kak istochnik po istorii Rossii v poslednei chetverti XVII veka." In *Materialy XXIV Vsesoiuznoi studencheskoi konferentsii 'Student i nauchno-tekhnicheskii progress.' Istoriia,* ed. Anatolii M. Shalagin et al., 27–30. Novosibirsk: Novosibirskii gos. universitet im. Leninskogo komsomola, 1986.

———. "'Zapiski o Moskovii' de la Nevillia: Avtor, rukopisi, pechatnoe izdanie." In *Kniga v Rossii XVI–serediny XIX v.: Materialy i issledovaniia,* ed. Aleksandra A. Zaitseva, 62–72. Leningrad: Biblioteka, 1990.

MADARIAGA, ISABEL DE, "Who was Foy de la Neuville?" *Cahiers du monde russe et soviétique* 28 (1987): 21–30.

OLEARIUS, ADAM (1603–1671; Holsteinian diplomat)

Studies: Adelung 2:299–306; ADB 24:269–76; DBI 3:1490.

BARON, SAMUEL H. "Krizhanich and Olearius." In *Juraj Križanič (1618–83): Russophile and Ecumenic Visionary,* ed. Thomas Eekman and Anté Kadič, 183–208. The Hague: Mouton, 1976. Rpt. in Baron, *Muscovite Russia,* chap. 13. London: Variorum Reprints, 1980.

———. "Olearius, Adam (1599–1671)." MERSH 25:240–43.

BELOKUROV, SERGEI A. *Adam Olearii o greko-latinskoi shkole Arseniia Greka v Moskve v XVII v.* Moscow: L. I. A. Snegirvy, 1888.

GOL'DBERG, ALEKSANDR L. "Adam Olearius, 1603–71." In *Wegbereiter der deutsch-slawischen Wechselseitigkeit,* ed. Eduard Winter and Gunter Jarosch, 7–15. Berlin: Akademie-Verlag, 1983.

———. "J. Krizhanich und Adam Olearius (Aus der Literarischen Polemik der 17. Jahrhunderts)." In *Studien zur Geschichte der russischen Literatur des 18. Jahrhunderts,* ed. Helmut Graßhoff and Gunter Jarosch, 2:93–113, 390–94. Berlin: Akademie-Verlag, 1968.

HEIN, LORENZ. "Adam Olearius und seine Begegnung mit der russisch-orthodoxen Kirche." *Kyrios,* n.s. 2 (1962): 1–17.

LISZKOWSKI, UWE. "Adam Olearius' Beschreibung des Moskauer Reiches." In *Russen und Rußland aus deutscher Sicht 9.–17. Jahrhundert,* ed. Mechthild Keller, 223–46. Munich: W. Fink, 1985.

LOHMEIER, DIETER. "Adam Olearius, Leben und Werke." In Adam Olearius, *Vermehrte Newe Beschreibung der Muscowitischen und Persischen Reyse* [1656], ed. Lohmeier. Facs. ed. Tübingen: Niemeyer, 1971.

————. "Nachwort." In Adam Olearius, *Vermehrte newe Beschreibung der Muscowitischen und Persischen Reyse* {1656}, ed. Lohmeier, 3–62. Facs. ed. Tübingen: Neimeyer, 1971.

SCHIEFNER, ANTON. "Ueber das Stammbuch von Adam Olearius." *Das Inland* 44 (1851): 767–72.

WEIL, H. H. "A Seventeenth-Century German Looks at Russia." *German Life and Letters* 8 (1954–55): 59–64.

PAUL OF ALEPPO (Syrian archdeacon)
Studies: Adelung 2:325.

KOWALSKA, MARIA. *Ukraina w połowie XVII wieku w relacji arabskiego podróżnika Pawła, syna Makarego z Aleppo.* Warsaw: Państwowe Wydawnictwo Naukowe, 1986.

SOKOL, EDWARD D. "Paul of Aleppo." MERSH 27:73–78.

PERRY, JOHN (1670–1732; English engineer)
Studies: Adelung, 2:401; DNB 15:921–22; BBI 3:1460.

PETREIUS, PETER [Peer Peerson] (1570–1622; Swedish diplomat)
Studies: Adelung 2:238–58.

ALMQUIST, HELGA K. H. *Sverige och Ryssland, 1595–1611.* Uppsala: Almqvist & Wiksells, 1907.

ORCHARD, G. EDWARD. "Petreius [Peer Peerson, or Peter Petreius, de Erlesunda] (1570–1622)." MERSH 28:18–19.

SMIRNOV, IVAN I. "Konrad Bussov i ego khronika." In Konrad Bussov, *Moskovskaia khronika, 1584–1613,* ed. and trans. Smirnov, 5–56. Moscow: Izd. Akademii nauk SSSR, 1961.

PEYERLE, HANS GEORG (German merchant)
Studies: Adelung 2:184–98.

DOLININ, NIKOLAI P. "K izucheniiu inostranykh istochnikov o krest. vosstanii pod rukovodstvom I. I. Bolotnikova." In *Mezhdunarodnye sviazi Rossii do XVII v.,* ed. Aleksandr A. Zimin and Vladimir T. Pashuto, 462–90. Moscow: Izd. Akademii nauk SSSR, 1961.

NAZAROV, VLADISLAV D. "Paerle (Peyerle), Gans Georg." In *Sovetskaia istoricheskaia entsiklopediia,* ed. E. M. Zhukov et al., 10:723. 16 vols. Moscow: Izdatel'stvo "Sovetskaia Entsiklopediia," 1961–76.

PIRCKHEIMER, WILLIBALD (1470–1530; German scholar; never in Muscovy)
Studies: ADB 26:810–19; DBI 3:1562.

ECKERT, WILLEHAD P., and Christoph von Imhoff. *Willibald Pirckheimer: Dürers Freund im Spiegel seines Lebens, seiner Werke und seiner Umwelt.* Cologne: Wienand, 1971.

GLOCK, KARL, and INGE MEIDINGER-GEISE, eds. *Willibald Pirckheimer, 1470/1970. Dokumente, Studien, Perspektiven.* Nuremberg: Glock & Lutz, 1970.

WEYRAUTHER, M. *Konrad Peutinger und Willibald Pirckheimer in ihren Beziehungen zur Geographie.* Münchner Geographische Studien 21. Munich, 1907.

PISO, JACOB (papal legate; never in Muscovy)
Studies: Florovskii, 368; Kappeler, 23; Lankau, 26–30.

POSSEVINO, ANTONIO (1533/34–1611; papal diplomat)
Studies: Adelung 1:321–50; Kappeler, 82–85.

AMMANN, ALBERT M. "Ein russischer Reisebericht aus dem Jahre 1581." *Ostkirchliche Studien* 10 (1961): 165–95, 283–300.

ARNDT, AUGUSTIN, S.J. "Ein päpstliches Schiedsgericht im 16. Jahrhundert." *Stimmen aus Maria-Laach* 31 (1886): 480–503.

BACKER, AUGUSTIN DE. *Bibliothèque de la Compagnie de Jésus*, ed. Carlos Sommervogel, S.J. 12 vols. Heverle-Louvain: Editions de la Bibliothèque S.J., 1960.

CACCAMO, DOMENICO. "Conversione dell'Islam e conquista della Muscovia nel'attività diplomatica e letteraria di Antonio Possevino." In *Venezia e Ungheria nel Renascimento a cura di Vittore Branca*, ed. Vittore Branca, 167–91. Florence: L. S. Olschki, 1973.

CRIVELLI, CAMILLO, S.J. "La disputa di Antonio Possevino con i Valdesi (26 luglio 1560) da una relazione del Possevino." *Archivum historicum Societatis Jesu* 7 (1938): 79–91.

DELIUS, WALTER. *Antonio Possevino S.J. und Ivan Groznyi: Ein Beitrag zur Geschichte der kirchlichen Union und der Gegenreformation des 16. Jahrhunderts*. Stuttgart: Evangelisches Verlagswerk, 1962.

GARSTEIN, OSKAR. *Rome and the Counter-Reformation in Scandinavia*. Vol. 1. Oslo: Universitetsforlaget, 1963.

GODOVIKOVA, L. N. "Istoricheskie sochineniia Possevino o Rossii." Candidate *dissertation*, Moskovskii gosudarstvennyi universitet, 1970.

GRAHAM, HUGH. "Possevino, Antonio (1533/34–1611)." MERSH 29:109–44.

HELK, VELLO. *Die Jesuiten in Dorpat, 1583–1625: Ein Vorpost der Gegenreformation in Nordosteuropa*. Odense: Odense, 1977.

KADIČ, ANTÉ. "Krizhanich and Possevino—Missionaries to Muscovy." In *Juraj Križanić (1618–1683): Russophile and Ecumenic Visionary*, ed. Thomas Eekman and Anté Kadič, 73–90. The Hague, Mouton: 1976.

KARTTUNEN, LIISI. *Antoine Possevin, un diplomate pontifical au XVIe siècle*. Lausanne, 1908.

LEONARD, EMILY V. "Muscovy in the Sixteenth Century: The Accounts of Sigismund von Herberstein and Antonio Possevino." Ph.D. dissertation, Indiana University, 1966.

LIKHACHEV, NIKOLAI P. "Delo o priezde v Moskvu Antoniia Possevina." *Letopis' zaniatii Arkheograficheskoi Komissii* 2 (1903).

LUKÁCS, LAJOS. "Die nördlichen päpstlichen Seminare und P. Possevino." *Archivum historicum Societatis Jesu* 14 (1955): 33–94.

PIERLING, PAUL, S.J. *Un Arbitrage pontifical au XVIe siècle entre Pologne et la Russie: Mission diplomatique du Possevino, S.J., 1581–82*. Brussels, n.d.

———. *Batory et Possevino: Documents inedits sur les rapports du Saint-Siège avec les Slaves*. Paris: E. Leroux, 1897.

———. *Un Nonce du Pape en Muscovie: Préliminaires de la trève de 1581*. Paris: E. Leroux, 1884.

POLCHIN, S., S.J. "Un Tentative d'union au XVIe siècle: La Mission religieuse du Père Antoine Possevino, S.J., en Moscovie." *Orientalia Christiana Analecta* 150 (1957): 1–142.

SCADUTO, MARIO, S.J. "Ivan il Terribile e Antonio Possevino." *Civiltà cattolica* 4 (1959): 292–96.

————. "Le missioni di A. Possevino in Piedmonte: Propaganda calvinista e restaurazione catolica, 1560–63." *Archivum historicum Societatis Jesu* (1959): 51–191.

STÖKL, GÜNTER. "Posseviniana." *Jahrbücher für Geschichte Osteuropas* 11 (1969): 223–36.

WOLTER, HANS, S.J. "Antonio Possevino (1533–1611). Theologie und Politik im Spannungsfeld zwischen Rom und Moskau." *Scholastic* 31 (1956): 321–50.

PRINTZ VON BUCHAU, DANIEL (1546–1608; Imperial diplomat)
Studies: Adelung 1:295–309; Brokgaus-Efron 5:112; DBI 3:1596; Jöcher 3:1775; Kappeler, 92–93; Kordt, 46.

REUTENFELS, JACOB (nephew of a court doctor)
Studies: Adelung 2:348–49; DBI 3:1627.

GOL'DBERG, ALEKSANDR L. "Reutenfels, Iakov." In *Sovetskaia istoricheskaia entsiklopediia,* ed. E. M. Zhukov et al., 11:995. 16 vols. Moscow: Izd. "Sovetskaia Entsiklopediia," 1961–76.

PIERLING, PAUL, S.J. "Novie materialy o zhizni i deiatel'nosti Iakova Reutenfelsa." *Chteniia v imperatorskom obshchestve istorii i drevnostei rossiiskikh pri Moskovskom universitete* 219, no. 4 (1906): 1–24.

SCHLICHTING, ALBERT (German translator)
Studies: Kappeler, 55–58.

GRAHAM, H. "Schlichting, Albert." MERSH 33:142–45.

STADEN, HEINRICH VON (b. 1542?; German mercenary)
Studies:

EPSTEIN, FRITZ. "Heinrich von Staden." *Westfälische Lebensbilder* 2 (1931): 51–70.

ESPER, THOMAS. "Staden, Heinrich von (1542?–?)." MERSH 37:57–58.

TANNER, BERNARD LEOPOLD FRANZ (Polish diplomat)
Studies: Adelung 2:363.

TAUBE, JOHANN, and ELBERT KRUSE (German-Livonian nobles)
Studies: Adelung 1:270–71; Kappeler, 73–77.

BRAUDO, A. I. "Poslanie Taube i Kruze k gercogu Ketleru (bibliograficheskaia zametka)." *Zhurnal Ministerstva narodnogo prosvieshcheniia* 271 (1890): 386–95.

DMITRIEV, LEV A. "Vnov' naidennoe sochinenie ob Ivane Groznom." *Trudy otdela drevnerusskoi literatury* 18 (1962): 374–408.

GRAHAM, HUGH. "Taube, Johann, and Kruse, Elbert." MERSH 38:203–8.

HANSEN, GOTTHARD VON. "Johann Taubes und Eilart Kruses Machinationen und die darauf durch 'König Magnus' erfolgte Belagerung Revals, 1570–71." *Beiträge zur Kunde Ehst-, Liv- und Kurlands* 3 (1886): 264–329.

ROGINSKII, MIKHAIL G. "Poslanie Ioganna Taube i Elberta Kruze kak istoricheskii istochnik." *Russkii istoricheskii zhurnal* 8 (1922): 10–59.

SCHIEMANN, TEODOR. "Johann Taube und Eilhard Kruse." In *Character-köpfe und Sittenbilder aus der baltischen Geschichte des sechzehnten Jahrhunderts,* 1–30. Hamburg-Mitau: Behre, etc., 1885.

TAUBE, MIKHAIL A. "Iogann Taube, sovetnik tsaria Ivana Groznogo." *Novyi zhurnal* 71 (1963): 170–89.

TRAKHANIOT, IURII (fl. 1486; Muscovite diplomat) (interviewed by Milanese officials)
Studies:

BARBIERI, GINO. *Milano e Mosca nella politica del Risascimento. Storia dele relazioni diplomatiche fra la Russie e el Ducato de Milano nell'epoca sforzesca.* Bari: Adriatica, 1957.

CROSKY, ROBERT, and E. C. RONQUIST, eds. and trans. "George Trakhaniot's Description of Russia in 1486." *Russian History/Histoire Russe* 17 (1990): 55–64.

GUKOVSKII, MIHAIL, ed. and trans. "Soobshchenie o Rossii Moskovskogo posla v Milan, 1486g." In *Voprosy istoriografii i istochnikovedeniia istorii SSSR. Sbornik statei,* ed. S, N. Valk, 648–55. Moscow and Leningrad, 1963.

ULFELDT, JACOB (d. 1593; Danish diplomat)
Studies: Adelung 1:273–84; Kappeler, 92.

GISSEL, S., ed. *Jacob Ulfelds jordebog på Ulfeldsholm, Selsø og Bavelse, 1588.* Copenhagen: I Kommission hos Rosenkilde og Bagger, 1964.

GRAHAM, HUGH. "Ulfeldt, Jacob." MERSH 40:178–82.

RASMUSSEN, KNUD. "Das *Hodoeporicon Ruthenicum* [1608] von Jacob Ulfeldt—eine Quelle zur russischen oder zur dänischen Geschichte?" In *Reiseberichte als Quellen europäischer Kulturgeschichte,* ed. Antoni Maczak and Hans Jurgen Teuteberg, 177–92. Wolfenbüttel: Herzog August Bibliothek, 1982.

SHCHERBACHEV, IURII N. "Dva posol'stva pri Ioanne Vasil'eviche." *Russkii vestnik* 7 (1887): 88–175.

TROELS-LUND, TROELS. *Jakob Ulfelds Sendefaerd til Russland, i Historiske Fortaellinger: Tider og Tanker.* Copenhagen, 1964.

WICKHART, CARL VALERIUS (Imperial diplomat)
Studies: Adelung 2:358–59.

Index

Aa, Abraham J. van der, 179
Abrusow, Leonid, 19, 26
Absolutism, ideology of:
  among European ethnographers, 106–7,
    145–46, 152
  among European political theorists,
    169–73, 184–85
Achenwall, Gottfried, 181
Adams, Clement, 43, 47–48, 68, 74–77,
    78, 80, 118, 128, 133, 149, 163,
    166
Adelung, Friedrich von, 133
Agapetus, 212, 217
Alef, Gustav, 13, 205–6, 208
Aleksei Mikhailovich (tsar of Russia), 69,
    75, 78, 86–87, 89, 105, 107, 140,
    146, 162–63, 183–85
Allodial estates (*votchiny*), 100
Alpatov, Mikhail A., 12
Ambassadorial Chancellery (*posol'skii
    prikaz*), 49, 183
Ambassadorial Court (*posol'skii dvor*), 44
Anchersen, Johann P., 181
Angermann, Norbert, 13
Anninskii, Sergei A., 26
Aristocracy, Russian. *See* Gentry, Russian
Aristotle, 6
  classification of constitutions, 152
  definition of commonwealth, 152
  definition of despotism, 155–56, 164
  definition of tyranny, 154–55
  early modern European interpretations
    of, 152–53
  influence on European political theo-
    rists, 152–57, 175–77, 179–80,
    188–89
  influence on travelers to Russia, 151–52,
    157–66

  knowledge of the *Politics* in early mod-
    ern Europe, 151
  See also Political concepts
Asia:
  despotism in, 155–56, 165–66, 180
  Russian customs from, 110, 166
  See also Oriental despotism
Assembly of the Land (*zemskii sobor*):
  European views of, 66–67, 103–4
Attendants (*pristavy*), 44–45, 48–49
Avril, Phillipe, 137

Bacon, Francis, 56–57, 188
Bakhrushin, Sergei V., 41
Barbaro, Josaphat, 27, 138
Barberino, Raffaelle, 42–43, 45–48, 52–
    53, 56, 58, 60, 62, 68–69, 71, 74–
    75, 77, 79–80, 82, 105, 136, 139–
    41, 148, 163
  biographical data, 147
  secondary sources on, 267
Barbieri, Gino, 18
Barkhudarov, Stepan G., 205
Baron, Samuel H., 7, 123, 135–36, 220
Barsov, Elpidifor V., 212
Basmanov, Petr F., 95
Batory, Stefan (king of Poland), 214
Behrens, B., 15
Belleforest, François de, 137–38
Belli, Nicolai, 179
Belokurov, Sergei A., 182
Benninghoven, Friedrich, 19
Bernard, Jean Féderic, 192
Berry, Lloyd E., 176
Bible:
  as a source of political theory in Russia,
    209, 217–18
  See also Political theory

DATE DUE

DEC ~~199~~			
			Printed in USA

HIGHSMITH #45230